T0176580

Digital Image Interpolation in MATLAB®

Digital Image Interpolation in MATLAB®

Chi-Wah Kok and Wing-Shan Tam
Canaan Semiconductor Limited
Hong Kong
China

Registered Offices
John Wiley & Sons, Inc., 111 River Street, Hoboken, NJ 07030, USA
John Wiley & Sons Singapore Pte. Ltd., 1 FusionopolisWalk, #07-01 Solaris South Tower, Singapore 138628

Editorial Office
The Atrium, Southern Gate, Chichester, West Sussex, PO19 8SQ, UK

For details of our global editorial offices, customer services, and more information about Wiley products visit us at www.wiley.com.

Wiley also publishes its books in a variety of electronic formats and by print-on-demand. Some content that appears in standard print versions of this book may not be available in other formats.

Limit of Liability/Disclaimer of Warranty
MATLAB® is a trademark of The MathWorks, Inc. and is used with permission. The MathWorks does not warrant the accuracy of the text or exercises in this book. This work's use or discussion of MATLAB® software or related products does not constitute endorsement or sponsorship by The MathWorks of a particular pedagogical approach or particular use of the MATLAB® software.

While the publisher and authors have used their best efforts in preparing this work, they make no representations or warranties with respect to the accuracy or completeness of the contents of this work and specifically disclaim all warranties, including without limitation any implied warranties of merchantability or fitness for a particular purpose. No warranty may be created or extended by sales representatives, written sales materials or promotional statements for this work. The fact that an organization, website, or product is referred to in this work as a citation and/or potential source of further information does not mean that the publisher and authors endorse the information or services the organization, website, or product may provide or recommendations it may make. This work is sold with the understanding that the publisher is not engaged in rendering professional services. The advice and strategies contained herein may not be suitable for your situation. You should consult with a specialist where appropriate. Further, readers should be aware that websites listed in this work may have changed or disappeared between when this work was written and when it is read. Neither the publisher nor authors shall be liable for any loss of profit or any other commercial damages, including but not limited to special, incidental, consequential, or other damages.

Library of Congress Cataloging-in-Publication Data

Names: Kok, Chi-Wah, author. | Tam, Wing-Shan, author.
Title: Digital image interpolation in MATLAB® / Dr. Chi-Wah Kok, Canaan Semiconductor Limited,
   Hong Kong, China, Dr. Wing-Shan Tam, Canaan Semiconductor Limited,
   Hong Kong, China.
Description: First edition. | Hoboken, NJ : John Wiley & Sons, Inc., 2019. |
   Includes bibliographical references and index. |
Identifiers: LCCN 2018043062 (print) | LCCN 2018045690 (ebook) | ISBN
   9781119119630 (Adobe PDF) | ISBN 9781119119647 (ePub) | ISBN 9781119119616
   (hardcover)
Subjects: LCSH: Image processing–Digital techniques–Data processing. |
   Interpolation. | MATLAB.
Classification: LCC TA1632 (ebook) | LCC TA1632 .K63 2019 (print) | DDC
   006.6/86–dc23
LC record available at https://lccn.loc.gov/2018043062

Cover Design: Wiley
Cover Image: Courtesy of Chi-Wah Kok and Wing-Shan Tam

Set in 10/12pt WarnockPro by SPi Global, Chennai, India
Printed in Singapore by C.O.S. Printers Pte Ltd

10 9 8 7 6 5 4 3 2 1

To my love Annie from Ted for putting up with it all once again
To mom Gloria Lee and the memory of dad, Simon Tam, dedicated by Wing-Shan

Contents

About the Authors

Chi-Wah Kok was born in Hong Kong. He was granted with a PhD degree from the University of Wisconsin–Madison. Since 1992, he has been working with various semiconductor companies, research institutions, and universities, which include AT&T Labs Research, Holmdel, SONY U.S. Research Labs, Stanford University, Hong Kong University of Science and Technology, Hong Kong Polytechnic University, City University of Hong Kong, Lattice Semiconductor, etc. In 2006, he founded Canaan Semiconductor Ltd., a fabless IC company with products in mixed-signal IC, high performance audio amplifier, and high-power MOSFETs and IGBTs. Dr. Kok embraces new technologies to meet the fast-changing market requirements. He has extensively applied signal processing techniques to improve the circuit topologies, designs, and fabrication technologies within Canaan. This includes the application of semidefinite programming to circuit design optimization, abstract algebra in switched capacitor circuit topologies, and nonlinear optimization method to optimize high voltage MOSFET layout and fabrication. He was MPEG (MPEG 4) and JPEG (JPEG 2000) standards committee member. He is the founding editor in chief of the journal *Solid State Electronics Letters* since 2017. He is also the author of three books by Prentice Hall and Wiley-IEEE and has written numerous papers on digital signal processing, multimedia signal processing, and CMOS circuits, devices, fabrication process, and reliability.

Wing-Shan Tam was born in Hong Kong. She received her PhD degree in electronic engineering from the City University of Hong Kong. She has been working in different telecommunication and semiconductor companies since 2004 and is currently the engineering manager of Canaan Semiconductor Ltd., where she works on both advanced CMOS sensor design and high-power device structure and process development. Dr. Tam has participated in professional services actively, in which she has been the researcher in different universities since 2007. She has been the invited speaker for different talks and seminars in numerous international conferences and renowned universities. She has served as guest editor in several journals published by IEEE and Elsevier. She is the founding editor of the journal *Solid State Electronics Letters* since 2017. She is the co-author of another Wiley-IEEE technology textbook and research papers with award quality. Her research interests include image interpolation algorithm, color enhancement algorithm and mixed-signal integrated circuit design for data conversion and power management, and device fabrication process and new device structure development.

Preface

The process of deriving real-world application from scientific knowledge is usually a very, very long process. However, with the advancement in complementary metal oxide semiconductor (CMOS) image sensor, and its application in handheld device, image interpolation has rapidly migrated from complex mathematics and academic publications to everyday applications in smartphones, laptops and tablets. Image interpolation has become a red-hot research topic in both academia and industry. One of the highly cited academic works in image interpolation is authored by Dr. Tam, which is an excerpt from her master thesis. Her work is also the origin of this book. However, this book is not intended to be a memoir of the work done by Dr. Tam and her research group; it is intended to be the course materials for senior- and graduate-level courses, training materials for engineers, and also a reference text for readers who are working in the field of digital imaging.

All the image interpolation algorithms discussed in this book will include both theories, where detailed analytic analysis are derived, and implementations through MAT-LAB into useful tools. Numerous algorithms are reviewed in this book together with detailed discussions on their origins, performances, and limitations. We are particularly happy with the numerical simulations presented for all the algorithms described in this book to clarify the observable but difficult to explain image interpolation artifacts, as the author shares the well-known Chinese saying that a picture is worth a thousand words. Furthermore, many of our unpublished works are included in this book, where new algorithms are developed to overcome various limitations.

This book is authored as much as it is collected. We have tried our best to cite references whenever we are aware of related works on the topics. However, we suspect that some topics may have been independently studied by many individuals, and thus we might have missed their citation. Over 30 years of research works are collected in one place, and we presented each selected topics in a self-contained format. If you are interested in further reading on any of these topics, you should look into the cited references and the Summary sections at the end of each chapter in this book. On a subject such as this one, which has been continuously investigated for over half a century, inevitably a number of valuable research results are not included in this book. It is nonetheless expected that the contents of this book will enable the careful readers to independently explore the more advanced image interpolation/processing technique.

Although much of the materials covered by this book are new to most students, our goal is to provide a working knowledge of various image interpolation algorithms without the need for additional course work besides freshman-level engineering mathematics and a junior-level matrix lab programming. To perform numerical simulation using computer, we must use a language that a computer can understand. This is why we choose to use MATLAB in this book, because MATLAB is not only a computer language. MATLAB, which is built with matrix data structure, is also a language of arithmetic. Once the MATLAB implementation of the algorithms have been learned, it will be fairly straightforward to implement them in other computer languages and VHDL for hardware synthesis. While almost all the MATLAB example codes presented in this book are co-developed from the basic and do not require any toolbox to run with, in Chapter 6, the author just cannot resist to make use of the wavelet toolbox developed by Prof. T.Q. Nguyen of UCSD who is also the PhD adviser of Dr. Kok back in the University of Wisconsin–Madison. The toolbox has made everything easy, which definitely helped the readers to understand the topics and ease their practical implementation tremendously.

The book is divided into nine chapters. Chapter 1 provides an account of basic signal processing and mathematical tools used in subsequent chapters. It also serves the purpose of getting the readers to be familiar with the mathematical notations adopted in the book. Chapter 2 introduces the important concepts of digital imaging and the operations that are useful to image interpolation algorithms. The quality and performance measures between the processed image and the original image are presented in Chapter 3. The human visual system that is first discussed in Chapter 2 will be extended here for the discussion of the *structural similarity* quality index. The nonparametric image interpolation algorithm developed around algebraic functions are presented in Chapter 4. This chapter ends with a discussion on the deficiency of nonadaptive interpolation methods. Chapter 5 discusses the interpolation by *Fourier* and other orthogonal series. We are particularly interested in interpolating image in the *discrete cosine transform* domain, which is motivated by current trends in international image compression and storage standards. The blocking noise resulted from transform domain zero padding interpolation with small block size is alleviated by variations of overlap and add interpolation techniques. An iterative algorithm is presented to improve the least squares solution of the conventional transform coefficients zero padding image interpolation algorithm. Note that iterative image interpolation algorithms are considered to be offline image interpolation algorithms. More about iterative interpolation algorithm that helps to maintain the original pixel values while improving the performance of the non-iterative image interpolation algorithms will be presented in subsequent chapters. Chapter 6 extends the block-based transform domain image interpolation to the wavelet domain. A number of the techniques presented in previous chapters are applicable to the wavelet domain image interpolation too, and various researchers have been given them different names in the literature. The performance of wavelet image interpolation can be improved by exploiting the scale-space relationships obtained by multi-resolution analysis through wavelet transform (a version of the human visual system). The explicit edge detection-based image interpolation methods discussed in Chapter 7 interpolate the image according to the edge-directed image perception property of human visual system. Various edge-directed interpolation methods will be discussed where edges are explicitly obtained by various edge detection methods discussed in Chapter 2, and implicit edge detection methods that the nature of the pixels to be interpolated is determined in the course of the estimation. The chapter concludes with discussions on the pros and cons of edge-directed image interpolation algorithm using explicit edge detection. Another type of edge-detected image interpolation method will be presented in Chapter 8, which is based on the edge geometric duality where a covariance-based implicit edge location and estimation method will interpolate the image along the edge to achieve good visual quality. Digital signal processing theory tells us that there is always room to improve the solutions of any estimation problem. Various improvements to the edge-directed interpolation problem will be discussed in this chapter to improve the preservation of edge geometric duality between the original image and the interpolated image, to reduce the interpolation error propagation by removing inter-processing dependence, and finally to improve the estimation solution through an iterative re-estimation algorithm. The book changes its course from linear statistical-based interpolation technique to fractal interpolation in Chapter 9.

It should be noticed that fractal is usually not considered to be a statistical-based interpolation algorithm. On the other hand, the generation of fractal map is based on similarity between image features, where the similarity is computed or classified via the statistics of the image or image blocks. Finally, an iterative algorithm is presented to improve the fractal image interpolation algorithm with the constraint that the original low-resolution image is the pivot of the interpolated image, i.e. the location and intensity invariance of the low-resolution image in the interpolation image is guaranteed. The advantage of such algorithmic constraint not only allows the preservation of the original low-resolution image pixel values in the interpolated image but also ensures the highest preservation of the structure property of the interpolated image. As a result, fractal image interpolation has been embedded in a number of successful image processing softwares. The book concludes with an appendix that lists all the MATLAB source codes discussed in the book.

Many people have contributed, directly or indirectly, over a long period of time, to the subjects presented in this book. Their contributions are cited appropriately in this book, and also in the *Summary* section at the end of each chapter. The Summary sections also aimed to detail the state-of-the-art development with respect to the topics discussed in each chapter. The exercises presented in the *Exercise* sections are essential parts of this text and often provide a discovery-like experience regarding the associated topics. It is our hope that the exercises will provide general guidelines to assist the readers to design new image interpolation algorithms for their own applications. The readers' effort spent on tackling the exercises will help them to develop a thorough consideration on the design of image processing algorithms for their future career in research and development in the field.

The book is definitely not meant to represent a comprehensive history about the development of image interpolation algorithms. On the other hand, it does provide a not so short review, which chronologically follows the evolution of some of the image interpolation algorithms that have direct implications on commercially available image processing softwares. In particular, we avoided with our best effort to provide a comprehensive survey of every image interpolation algorithms in literature and market. Instead, our selection of topics is on the importance of the algorithms with respect to their applications in image processing softwares in today's or near-future market. Our hope is that the book offers the readers a range of interesting topics and the current state-of-the-art image interpolation methods. In simple terms, image interpolation is an open problem that has no definite winner. Analyzing the design and performance trade-offs and proposing a range of attractive solutions to various image interpolation problems are the basic aims of this book. The book will underline the range of design considerations in an unbiased fashion, and the readers will be able to glean information from it in order to solve their own particular image interpolation problems. Most of all, we hope that the readers will find it an enjoyable and relatively effortless reading, providing them with intellectual stimulation.

Hong Kong, August 2018   *Chi-Wah Kok*
                                                          Wing-Shan Tam

Acknowledgments

Dr. Kok would like to thank his wife Dr. Annie Ko, an extraordinary woman with abiding faith in Christianity. He has acknowledged her in his previous book for her enormous contributions to his life – and still do. He thanks her for her encouragement, and she created enough time for him to write the book while being granted with *tenure* and awarded the *best teaching award* in her university. She has been his inspiration and motivation for continuing to improve his knowledge and move his career forward.

Dr. Kok would also like to thank Dr. Cindy Tam for allowing him to put up with far too many side projects while writing this book. He appreciates her belief in him to provide the leadership and knowledge to make this book a reality. She has provided research insights along the way, working with him to complete each chapter with the appropriate MATLAB sources and analytic details through revision and re-revision, pouncing on obscurities, decrying omissions, correcting misspelling, redrawing figures, and often making her life very much more difficult by his unrelenting insistence that the text and figures could be more literate, accurate, and intelligible. He is very pleased to see his illegible red marginalia have found their way into the text of this book. The last but not the least, he would like to thank her for contributing the beautiful photo of "BeBe" both as the designated simulation image source for all the examples and also the cover image of the book. This lovely cat is Dr. Tam's domestic cat, and the best model for image interpolations, because it contains all the necessary image features that can demonstrate the visual artifacts and performance of various image interpolation algorithms.

Dr. Tam is glad to write her second book with the topic on image interpolation, the same topic as her master thesis. This book project gives her precious opportunities to review the work done in her early years of research and a chance to refresh her knowledge with the ongoing technology development and to explore new research breakthroughs in the field. An interesting research topic always begins with some extraordinary idea. Dr. Tam would like to thank her best mentor and collaborator, Dr. Kok, who introduced and inspired her in this interesting topic.

Dr. Tam would not be able to finish her master thesis, and all other industrial and research projects, without the patience and guidance of Dr. Kok. Though sometimes the collaboration is challenging and bumpy, Dr. Tam believes all the experience and knowledge gained from their collaboration have laid the cornerstone for her future, both personally and professionally.

Dr. Tam would not be able to continue her research career without the love and support from her family. She would like to thank her mother, Gloria, for her love and support, offering her a warm shelter to rest her tired and frustrated body and mind for all these years, and her father, Simon, now in heaven watching and praying for her. Dr. Tam has inherited her father's spirit in striving for perfection, which keeps her moving and be a better researcher.

Her father would be happy to see the publication of her second book and all her research papers. Thanks also go to her sister Candy, brother-in-law Kelvin, niece Clarice, and nephew Kayven who have brought much happiness and laughter to her, the natural booster to keep her energetic year round.

We are in debt to many people, too numerous to mention. Our sincere gratitude is due to the numerous authors listed in the bibliography, as well as to those whose works were not cited due to space limitations. We are grateful for their contributions to the state of the art; without their contributions this book would not have materialized. In particular, we have to express exceptional and sincere gratitude to Dr. Min Li (of University of California, San Diego, and now Qualcomm) for her PhD research work contributed to the development of Markov random field-based edge-directed image interpolation. We are very sorry for the last minute decision to exclude the chapter about Dr. Li's work from the book. But our personal communications have made the book to be much better for the readers.

Despite the assistance, review, and editing by many people, both authors have no doubt that errors still lurk undetected. These are undoubtfully the authors' sin, and it is our hope that the readers of this book will discover them and bring them to our attention, so that they all may be eradicated. Finally, we acknowledge our thanks to God, who blessed this book project, through the words of the psalmist, "Give thanks to the Lord, for He is good; His love endures forever" (Psalms 107:1, NIV).

Chi-Wah Kok
Wing-Shan Tam

Nomenclature

$[x]$:   ceiling operator that returns the smallest integer larger than or equal to x

$\mathbb{Z}$:   the set of integers

$\mathbb{Z}^+$:   the set of positive integers (great than 0)

$\mathbb{R}$:   the set of real numbers

$\mathbb{C}$:   the set of complex numbers

$\mathbf{A}_{M,N}$:   arbitrary matrix of size $M \times N$ constructed by matrix entrance $a(m, n)$ with $\mathbf{A}_{M,N} = [a(m, n)]_{m,n}$ where $0 \leq m \leq M - 1$, and $0 \leq n \leq N - 1$

$\mathbf{I}_N$:   identity matrix of size $N \times N$

ℓ_2:   the space of all squares summable discrete functions/sequences

$\mathcal{L}^2$:   the space of all Lesbesgue squares integrable functions

$\mathcal{R}$:   real part of a number, matrix, or a function

$\mathcal{I}$:   imaginary part of a number, matrix, or a function

$\mathbf{sinc}(x)$:   Sinc function $\left(\frac{\sin(x)}{x} \right)$

δ: Kronecker delta, or Dirac-delta function, or unit impulse with infinite size

j: root of -1 and is equal to $\sqrt{-1}$

W_N: Nth root of unity and equals to $e^{\frac{-j2\pi}{N}}$

$\mathcal{F}$:   discrete Fourier transform operator

$\mathcal{F}^{-1}$:   inverse discrete Fourier transform operator

$\mathbf{W}_N$:   discrete Fourier transform matrix of size $N \times N$; $\mathbf{W}_N = [W_N^{k,\ell}]_{k,\ell}$ with $0 \leq k, \ell \leq N - 1$. The Fourier matrix is of arbitrary size when N is missing

$C_{M \times N}$:   discrete cosine transform matrix of size $M \times N$; the cosine matrix is of arbitrary size when $M \times N$ is missing

$\otimes$:   convolution operator

Δ_x: interval in domain x; the interval domain is arbitrary when x is missing

ω: angular frequency

ω_x: spatial angular frequency in domain x

ω_{Δ_x}:   sampling angular frequency with sampling interval Δ_x in domain x $\left(= \frac{2\pi}{\Delta_x}\right)$

$h_c(x, \Delta_x)$:   comb filter impulse response function in domain x with Δ_x being the separation between adjacent impulses in the comb filter; $h_c(x, \Delta_x) = \sum_{k=-\infty}^{\infty} \Delta_x \delta(x - k\Delta_x)$

$H_c(\omega, \Delta_x)$:   frequency response of the comb filter $h_c(x, \Delta_x)$, i.e.
$$H_c(\omega, \Delta_x) = \mathcal{F}(h_c(x, \Delta_x))$$

$f(x, \Delta)$:   impulse train in analog domain x with Δ being the separation between adjacent indices $= \Delta \sum_{m=-\infty}^{\infty} \delta(x - m\Delta)$, with
$$\delta(k) = \begin{cases} 1/\Delta & \text{for } k = 0, \\ 0 & \text{otherwise.} \end{cases}$$

$f[k, N]$:   discrete impulse sequence $= N \sum_{m=-\infty}^{\infty} \delta[k - mN]$, with
$$\delta[k] = \begin{cases} 1/N & \text{for } k = 0, \\ 0 & \text{otherwise.} \end{cases}$$

A word on notations
1. (Indices) We denote continuous variable (m) and discrete variable $[n]$ induced signals as $x(m)$ and $x[n]$, respectively.
2. (Vector-matrix) The blackboard bold $(\mathbf{A})$ is used to represent matrix-valued signal and function, and $(\mathbf{x})$ is used to represent the vector-valued signal and function. The normal characters (x) are used to represent signal in scalar form.
3. (Rows versus columns) For vector-matrix multiplication written as $\mathbf{xA}$, we may take vector $\mathbf{x}$ as a row vector.

Abbreviations

1D:	one-dimensional
2D:	two-dimensional
ADC:	analogue-to-digital converter
CFA:	color filter array
dB:	decibel
DCT:	discrete cosine transform
DFT:	discrete Fourier transform
DoG:	difference of Gaussian
DTFT:	discrete time Fourier transform
DWT:	discrete wavelet transform
FFT:	fast Fourier transform
FIR:	finite impulse response
FOH:	first-order hold
FRIQ:	full-reference image quality index
HR:	high-resolution
HVS:	human visual system
IDCT:	inverse discrete cosine transform
IDFT:	inverse discrete Fourier transform
IFS:	iterated function system
IIR:	infinite impulse response
JPEG:	joint photographic experts group
LoG:	Laplacian of Gaussian
LPF:	low-pass filter
LR:	low-resolution
MATLAB:	high-level technical computing language by MathWorks Inc.
MEDI:	modified edge-directed interpolation [59]
MOS:	mean opinion score
MRF:	Markov random field
MSE:	mean squares error
MSSIM:	mean structural similarity [63]
NEDI:	new edge-directed interpolation [40]
NRIQ:	no reference image quality index
PDF:	probability density function
PIFS:	partitioned iterated function system
PSNR:	peak signal-to-noise ratio

QMF: quadrature mirror filter
RGB: red, green, and blue color space
RMSE: root mean squares error
RRIQ: reduced reference image quality index
SNR: signal-to-noise ratio
SSIM: structural similarity [63]
YCbCr: luminance, blue chrominance, red chrominance color space
ZOH: zero-order hold

About the Companion Website

The companion website for this book is at:

www.wiley.com/go/ditmatlab

The website includes:

- MATLAB soruce code and figure inventory. Figure inventory includes certain figures from the book in PNG format for the convenience of the readers.
- PowerPoint file for lecturers[1]
- Solution manual[1]

Scan this QR code to visit the companion website.

---

1 PowerPoint file and Solution manual are available under subscription for professors/lecturers who intent to use this book in their courses.

1

Signal Sampling

We are living in an analog world that makes it fairly easy to overwhelm our computation system to process the vast information carried by the analog signal. To process the analog signal, it will have to be sampled in a way that the sampled signal can be handled by our computation system. The sampled signal should be able to faithfully represent the analog signal. With this, it is natural to ask: "Is it possible to reconstruct the analog signal from the samples?" Such an important question has been answered by the *sampling theorem* [56]. The sampling theorem considers the signal sequence $f[k]$ obtained by uniformly sampling an analog function $f(x)$ with a sampling interval Δ_x, such that

$$f[k] = f(x)\delta(x - k\Delta_x) = f(k\Delta_x), \quad \forall k \in \mathbb{Z}, \tag{1.1}$$

where $\delta(\cdot)$ is a Dirac delta function and $\mathbb{Z}$ is the set of integers. The sampling theorem tells us when and how to reconstruct the analog signal $f(x)$ from the sampled signal sequence $f[k]$. At the same time, the signal sequence $f[k]$ to be handled by the computation system is not only a sampled version of $f(x)$ along x; the amplitude of the signal is also "*sampled*" by a process known as *quantization*. We shall discuss the x domain (also known as the time domain) sampling process in the next section and the quantization process in Section 1.3. Following the presentation of the sampling theorem, the signal reconstruction problem is alleviated by means of interpolation and/or approximation. Other problems that affect the signal reconstruction accuracy, including quantization, will be discussed in Section 1.3. The quantization problem is an important problem because the quantization process is lossy, which poses tremendous difficulties in the recovery of the analog signal. A number of reconstruction methods for *imperfect signal* will be discussed subsequently.

1.1 Sampling and Bandlimited Signal

The readers should have studied Engineering Mathematics in their freshman year; therefore, we shall not discuss the Fourier theorem in detail. Nevertheless, the discrete Fourier transform (DFT) of sampled signal sequence will be introduced in Section 1.2.1 to familiarize the readers with the mathematical notations used in this book. This book also assumes the readers have already acquired the basic knowledge about spectral domain signal processing, and, therefore, this section starts with a formal definition

Digital Image Interpolation in MATLAB®, First Edition. Chi-Wah Kok and Wing-Shan Tam.
© 2019 John Wiley & Sons Singapore Pte. Ltd. Published 2019 by John Wiley & Sons Singapore Pte. Ltd.
Companion website: www.wiley.com/go/ditmatlab

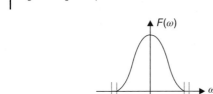

(a)

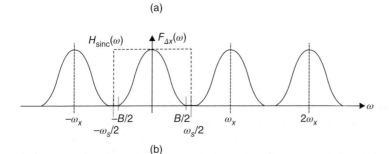

(b)

Figure 1.1 (a) Spectrum of a bandlimited signal $f(x)$ with bandwidth B; (b) sampled with rate $\Delta_x = \frac{2\pi}{\omega_s}$ with $B \leq \omega_x$ can be recovered with a sinc filter with bandwidth ω_s.

of bandlimited signal. A signal $f(x)$ is said to be bandlimited with bandwidth B if and only if it does not contain any frequency components outside the spectral range of $-B/2 \leqslant \omega \leqslant B/2$, where ω is the angular frequency. An example of bandlimited signal is shown in Figure 1.1, where the B bandlimited signal $f(x)$ has its Fourier transform $F(\omega)$ equal 0 with $|\omega| > B/2$.

The sampling theorem tells us the sufficient conditions for the reconstructed signal $g(x)$ obtained from

$$g(x) = f[k] \otimes h(x) = \sum_{k=-\infty}^{\infty} f(k\Delta_x)h(x - k\Delta_x), \tag{1.2}$$

where $h(x)$ is the reconstruction function and the sample sequence $f[k] = f(k\Delta_x)$ with $k \in \mathbb{Z}$ and $\Delta_x > 0$ (as discussed in Eq. (1.1)) is lossless, such that $g(x) = f(x)$, with $f(x)$ being bandlimited by B with sampling frequency $\omega_x = \frac{2\pi}{\Delta_x} \geqslant B$. A formal and also one of the oldest definition of the sampling theorem is given by the following

---

Theorem 1.1 *Sampling theorem:* *Consider a sampled signal $f[k]$ with samples taken at a B-bandlimited function $f(x)$ at sampling period Δ_x. The reconstructed signal,*

$$g(x) = \sum_{k=-\infty}^{\infty} f[k]\mathrm{sinc}\left(\frac{\pi(x - k\Delta_x)}{\Delta_x}\right) = \sum_{k=-\infty}^{\infty} f[k]\mathrm{sinc}\left(\frac{\omega_x}{2}(x - k\Delta_x)\right), \tag{1.3}$$

with $\omega_x = \frac{2\pi}{\Delta_x}$ being the sampling frequency and $\mathrm{sinc}(a) = \sin(a)/a$ being a sinc function, is an exact reconstruction of $f(x)$ when $\omega_s \geqslant B$. It should be noted that both ω_x and B are in radian and $\omega_x = B$ is known as the Nyquist frequency *or* Nyquist rate.

To understand Eq. (1.3) of the sampling theorem, we can make use of the *discrete time Fourier transform* (DTFT) to examine the reconstructed signal $g(x)$.

$$G(\omega) = \sum_k f[k]e^{-2j\omega k} \times \mathcal{F}\left(\text{sinc}\left(\frac{\omega_s}{2}(x - k\Delta_x)\right)\right),$$

$$= \frac{H_{\text{sinc},\Delta x}(\omega)}{\Delta_x} \sum_{k=-\infty}^{\infty} F(\omega - k\omega_s), \tag{1.4}$$

where $H_{\text{sinc},\Delta x}(\omega)$ is the DTFT of $\text{sinc}(\cdot)$ that is a box function of height Δ_x in the spectral domain from $[-\omega_x/2, \omega_x/2]$, and zero everywhere else, and $\mathcal{F}$ is the Fourier transform operator. It is vivid from Eq. (1.4) that the spectrum of the sampled signal is a series of duplications of the original analog signal spectrum of $F(\omega)$ located at spectral locations $k\omega_x$ with $k \in \mathbb{Z}$ as shown in Figure 1.1b. Therefore, when the bandwidth of $f[k]$ is smaller than ω_s, the contributions of the duplicated spectral components $F(\omega - k\omega_x)$ at different k will not overlap (also known as *aliasing*-free). Otherwise, as shown in Figure 1.2b, when the signal spectrum of $f(x)$ has a bandwidth wider than ω_s as shown in Figure 1.2a, the spectral contributions of the sampled signal spectra at different k will overlap. As a result, the reconstructed signal obtained by filtering with $H_{\text{sinc}}(\omega)$ will be a distorted signal $\hat{F}(\omega)$ (not the same as $F(\omega)$). Such kind of distortion is known as the *aliasing distortion*. This helps to illustrate the *Nyquist frequency* ($\omega_x = B$) as a *sufficient* condition to perfectly reconstruct the analog function $f(x)$ from its sample sequence $f[k]$ at a sampling rate $\Delta_x = \frac{2\pi}{B}$.

The sampling theorem (Theorem 1.1) stated that a bandlimited signal $f(x)$ can be sampled at a rate equal to or higher than the Nyquist rate and then reconstructed from its sample sequence without loss by passing the sample sequence $f[k]$ through a noncausal

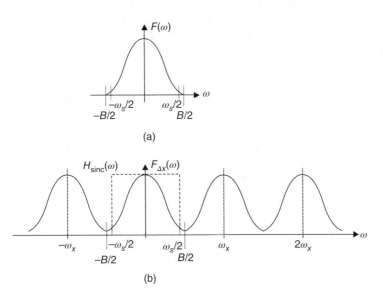

(a)

(b)

Figure 1.2 (a) Spectrum of a bandlimited signal $f(x)$ with bandwidth B; (b) sampled with rate $\Delta_x = \frac{2\pi}{\omega_x}$ with $B > \omega_s$ will suffer from spectrum overlap error, also known as aliasing noise, which makes it difficult to be recovered by a sinc filter with bandwidth ω_s.

filter with the impulse response equal to a sinc function. In reality, Eq. (1.3) is of theoretical interest only because the equation is numerically ill conditioned (the range of $f[k]$ includes both causal and noncausal components). However, it is intuitively clear that the analog function could be closely reconstructed from the sampled sequence using practical reconstruction function (provided that the signal does not change too rapidly and hence bandlimited), and the sampling frequency is relatively high when compared with that of the signal (in that case the sampling frequency is higher than that of the signal bandwidth).

1.2 Unitary Transform

The DTFT can be applied to signal sequence with infinite length to represent the signal in frequency domain. For finite length signals, the concept of spectral (Fourier) domain representation is generalized to transform domain representation with unitary transforms. Let us consider a length N finite duration sequence

$$\mathbf{f} = [\ f[0] \quad f[1] \quad \cdots \quad f[N-1]\ ]^T, \tag{1.5}$$

where $\mathbf{f}$ can be a vector in either $\mathbb{R}^{N\times1}$ or $\mathbb{C}^{N\times1}$. Similarly, consider an invertible matrix $\mathbf{U}$ that is in either $\mathbb{R}^{N\times N}$ or $\mathbb{C}^{N\times N}$, which is known as the *basis matrix* or *kernel matrix*. A linear transform and the associated inverse transform of $\mathbf{f}$ by $\mathbf{U}$ are defined to be

$$\mathbf{F} = \mathbf{U} \cdot \mathbf{f}, \tag{1.6}$$

$$\mathbf{f} = \mathbf{U}^{-1} \cdot \mathbf{F}, \tag{1.7}$$

with $\mathbf{F} \in \mathbb{R}^{N\times1}$ or $\mathbb{C}^{N\times1}$ being the transform coefficient vector of $\mathbf{f}$. In other words, the signal vector $\mathbf{f}$ is represented by $\mathbf{F}$ in a domain described by the basis matrix $\mathbf{U}$. The transform defined by the set of Eqs. (1.6) and (1.7) is said to be a *unitary transform* pair when $\mathbf{U} \in \mathbb{R}^{N\times N}$ and

$$\mathbf{U}^{-1} = \mathbf{U}^T \quad \rightleftharpoons \quad \mathbf{U}\mathbf{U}^T = \mathbf{I}. \tag{1.8}$$

In the case of $\mathbf{U} \in \mathbb{C}^{N\times N}$, the basis matrix $\mathbf{U}$ is a unitary transform when it satisfies

$$\mathbf{U}^{-1} = \mathbf{U}^\dagger \quad \rightleftharpoons \quad \mathbf{U}\mathbf{U}^\dagger = \mathbf{I}, \tag{1.9}$$

where the superscript $\dagger$ denotes the complex conjugate transpose operation and the resulting matrix is known as the Hermitian matrix. The following will present an example of the complex unitary transform, the DFT.

1.2.1 Discrete Fourier Transform

The DFT is derived from the DTFT by assuming $f[n]$ is periodic, which implicitly defines a mapping from $\mathbb{C}^N$ to $\mathbb{C}^N$ between $f[n]$ and $F[k]$ as

$$f[n] \xrightarrow{\ \mathcal{F}\ } F[k] = \sum_{n=0}^{N-1} e^{\frac{-j2\pi kn}{N}} f[n], \qquad \forall k = 0, \dots, N-1, \tag{1.10}$$

with $j = \sqrt{-1}$. The inverse discrete Fourier transform (IDFT) of the sequence $F[k]$ is given by

$$F[k] \xrightarrow{\mathcal{F}^{-1}} f[n] = \sum_{k=0}^{N-1} e^{\frac{j2\pi kn}{N}} F[k], \qquad \forall n = 0, \dots, N-1. \tag{1.11}$$

In the form of unitary transform, the transform kernel of the DFT is given by the $N \times N$ DFT (Fourier) matrix $\mathbf{W}_N$, where the subscript N indicates the kernel size.

$$\mathbf{W}_N = \left[e^{\frac{-j2\pi kn}{N}} \right]_{0 \leqslant k,n < N}. \tag{1.12}$$

If we denote $W_N^k = e^{\frac{-j2\pi k}{N}}$, the Nth root of unity, then the Fourier matrix can be expressed as a Vandermonde matrix in W. As an example, the 3×3 Fourier matrix is given by

$$\mathbf{W}_3 = \begin{bmatrix} W_3^0 & W_3^0 & W_3^0 \\ W_3^0 & W_3^1 & W_3^2 \\ W_3^0 & W_3^2 & W_3^4 \end{bmatrix} = \begin{bmatrix} 1 & 1 & 1 \\ 1 & W_3^1 & W_3^2 \\ 1 & W_3^2 & W_3^1 \end{bmatrix}. \tag{1.13}$$

Therefore, one can view the computation of $F[k]$ from $f[n]$ as a matrix vector product of

$$\mathcal{F}(f) = \mathbf{W}_N \mathbf{f} = \mathbf{F}. \tag{1.14}$$

The IDFT can be easily obtained by multiplication of $\mathbf{W}_N^{-1}$ to Eq. (1.14). Since the matrix $\mathbf{W}_N$ is an orthogonal matrix, therefore, $\mathbf{W}_N^{-1} = \mathbf{W}_N^{\dagger}$ as given by Eq. (1.9). In image interpolation, N is usually very large, and an efficient method to compute the DFT is required. In MATLAB, an efficient computation of the DFT is available by means of the *fast Fourier transform* (FFT) command `fft`.

It is vivid that the kernel of the Fourier matrix $\mathbf{W}_N$ is a function of $j = \sqrt{-1}$, which makes this kernel complex. As a result the power of the signal in frequency domain (Fourier domain) given by the power spectrum $P[u]$ is obtained as the sum of squares of the real and imaginary part of the DFT

$$P[u] = |F[u]|^2 = (R^2(\mathcal{F}[u]) + I^2(\mathcal{F}[u])), \tag{1.15}$$

which measures the power of individual sinusoidal components contained in the signal.

1.3 Quantization

The time domain (x domain) sampled signal has a continuum of values, as can be observed from the solid line in Figure 1.3. However, the sampled analog signal must be representable in digital form for storage or transmission. Since the number of bits (binary digits) for representing each signal sample is limited, the analog samples must be *quantized* to a finite number of levels before it can be coded in the form of binary numbers. As a result, the quantization process compresses the continuum of analog values to a finite number of discrete values. It is vivid that the quantization process will introduce distortion into the quantized signal when compared with the original

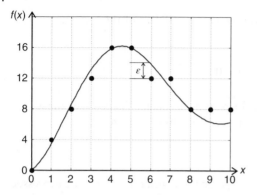

Figure 1.3 Sampling and quantization of a one-dimensional continuous signal.

analog signal. This kind of distortion is known as *quantization noise*. In simple terms, a scalar quantizer for real signal is a mapping from $\mathbb{R}$ to a finite set of discrete values on the real number line. The quantized value is chosen to be the closest approximation to the amplitude of the input signal within the finite set. Formally, a scalar quantizer $Q(\cdot)$ defines the mapping of the input *decision intervals* ($d_k : k = 0, 1, \ldots, L$) to output or *reconstruction levels* ($r_k : k = 0, \ldots, L - 1$). The quantized signal is given by

$$f_Q(x) = Q(f(x)) = r_k \quad \text{with } d_k \leqslant f(x) < d_{k+1} \qquad \text{for } k = 0, \ldots, L - 1. \tag{1.16}$$

Without loss of generality, the decision levels are chosen such that

$$d_0 < d_1 < \cdots < d_L. \tag{1.17}$$

Furthermore, d_0 and d_L are selected to be the minimum and maximum possible input signals. It should be noted that $d_0 = -\infty$ and $d_L = \infty$ are valid and are being chosen for most of the quantizers applied in practice. As a result, the number of bits required to address any one of the output levels is $\lceil \log_2 L \rceil$ bits with $\lceil \cdot \rceil$ being the ceiling operator that returns the smallest integer equal to or larger than $\log_2 L$. There exist a lot of quantizers (a particular choice of d_k and r_k) that are optimal for different applications. Without loss of generality and limitation in our discussions, we shall focus on uniform quantizer in this book, where the difference between decision levels of the quantizer equals to a constant step size Δ_Q.

$$\Delta_Q = d_k - d_{k-1}, \qquad \forall k \in \mathbb{Z}^+. \tag{1.18}$$

An example of an analog signal being sampled and quantized is shown in Figure 1.3, where the analog signal plotted in the figure is a damped cosine function.

$$f(x) = 10e^{-x/10} \cos\left(\frac{x}{10}\omega - \theta\right) - \gamma, \tag{1.19}$$

with $\omega = 2\pi$, $\theta = 3$, and $\gamma = -9.9$. The sampled and quantized signal samples are plotted in Figure 1.3 by black dots together with the analog signal $f(x)$ by solid line. It can be observed that the sampled signal can faithfully represent the analog signal with quantization error $\epsilon(x)$ (also known as quantization noise as marked in Figure 1.3 for the case of $x = 6$). The quantization error is highly correlated with the number of bits applied to quantize the signal. Shown in Figure 1.4 is the same signal being sampled with the same

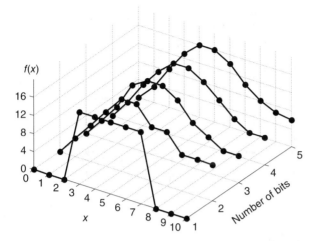

Figure 1.4 Signal sampling with different quantization bit depths.

sampling rate and quantized with a uniform quantizer under different numbers of bits. It can be observed from Figure 1.4 that the "*quality*" of the sampled and quantized signal sequence improves rapidly with small increases in the number of bits being applied to the uniform quantizer. The higher the *quality*, the better the sampled and quantized signal sequences resemble the analog signal, both visually and also in least squares sense. In fact, the improvement is very efficient in particular for the case of increasing the number of quantization bits from 2 bits to 3 bits. This visual evidence leads us to conjecture that there exists a close relationship between the sampling rate and the quantization bit length that affects the quality of the sampled signal.

1.3.1 Quantization and Sampling Interaction

The interaction between sampling and quantization can be revealed by observing the sampling and quantization results shown in Figure 1.5. Shown in Figure 1.5a is the damped cosine function as depicted in Eq. (1.19) being sampled and quantized with a particular rate and bit length. Figure 1.5b shows the same damped cosine function sampled with doubled sampling rate but quantized with the same bit length as that in Figure 1.5a. It can be observed that the quality of the sampled signal does not improve significantly. In other words, the *quality* of the sampled signal sequence cannot be improved by increasing the sampling rate alone. It requires the increment of both the sampling rate and the quantization bit length to improve the *quality* of the sampled signal as shown in Figure 1.5c, where the damped cosine function is sampled with doubled sampling rate and quantized with one more bit when compared with that in Figure 1.5a. In the rest of this book, we shall assume that adequate number of quantization bit length is applied to all the image processing and interpolation problems, such that the quality of different image processing and interpolation problems will be independent of the quantization bit length.

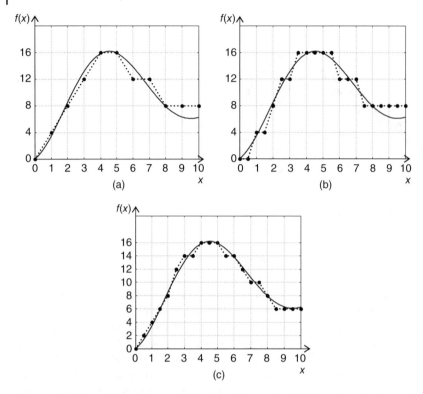

Figure 1.5 Effects of sampling rate and number of quantization bit on the sampling quality of a one-dimensional continuous signal: (a) a damped cosine function sampled with a particular sampling rate and number of quantization bit, (b) the same function sampled with doubled sampling rate but the same number of quantization bit length, and (c) the same function with the same sampling rate as that in (b) and increased number of quantization bit by one.

1.4 Sampled Function Approximation: Fitting and Interpolation

Theoretically the sampled signal can be perfectly reconstructed by Eq. (1.3). However, the filter in Eq. (1.3) is noncausal and thus cannot be used in practice. Furthermore, the samples are obtained with sampling rate that may not satisfy the sampling theorem. Even if the above two conditions are satisfied, the sampled signal will suffer from quantization error. As a result, exact signal reconstruction is difficult, if not impossible. In practice, the signal reconstruction problem is very often reformulated as a *function approxima-tion* problem that extracts a function representation from the given signal samples. The function approximation can be roughly classified into two categories: *interpolation* and *fitting*. The fundamental difference between these two techniques is that the interpola-tion function passes through all the given signal samples, while the fitting function may not pass all the signal samples. Figure 1.6 is an example illustrating the fundamental dif-ference between interpolation and fitting. The dots lying on the sampling grid are the data points sampled from the original damped cosine function depicted in Eq. (1.19). The solid line is the curve obtained by interpolation, while the dashed line is the result

Figure 1.6 Reconstructing the analog signal from its samples through *interpolation* (solid line) and *fitting* by *least squares approximation* (dashed line).

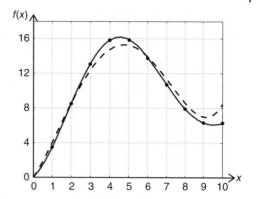

obtained by fitting. It can be observed that the interpolation curve does pass through all data points, while the fitting curve does not. Formally, we can define the interpolation problem as a constrained functional fitting problem, such that the fitting function is constrained to pass through all the given signal samples. There exist a lot of functions that can be applied to the interpolation (function approximation) problem. In particular the one shown in Figure 1.6 is obtained by minimizing the least squares difference between the given samples with a set of predefined basis functions. One of such function is a degree n polynomial $P_n(x)$. The Weierstrass theorem formulated the function approximation problem between $f(x)$ and $P_n(x)$ as a least squares problem that minimizes ϵ with

$$|f(x) - P_n(x)|_2 \leqslant \epsilon, \qquad x \in [0, N], \tag{1.20}$$

with $|\cdot|_2$ being the $\mathcal{L}_2$ norm operator and $\epsilon > 0$ being a predetermined small quantity also known as the *approximation error*. If the problem is further constrained to satisfy

$$\text{comb}(x, \Delta_x)f(x) = \text{comb}(x, \Delta_x)P_n(x). \tag{1.21}$$

Then the function approximation problem is equivalent to an interpolation problem, where $P_n(k\Delta_x) = f[k]$. The comb function $\text{comb}(x, \Delta_x)$ is given by

$$\text{comb}(x, \Delta_x) = \sum_{k=-\infty}^{\infty} \delta(x - k\Delta_x), \tag{1.22}$$

which is equivalent to a pulse train function. If n is sufficiently large, a polynomial $P_n(x)$ can be found to satisfy Eq. (1.21), which in our example is plotted with a solid line in Figure 1.6. On the other hand, when the order of the polynomial is not large enough, $P_n(x)$ may not be able to satisfy Eq. (1.21), and the best $P_n(x)$ that satisfies Eq. (1.20) will be similar to that plotted in Figure 1.6 with a dashed line, which does not pass through all the given sample points.

It is vivid that it is impractical to apply polynomial function with a given degree n to interpolate any given set of signal samples within a predefined interval. As a result, interpolation by polynomial functions is always performed in a piecewise fashion, such as those shown in the following sections, where two frequently used signal reconstruction techniques (which involve the application of two polynomials with degrees 0 and 1) are presented. These two methods are simple and easy to use and are thus adopted in many real-life applications, even though the reconstruction results are far from satisfactory in many cases.

1.4.1 Zero-Order Hold (ZOH)

One practical reconstruction method that has been applied in many applications is the zero-order hold (ZOH) method. The ZOH method is also known as the *nearest neighbor* method, where the interpolated signal samples are filled with the same value as that of the signal sample on the left (time or x domain index smaller than that of the signal location under concern) of it. For theoretical and sometimes practical purposes, it is useful to model the interpolation method by a convolution process. The ZOH interpolation method follows the signal reconstruction Eq. (1.2) with the reconstruction filter $h(x) = h_0(x)$ given by

$$h_0(x) = \begin{cases} 1, & \text{for } 0 \leqslant x \leqslant \Delta_x, \\ 0, & \text{elsewhere.} \end{cases} \tag{1.23}$$

This interpolation kernel is plotted in Figure 1.7a. The filtering can be evaluated between $f_{\Delta_x}(x)$ and $h_0(x)$ in time domain through convolution to obtain the reconstructed signal $g(x)$ as

$$g(x) = h_0(x) \otimes f_{\Delta_x}(x) = \int_0^{\Delta_x} \sum_{k=-\infty}^{\infty} f[k]\delta(x - k\Delta_x - \ell)d\ell$$

$$= \sum_{k=-\infty}^{\infty} f[k](u(x - k\Delta_x) - u(x - (k+1)\Delta_x)), \tag{1.24}$$

with $u(\cdot)$ being the step function. The difference between the two-step functions in Eq. (1.24) will lead to a $g(x)$ that looks like staircase approximation as shown in Figure 1.7b for the sampled damped cosine function $f(x)$ in Eq. (1.19).

1.4.2 First-Order Hold (FOH)

Another frequently used interpolation method constructs an analog signal by connecting adjacent signal samples using a straight line. This is equivalent to interpolate the missing signal as a weighted sum of adjacent signal samples where the weight equals the distance between the missing signal and the two adjacent signal samples. Following Eq. (1.2), the interpolation can be accomplished by passing $f[k]$ through the first-order hold (FOH) (noncausal) but finite in length filter $h(x) = h_1(x)$ given by

$$h_1(x) = \text{tri}\left(\frac{x}{\Delta_x}\right) = \begin{cases} 1 - \frac{|x|}{\Delta_x}, & \text{for } |x| \leqslant \Delta_x, \\ 0, & \text{otherwise,} \end{cases} \tag{1.25}$$

with Δ_x being the distance between two signal samples. The interpolation kernel in Eq. (1.25) is equivalent to a triangular function (tri($\cdot$)), and its impulse response is plotted in Figure 1.7c. The reconstructed signal $g(x)$ is thus given by

$$g(x) = h_1(x) \otimes f_{\Delta_x}(x)$$

$$= \sum_{k=-\infty}^{\infty} f[k]\text{tri}\left(\frac{x - k\Delta_x}{\Delta_x}\right). \tag{1.26}$$

The reconstructed signal of the sampled damped cosine function in Eq. (1.19) is shown in Figure 1.7d. It can be observed that the FOH gives much better interpolation results than

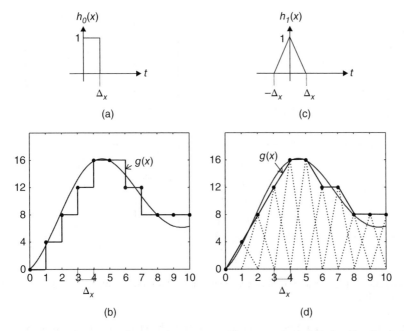

Figure 1.7 Illustration of (a) impulse response of a zero-order hold (ZOH) filter $h_0(x)$; (b) the sampled signal $g(x)$ reconstructed using the ZOH filter $h_0(x)$; (c) impulse response of a first-order hold (FOH) filter $h_1(x)$; (d) the reconstructed signal filtered by $h_1(x)$.

those obtained by ZOH. If we consider the ZOH and FOH filters in spectral domain, which are given by

$$h_0(x) \overset{\mathcal{F}}{\leftrightarrow} H_0(j\omega) = \frac{2}{\omega} \sin\left(\frac{\omega \Delta_x}{2}\right) e^{-j\omega \Delta_x/2}, \qquad (1.27)$$

$$h_1(x) \overset{\mathcal{F}}{\leftrightarrow} H_1(j\omega) = \frac{4}{\omega^2 \Delta_x} \sin^2\left(\frac{\omega \Delta_x}{2}\right), \qquad (1.28)$$

and are plotted in Figure 1.8b,c, respectively, for the case of $\Delta_x = 1$, it is vivid that both the time and spectral domain responses of the filter kernels of ZOH and FOH are the approximation to that of the sinc filter with a finite kernel size as shown in Figure 1.8a. The FOH is observed to produce better interpolation result in Figure 1.7d, and at the same time, the FOH kernel (in both time and spectral domains) also achieves better approximation to that of the sinc filter. This observation led us to draw the conclusion that the quality of the interpolated signal not only depends on how well the interpolation filter mimics the sinc filter but also depends on how well the time and spectral responses of the interpolation filter match the time and spectral responses of the analog signal. High-order polynomial interpolation kernel can provide very good mimic to the sinc interpolator. It is, however, the signal reconstructed by higher-order polynomial filter that has a higher-order differentiability. The higher the order of the filter kernel, the faster the decay rate of the filter response in high frequency than that of lower degree filter kernel. As a result, these filters help to minimize the introduction of high frequency interpolation error. But at the same time, they may also remove some high frequency components of the original signal. We shall discuss the two-dimensional (2D) digital

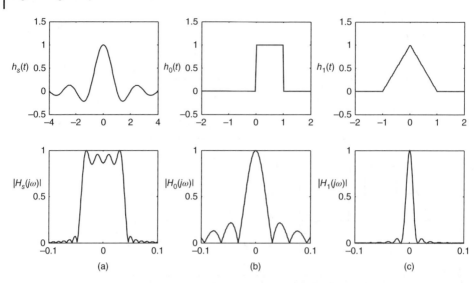

Figure 1.8 Time and spectral responses for various reconstruction filters: (a) Sinc filter; (b) Zero-order hold; and (c) First-order hold.

image interpolation in a sequel, where it is concluded that the sharpness of the interpolated image is being traded for edge blurring as the degree of the interpolation kernel increases. Disregarding the kind of performance trade-off, it is the purpose of the rest of this book to introduce interpolation kernels and methods that aim at interpolating the sampled signal with the best performance trade-off to reconstruct a signal that closely mimics the analog signal.

1.4.3 Digital Interpolation

Instead of reconstructing the analog signal, most of the digital signal applications only interested in *digital interpolation*. The objective of digital interpolation is to obtain a new sequence that is a close approximation to the sampled sequence obtained from sampling the associated analog signal with high sampling rate. Such process is sometimes known as *up-sampling*. The digital interpolation is considered to be computationally efficient, as it avoids the analog function reconstruction problem. As an example, the digital interpolation by a factor of r through linear filtering can be achieved through a two-stage process, where (i) $r - 1$ zeros are inserted between every two samples of $f[k]$ in the first stage and then (ii) filter the zero-inserted signal by a digital filter (the interpolated kernel). Two possible filters (ZOH and FOH) are introduced in previous sections as depicted in Eqs. (1.23) and (1.25). More interpolation filters and their properties will be discussed in subsequent chapters.

1.5 Book Organization

In Chapter 2, the fundamental theories of digital and analog images and related mathematical manipulations will be presented, together with a formal definition of the image interpolation problem. We shall also discuss the application of MATLAB to manipulate digital images in a PC environment. The performance of the interpolation algorithm should be determined by human; however, such quality assessment method is either biased due to small sample size (human observers) or very expensive and slow when the sample size is large (a large group of human observers). Instead, various analytical quality measures are developed, where some are developed specifically to mimic the human visual system to provide limited subjective quality measure. Some of the frequently used quality measures will be discussed in Chapter 3 to assist the performance evaluation of various image interpolation algorithms to be presented in subsequent chapters.

The rest of the book is formally divided into three parts: the traditional nonadaptive image interpolation methods, the model-based image interpolation methods, and the fractal-based interpolation methods. Many other arrangements could be adopted; however, the authors have chosen this framework because they believe that it is the most natural way for the readers to first learn the conventional image interpolation methods and work their way up to the advanced image interpolation methods. Algorithms presented in Chapter 4 are pure nonadaptive interpolation methods, where the image is interpolated with only one assumption, that is, the sampled signal (image) is bandlimited. Chapter 4 derives the traditional nonadaptive linear filtering-based interpolation methods from sampling theorem. Some of the interpolation algorithms are very effective in interpolating texture-rich areas, which will be integrated as part of the model-based image interpolation methods to be presented in later chapters. Chapter 5 is devoted to the discussion of image interpolation in the spectral domain. The basic theoretical performance is the same as the corresponding nonadaptive methods presented in Chapter 4. However, the implementation in frequency domain through block-based transformation allows the change of interpolation kernels (transform basis) on the fly and thus can achieve mixed-basis interpolation with ease. Furthermore, we shall also present iterative interpolation methods, which can be considered as a back propagation algorithm that helps to improve the interpolated image quality.

Chapter 6 extends the image interpolation problem from spatial to spectral domain and then to scale-space. Traditionally wavelet transform can be viewed as conventional transform as those discussed in Chapter 5. However, the multi-resolution decomposition method adopted by wavelet transform allows us to construct a scale-space representation of the image where the transform kernel adopts to the changing scales. Features that are important to the human visual system can be easily located in scale-space. The application of across scale information is the first step to apply model-based image interpolation. The advantage of model-based image interpolation is fully revealed in subsequent chapters.

The model-based image interpolation methods that preserve the structure and edges of the image using explicit edge maps obtained from edge detectors are presented in Chapter 7. The interpolated image quality can be greatly improved; however, their performance is limited by the accuracy of the edge map. Due to the existence of image noise (which includes the quantization noise) and the complexity of the edges in two dimensions, it is difficult to obtain good edge localization and completeness. Edge-directed image interpolation methods that make use of implicit edge information, such as scale-invariant geometric duality in second-order statistics, are presented in Chapter 8.

The iterative interpolation algorithm first discussed in Chapter 5 can be implemented in all model-based algorithms to improve the image interpolation results. This is because subsequent interpolation loop helps to correct the interpolation error resulted from the previous loop. Similar iterative approach will be applied to the model-based method in Chapter 8.

The fractal image interpolation method presented in Chapter 9 is the ultimate iterative image interpolation method. Instead of modeling the image as composed with edges and filled with texture in between, fractal image coding models the image as self-organized low-resolution fractal images. As a result, interpolation is just as simple as growing the fractal image to the desired resolution. However, fractal image interpolation

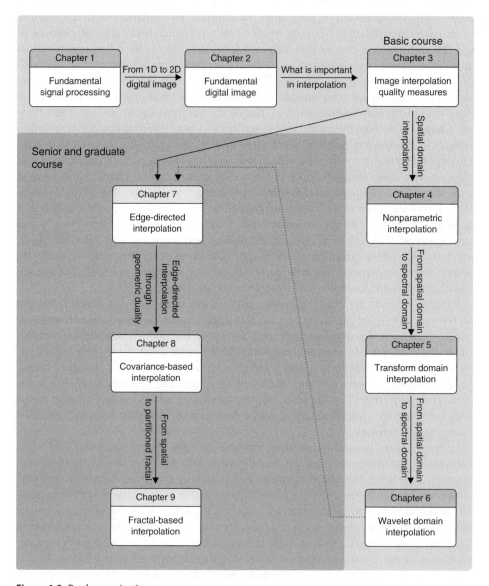

Figure 1.9 Book organization.

is probabilistic and does not guarantee the original image pixel intensities that are preserved in the interpolation process. An appropriate modification of the conventional fractal reconstruction algorithm is required to preserve the low-resolution image pixel values to achieve image interpolation instead of fitting.

This text is intended for use as a senior course in image processing. The above topics can be arranged in many ways in the lectures, depending on the coverage required in the course. Shown in Figure 1.9 is the suggested course material arrangement. A useful approach for undergraduate teaching will cover the materials from Chapters 1 to 6 to provide the understanding of image interpolation from basic signal processing algorithms and interpolated image quality evaluations to nonadaptive image interpolation methods. Chapters 7–9 are advanced topics on image interpolation. In particular, we focus on edge-directed image interpolation methods. A senior undergraduate course can be easily organized from materials presented in Chapters 1 –5 and 7. Chapters 6, 8, and 9 involve graduate-level understanding of image processing using high-order statistics, wavelet, and fractal image processing. The materials presented in Chapters 5–9 will form a one-semester graduate-level course, where Chapter 5 will provide the necessary review of the transform domain image processing.

In our experience, students learn more when they are given realistic assignments to carry out. To this end, we would encourage substantial assignments on, for example, the MATLAB implementation of the studied image interpolation methods and tweaking those algorithms to achieve the desired subjective performance. This work should be designed to demonstrate and reinforce the techniques taught. It is important that students actually participate and attend lectures to gain the best from the course.

1.6   Exercises

1.1   Consider the inverse DFT with $N = 5$.
1. Find the inverse Fourier matrix $\mathcal{F}^{-1}$.
2. Verify that it is the inverse of $\mathcal{F}$, that is, show $\mathcal{F}\mathcal{F}^{-1} = \mathbf{I}$.

1.2   Develop a MATLAB program that accepts $N + 1$ pairs of data points $(x_0, y_0), \ldots, (x_N, y_N)$ and generates a $1 \times N$ vector $[a_N \; a_{N-1} \; a_0]$ such that the polynomial $P(x) = a_N x^N + a_{N-1} x^{N-1} + \cdots \; a_0$ will pass through the given data points.

1.3   Develop a MATLAB program that accepts N data points and generates $2 \times N$ data points by resampling the first-order hold function constructed with the given N data points.

2

Digital Image

An image is a two-dimensional (2D) light intensity function $f(x, y)$, where (x, y) is a coordinate system of interest. Without loss of generality, and to simplify our discussions, the rest of the book will concentrate on the case of 2D Cartesian coordinate. The value of f at the coordinates (x, y) is proportional to the brightness of the image at that point. While digital images can be generated/acquired by a number of methods, primarily, the image f is converted to a digital image through cameras using a 2D image sensor array, which are typically constructed with *charge-coupled devices* (CCD) and *complementary metal oxide semiconductor* (CMOS) technologies. Camera constructed with CCD or CMOS works in a similar fashion, where the light reflected from an object $f(x, y)$ will impinge onto the face of the sensor array, such that the $f(x, y)$ will be converted into an electrical signal. Figure 2.1 illustrates the construction of a color digital camera that is used to capture the *Cat* image. The light bounced off from the *Cat* will be focused onto the sensor array through the lens. Considering a sensor array with M-rows and N-columns, the output of the sensor array will be an $M \times N$ matrix, where each of the element represents the light intensity exposed to the corresponding sensor location. The output of the sensor array is not a digital image yet. The subsequent *analog-to-digital converter* (A/D converter) accomplishes the quantization processes (as discussed in Section 1.3) of the light intensity at each (x, y) location to generate the digital image.

The arrangement of the image sensor array is also known as the *sampling grid*, where the intersection of a row and a column will be assigned with an integer coordinates $[m, n]$ with $0 \leqslant m \leqslant M - 1$ and $0 \leqslant n \leqslant N - 1$. The sampled image obtained from the sampling and quantization process as shown in Figure 2.2a,b is the discrete image that forms a matrix $[f[m, n]] : m, n \in \mathbb{Z}^+; 0 \leqslant m \leqslant M - 1, 0 \leqslant n \leqslant N - 1$. Each entry in this array, $f[m, n]$, records the sensing data of the corresponding sensor in the arrays and is termed a *pixel*. Thus, a digital image will look like

$$\left[f[m, n] \right] = \begin{bmatrix} f[0, 0] & f[0, 1] & \cdots & f[0, N-1] \\ f[1, 0] & f[1, 1] & \cdots & f[1, N-1] \\ \vdots & \vdots & \ddots & \vdots \\ f[M-1, 0] & f[M-1, 1] & \cdots & f[M-1, N-1] \end{bmatrix}. \tag{2.1}$$

The values assigned to every pixels are the brightness recorded by the image sensor, which is also interpreted as the pixel *intensity* (also known as the *gray* level or

Digital Image Interpolation in MATLAB®, First Edition. Chi-Wah Kok and Wing-Shan Tam.
© 2019 John Wiley & Sons Singapore Pte. Ltd. Published 2019 by John Wiley & Sons Singapore Pte. Ltd.
Companion website: www.wiley.com/go/ditmatlab

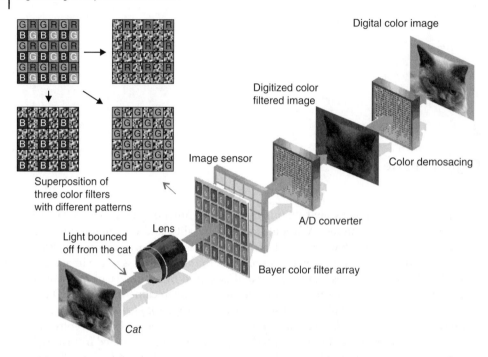

Figure 2.1 Illustration of capturing an image by digital camera. (*See insert for color representation of this figure.*)

grayscale.[1] To store, transmit, and visualize the discrete image, the pixel intensity of the discrete image will be rounded to the nearest integer value within L different gray levels through quantization performed within the A/D converter. This process will produce the digital image, which can be visualized as a shade of gray denoted as the *grayscale* or *gray level* value ranging from black (0) to white ($L - 1$). Figure 2.2b shows the pixel values of an extract from the image $f[m, n]$. It can be observed that the higher the intensity value, the brighter the image pixel. More details will be discussed in Section 2.1.

The discrete image is arranged with each pixel $f[m, n]$ being located at the mth row and nth column starting from the top left image origin (as shown in Figure 2.2a) with respect to the MATLAB convention. The readers may have already noticed from Figure 2.2a that the matrix indices in the figure are different from that in Eq. (2.1). This is one of the irritating features of MATLAB; notwithstanding the similarity between the arithmetic and the language of MATLAB, all matrices within MATLAB are indexed with the top left-hand entry as $[1, 1]$ instead of $[0, 0]$ and hence the discrepancy between Figure 2.2a and Eq. (2.1). The rest of the book will assume this difference to be natural and will no longer discuss the difference between the MATLAB implementation and the analytical analysis with respect to the indexing problem. The digital representation of images in MATLAB will be detailed in Section 2.1.

---

1 The authors do not want to join the fight between "greyscale" and "grayscale." It is however, MATLAB adopted "grayscale" and we adopted MATLAB, and thus this book will use "grayscale."

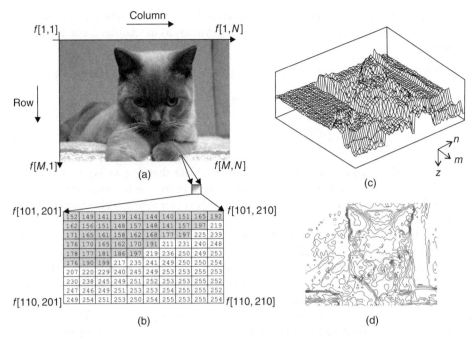

Figure 2.2 Representation of the digital image *Cat*: (a) a grayscale printout of *Cat*, which is described by an *M* × *N* 2D array within the computation system with each matrix element representing the intensity of a pixel taking a value in the quantizer (in this case, it is [0, 255] for *Cat* is a 8-bit quantized image); (b) a pixel intensity map of the selected region in the image, where the pixel intensity at [101, 201] is 152; and the intensity variation across the complete image by viewing (c) the 2D vector mesh of the image on a plane with the height (*z*-axis) being the pixel intensity (note the direction of the *z*-axis is inverted to display the *Cat* more vividly) or through (d) the contour map, where the pixel with same intensities are located on the same contour lines.

Reader may wonder the functions of *Bayer color filter array* (CFA) and *color demosaicing block* in Figure 2.1. These two modules are essential in capturing images with color. To be more precise, Bayer CFA is a typical construction of CFA, which is commonly applied to the photosensor arrays in modern camera. The filter is arranged in Bayer pattern, which is a combination of red, green, and blue filters in checker board format. The size of the CFA is identical to the sensor array, and each color filter has a narrow pass-band and will only allow the light component with the same color tone as that of the filter to pass through. Therefore, each pixel in the "digitized color filtered image" is the intensity of one of the three color tones of a color pixel. The color demosaicing block takes the role to restore the color image by superimposing the red, green, and blue pixels to form a complete color image with red, green, and blue panes. The details of digital color imaging will be discussed in Section 2.8.

Some might noticed that the digital image can be represented by other forms that are not pixel oriented. For example, the JPEG image [52] is not stored in a pixel array form to achieve a compact storage size. Nonetheless, pixels are still the central concept in digital imaging. The quality of the digital image grows with the spatial, spectral, radiometric, and time resolutions of the digitization process. This image model allows us to identify the set of digital images with complex vector space $\mathcal{L}^2(\mathbb{Z}_M \times \mathbb{Z}_N)$, where complex space is used because we are preparing for the transform analysis in Chapter 5 and the rest of the book.

$$\mathcal{L}^2(\mathbb{Z}_M \times \mathbb{Z}_N) = \{f \; : \; \{0, \dots, M-1\} \times \{0, \dots, N-1\} \to \mathbb{C} : f \text{ is a map}\}, \qquad (2.2)$$

which also defines the following scalar product

$$\langle f, g \rangle = \sum_{m=0}^{M-1} \sum_{n=0}^{N-1} f[m,n]\overline{g[m,n]}, \qquad (2.3)$$

where the overline denotes complex conjugation. Note that f, g in Eq. (2.3) are two matrices of the same size. Since an image is presented in this vector space through spatial coordinates $[m, n]$, therefore, the domain of this vector space is also termed as the *spatial* domain.

The row-by-column dimensions of the digital image defines the number of pixels used to represent the analog image, which is known as the sampling rate and also referred to as the pixel or *spatial resolution* (also known as *geometric resolution*) of the digital image. The notation $M \times N$ is commonly used to denote the spatial resolution. The variation in intensity across the image pixels can form a vector valued mesh on a plane, where the mesh location is defined by the pixel location. An example of the functional plot of the mesh defined by the image $f[m, n]$ in Figure 2.2a is shown in Figure 2.2c. However, the spatial resolution does not tell us much about the actual appearance of the image as realized on a physical device. The *resolution density*, which gives the number of pixels per unit length, such as the *pixels per inch* (ppi) or the *dots per inch* (dpi), is the common unit that enables us to obtain the dimensions of the image. Such that when specified together with the spatial resolution, the actual image size will be determined.

It should be noted that $f[m, n]$ is a three-dimensional (3D) discrete function. Furthermore, it is constrained to be a nonnegative function. Due to the digitization process, this function will only take on a finite number of values (in our case, L different values). The number of quantization levels will affect the *radiometric resolution* of the digitized image that measures the number of distinguishable gray levels in the digital image. An effective method to display the quantization effect of the image is by means of image isophotes, which are curves of constant gray value, such that $f[m, n] = c$ for a given c, with analogy to iso-height lines on a geometric map. An image isophote plot of the *Cat* image in Figure 2.2a is shown in Figure 2.2d.

The spatial resolution and the radiometric resolution are the two factors affecting the quality of the digital image. These two factors can be altered by users during the image capturing processes. Besides, the *spectral resolution* that specifies the bandwidth of the light frequencies captured by the sensor and the *time resolution* that measures the interval between time samples at which images are captured are technology dependent and are therefore seldom discussed in digital image processing, but rather in the semiconductor device and circuit of the image capturing devices.

Besides capturing natural images using digital camera, digital images can also be generated synthetically. Shown in Figure 2.3 is a synthetic image of the letter A that is black in color and on top of a white background with a gray shadow. Synthetic image usually has sharp edges and uniform texture area without noise. Digital color image can be synthesized in a similar fashion.

Figure 2.3 Synthetic grayscale image: Letter *A*.

2.1 Digital Imaging in MATLAB

Digital images can be stored in computer with a number of formats, such as "bmp" (bit map), "tiff" (tagged image file format), "jpg" (joint photographic experts group), "pcx" (PC paintbrush), "png" (portable network graphics), etc. MATLAB can use the built-in function imread to import the digital image into the computer system.

MATLAB 2.1.1—Import digital image.

```
>> f = imread('cat.jpg','jpeg');
```

The imported image is stored in the $M \times N$ array f=[f(m,n)], with line index $1 \leqslant m \leqslant M$ representing the vertical position and column index $1 \leqslant n \leqslant N$ representing the horizontal position of each pixel within the image array, where $m, n \in \mathbb{Z}^+$. Please note that all the matrices and vectors in MATLAB are indexed from 1 and onward, while our analytical derivations will manipulate signal vectors and matrices from 0 and onward. These unmatched indices will have to be taken good care of when coding image processing algorithms using MATLAB.

The spatial resolution of the image f can be examined in MATLAB by the command whos as shown in Listing 2.1.2.

MATLAB 2.1.2—Digital image details.

```
>> whos f
   Name      Size           Bytes      Class
   f         1400x2000      2800000    uint8
```

Note that the data type of f in this example is uint8 (*8-bit unsigned integer*). The number 8 that specifies the number of binary bits required for storage at a given quantization level is known as the *bit resolution*, which works hand in hand with radiometric resolution to specify the clarity of the captured image to be observed by human. For instance, a binary image has just two pixel values (black or white) and has 1-bit resolution. A grayscale image commonly has 256 different gray levels ranging from black to white and is therefore has 8-bit resolution, which means that each pixel (each entry in the array f(m,n)) takes value in one of the integers between 0 and $2^8 - 1$ (8-bit encoding). Within these 256 levels, 0 is black, and 255 is white in the convention of

MATLAB. The bit resolution of a digital image is also referred to as the *dynamic range* of an image. The quantization effect of the 1D signal that we have discussed in Section 1.3 as shown in Figure 1.4 will have the same effect in the 2D digital image. As a result, digital image with low dynamic range will look blocky just as that in Figure 1.4.

The image array f with data type uint8 can be printed or displayed by electronic devices, such as printer and computer screen. The Listing 2.1.3 applies the MATLAB built-in function imshow to display f on computer monitor. The MATLAB command imwrite can be applied to store the image into the PC file system with a selected image format. The example in Listing 2.1.4 saves the uint8 image array f in png format with filename 'image.png'.

MATLAB 2.1.3—Display digital image.

```
>> imshow(f);
```

MATLAB 2.1.4—Saving a digital image f to a png file with filename "image.png."

```
>> imwrite(f,'image.png','png');
```

The readers may have noticed that we have placed special attention to the data type of the image array f. This is because the uint8 data type can take value in one of the integers within the range of 0–255. The data type uint8 uses 8-bit of information to represent integers from 0 to 255. In general image processing application, different mathematical computations will be applied to the pixel values, resulting in intermediates floating point or negative values, which cannot be fully represented by the uint8 data and results in overflow or known as data type error in MATLAB. As a result, it is a common practice to convert the uint8 data into double to render the data type error problem for any computation in MATLAB. double refers to a double-precision data that uses 64-bit to represent the data.

There are series of built-in data conversion functions in MATLAB. typecast is the general data conversion function that supports lossless conversion in between different data types. However, it is more common to use the typecasting functions double and uint8 for direct conversion. It should be noted that the data in double data type has 64-bit data and it may contain floating point information; the direct conversion of a double data to a uint8 data will truncate and round off the data to the nearest integer in the range of [0, 255]. The truncation is system dependent such that the result of direct conversion may be different from system to system. However, the difference is not noticeable in most of the cases. Listings 2.1.5 and 2.1.6 show the usage of the conversion functions uint8 and double, respectively.

MATLAB 2.1.5—Data type conversions from uint8 to double.

```
>> f = double(f);
```

```
>> f = uint8(f);
```

The readers may have also noticed that the images in the example are of size 256×256 and 512×512. This is because many operations and arithmetic with images can be simplified when the dimension (both row and column) of the image is of power of 2. However, the readers should understand that all operations discussed in this book are applicable to images with arbitrary size through some small and necessary modifications.

2.2 Current Pixel and Neighboring Pixels

After we have imported an image into MATLAB as an array, we can manipulate it as any other numeric vectors and matrices. Such manipulation is termed as *image processing*. To ease our discussions on the pixel under processing to other pixels in the same image, we define the term *"current pixel"* to describe this particular pixel. In the case of image interpolation, the *current pixel* can have an unknown value and is to be estimated from the *image interpolation algorithm* using *a priori* knowledge of its surrounding pixels, also known as *"neighboring pixels."* The collection of the *neighboring pixels* can be very different for each interpolation algorithm. The collection of *neighboring pixels* is sometimes referred to as the *training window*. For example, a 3×5 rectangular window is drawn in Figure 2.4, which encloses the *neighboring pixels* of the *current pixel* (the pixel with a gray color background). Besides rectangular window, the shape of the window can be in circular or other shape as desired. It is a common practice to form a training window to have odd numbers of rows and columns, such that the *"current pixel"* is located at the center of the window. In any special case where the window has even numbers of

Figure 2.4 Current pixels and its neighborhood.

rows or columns, or both, the location of the *"current pixel"* should be clearly specified to avoid ambiguity.

2.3 Frequency Domain

The mathematical tools that are applied to describe and manipulate digital images have their roots in linear system theory, integral transforms, discrete mathematics, and the theory of stochastic processes. All these tools can be applied to the digital image $f[m, n]$ if it is treated as a deterministic function or as a realization of stochastic process. In particular the integrable image vector space defined in Eq. (2.2) has a standard basis in the space $\mathcal{L}^2(\mathbb{Z}_M \times \mathbb{Z}_N)$ as

$$\mathbf{U} = \{\mathbf{U}_{k,\ell}\}, \quad \text{with } 0 \leqslant k < M, 0 \leqslant \ell < N, \text{ and } k, \ell \in \text{ real number,} \tag{2.4}$$

where

$$\mathbf{U}_{k,\ell}[m, n] = \begin{cases} 1, & \forall [k, \ell] = [m, n], \\ 0, & \text{otherwise.} \end{cases} \tag{2.5}$$

This basis specifies the spatial domain, such that the digital image can be expressed as

$$f = \sum_{k=0}^{M-1} \sum_{\ell=0}^{N-1} \sum_{m=0}^{M-1} \sum_{n=0}^{N-1} f[m, n] \mathbf{U}_{k,\ell}[m, n]. \tag{2.6}$$

Similar to the case of digital 1D signals in Chapter 1, there exists an orthogonal basis that represents the image by summation of a series of sinusoids. This alternative representation of an image is known as *frequency* domain. This basis is given by $\mathbf{W}_{k,\ell}$ with $0 \leqslant k < M$ and $0 \leqslant \ell < N$, where

$$\mathbf{W}_{k,\ell}[m, n] = e^{2\pi j \left(\frac{km}{M} + \frac{\ell n}{N} \right)}. \tag{2.7}$$

The transformation that converts the image from spatial domain to frequency domain is known as the *forward* 2D *discrete Fourier transform* (2D DFT), and from frequency domain to spatial domain is known as the *inverse* 2D DFT, and they are given mathematically as

$$F[u, v] = \frac{1}{MN} \sum_{m=0}^{M-1} \sum_{n=0}^{N-1} f[m, n] e^{-2\pi j \left(\frac{mu}{M} + \frac{nv}{N} \right)}, \quad \begin{array}{l} u = 0, 1, \ldots, M - 1, \\ v = 0, 1, \ldots, N - 1, \end{array} \tag{2.8}$$

$$f[m, n] = \sum_{u=0}^{N-1} \sum_{v=0}^{N-1} F[u, v] e^{2\pi j \left(\frac{mu}{M} + \frac{nv}{N} \right)}, \quad \begin{array}{l} m = 0, 1, \ldots, M - 1, \\ n = 0, 1, \ldots, N - 1, \end{array} \tag{2.9}$$

with u and v being the spatial frequencies. Note that

$$\exp\left(2\pi j \left(\frac{mu}{M} + \frac{nv}{N} \right) \right) = \exp\left(2\pi j \frac{mu}{M} \right) \exp\left(2\pi j \frac{nv}{N} \right). \tag{2.10}$$

The first term in the above product, $\exp(2\pi j \frac{mu}{M})$, depends on m and u only and is independent of n and v. Similarly, the second product term, $\exp(2\pi j \frac{nv}{N})$, depends on n and v only and is independent of m and u. It means that we can breakdown the forward

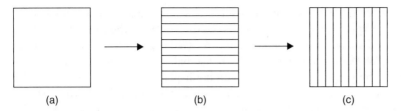

(a)   (b)   (c)

Figure 2.5 Calculating a 2D DFT by row–column technique; (a) Original image; (b) DFT of each row of (a); and (c) DFT of each column of (b).

transform in Eq. (2.8) to simpler formula that works on rows or columns separately as

$$F[u, v] = \frac{1}{N} \sum_{n=0}^{N-1} \left(\frac{1}{M} \sum_{m=0}^{M-1} f[m, n] e^{-2\pi j \frac{mu}{M}} \right) e^{-2\pi j \frac{nv}{N}}. \qquad (2.11)$$

The above further implies the 2D DFT can be computed separately with 1D DFT on each value of m within the parenthesis and then performs another 1D DFT again on the results with respect to the index n. In other words, by making use of the *"separability"* property of 2D DFT, the 2D DFT can be computed by first the DFT of all the rows and then the DFT of all the columns of the first DFT result, as shown in Figure 2.5. The MATLAB implementation listed in Listing 2.3.1 makes use of the MATLAB function `fft` on the transpose array of the `fft` result of the image array f to obtain the 2D DFT of f. Further note that a transposition, `'`, is required to apply the `fft` in a row and then column fashion. Finally, another transposition is applied to get the matrix in the right row–column orientation.

MATLAB 2.3.1—2D DFT by two 1D-DFT.

```
>> F = fft(fft(f)')';
```

The inverse transform can be implemented similarly by using consecutive `ifft` functions as listed in Listing 2.3.2. There also exists the `fft2` and `ifft2` functions in MATLAB that perform the forward and inverse 2D DFT transform operations, respectively. The readers should note that `fft` and `fft2` are both not averaged with the image size $M \times N$. Taking `fft2` as an example, to obtain the same results as that given by Eq. (2.8), we shall have F=fft2(f)/(M * N) in MATLAB, while the inverse transform is obtained as f=ifft2(F*M*N).

MATLAB 2.3.2—2D IDFT by two 1D-IDFT.

```
>> f = ifft(ifft(F)')';
```

The 2D DFT result is a complex-valued 2D spectrum of the digital image. The spectrum has the same resolution as the spatial resolution of the digital image. However, the values in both real and imaginary parts of the spectrum usually span a bigger range, perhaps millions, for an input image with pixel intensity in the range of [0, 255]. The existence of real and imaginary components with values spanning over several orders of magnitude makes the spectrum difficult to be visualized on computer screen. Simply displaying the spectrum using a simple constant scalar normalized spectrum will only result in dark and low contrast image. To enhance the contrast, the magnitude of the spectrum is usually displayed in decibel scale or expressed in $\log(|F(u, v)| + 1)$ for visual inspection. To display the spectrum in MATLAB, we shall have to map the decibel scale spectrum value to the grayscale such that it can be displayed on the screen using the MATLAB function `mat2gray` image with values spanning from 0 (black) to 1 (white), where all elements in the matrix `f` are scaled in ratio and completely fall within the eligible range for display.

Example 2.1 The spatial frequency content can be displayed in a similar way as that of the 1D spectral response, where it is preferable to display the frequency range between 0 and 1/2. The following script computes and displays the 2D spatial frequency of a portion of the letter A in Figure 2.3 as shown in Figure 2.7, where the MATLAB command `fftshift` has been applied to move the frequency location (0,0) to the center of the spectral plot.

MATLAB 2.3.3—Spatial frequency of a selected portion of the A in Figure 2.3 displayed in Figure 2.7.

```
>> Fqs=fftshift(fft2(f,M,N));
>> NFqs = uint8(log(abs(Fqs)+1));
>> mu=(0:M-1)/M; nu=(0:N-1)/N;
>> subplot(1,2,1); imagesc((0:N-1),(0:M-1),mat2gray(f)); axis('
    square');
>> subplot(1,2,2); imagesc(nu,mu,mat2gray(NFqs')); axis('square');
```

Furthermore, the definition of 2D DFT in Eq. (2.8) indicates that the spatial frequency coordinates run from the origin at the top left corner of the array, increasing as we move across right and down. It is a custom to visualize a centered spectrum, where the center of the 2D spectrum is the DC component of the spectrum, while the high frequency components are located close to the corners. Such a spectral display can be achieved by *shifting* the origin to the center of the array such that the centered 2D DFT $F(\hat{u}, \hat{v})$ is given by

$$F(\hat{u}, \hat{v}) = F\left[u - \frac{M}{2}, v - \frac{N}{2}\right]$$

$$= \frac{1}{MN} \sum_{m=0}^{M-1} \sum_{n=0}^{N-1} f[m, n] e^{-2\pi j \left(\frac{m(u-(M/2))}{M} + \frac{n(v-(N/2))}{N}\right)}$$

$$= \frac{1}{MN} \sum_{m=0}^{M-1} \sum_{n=0}^{N-1} ((-1)^{m+n} f[m, n]) e^{-2\pi j \left(\frac{mu}{M} + \frac{nv}{N}\right)}, \tag{2.12}$$

which is, by definition, the 2D DFT of the product $(-1)^{m+n} f[m, n]$. Figure 2.6 illustrates the shifting operation depicted in Eq. (2.12). Figure 2.6a is the 2D DFT spectrum obtained by Eq. (2.8), where the spectrum consists of four symmetrical quadrants A, B, C, and D, with the DC components located at the four corners of the spectrum (see the block boxes). Eq. (2.12) shifts the origin of the spectrum by swapping the spectral

Figure 2.6 (a) The four quadrants of the original spectrum of a digital image obtained by 2D DFT. (b) The centered spectrum obtained through swapping quadrants.

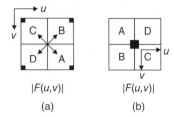

$|F(u,v)|$ $|F(u,v)|$

(a)   (b)

location of quadrant A with quadrant C, and that of quadrant B with quadrant D, such that the DC component will all appear in the center of the spectrum as shown in Figure 2.6b. Instead of going through the complicated computation as depicted in Eq. (2.12), MATLAB provides a simple function `fftshift` to perform the same operation.

Example 2.1 showcases the usage of the MATLAB functions `fft2` and `fftshift`. Fqs is the output of the 2D spatial frequency spectrum of the input image f, where the command `fft2(f,M,N)` realizes Eq. (2.8). The function `fftshift` shifts the origin of the output of `fft2(f,M,N)` to the center. To enhance the contrast and facilitate the display of the spectrum, the 2D spectrum Fqs is converted into log scale, and the data type is also converted to the image compatible form of `uint8` as shown in the second line of the code in the example. Both the original image f and the output spectrum NFqs are mapped to the grayscale display via the function `mat2gray` and displayed using the image handling function `imagesc`. Figure 2.7 is the output for considering portion of letter *A* as the input image to Example 2.1, where the original portion of the image is shown in Figure 2.7a and the output spectrum NFqs is shown in Figure 2.7b.

It is not mandatory to center the DFT spectrum. However, it seems natural to shift the spectrum for visualization, as the frequency range of the shifted spectrum is $(-M/2, M/2) \times (-N/2, N/2)$, which is more akin to the continuous space that has equal distribution of positive and negative components. On the other hand, readers will find that `fftshift` has other use in the later chapters.

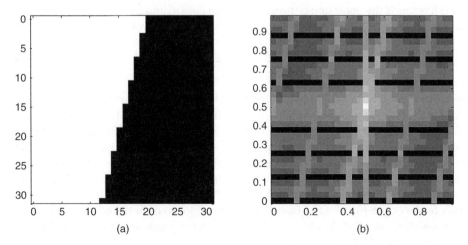

Figure 2.7 (a) A 30 × 30 portion of the letter *A* and (b) the associated 2D DFT spatial frequency magnitude.

2.3.1 Transform Kernel

The Fourier transform is a particular case of the general linear transformation where the forward transform is given by

$$F[u,v] = \frac{1}{MN} \sum_{m=0}^{M-1} \sum_{n=0}^{N-1} f[m,n]p[m,n,u,v], \qquad (2.13)$$

and the inverse transform is given by

$$f[m,n] = \sum_{u=0}^{M-1} \sum_{v=0}^{N-1} F[u,v]q[m,n,u,v], \qquad (2.14)$$

with $p[m,n,u,v]$ and $q[m,n,u,v]$ known as the forward and inverse transform kernels, respectively. As an example, the forward and inverse Fourier transform kernels are given by Eqs. (2.8) and (2.9), respectively. These kernels act like sets of basis functions. If the kernel $p[m,n,u,v] = p_1[m,u]p_2[n,v]$, the kernel and thus the transformation are said to be separable in dimension or simply separable. In addition, if the functional forms of p_1 and p_2 are identical, then the kernel and thus the transformation are said to be symmetric. As an example, the 2D Fourier forward transformation kernel is given by

$$p[m,n,u,v] = \exp\left(-j2\pi\left(\frac{um}{M} + \frac{vn}{N}\right)\right), \qquad (2.15)$$

$$= \exp\left(-j2\pi\left(\frac{um}{M}\right)\right)\exp\left(-j2\pi\left(\frac{vn}{N}\right)\right).$$

It is vivid that the Fourier transformation kernel is separable and symmetric. In a similar fashion, it is easy to show that the inverse Fourier transform kernel $q[m,n,u,v]$ and thus the inverse transform are also symmetric and separable.

2.4 2D Filtering

The 2D filtering is the operation between the image $f[m,n]$ and the 2D filter $h[m,n]$ that generates the filtered image $g[m,n]$ through the following convolution equation.

$$g[m,n] = (f \otimes h)[m,n] = \sum_{k=M_1}^{M_2} \sum_{\ell=N_1}^{N_2} f[m-k,n-\ell]h[k,\ell], \qquad (2.16)$$

where the range of the convolution is determined by both the data array size and the kernel size of the filter. In the case of Eq. (2.16), the filter kernel spans $([M_1,M_2] \times [N_1,N_2])$.

The operation of 2D image convolution is geometrically illustrated in Figure 2.8, where the convolution $(f \otimes h)[m,n]$ at the pixel $[m,n]$ is obtained by shifting the filter kernel $h[m,n]$ across the input image $f[m,n]$ with different offsets; then superimposed values at each offset are multiplied together, summing up all products. The summation results at each offset are the value of the output image $g[m,n]$ where the location $[m,n]$ corresponds to the origin $[0,0]$ of the filter kernel $h[m,n]$ located on top of the pixel of the input image $f[m,n]$. All of the above operations can be implemented with the MATLAB command `filter2(h,f)`.

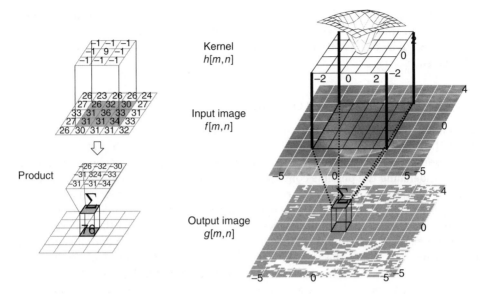

Figure 2.8 Illustration of 2D image convolution.

The equivalent operation in spectral domain for the convolution operator is the element-wise product and is given by

$$\mathcal{F}\{f \otimes h\} = F[u, v] \odot H[u, v], \tag{2.17}$$

where $F[u, v]$ and $H[u, v]$ are the 2D DFT of $f[m, n]$ and $h[m, n]$, respectively. The operator $\odot$ is an element-wise product (not a matrix product). This equation, called the Fourier convolution theorem, gives insight into what the filter mask does to an arbitrary image. It scales and phase shifts each unique frequency component of the image, $F[u, v]$, by the spectral coefficients of the filter at the same spectral indices. In fact, one can manually manipulate the image in the spectral domain and then inverse transform the result to obtain the filtered image and skip constructing the filter nor the convolution step all together.

Figure 2.8 illustrates a 2D image convolution as depicted in Eq. (2.16). We shall consider the sub-block image of the eye of the *Cat* image in this example. The convolution operation is graphical illustrated on the right column of Figure 2.8. The output of the convolution is a scalar that is the sum of the output of the multiplication of two matrices (the filter $h[m, n]$ and the input image $f[m, n]$). The sizes of the matrices are the same, and the center of the filter should align with the output pixel spatial location. A numerical example is illustrated on the left-hand side of Figure 2.8 with the filter kernel being a simple box filter for illustration purposes.

The extension of the convolution to color image can be as simple as repeating the convolution (filtering) operations three times to each color component of the image, as if each component is an independent grayscale image. The above assumes the color image has separable component images. However, it has been shown that serious artifacts can be resulted from treating the RGB color space separately in filtering. To reduce distortion, we can perform higher dimensional filtering, by going from 2D to 3D filtering, or we can transform the color image from RGB color space to other perceptual color spaces (to be discussed in Section 2.8.2) where the color components are almost independent.

2.4.1 Boundary Extension and Cropping

When we examine the convolution sum in Eq. (2.16), the following question arises: what should $f[m, n]$ be when $m < 0, m \geqslant M, n < 0$, or $n \geqslant N$? There is no absolute "*answer*" to this question. There are only alternatives among which we are free to choose assuming that we understand the possible consequences of our choice. The standard alternatives are to (i) extend the images with a constant (possibly zero) brightness, (ii) extend the image periodically, (iii) extend the image by mirroring it at its boundaries, (iv) extend the pixel brightness at the boundaries indefinitely, or (v) only consider the center portion of the original image by cropping. The alternatives (i)–(iv) are illustrated in Figure 2.9, where Figure 2.9a shows the portion of the original letter *A* image, with the boundary extended images using methods (i)–(iv) being illustrated in Figure 2.9b–e, respectively. The alternative (v) is illustrated by Figure 2.10, which shows the *Cat* image with its boundary cropped. Each method and their implementation using MATLAB will be detailed in the following sections.

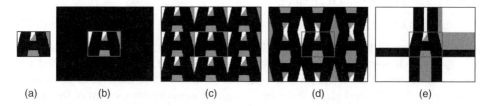

(a)   (b)   (c)   (d)   (e)

Figure 2.9 Boundary extensions applied to finite length 2D image (a portion of the letter *A* in Figure 2.3 in (a)); (b) zero padding; (c) periodic extension; (d) symmetric extension; and (e) constant extension; with the sub-image enclosed by the box being the original image shown in (a).

Figure 2.10 Cropping to avoid undefined boundary signal in 2D filtering.

2.4.1.1 Constant Extension

This method extends the image boundary by a constant. The most frequently used constant is zero, and the extension method is known as *zero padding*. This is a very popular extension method because it does not alter the total energy of the image under consideration. The application of any other constant will increase the total energy and may get awkward result. In the case of 2D image, the image is extended for each row and then each column separately as shown in Figure 2.9b, where the sub-image inside the box is the original 2D image (Figure 2.9a). The zero padding is analytically defined as

$$
\mathbf{g} = \begin{bmatrix} \mathbf{0} & \mathbf{0} & \mathbf{0} \\ \mathbf{0} & \mathbf{f} & \mathbf{0} \\ \mathbf{0} & \mathbf{0} & \mathbf{0} \end{bmatrix},
\tag{2.18}
$$

where **0** is a matrix with the same size as that of **f** and all with its elements have 0 value. Listing 2.4.1 is the MATLAB source code example that implements Eq. (2.18), where the function `zeros(M,N)` defines the **0** matrix in Eq. (2.18).

> **MATLAB 2.4.1—Constant extension of image as illustrated in Figure 2.9b.**
>
> ```
> >> [M N] = size(f);
> >> g = [  zeros(M,N)   zeros(M,N)   zeros(M,N);
>          zeros(M,N)   f            zeros(M,N);
>          zeros(M,N)   zeros(M,N)   zeros(M,N)];
> ```

Besides the preservation of total energy, the zero padding method is also simple to implement. However, the inserting zeros will also insert discontinuity into the image, unless $f[0, :] = f[N - 1, :] = f[:, 0] = f[:, M - 1] = 0$.

2.4.1.2 Periodic Extension

This method extends the image boundary to form a periodic function. In the case of 2D image, the image is extended for each row and then each column separately as shown in Figure 2.9c, where the sub-image within the box is the original 2D image (Figure 2.9a). The advantage of periodic extension is that it mimics the periodic extension structure of the DFT. As a result, filtering the extended image by linear filter can be achieved by circular convolution, which helps to lower the computational complexity. Furthermore, it does not introduce new type of discontinuity to the boundary extended image. However, it is vivid from Figure 2.9c that the extended image has discontinuity at the boundary between the original image and the extended sub-images, similar to that of zero padding, unless $f[0, :] = f[M - 1, :]$ and $f[:, 0] = f[:, N - 1]$ (which implies the top and bottom rows of the image are the same and the left and right columns of the image are the same). The analytical function of the extended image **g** is given by

$$
\mathbf{g} = \begin{bmatrix} \mathbf{f} & \mathbf{f} & \mathbf{f} \\ \mathbf{f} & \mathbf{f} & \mathbf{f} \\ \mathbf{f} & \mathbf{f} & \mathbf{f} \end{bmatrix}.
\tag{2.19}
$$

The MATLAB Listing 2.4.2 is an example that implements Eq. (2.19), which applies the MATLAB built-in function `repmat(f,k,l)` to replicate the matrix **f** to form $k \times \ell$ tiling. The example in Figure 2.9c replicates the original image into a 3×3 array ($k=3$ and $l=3$) of $M \times N$ matrices.

MATLAB 2.4.2—Periodic extension of image as illustrated in Figure 2.9c.

```
>> k = 3; l = 3;
>> g = repmat(f, k, l);
```

2.4.1.3 Symmetric Extension

The *symmetric extension* is proposed to remedy the signal boundary discontinuity problem and at the same time obtain a periodic signal after extension. Figure 2.9d shows the symmetric extension result of the letter A, where the sub-image within the box is the original 2D image (Figure 2.9a). It can be observed in this example that the extended image follows certain symmetry by concatenating the mirrored version of the original image. The mirroring is applied in both horizontal and vertical directions, such that the image continuity in the extended image can be preserved. The symmetric extended image $\mathbf{g}$ from $\mathbf{f}$ is given by

$$
\mathbf{g} = \begin{bmatrix} \mathbf{f}_x & \mathbf{f}_{ud} & \mathbf{f}_x \\ \mathbf{f}_{lr} & \mathbf{f} & \mathbf{f}_{lr} \\ \mathbf{f}_x & \mathbf{f}_{ud} & \mathbf{f}_x \end{bmatrix},
\tag{2.20}
$$

where $\mathbf{f}_{lr}$ is the horizontally flipped version of $\mathbf{f}$ (flipping $\mathbf{f}$ left to right), $\mathbf{f}_{ud}$ is the vertically flipped version of $\mathbf{f}$ (flipping $\mathbf{f}$ top to down), and $\mathbf{f}_x$ is the horizontally flipped version of $\mathbf{f}_{ud}$ (flipping $\mathbf{f}_{ud}$ left to right).

The MATLAB source code listed in Listing 2.4.3 makes use of the MATLAB built-in functions `fiplr(f)` and `flipud(f)` to flip the matrix f in left-to-right direction and in up-to-down direction, respectively, to obtain a symmetrically extended image g from f.

MATLAB 2.4.3—Symmetric extension of image as illustrated in Figure 2.9d.

```
>> flr = fliplr(f);
>> fud = flipud(f);
>> fx = fliplr(fud);
>> g = [ fx fud fx;
         flr  f   flr;
         fx fud fx ];
```

2.4.1.4 Infinite Extension

Similar to periodic extension, infinite extension extends an image by titling up multiple images with same size as that of the original image, whereas the titled images are not the replica of the original image but only repeating the outermost row/column of the original image adjacent to the titling image. Figure 2.9e shows an example of an extended image formed by infinite extension, where the sub-image within the box is the original 2D image (Figure 2.9a). This method preserves the image structure without introducing any discontinuity at the boundary of the extended image. It should be noted that the four corners of the extended image is padded with white pixels. In the case of a `uint8` image f, the extended image g is given by

$$
g = \begin{bmatrix} 255_{M\times N} & f_U & 255_{M\times N} \\ f_L & f & f_R \\ 255_{M\times N} & f_D & 255_{M\times N} \end{bmatrix}, \tag{2.21}
$$

where $255_{M\times N}$ defines a constant matrix of white pixels (with pixel value 255 for an image with 8-bit per pixel) titling at the four corners of the extended image and f_U, f_R, f_D, and f_L are the titling images to the upper, right, lower, and left of the original image, respectively. Other values can be used to fill in the corners with the objective of alleviating the discontinuity problem in the extended image.

The MATLAB source code listed in Listing 2.4.4 defines the constant matrices fC to be $255_{M\times N}$. The built-in function repmat is applied to repeat the outermost row/column of the original image to form the required image block for fU, fR, fD, and fL in Listing 2.4.4.

MATLAB 2.4.4—Infinite extension of image as illustrated in Figure 2.9e.

```
>> [M N] = size(f);
>> fC = 255*ones(M,N);
>> fU = repmat(f(1,:),M,1);
>> fR = repmat(f(:,N),1,N);
>> fD = repmat(f(M,:),M,1);
>> fL = repmat(f(:,1),1,N);
>> g = [ fC fU fC;
         fL f  fR;
         fC fD fC ];
```

2.4.1.5 Cropping

Besides extending the image boundary, the undefined boundary problem can be rendered by image cropping. By cropping, only part of the image will be considered as operable region, usually the center of the image, and the rest of the pixels will be considered as boundary pixels. Figure 2.10 illustrates an example of image cropping, where only the center of the *Cat* image will be considered for image manipulation, while those shaded pixels are considered as boundary pixels. It should be noted that the cropped image **g** has a smaller size than that of the original image **f**. Consider the original image **f** consisting of M-row and N-column. A cropped image with size $(M - p) \times (N - q)$ can be constructed by cropping p-row from both the top and bottom of **f** and q-column from both the leftmost and rightmost of **f**. The cropped image **g** is analytically defined to be

$$
g = \begin{bmatrix} f[p,q] & f[p,q+1] & \cdots & f[p,N-q] \\ f[p+1,q] & f[p+1,q+1] & \cdots & f[p+1,N-q] \\ \vdots & \vdots & \ddots & \vdots \\ f[M-p,p] & f[M-p,q+1] & \cdots & f[M-p,N-q] \end{bmatrix}. \tag{2.22}
$$

It should be noted that it is a common practice to have $p = q$ in image cropping, such that the cropped image will be taken from the center of the original image. The MATLAB Listing 2.4.5 implements the image cropping.

MATLAB 2.4.5—Image cropping.

```
>>  [M,N]=size(f);
>>  g = f(p:M-p,q:N-q);
```

The advantage of using cropped image in image manipulation is that it will not introduce any unnatural discontinuities in the processed image through the convolution process in Eq. (2.16) on **g**. The disadvantage is, of course, a reduction in size of the image and thus the filtered image.

2.5 Edge Extraction

Besides viewing the image as a collection of pixels, it can also be viewed as a collection of texture patches. Pixels within the patch are homogeneous, such that they have the same texture property, or simply similar in intensity. The boundaries of the patches are known as edges, which are groups of pixels with the brightness of its neighboring pixels change abruptly. As a result, pixels next to the edge pixels will contain large local contrast. A third way to view the image edges is the 2D functional views. When the image is considered as a 2D function, the edges are located at the function with large slope or large (absolute) derivative. As a result, edge pixels can be found by any processes that calculate the gradient magnitude and edge direction.

Shown in Figure 2.11a is an enlarged image block from the ear of the *Cat* (see the enclosed region in Figure 2.11b), where an edge example is found along the boundary

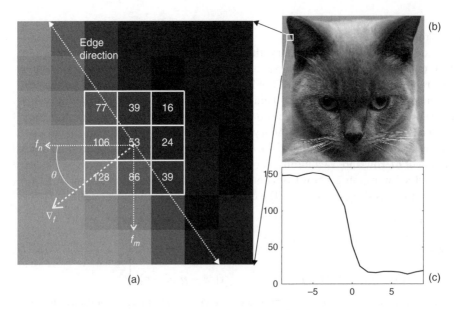

Figure 2.11 The edge information contained in the block of the *Cat* image.

of the ear (the group of dark pixels) and the background (the group of gray pixels). We can describe an edge by its orientation, position, and strength. Considering the pixel with the intensity "53" in Figure 2.11a, an abrupt intensity change can be observed in its neighboring pixels. The intensity changes around the neighboring pixels are not random, but the largest change is observed across a certain line, which is known as an edge, where the arrow heads at the two ends of this line in Figure 2.11a indicate the "*edge direction*." As the edge sits on the pixel with intensity of "53," we can name the location of this pixel $(\hat{m}, \hat{n})$ as "*edge position*" or "*edge center*." Besides the edge orientation and the edge position, it is most common to investigate the maximum intensity change across the edge and also the related strength. This is because they provide important information for edge extraction. The unit vector perpendicular to the edge direction is known as the "*edge normal*" (the direction indicated by the arrow "∇f" in Figure 2.11a), which gives the direction of maximum intensity change. Shown in Figure 2.11c is the pixel intensity along the ∇f direction as indicated in Figure 2.11a, where the "0" position indicates the edge center pixel (pixel with intensity of "53"). It is vivid that the edge is located at the transition between patch with pixel intensities around 150 and another patch with pixel intensities around 15. The "*edge strength*" is defined as the magnitude of the local contrast (rate of change in intensity) at the edge center pixel along the edge normal ($|\nabla f|$). It should be noted that an image is a 2D data in spatial domain. The rate of change of the pixel intensity can be obtained by considering the first-order derivative or second-order derivative of the 2D intensity map. Moreover, we can break the vector-based deviates into the ∇f_m (vertical) and ∇f_n (horizontal) components. In some applications, we need to quantify the edge orientation for further analysis. To simplify the discussion, we take the direction in ∇f_n as a reference and the edge center $(\hat{m}, \hat{n})$ as the origin, such that the angle of $|\nabla f|$ departing from ∇f_n in anticlockwise direction is the gradient direction in this book. The qualitative definition of ∇f, θ, ∇f_m, and ∇f_n will be discussed in the later sections.

The conventional edge detection methods convolve an image with a 2D filter such that the gradient across edges and zero in uniform region will be returned. The 2D filter is also known as "*edge detection operator*" that transforms a given image into an edge image (also known as "*edge map*"). There are large number of edge detection operators reported in literature, which are designed to detect edges in different natures, e.g. to be sensitive to edge orientation, to edge structure, to detect edges under noisy environment, etc. However, the transition between image patches may not be as sharp as that shown in Figure 2.11. Shown in Figure 2.12a,c are examples of edge images, and the associated pixel intensity across transitions of the edges between image patches is

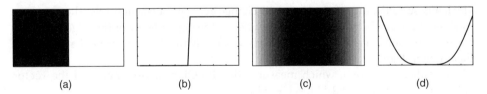

(a)   (b)   (c)   (d)

Figure 2.12 Two types of grayscale image brightness variations (a) and (c) and the corresponding 1D plots in (b) and (d), respectively.

shown in Figure 2.12b and d, respectively. For the sharp edge shown in Figure 2.12a, the transition is sharp, and the slope of the intensity change can be easily determined by computing the magnitude of the first-order derivative at each pixel. On the other hand, the edge in Figure 2.12c is not sharp, and the edge is considered to be thick and spanning over several pixels. The change in magnitude of the first-order derivative at each pixel is not significant; thus the actual sharpness of the edge can only be formally determined by the edge strength (by applying a threshold to the magnitude of the first-order derivative) or by extracting the second-order derivative of the edge to locate the exact transitional point (the zero-crossing point).

It should be noted that different edge operators are designed with different mathematical tools to achieve their goal of extracting the edge map. The edge operators are required to work with other post-processing steps (*thresholding*) or multiple operators to be used adaptively to extract the edge more accurately. In the following sections, we shall discuss both the concept of first-order derivative and second-order derivative operators, through basic mathematical derivation, while some common edge detection techniques will be presented in sequel.

2.5.1   First-Order Derivative Edge Detection Operators

First-order derivative-based method, also known as gradient magnitude-based method, finds the rate of pixel intensity change along the edge normal. The rate of pixel intensity change can be retrieved from the gradient vector ($|\nabla f|$) at each pixel, which can be obtained by convolving the image with first-order horizontal and vertical derivative filters ($\partial f[m, n]/\partial n$ and $\partial f[m, n]/\partial m$, respectively). In spatial domain, the horizontal and vertical derivative filters form a 2D filter, known as edge operator in common practice. The gradient vector along the pixel $[\hat{m}, \hat{n}]$ within an image block f is defined as

$$\nabla f[\hat{m}, \hat{n}] = \left[\frac{\partial f[\hat{m}, \hat{n}]}{\partial m}, \frac{\partial f[\hat{m}, \hat{n}]}{\partial n} \right], \tag{2.23}$$

where the definition of $\frac{\partial f[\hat{m}, \hat{n}]}{\partial m}$ and $\frac{\partial f[\hat{m}, \hat{n}]}{\partial n}$ depends on the edge filters being used. Consider the derivative operator defined by finite differences, such that

$$\frac{\partial f[m, n]}{\partial m} = f[m + 1, n] - f[m, n], \tag{2.24}$$

$$\frac{\partial f[m, n]}{\partial n} = f[m, n + 1] - f[m, n], \tag{2.25}$$

which measures the rate of pixel intensity change between adjacent pixels. The two components of the gradient vector $\nabla f[\hat{m}, \hat{n}]$ refer to the dependency of the edge along the m (vertical) and n (horizontal) dimensions separately for the pixel located at $[\hat{m}, \hat{n}]$ (as illustrated in Figure 2.11a).

The gradient direction, which measures the direction or orientation of the vector $\nabla f(\hat{m}, \hat{n})$ shown in Figure 2.11a, is given by

$$\theta = \tan^{-1} \left(\frac{\partial f[\hat{m}, \hat{n}]}{\partial m} \bigg/ \frac{\partial f[\hat{m}, \hat{n}]}{\partial n} \right), \tag{2.26}$$

which is perpendicular to the edge direction.

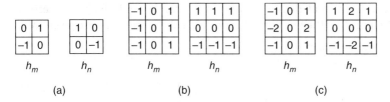

Figure 2.13 The vertical derivative operator, h_m, and horizontal derivative operator, h_n, of (a) Robert operator, (b) Prewitt operator, and (c) Sobel operator.

The magnitude of the gradient indicates the strength of the edge and is given by

$$|\nabla f| = \sqrt{\left(\frac{\partial f}{\partial m}\right)^2 + \left(\frac{\partial f}{\partial n}\right)^2}. \tag{2.27}$$

There exist many other gradient operators in literature that have their pros and cons in locating the edges between image patches. Eqs. (2.24) and (2.25) are the simplest computations. However, the operator that adopts Eqs. (2.24) and (2.25) is sensitive to small changes, such that "unwanted noise" with intensity changes close to the real edge would be faulty determined as edge and results in false detection. Therefore, to render the requirement of different edge detections, the implementation of the horizontal and vertical derivatives can be different, such that $\partial f[m, n]/\partial m$ and $\partial f[m, n]/\partial n$ can be different from that depicted in Eqs. (2.24) and (2.25), respectively.

There are a wide variety of first-order derivative-based edge operators. The detection performance of the operators can be highly influenced by the nature of the edge. Figure 2.13 shows the horizontal and vertical derivatives of three first-order derivative operators commonly applied in literature. The *Robert operator* (see Figure 2.13a) enhances the detection by computing the gradient along the diagonal direction. However, it is still sensitive to small changes due to its small kernel size (2 × 2) (see Figure 2.13b) even though the edge position can be located accurately. The *Prewitt operator* uses a 3 × 3 kernel, which approximates the gradient vector in both horizontal and vertical dimensions. However, it is not sensitive to diagonal edges. Therefore, it is more common to apply the *Sobel operator* for edge detection in commercial image processing tools. The Sobel operator has a 3 × 3 kernel (see Figure 2.13c). However, it is known that there is no significant difference in the edge maps generated from the Prewitt operator and that of the Sobel operator. In this book, we shall focus our discussions using the Sobel operator.

As the rate of pixel intensity change is not always sharp and the image edge can span a large region (so-called a thick edge), it is difficult to identify the exact location and orientation of the image edge. Therefore, the first-order derivative-based edge detection operator will keen to advance the detection by detecting also the edge strength. This can be achieved by comparing the magnitude of the gradient ($|\nabla f|$) with a (threshold), such that an edge is regarded to be presented when $|\nabla f| \geqslant$ threshold. We shall investigate the effect of threshold on the edge map obtained by the Sobel operator.

2.5.1.1 Sobel Operator

The Sobel operator is a first-order derivative operator that uses *gradient filters* ($\mathbf{h}_n$ and $\mathbf{h}_m$) through a convolution operation to the original image to obtain the first-order derivative along the horizontal direction using the filter $\mathbf{h}_n$ and along the vertical direction using the filter $\mathbf{h}_m$. The gradient filters used in both directions are given by

Estimate gradient

Smoothing

$$\mathbf{h}_n = \frac{1}{2+\lambda} \begin{bmatrix} 1 & 0 & -1 \\ \lambda & 0 & -\lambda \\ 1 & 0 & -1 \end{bmatrix}, \tag{2.28}$$

Smoothing

Estimate gradient

$$\mathbf{h}_m = \frac{1}{2+\lambda} \begin{bmatrix} 1 & \lambda & 1 \\ 0 & 0 & 0 \\ -1 & -\lambda & -1 \end{bmatrix}, \tag{2.29}$$

with $2 + \lambda$ being the normalization factor, where $\lambda \geqslant 1$. It should be noted that the above gradient filters can be constructed as the Prewitt operator with $\lambda = 1$ and can also be constructed as the Sobel operator with $\lambda = 2$.

As ∇f_m and ∇f_n are orthogonal, the Sobel operator is separable and is given by

$$\mathbf{h}_n = \frac{1}{4} \begin{bmatrix} 1 & 0 & -1 \\ 2 & 0 & -2 \\ 1 & 0 & -1 \end{bmatrix} = \frac{1}{4} \begin{bmatrix} 1 \\ 2 \\ 1 \end{bmatrix} \begin{bmatrix} 1 & 0 & -1 \end{bmatrix} = \mathbf{h}_m^T. \tag{2.30}$$

It is vivid from the separable filter form of the Sobel operator that it will perform smoothing along one direction by the vector [1 2 1]/4 and the derivative function in the other direction by the vector [1 0 −1]/4. Moreover, the filters applied to the horizontal direction and the vertical direction are the transpose of each other (with $\mathbf{h}_n = \mathbf{h}_m^T$). Therefore, the implementation of the first-order derivative in vertical and horizontal directions (by $\frac{\partial f_m}{\partial m}$ and $\frac{\partial f_n}{\partial n}$) is different when compared with that depicted in Eqs. (2.24) and (2.25), where

$$\frac{\partial f_m}{\partial m} = \frac{1}{4}[(f[m-1,n+1] + 2f[m,n+1] + f[m+1,n+1])$$
$$-(f[m-1,n-1] + 2f[m,n-1] + f[m+1,n-1])] \tag{2.31}$$

and $\quad \dfrac{\partial f_n}{\partial n} = \dfrac{1}{4}[(f[m-1,n-1] + 2f[m,n-1] + f[m+1,n-1])$
$$-(f[m+1,n-1] + 2f[m+1,n] + f[m+1,n+1])]. \tag{2.32}$$

The operation of Sobel filter is similar to the Prewitt filter, but with a larger weighting on the center pixel, which helps to provide better localization of the edges of the image by also considering the diagonal edges. The Sobel edge detector can be implemented with the MATLAB function sobel (f, threshold) (see Listing 2.5.1), which returns an edge image edge of the same size as that of the input image. The edge image has 0 as the entry for all pixel locations that are not edges and 255 for all pixel locations that are edges determined by the threshold operation on the gradient results. hn and hm are the gradient filters as depicted in Eq. (2.30). Instead of implementing Eqs. (2.31) and

(2.32), the original image block is convolved with the 2D filters hn and hm directly to give gn and gm, respectively. The strength of the gradient vector is computed to give s by applying Eq. (2.27). Since not all edges in natural image are sharp edges, the edge image is screened by thresholding the gradient map of the input image by an appropriately assigned threshold.

MATLAB 2.5.1—Sobel edge image extraction.

```
function edge=sobel(f,threshold)
    hn = [1 2 1; 0 0 0; -1 -2 -1];
    hm = hn';
    gn = conv2(double(f),hn, 'same');
    gm = conv2(double(f),hm, 'same');
    s = sqrt(gn.*gn + gm.*gm);
    edge = uint8((s>threshold)*255);
end
```

Figure 2.14 shows the edge maps extracted from the *Cat* image using Sobel filter with different threshold values. In Figures 2.14a–c, only the lower bound of the threshold (threshold) is considered. When threshold is being low, many edges are extracted (see Figure 2.14a). The extracted edges are thick (the outlines of ears) and noisy at the texture-rich regions (such as the forehead of the *Cat*), which hardly reflects the exact position of the edges. On the other hand, with increasing threshold, it is vivid that the remaining edge pixels have large gradient vector strength, such that the resulted edges are thinner. Furthermore, the texture-rich region will be considered as homogeneous and has very few edge pixels. However, some soft edges (e.g. the outline of iris, the upper outline of head, and the outline of right ear) will be omitted (see Figure 2.14b,c). Therefore, selecting an appropriate threshold is especially problematic. Theoretically, the threshold should be chosen according to the just noticeable detection of *human visual system* (HVS). However, natural images are noisy. To improve the detection efficiency, prefiltering is often applied to reduce the noise content of the image. On the other hand, smoothing filter flattens gradient, which will make edges both wider and harder to detect by a single threshold.

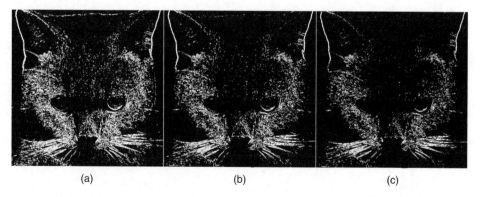

| (a) | (b) | (c) |

Figure 2.14 The edge maps of *Cat* extracted by Sobel filtering at different thresholds: (a) threshold = 80, (b) threshold = 100, and (c) threshold = 120.

2.5.2 Second-Order Derivative and Zero-Crossing Edge Detector

There are a large variety of edges in natural image. We have reviewed the first-order derivative methods to extract image edges, and it is found that those methods are efficient in detecting sharp edges, which has abrupt intensity change. For the edges with gradual intensity change and the edge that spans over several pixels, it is difficult if not impossible to extract the exact location of the edge, where multiple edge operator, thresholding, or post-processing steps are required to alleviate the problem. *Second-order derivative*-based edge detection method is adopted to obtain more accurate detection. When a second-order derivative filter is applied over the edges in the spatial domain, a function of the rate of change in the gradient along edges will be generated. The zero crossings of the output function indicate the maximum rate of change in gradient locations. The zero-crossing location is the exact location of the edge. The second-order derivative method is also efficient in detecting edges with small intensity change, as the detection is determined by the zero crossings of second-order derivative output, rather than the magnitude of gradient vector. This is because the magnitude of the gradient vector is relatively small in regions with low contrast and can be easily masked by a poorly chosen detection threshold.

Figure 2.15 compares the operation of first-order derivative method and second-order derivative method. Figure 2.15a plots the intensity along the edge normal, and the output of the first-order derivative edge operator and that of the second-order derivative operator are shown in Figure 2.15b and c, respectively. Figure 2.15b shows that the output elevates from 0 to a peak value with the changes of the pixel intensity. Therefore, if we map a value "1" to the binary edge map for the filter output with values greater than 0, the resulted edge will be a thick line in the map, and it is difficult to determine the exact edge location. In Section 2.5.1, we have introduced the idea of applying a threshold to the operator output, such that the output with values greater than `threshold` will be mapped to "1" in the edge map. In this

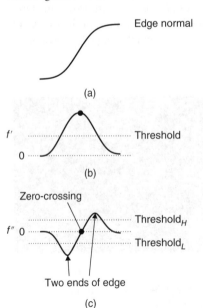

Edge normal

(a)

f' .... Threshold

0

(b)

Zero-crossing

f'' 0 .... Threshold$_H$

.... Threshold$_L$

Two ends of edge

(c)

Figure 2.15 Comparison of first-order and second-order derivative edge detection: (a) edge normal, (b) first-order derivation, and (c) second-order derivation.

case, the edge localization will be more precise. The precision could be improved by increasing the threshold further to make it as high as the peak value of the output. However, setting threshold too high will possibly mask other edges with lower gradient in the same image. The zero-crossing point indicates the exact location of the peak of gradient change in Figure 2.15b, which in fact is the exact edge location. Figure 2.15c shows the output of the edge normal filtered with the second-order derivative operator, where the output goes over or under the value of 0 depending on whether the rate of pixel value gradient change is increasing or decreasing. Therefore, it shows that the second-order derivative method provides more precise extraction and the image edges can be outlined with thin lines in the edge map. To accommodate the requirement of different applications, e.g. edge enhancement, we shall need to know both the exact edge location and the span of the edge. The trove and valley in Figure 2.15c show two ends of the edge normal, which is the extra information that could not be extracted by first-order derivative method. We can further distinguish weak and strong edges by applying a lower-bound threshold (threshold_L) and upper-bound threshold (threshold_H) to the second-order derivative output, such that edge with specific rate of change in gradient could be reflected in the final edge map.

2.5.2.1 Laplacian Operator

The *Laplacian operator* $\nabla^2 f$ that is defined on the space of twice-differentiable functions of two variables

$$\nabla^2 f = \frac{\partial^2 f}{\partial m^2} + \frac{\partial^2 f}{\partial n^2} \tag{2.33}$$

is a high-pass filter. To understand how to implement the Laplacian operator, let us consider Taylor's expansion of $f[m+1, n]$ or simply $f[m+1]$

$$f[m+1] = f[m] + f'[m] + \frac{1}{2}f''[m_0], \quad \text{for } m < m_0 < m+1, \tag{2.34}$$

which can be approximated as

$$f[m+1] \approx f[m] + f'[m] + \frac{1}{2}f''[m]. \tag{2.35}$$

Since $f'[m] \approx f[m] - f[m-1]$, it follows that

$$f[m+1] \approx 2f[m] - f[m-1] + \frac{1}{2}f''[m]. \tag{2.36}$$

By rearranging the terms

$$f''[m] \approx 2f[m+1] - 4f[m] + 2f[m-1]. \tag{2.37}$$

As a result, apart from the proportionality factor $\frac{1}{2}$, we define

$$\frac{\partial^2 f}{\partial m^2} \approx f[m+1] - 2f[m] + f[m-1]. \tag{2.38}$$

The discrete Laplacian is therefore given by

$$\nabla^2 f = f[m+1, n] - 2f[m, n] + f[m-1, n] + f[m, n+1] - 2f[m, n] + f[m, n-1], \tag{2.39}$$

which defines a 3×3 filter kernel

0	1	0
1	−4	1
0	1	0

The locations of the edge in the image is located at which $\nabla^2 f$ goes from positive to negative (or vice versa), also known as the zero crossing (as illustrated in Figure 2.15c). The intensity of the edge is proportional to the contrast on the two sides of the zero crossing. This kind of zero-crossing edge detector is also known as Laplacian edge detector, which was developed based on the belief on how the human eye processes edges. However, as the Laplacian operator is sensitive to small intensity change, false detection on noisy image would be resulted. Therefore, image smoothing is often applied before the Laplacian operator to eliminate the noises that would otherwise appear as false contours after the edge detector. One of the frequently applied smoothing filters is the Gaussian filter. Such kind of edge detection method is known as the Laplacian of Gaussian (LoG) method.

2.5.2.2 Gaussian Smoothing

The circular symmetric 2D Gaussian smoothing operator $h_{Gau}(m, n)$ (also called a Gaussian filter or simply a Gaussian) is given by

$$h_{Gau}(m, n) = e^{-(m^2+n^2)/2\sigma^2}, \tag{2.40}$$

where σ is a standard deviation of the associated probability distribution. In some literature, the filter is normalized as

$$h_{Gau}(m, n) = \frac{1}{2\pi\sigma^2}e^{-(m^2+n^2)/2\sigma^2}, \quad \text{or} \quad h_{Gau}(m, n) = \frac{1}{\sqrt{2\pi\sigma^2}}e^{-(m^2+n^2)/2\sigma^2}. \tag{2.41}$$

For simplicity, this book will consider h_{Gau} without the normalization factor as defined in Eq. (2.40). The standard deviation σ parametrizes the 2D Gaussian filter to achieve tunable smoothing. Such that pixels far away from the center of the operator will have smaller influence to the smoothing filtering result, and pixels farther than 3σ from the center will have negligible influence. This smoothing property is important for the application of Laplacian operator ∇^2 to digital image, which gives nondirectional (isotropic) second derivative.

To understand how σ can be applied to fine-tune the Laplacian operation result, we shall consider the Laplacian of an image $f[m, n]$ smoothed by a Gaussian (expressed using a convolution operator), also known as LoG

$$\nabla^2(h_{Gau}(m, n, \sigma) \otimes f[m, n]). \tag{2.42}$$

The order of performing differentiation and convolution can be interchanged because of the linearity of the operators involved.

$$(\nabla^2 h_{Gau}(m, n, \sigma)) \otimes f[m, n]. \tag{2.43}$$

The derivative of the Gaussian filter $\nabla^2 h_{Gau}$ can be precomputed analytically, since it is independent of the image under consideration. Thus, the complexity of the composite operation is reduced. For simplicity, let us consider $r^2 = m^2 + n^2$, where r measures distance from the origin; this is reasonable, as the Gaussian is circularly symmetric.

This substitution converts the 2D Gaussian in Eq. (2.40) into a 1D function that is easier to differentiate

$$h_{Gau}(r) = e^{-r^2/2\sigma^2}.$$ (2.44)

The first derivative $h'_{Gau}(r)$ is given by

$$h'_{Gau}(r) = -\frac{1}{\sigma^2} r e^{-r^2/2\sigma^2},$$ (2.45)

and the second derivative $h''_{Gau}(r)$, the LoG, is obtained as

$$h''_{Gau}(r) = \frac{1}{\sigma^2}\left(\frac{r^2}{\sigma^2} - 1\right)e^{-r^2/2\sigma^2}.$$ (2.46)

To obtain $\nabla^2 h_{Gau}(r)$, we shall consider the differentiation of r^2 with respect to m, to obtain $2r\partial r/\partial m = 2m$, whence $\partial r/\partial m = m/r$, and also

$$\partial h_{Gau}(r)/\partial m = \partial h_{Gau}/\partial r \cdot \partial r/\partial m = m(h'_{Gau}(r)/r),$$ (2.47)

$$\begin{aligned}\partial^2 h_{Gau}(r)/\partial m^2 &= h'_{Gau}(r)/r + m(\partial/\partial m)(h'_{Gau}(r)/r)\\ &= h'_{Gau}(r)/r + (m^2/r)\partial/\partial r)(h'_{Gau}(r)/r)\\ &= h'_{Gau}(r)/r + (m^2/r)(rh''_{Gau}(r) - h'_{Gau}(r))/r^2.\end{aligned}$$ (2.48)

Similarly for $\partial^2 h_{Gau}(r)/\partial n^2$ and adding the two parts and simplifying by $m^2 + n^2 = r^2$, we shall obtain

$$\nabla^2(h_{Gau}(r)) = h''_{Gau}(r) + h'_{Gau}(r)r.$$ (2.49)

Substituting Eqs. (2.45) and (2.46) into Eq. (2.49) will yield the LoG operator

$$\nabla^2 h_{Gau}(r) = \frac{r^2 - 2\sigma^2}{\sigma^4} h_{Gau}(r).$$ (2.50)

Figure 2.16a plots the LoG filter with $r = 10$ and $\sigma = 2$, while Figure 2.16b plots the Gaussian filter with same r and σ. It can be observed that the LoG filter is an inverted version of Gaussian filter. It is interesting to note that because of the shape of the Gaussian filter, it is also commonly called a *Mexican hat*.

The Gaussian smoothing effectively suppresses the influence of the pixels that are more than a distance of 3σ from the current pixel. As a result, the smoothing property of Gaussian filter depends on the variance σ. Increasing σ will increase the effective

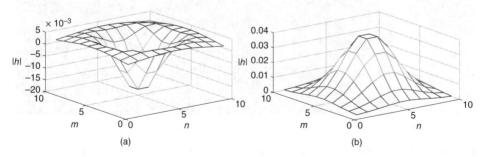

Figure 2.16 Smoothing filters: (a) a 10×10 Laplacian of Gaussian (LoG) filter with $\sigma = 2$ and (b) a 10×10 Gaussian filter with $\sigma = 2$.

width of the Gaussian filter kernel, which helps to reduce the edge detector's sensitivity to noise, at the expense of losing some of the fine details in the image. The localization error in the detected edges also increases slightly as the effective Gaussian filter kernel width increases.

The Laplace operator is an efficient and stable measure of changes in the image. After image convolution with $\nabla^2 h_{Gau}$, the locations in the convolved image where the zero level is crossed correspond to the positions of edges. The advantage of this approach when compared with classical edge operators of small size is that a larger area surrounding the current pixel is taken into account; the influence of more distant points decreases according to the σ of the Gaussian. In other words the scale at which edges are detected is controlled by the smoothing filter and so can be tuned easily. Moreover, the edge locations tend to be very precise, especially if the zero crossings are detected by using interpolation to get sub-pixel accuracy. In the ideal case of an isolated step edge, the σ variation does not affect the location of the zero crossing.

Listing 2.5.2 shows the usage of the built-in MATLAB function for edge detection using the LoG filter, where the function `edge` returns a binary image `map` containing 1s for the edge extracted from the input image `f`. The edge operator applied is defined by the second input parameters, where `'log'` is supplied to apply LoG filter for detection. The third input parameter `threshold` defines the sensitivity threshold, which will be automatically assigned according to the input image `f`. The fourth input parameter defines the value of σ in the LoG filter as depicted in Eq. (2.50), where the default value is 2 for the case of LoG operator. The size of the LoG filter generated by the function is proportional to the value of `sigma`.

> **MATLAB 2.5.2—Built-in MATLAB edge detection function using Laplacian of Gaussian (LoG) filter method.**
>
> ```
> >> map = edge(f,'log', threshold, sigma);
> ```

Figure 2.17a shows the edge map extracted by LoG filter with `threshold` and `sigma` being 0 and 0.8, respectively. It can be observed that any occurrence of intensity changes will be determined as edges if we consider all zero-crossing points as the edge location, where some edges are not important in describing the image object (e.g. the edges at the background of the *Cat* image). By having a fixed `threshold` to be 0.03 and

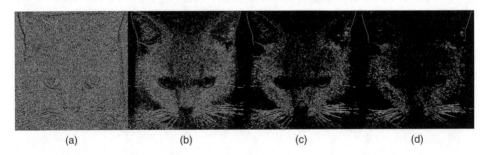

(a)　　　　　(b)　　　　　(c)　　　　　(d)

Figure 2.17 The edge of *Cat* extracted by Laplacian of Gaussian (LoG) filter with different `threshold` and σ: (a) at zero-crossing points with $\sigma = 0.8$, (b) `threshold` = 0.03 and $\sigma = 0.8$, (c) `threshold` = 0.03 and $\sigma = 1$, and (d) `threshold` = 0.03 and $\sigma = 1.2$.

different `sigma` values at 0.8, 1, and 1.2, the three corresponding edge maps are shown in Figure 2.17b–d, respectively. By setting a higher `threshold`, the small intensity variation at the image background is bypassed in the edge detection, such that the edges representing the features of the *Cat* face can be outlined. It can be further observed that by increasing `sigma`, the filter size is increased while the effect of smoothing is also increased, such that more high frequency components (short edges or edges with low contrast) will be bypassed by the filter. As a result, less edges are detected with increasing `sigma`. Therefore, same as the first-order derivative filter, an appropriate choice of parameter setting is critical for edge detection in the second-order derivative detection method too.

2.6 Geometric Transformation

In the previous section, we have reviewed different edge extraction methods and discussed how they help to locate an important image feature in human vision, the edges. Edges outline the boundary of an object and provide the geometric information of an object, which can be easily perceived by human vision. The boundary of an object defines the "*shape*" of an object. Geometric transformation is an operation to transform the placement and orientation of an object. With *shape* defines the geometric information of an object, such information should be preserved after the transformation in order to preserve the image contents. In the following we shall use *shape* and *object* indistinguishably; as to this book, they merely mean the same things, even though they are different in other mathematics or computer graphic subjects.

In mathematical points of view, *shape* can be presented by the collection of N edge pixels that defines the object boundary, with the coordinates of the edge pixels oriented within an ordered matrix $\mathbf{S}$ given by

$$\mathbf{S} = \begin{bmatrix} m_1 & m_2 & m_3 & \cdots & m_N \\ n_1 & n_2 & n_3 & \cdots & n_N \end{bmatrix}, \tag{2.51}$$

where the first row elements are the coordinates of the edge pixels in the row direction and the second row elements are the corresponding coordinates of the edge pixels in the column direction. The appearance sequence of the coordinate pairs within the matrix $\mathbf{S}$ will outline the *shape* of the object. The shape of the object can be deformed by geometric transformations, which finds applications such as in image restoration to help to eliminate geometric distortion aroused during the time of image capturing, or due to lens imperfection, or irregular movement of the sensors during image capturing. It is also useful in image comparison, where images of different viewpoints can be compared after they are transformed to a unified viewpoint. It also finds applications in image registration.

The 2D geometric transformation transforms the original shape presented by the matrix to transformed shape $\hat{\mathbf{S}}$ through vector matrix multiplications and additions, where the transformed *shape* is expressed as

$$\hat{\mathbf{S}} = \mathbf{T}_1 \mathbf{S} + \mathbf{T}_2, \tag{2.52}$$

with both $\mathbf{T}_1$ and $\mathbf{T}_2$ being the transformation matrices. The transform matrix $\mathbf{T}_1$ governs the size and orientation of the transformed object, while $\mathbf{T}_2$ governs the displacement of the object from its original spatial position. The operation is known to be a homogeneous transformation if the input object and the transformed object have the same dimension and in the same coordination space. Eq. (2.52) illustrates a homogeneous transformation in 2D space. It should be noted that Eq. (2.52) is a 2D operation, while the geometric transformation can also be applied in 3D space. There are some special operations that transform 2D objects to 3D objects, which will require the definition of nonexisting dimension of the 2D input object to be zero in order to preserve the homogeneity of the transformation. However, with grayscale image being always in 2D, we shall focus on 2D transformations in this book. In the following sections, we shall discuss the mathematics of some basic homogeneous transformations. Some transformation matrices can be applied to each pair of the coordinates independently within **S**. Hence, the transformed coordinate pair $[\hat{m},\hat{n}]$ can be written as a function of the original coordinate pair $[m_k,n_k]$ and the transformation matrices T_1 and T_2 as

$$\begin{bmatrix} \hat{m} \\ \hat{n} \end{bmatrix} = \mathbf{T_1} \begin{bmatrix} m \\ n \end{bmatrix} + \mathbf{T_2}, \tag{2.53}$$

where

$$\mathbf{T_1} = \begin{bmatrix} a & b \\ c & d \end{bmatrix}, \quad \text{and} \quad \mathbf{T_2} = \begin{bmatrix} e \\ f \end{bmatrix}, \tag{2.54}$$

with a, b, c, d, e, and f being real numbers. The matrix $\mathbf{T_1}$ is the multiplicative factor governing the scaling and the rotation of the object. The matrix $\mathbf{T_2}$ is the additive factor governing the translation of the object. In the following sections, we shall explain the different geometric transformations by considering a single coordinate pair to simplify the discussions. But before the discussions, let us formally define some terms used in geometric transformations.

2.6.1 Translation

Translation can be regarded as the most basic geometric transformation that involves the displacement of an object from one location to another as illustrated in Figure 2.18a, where the gray triangle is the object under discussion. Let us consider the vertex $[m, n]$ is translated to a new location $[\hat{m}, \hat{n}]$ with the displacement of e in the horizontal direction

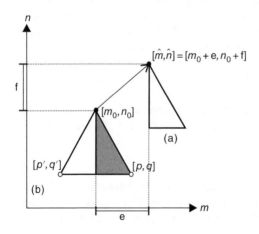

Figure 2.18 Geometric transformation: (a) translation and (b) reflection.

and f in the vertical direction, such that $\hat{m} = m + e$ and $\hat{n} = n + f$. Such operation can be expressed in matrix form with Eq. (2.53), where

$$\mathbf{T}_1 = \begin{bmatrix} 1 & 0 \\ 0 & 1 \end{bmatrix}, \qquad \text{and} \quad \mathbf{T}_2 = \begin{bmatrix} e \\ f \end{bmatrix}. \tag{2.55}$$

The displacement direction of the vertex of the object is determined by the values of e and f. For example, when both e and f have positive values, the vertex will move to right and upward. However when both e and f have negative values, the vertex will move toward left and downward. It should be noted that $\mathbf{T}_1$ in Eq. (2.55) is an identity matrix, such that Eq. (2.53) can be rewritten as

$$\begin{bmatrix} \hat{m} \\ \hat{n} \end{bmatrix} = \begin{bmatrix} m \\ n \end{bmatrix} + \begin{bmatrix} e \\ f \end{bmatrix} = \begin{bmatrix} m + e \\ n + f \end{bmatrix}, \tag{2.56}$$

which shows the translation is a pure addition operation. By applying the same operation to all other vertices of the triangle, the gray triangle will be moved to the white triangle position as shown in Figure 2.18a.

2.6.2 Reflection

Reflection is the geometric transformation that produces the mirror image of the object under transformation. The mirror image is perfectly symmetric to the original object along a vertical or horizontal reference axis. Consider the gray triangle in Figure 2.18a, where this triangle is reflected along the vertical axis at $m = m_0$ to produce the transformed white triangle (see Figure 2.18b). To illustrate the mathematical operation of *Reflection*, let us consider the vertex $[p, q]$ of the gray triangle. We can apply Eq. (2.53) to find the new location $[p', q']$ for this vertex. In this example, we shall set $e = m_0$, such that the *reflection* is in the horizontal direction along the axis $m = m_0$. The reflection operation can be written in the form of Eq. (2.53) as

$$\begin{bmatrix} p' \\ q' \end{bmatrix} = \mathbf{T}_1 \begin{bmatrix} p \\ q \end{bmatrix} + \mathbf{T}_2,$$

$$= \begin{bmatrix} -1 & 0 \\ 0 & 1 \end{bmatrix} \begin{bmatrix} p \\ q \end{bmatrix} + \begin{bmatrix} m_0 \\ 0 \end{bmatrix}. \tag{2.57}$$

The transformation matrix $\mathbf{T}_1$ controls the direction of the *reflection*, where b and c are zero, whereas a and d are set to be 1 and -1, respectively, for the *reflection* in horizontal direction. For the case of *reflection* in the vertical direction, a and d should be 1 and -1, respectively. The transformation matrix $\mathbf{T}_2$ controls the translation of the object. $\mathbf{T}_2$ can be ignored if the centroid of the object is located at $[0, 0]$. Otherwise, the values of e and f should be chosen such that the reference axis for the *reflection* would remain unchanged after the transformation. For example, if the *reflection* is in vertical direction with the reference point at $[m_0, n_0]$, the values of e and f should equal 0 and n_0, respectively.

2.6.3 Scaling

Scaling is generally used to resize an image or an object. The common application of scaling is zooming. An image/object can enlarge or shrink via zoom-in or zoom-out operations, respectively, which involves resampling to preserve the details of the image/object under resizing. Image size reduction is also known as *"subsampling"* (or down-sampling as used in this book), where the sampling rate is reduced by discarding redundant pixels and/or replacing the intensity of the remaining pixels with the interpolated results from its neighborhood. The reverse of image size reduction is image size enlargement, where the sampling rate increases and is known as *"up-sampling"* (or interpolation as used in this book). The new samples in the denser sampling grid are obtained from interpolation, such as pixel replication. More about image interpolation will be discussed in Section 2.7. However, no matter the sampling rate is increased or decreased, the outline (the shape) of the object should not be altered in the *scaling* operation, which can be easily preserved by using the geometric transformation that mapping the shape coordinate pairs through the matrix operation in Eq. (2.53) with b = c = 0, such that the new coordinates of the vertices of the scaled object are given by

$$
\begin{bmatrix} \hat{m} \\ \hat{n} \end{bmatrix} = \mathbf{T}_1 \begin{bmatrix} m_0 \\ n_0 \end{bmatrix} + \mathbf{T}_2,
$$

$$
= \begin{bmatrix} a & 0 \\ 0 & d \end{bmatrix} \begin{bmatrix} m \\ n \end{bmatrix} + \begin{bmatrix} e \\ f \end{bmatrix}, \tag{2.58}
$$

where a and d determine the scaling factor to m in horizontal direction and to n in vertical direction, respectively, and e and f aim to translate the locations of the transformed coordinate pairs to appropriate locations such that the location of the reference point of the transformation remains unchanged.

Let us consider the operation on the vertex $[m_0, n_0]$ of the gray triangle shown in Figure 2.19, where the reference point of the transformation is $[p, q]$. We shall apply a scaling factor a and d to m_0 and n_0, respectively. To maintain the reference point to remain at same location $[p, q]$, e = −ap and f = −dq are adopted. Therefore, Eq. (2.58) is written as

$$
\begin{bmatrix} \hat{m} \\ \hat{n} \end{bmatrix} = \begin{bmatrix} a & 0 \\ 0 & d \end{bmatrix} \begin{bmatrix} m_0 \\ n_0 \end{bmatrix} + \begin{bmatrix} -ap \\ -dq \end{bmatrix}. \tag{2.59}
$$

It should be noted that the values and relation between a and d determine the overall scaling operations. If the scaling in the horizontal and vertical directions are not identical, the object will be skewed, and the final *"shape"* of the transformed object may not be the same as that of the original object. Such special kind of *"scaling"* is known as

Figure 2.19 Geometric transformation: scaling.

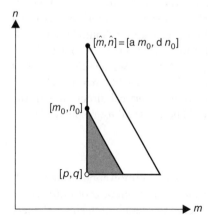

$[\hat{m}, \hat{n}] = [a\, m_0, d\, n_0]$

$[m_0, n_0]$

$[p, q]$

Table 2.1 Effect of the scaling parameters.

Parameters a and d	Effect
a = d	Uniform scaling
a ≠ d	Nonuniform scaling
a, d < 1	Object size reduction
a, d > 1	Object size enlargement
a = d = 1	Object size unchanged

"*shearing.*" The image scaling effects caused by different choices of a and d are summarized in Table 2.1.

2.6.4 Rotation

Rotation is a geometric transformation that maps a pixel from its original location to a new location by rotating it through a user-defined angle about the origin of the Cartesian coordinate system. Consider the pixel at one of the vertices of the gray triangle in Figure 2.20 with the coordinate $[m_0, n_0]$. The pixel makes an angle θ with the x-axis and a distance of r away from the origin $[0, 0]$ as shown in the same figure. Therefore, the coordinates m_0 and n_0 can be written as

$$m_0 = r\cos(\theta), \tag{2.60}$$

$$n_0 = r\sin(\theta). \tag{2.61}$$

In the example shown in Figure 2.20, the gray triangle is being transformed by rotation of ϕ in anticlockwise direction with respect to the origin. In the course of the rotation transformation, all the vertices of the gray triangle will undergo the same operation.

Figure 2.20 Geometric transformation: rotation.

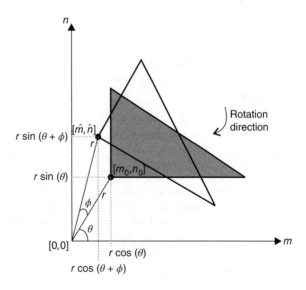

To simplify the discussion, let us consider the vertex at $[m_0, n_0]$. After rotation, the new coordinate of this vertex will be at $[\hat{m}, \hat{n}]$, where $\hat{m}$ and $\hat{n}$ are given by

$$
\begin{aligned}
\hat{m} &= r \cos(\theta + \phi), \\
&= r \cos(\theta) \cos(\phi) - r \sin(\theta) \sin(\phi), \\
&= m_0 \cos(\phi) - n_0 \sin(\phi),
\end{aligned}
\tag{2.62}
$$

and

$$
\begin{aligned}
\hat{n} &= r \sin(\theta + \phi), \\
&= r \cos(\theta) \sin(\phi) + r \sin(\theta) \cos(\phi), \\
&= m_0 \sin(\phi) + n_0 \cos(\phi),
\end{aligned}
\tag{2.63}
$$

respectively. Eqs. (2.62) and (2.63) can be expressed in matrix form with transform matrix given by

$$
\mathbf{T}_1 = \begin{bmatrix} \cos(\phi) & -\sin(\phi) \\ \sin(\phi) & \cos(\phi) \end{bmatrix},
\tag{2.64}
$$

with $a = \cos(\phi)$, $b = -\sin(\phi)$, $c = \sin(\phi)$, and $d = \cos(\phi)$ in Eq. (2.53). The readers may be curious about what is the appropriate $\mathbf{T}_2$ when applying Eq. (2.53) in this example. As the rotational center for the rotation operation is set at the origin $[0, 0]$, therefore, we can simply set $e = f = 0$ in $\mathbf{T}_2$ in this example. In general, the values of e and f should be chosen such that the rotational center relative to the object under the rotation operation should remain unchanged.

The *rotation* can be reverted from anticlockwise direction to clockwise direction by replacing the positive rotation angle ϕ to a negative value and the transform matrix $\mathbf{T}_1$ as

$$
\mathbf{T}_1 = \begin{bmatrix} \cos(-\phi) & -\sin(-\phi) \\ \sin(-\phi) & \cos(-\phi) \end{bmatrix}.
\tag{2.65}
$$

The pixel on the 2D Cartesian coordination system is now mapped to a polar coordination system after the transformation, where the new coordinates may not be on the grid of the original 2D Cartesian coordination system or the new coordinates may overlap with that of other pixels on the 2D Cartesian coordination system. Therefore, special approximation techniques are required to approximate the final locations of the transformed pixels back to the 2D Cartesian coordination system to make them fall perfectly onto the grid of the original system. The detail of such mapping will be discussed in Section 4.4.

2.6.5 Affine Transformation

Affine transformation can be regarded to be an arbitrary geometric transformation, where it invokes concatenation of parts of or all of the above-discussed geometric transformation operations to accomplish the object transformation; however, the final "*shape*" of the transformed object may not be the same as that of the original object. It is because only the straight lines of an object will remain straight and parallel lines will remain in parallel after the transformation. This can be more clearly explained by considering a rectangle. The rectangle might become a parallelogram upon affine transformation, with all the four edges remain straight and the two pairs of parallel edges remain in parallel. As a result, the perception of the "*shape*" of the transformed object will not be the same as that of the original object. Affine transformation is usually applied in image processing application to alter the "*shape*" of an object intentionally to accommodate a desired viewing perspective, which finds applications in mapping 2D image to a 3D image in a particular perspective viewpoint, image registration and holography, etc.

The affine transformation is usually applied to an image together with other image processing techniques. In Section 4.4, we shall showcase a special affine transformation that is a combination of image resizing and rotation to adjust the orientation of an image without unwanted missing pixels in spatial domain. We shall also discuss the application of affine transformation to image interpolation in Chapter 9.

2.7 Resize an Image

Image resizing is about the manipulation of the spatial resolution of an image. The process can be generalized to two operations: "*decimation*" and "*interpolation.*" Decimation is to down-sample, which will reduce the spatial resolution of the image. Interpolation is to up-sample, which will improve the spatial resolution of the image. In the context of digital camera, the decimation results enumerate the images captured by digital camera with smaller number of image sensing elements, while the interpolation results enumerate the images captured by digital camera with larger number of image sensing elements.

2.7.1 Interpolation

Image interpolation is the process of producing a high-resolution image from its low-resolution counterpart. Image interpolation extends the 1D interpolation problem discussed in Chapter 1 to 2D as shown in Figure 2.21. In the case of 2D interpolation, the intensity of a pixel in the denser sampling grid that is not available in the original sampling grid will be estimated (interpolated) from the pixels in the original sampling grid,

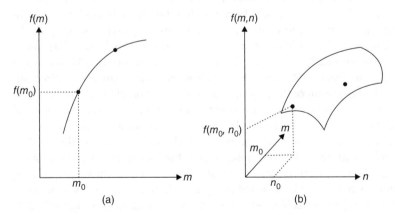

Figure 2.21 (a) 1D interpolation estimates a point on a line. (b) 2D interpolation estimates a point on a surface.

such that all the pixels (both new and old) will be laid on the same surface (in the denser grid) constructed by the 2D fitting function/functions.

The applications of image interpolation range from the image viewing to the more sophisticated magnification of medical and deep space images. With the increasing sophistication of consumer-based digital photography, users expect to have a greater control over their digital images. Digital image interpolation has a role in picking up clues and details in surveillance images and videos. As high-definition television (HDTV) technology enters the marketplace, engineers are interested in fast interpolation algorithms for viewing traditional low-definition programs on HDTV. Astronomical images from rovers and probes are received at an extremely low transmission rate (about 40 bytes per second); interpolation makes the transmission of high-resolution image infeasible. In medical imaging, neurologists would like to have the ability to interpolate the images on specific parts of brain tomography images. This is just a shortlist of applications, but the wide variety cautions us that our desired interpolation result could vary depending on the application and user.

Almost every image processing software implements some interpolation technique for transformations, rotations, and many other manipulations performed on an image. Consider one of the most common applications, image *"resolution enhancement"* or simply known as *"image enlargement."* One may wonder what makes *resolution enhancement* important. HVS perceives and resolves objects in a captured digital image depending on many factors, among which the spatial resolution is of great importance, thus determining the perceptual quality of a digital image. The higher the spatial resolution of an image, the better the reproduction of fine structures in the captured image. To demonstrate the relation of spatial resolution on image quality, the readers are invited to compare two images of the same scene but of different spatial resolutions in Figure 2.22a,b, where the image on the right is a high-resolution version (with spatial resolution four times greater) of the image shown on the left. The high-resolution image is expanded from the low-resolution image by interpolation (enlarged from the size of $M \times N$ to $2M \times 2N$); therefore, the high-resolution image contains some approximated information, but nothing new has been added. However, HVS will give the interpretation that the high-resolution image contains more information than that of the low-resolution one, e.g. the whiskers and the hair are vivid in the high-resolution image, the sharper contrast around the ears. It should be noted that the approximated information "seems" to provide more information, but it does not necessarily make the image looks more pleasant. This can be better illustrated with an example of the detail enlargement process as shown in Figure 2.22c–e. Figure 2.22c is taken from the original $M \times N$ image (the enclosed region in Figure 2.22a), in which a clear edge along the arrow direction can be observed. The resolution of the original image is first expanded by inserting new pixels with zero value (zero padding is applied in this example) in between the original pixels along the direction m and followed by the zero insertion along the direction n. The resulting zero-padded image is shown in Figure 2.22d. The values of the additional "zeros" will then be filled with the value interpolated from the known pixels in the original image. Figure 2.22e shows the interpolated result of Figure 2.22c, and the corresponding region in the interpolated image is enclosed in Figure 2.22b. It can be observed from the zoom-in image that the edge is blurred in the interpolated image (see Figure 2.22d).

The example illustrated in Figure 2.22 shows that additional pixels are interpolated from the neighboring known pixels that do not bring in any extra information to

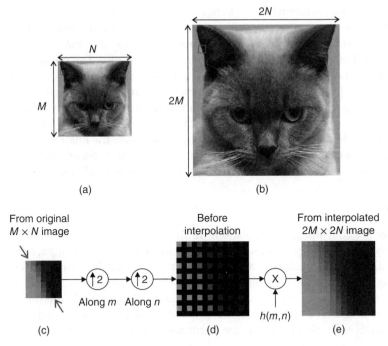

Figure 2.22 Example illustrates image enlargement by interpolation: (a) the original $M \times N$ image, (b) the enlarged image with spatial resolution of $2M \times 2N$, (c) the zoom-in of the enclosed region in (a), (d) unknown pixels are added before interpolation, and (e) the zoom-in of the enclosed region in the enlarged image in (b).

the interpolated image. As a result, the estimation of the unknown pixels will have unavoidable estimation error, and hence the interpolated image obtained from any interpolation process will be a distorted reproduction of the actual high-resolution image. The kinds of distortion and levels of degradation imposed on the interpolated image depend on the interpolation algorithm involved, as well as the prior knowledge of the original image. It is very important that the interpolation method has a very low computational cost in terms of both time and memory utilization since they are usually implemented in some intermediate step of subsystem in the application. At the same time, it is necessary for the interpolation method to yield good and accurate results, or else it could jeopardize the overall application. Therefore, there are many reasons to be interested in interpolating an image to retain as much as possible of the information it contains. One of the major technical challenges in image interpolation is to reconstruct the high frequency components or fine textures. Based on Nyquist–Shannon sampling theorem, continuous signals with limited frequency bandwidth are recoverable at specific sampling rate. However around sharp edges and boundaries of objects, due to rapid changes of the light field, the 2D image waveform has unlimited bandwidth, and hence mathematically it is impossible to completely reconstruct the original sampled signal by a set of limited number of pixels. To aggravate the difficulty of reproducing the edges, the HVS is highly sensitive to edges that signify attributes of an object (e.g. shape, boundaries, surface, and other visual characteristics). Even small interpolation errors around edges are highly visible and thus drastically degrading the visual quality of the entire image. As such, the performance of image interpolation techniques is largely determined by how well they preserve edges and fine structures in the image. Many image interpolation algorithms try to fit the 2D image waveform to a mathematical model and use the model to estimate the high frequency components of an image.

There are a variety of image interpolation methods presented in literature, which can be roughly categorized into two classes: the nonparametric and model-based image interpolations. The nonparametric interpolation techniques do not require any a priori information of the given image, and all pixels in the image are treated in same manner. On the other hand, model-based interpolation techniques estimate the unknown pixel values according to a priori information. A selected set of interpolation techniques from both categories will be the main topics of the rest of the chapters in this book.

2.7.2 Decimation

Though this book is about image interpolation, we intended to reserve a section to discuss its reverse process, *image decimation*. In later chapters, we shall compare the performance of different interpolation methods objectively using different metrics, where decimating the interpolated images is a necessary step. Image decimation is about reducing the spatial resolution of the image. Figure 2.23 illustrates the image decimation process in spatial domain, where the original image $g[m, n]$ is filtered with a 2D low-pass filter $h[m, n]$, also known as the decimation filter, to generate a filtered image $\hat{g}[m, n]$ with

$$\hat{g}[m, n] = h[m, n] \otimes g[m, n]. \tag{2.66}$$

Upon this stage, the filtered image $\hat{g}[m, n]$ still has the same size as that of the original image $g[m, n]$ but a blurred/distorted approximation. It would be easier if we consider in frequency domain that the high frequency components defining sharp edges/features in $g[m, n]$ are filtered out by the low-pass filter $h[m, n]$. To complete the decimation process, the filtered image $\hat{g}[m, n]$ is passed to a down-sampler to rectify the image spatial

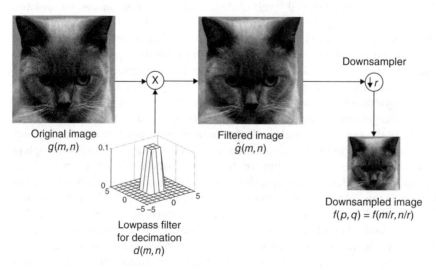

Original image
$g(m, n)$

Lowpass filter
for decimation
$d(m, n)$

Filtered image
$\hat{g}(m, n)$

Downsampler

Downsampled image
$f(p, q) = f(m/r, n/r)$

Figure 2.23 Image decimation by filtering.

resolution as desired and form the decimated image (low-resolution image) f, where

$$f[k, \ell] = \hat{g}[\text{round}(m/r), \text{round}(n/r)], \quad \text{for } m = 0, \ldots, M - 1; \quad n = 0, \ldots, N - 1,$$

$$(2.67)$$

with round(x) being a function that rounds x to the nearest integer and $k = \text{round}(m/r)$ and $\ell = \text{round}(n/r)$ with r being the down-sampling ratio. It is obvious that the decimated image will be governed by the decimation filter $h[m, n]$ applied. In the following sections, we shall discuss the pros and cons of different decimation filters and how we could implement the decimation filters.

2.7.2.1 Direct Subsampling

The most widely used decimation filter is the delta function filter.

$$h(m, n) = \delta(m, n), \tag{2.68}$$

where $\delta[m, n]$ has a magnitude of 1 at $m = n = 0$ and equals 0 in all other locations. It is interesting that the $\delta[m, n]$ filtered image $\hat{g}[m, n]$ is identical to that of the original image $g[m, n]$. When the subsampler is applied to $\hat{g}[m, n]$, a pixel will be taken from the $\hat{g}[m, n]$ in every r-pixel and placed into the final image $f[k, \ell]$; therefore, this decimation method is also called *"direct down-sampling."* This method requires very low computation effort; however, it suffers from sever aliasing problem. The cause of the aliasing can be more easily explained in the frequency domain, where the delta function, δ, is a Gaussian function in frequency domain and the aliasing is due to the overlapping of the tail of the Gaussian function after reducing the sampling frequency.

As the filtered image $\hat{g}[m, n]$ has identical pixel intensity with the corresponding pixels in the original image $g[m, n]$ through direct down-sampling, we can simplify the implementation by applying the original image to the sampler directly by dropping every $(r - 1)$ pixels periodically in every row/column to form the filtered image $\hat{g}$. Listing 2.7.1 shows the MATLAB code for the down-sampler with r being the down-sampling ratio, g being the input image, and f being the output image.

MATLAB 2.7.1—Down-sampler with down-sampling ratio $1/r$.

```
function f = directds(g,r)
  [M N]=size(g);
  f = g(1:r:M,1:r:N);
end
```

If we do not consider the aliasing problem, the direct down-sampling method does closely mimic the low-resolution image digitizer to obtain a low spatial resolution image and is therefore applied to generate low-resolution image for performance evaluation of various image interpolation methods presented in this book.

2.7.2.2 Sinc Filter

Among all the decimation filters, sinc function filter is known to be an ideal choice of filter because the frequency response of a sinc function is a box function; therefore this filter can be considered as ideal low-pass filter for any signal with bandwidth well within the box. Figure 2.24 shows the 2D plot of the sinc filter in spatial domain. The 2D sinc

Figure 2.24 Sinc function filter.

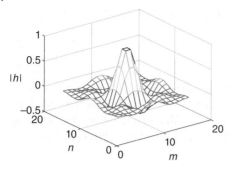

filter is separable in dimensions and is therefore constructed by Kronecker product of two 1D sinc filters as

$$h[m, n] = \frac{1}{r^2} \text{ sinc}\left(\frac{m}{r}\right) \text{ sinc}\left(\frac{n}{r}\right). \tag{2.69}$$

However this filter has infinite kernel size (support) and is therefore non-realizable. A realizable 2D sinc filter can be easily obtained by sampling and truncating the function in Eq. (2.69). The symmetry of the 2D sinc filter will be maintained when the support size and sampling density along m and n dimensions are the same. Shown in Listing 2.7.2 is the MATLAB implementation of the 2D sinc filter by multiplying a 1D sinc filter to its transpose.

> **MATLAB 2.7.2—Image decimation by sinc filter with scaling factor $1/r$ where $r = 2$.**
>
> ```
> >> y=sinc(a);
> >> h=y'*y;
> >> g_hat=filter2(h,g);
> >> f=directds(g_hat,2);
> ```

where a is the kernel size of the 1D sinc filter returned by the MATLAB built-in function sinc(a). However, 2D filtering using sinc filter is heavy in computation and is therefore less favorable in practice. Reader should also notice that the direct down-sampling function directds is applied in Listing 2.7.2 to generate the low-resolution image f from the filtered image g_hat.

2.7.2.3 Block Averaging

Another commonly used decimation filter is the block averaging filter, which defines the pixel intensity by taking average of the pixel intensities of the neighboring pixels in the original image. The size of the block averaging filter depends on the size of the window of neighboring pixels to be considered. Considering a 3×3 window, the block averaging filter is given by

$$h(m, n) = \frac{1}{3^2} \begin{bmatrix} 1 & 1 & 1 \\ 1 & 1 & 1 \\ 1 & 1 & 1 \end{bmatrix}. \tag{2.70}$$

Figure 2.25 is a graphical illustration of the 3×3 block averaging factor and the source code to down-sample an image by block averaging filter is shown in Listing 2.7.3.

Figure 2.25 Block averaging filter.

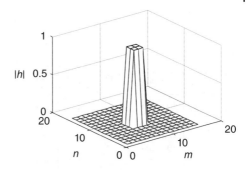

```
>> h=[1 1 1; 1 1 1; 1 1 1]./(3*3);
>> g_hat=filter2(h,g);
>> f=directds(g_hat,2);
```

Similar to sinc filter-based image down-sampling, `directds` is applied in Listing 2.7.2 to generate the low-resolution image `f` from the filtered image `g_hat`. Decimation by using block averaging filter has the advantage of easy to implement and requires less computation effort when compared with the sinc filter function. Though it will also suffer from aliasing problem, it is less sever when compared with that in direct down-sampling.

On the other hand, the convolution-based decimation may cause structural damage to the down-sampled image that cannot be recovered easily. Shown in Figure 2.26a is an excerpt of the image that lists the intensity of each pixel, and is decimated by direct down-sampling, and averaging with the result shown in Figure 2.26b. The down-sampled result is interpolated by nearest neighbor and linear interpolation methods with the results shown in Figure 2.26c, where the nearest neighbor interpolation estimates the unknown pixel intensity by replicating the neighboring data and the linear interpolation takes the average of neighboring data to fill up the unknown pixel intensity. The details of these two interpolation methods will be explained in Chapter 4. It is vivid that the averaging decimation method has ruined the structure of the image, which cannot be recovered by interpolation as shown in Figure 2.26c, no matter which interpolation methods have been applied. On the other hand the interpolation of the direct down-sampling results in Figure 2.26c has been shown to be able to resemble the original image fairly, in particular for the case of linear interpolation. In the rest of this book, we shall keep using direct down-sampling to generate low-resolution image for analysis in order to avoid the potential image structural damage.

2.7.3 Built-in Image Resizing Function in MATLAB

The MATLAB image processing toolbox is packed with `imresize`, which is a powerful image resizing function that supports both interpolation and decimation. An example that demonstrates the application of `imresize` is listed in Listing 2.7.4. In this example, the resizing ratio (scaling factor) is specified by the variable `r`, which can be any positive

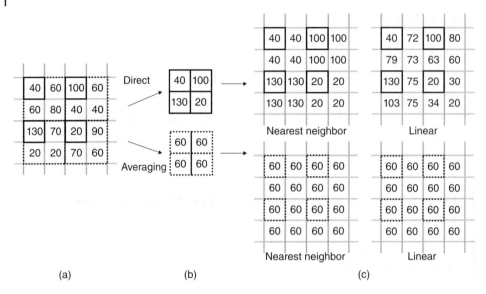

Figure 2.26 The effects of direct and block averaging down-sampling on image reconstruction through interpolation. (a) original image block; (b) down-sampled image blocks obtained from direct and averaging down-samplings; (c) image blocks obtained by interpolation using nearest neighbor and linear interpolation methods.

real number greater than 0. In our example, r=0.5, which means that the output image g has half the size in both *m* and *n* dimensions as that of the input image f. As specified by the parameter "bilinear," the original image is filtered with bilinear filter before decimation. In a similar manner, an output image with double the size of that of the input image interpolated by bilinear filter can be obtained by setting r=2. Besides the bilinear filter, there exists other decimation/interpolation filter defined in imresize, including the nearest neighboring, B-spline, bicubic, etc. If this parameter is missing, the bicubic filter is the default filter to be used.

MATLAB 2.7.4—Example of image resizing in MATLAB.

```
>> r=0.5;
>> g=imresize(f,r,'bilinear');
```

2.8   Color Image

Why do most image interpolation algorithms refer to grayscale images, while most images we come across are color images? The image interpolation algorithm that we apply to a grayscale image can be easily extended to a color image by applying them to each spectral component separately. A lot of the information conveyed by an image is expressed in its grayscale form, and so color is not necessary for its extraction. That is the reason why black and white television receivers have been perfectly acceptable to the public for many years and black and white photography is still popular with many photographers.

Nevertheless, color is an important property of the natural world, and so we shall examine its role in image processing in this section. As pointed out by Sir Isaac Newton, color is a property of the mind between the interaction of light sources, objects, and the visual system, which adds a subjective layer on top of the underlying objective physical properties – the wavelength of the electromagnetic radiation carried by color signal. The color signal is received by light sensitive cells in the human eye. Hering's experimental results and the discovery of three different types of photosensitive molecules in the human eye [66] led us to the modern color perception theory, where color is perceived through a *luminance* (grayscale) and two *chrominance* (color) components. This is the basis of trichromacy, the ability to match any color with a mixture of three suitably chosen primaries. The basic principles of color additivity have led to a number of useful trichromatic descriptions of color, which is also known as the *color space*.

Among various color spaces, the RGB and the YCrCb are most popular. In particular, the RGB color spaces have been widely employed in digital cameras and monitors to capture and display digital color images. This is because the RGB space conveniently corresponds to the three primary colors, which are mixed for display on a monitor or similar device. A digital color image in the RGB space is similar to a digital monochrome (grayscale) image, except that it requires a 3D vector to represent each pixel, and thus three $M \times N$ arrays are required to represent the whole image. Each of this $M \times N$ array represents one of the RED, GREEN, and BLUE primitive color components. The RED, GREEN, and BLUE components of an RGB image can be viewed separately as a monochrome image by considering the corresponding $M \times N$ array alone as shown in Figure 2.27. When the three color components are superposed, it produces the rightmost color image in Figure 2.27.

The digitization of the color image will quantize the RED, GREEN, and BLUE components separately similar to that operated on that monochrome image in Section 2.1. As a result, in the case of each component, images are encoded with data type `uint8`; the total number of bits required to represent each pixel will be 8 bits × 3 bits = 24 bits. This is also the default representation adopted by MATLAB for the three color triplets, and such type of image is known as the *true color* image. Disregarding the digital color

Figure 2.27 Three separate RED, GREEN, and BLUE channels are combined to create a final, full-color image. (*See insert for color representation of this figure.*)

image format, the MATLAB function `imread` can be used to import the image directly from the image file stored in the hard disk as shown in Listing 2.8.1.

MATLAB 2.8.1—Digital image details.

```
>> f = imread('cat_color.jpg','jpeg');
>> whos f
   Name       Size            Bytes      Class
   f          2000x1400x3     8400000    uint8 array
```

2.8.1   Color Filter Array and Demosaicing

It is vivid that three sensors, each sensor measures one of the three colors, respectively, are required to capture the RED, GREEN, and BLUE component images. A cheaper alternative to the three-sensor camera system is to have one sensor only. In this case, each photosensor in the sensor array is made to be sensitive to one of the three colors (ranges of wavelengths). This can be done in a number of different ways. A popular method in modern camera is to cover the photosensor array with a *Bayer pattern* color filter as shown in Figure 2.1. A Bayer filter array is constructed with 50% of the filter cell being green, while the remaining filter cells are divided equally between red and blue. The reason behind is that the human eye is most sensitive to green, and less to red, and least to blue. This property has been applied in the layout of the filter cells as illustrated in Figure 2.1 back in 1976 [9]. Each pixel only captures one color, and the two other colors of a particular pixel must be inferred from the neighbors.

An example of a 6 × 6 *Bayer pattern* color filter arrangement is shown in Figure 2.28, which can be separated into three images containing the RED, GREEN, and BLUE pixels separately with some undefined pixel values (as shown by the shaded box in the figure). A full-color image needs the information of all the three colors in each pixel location. As a result, it is essential to interpolate the missing two colors in each pixel location using the information of the neighboring pixels. The methodology to recover these missing color components is known as *color demosaicing*. Although complicated algorithms do exist, most color demosaicing algorithms consider each primitive color image separately, and the missing pixels in each color component are interpolated independently.

2.8.2   Perceptual Color Space

Most digital image processing algorithm makes use of a simplified RGB color model (based on the CIE color standard of 1931) that is optimized and standardized toward graphical displays. However, the primary problem with RGB is that it is perceptually nonlinear. By this we mean that moving in a given direction in the RGB color cube does not necessarily produce a color that is perceptually consistent with the change in each of the channels. For examples, starting at white and subtracting the blue component produces yellow; similarly, starting at red and adding the blue component produces magenta. For this reason, RGB space is inherently difficult for humans to work with, because it is not related to the natural way we perceive colors. As an alternative, we may use perceptual color representations, such as YCbCr color space.

Although color is typically thought of as being 3D due to the trichromatic nature of color matching, five perceptual attributes are needed for a complete specification of

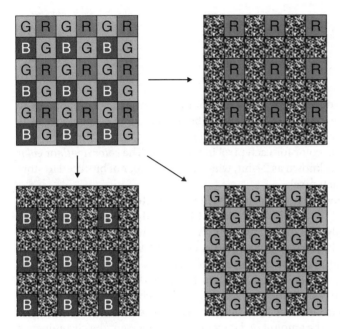

Figure 2.28 Red, green, and blue samples obtained from *Bayer pattern* color filter. (*See insert for color representation of this figure.*)

color appearance. These are *brightness*, the attribute according to which an area appears to be more or less intense; *lightness*, the brightness of an area relative to a similarly illuminated area that appears to be white; *colorfulness*, also known as *chromaticness* that describes the attribute according to which an area appears to be more or less chromatic; *chroma*, the colorfulness of an area relative to a similarly illuminated area that appears to be white; and *hue*, the attribute of a color denoted by its name such as blue, green, yellow, orange, etc. In some cases, the attribute *saturation* that describes the colorfulness of an area relative to its brightness may be provided, which can be derived from the previous five attributes, and is therefore considered to be redundant.

The HVS is less sensitive to chromatic than luminance. In the RGB color space, the three primitive colors are equally important, and so are usually all stored at the same resolution. It is possible to represent a color image more efficiently by separating the luminance from the color information and representing luma with a higher resolution than color. The YCbCr color space and its variations are popular ways to efficiently representing color images. Y is the luminance (luma) component and can be calculated as a weighted average of R, G, and B as

$$Y = k_r R + k_g G + k_b B, \tag{2.71}$$

where the k's are the weighting factors. The color information can be represented as *color difference* (chrominance or chroma) components, where each chrominance component is the difference between R, G, or B and the luminance Y as

$$C_b = \frac{0.5}{1 - k_b} B - Y + 128, \tag{2.72}$$

$$C_r = \frac{0.5}{1 - k_r} R - Y + 128, \tag{2.73}$$

$$C_g = \frac{0.5}{1 - k_g} G - Y + 128, \tag{2.74}$$

where the constant 128 is added to shift the range of the chrominance components to the range of [0,255] with the input RGB signal range being [0,255]. In other words, each color component in a color pixel would require 8 bits, and a total of 8 bits $\times$ 3 = 24 bits are used to represent the color for each pixel in the image. The *color depth* or *color resolution* of such an image is known as 24-bit, which is the number of bits used to store the color information for each pixel.

In the case of YCbCr color space, the color image is completely described by Y (the luminance component) and three color differences C_b, C_r, and C_g. Since $C_b + C_r + C_g$ is proportional to Y, so only two of the three chroma components need to be stored or transmitted, as the third component can always be calculated from the other two together with Y. As a custom, the blue and red chromas (C_b, C_r) are selected in the YCbCr color space, and C_g will be computed from these two color chromas. YCbCr has an important advantage over RGB, that is, the C_r and C_b components may be represented with a *lower resolution* than Y because the HVS is less sensitive to chroma than luminance. This reduces the amount of data required to represent the chrominance components without having an obvious effect on visual quality. As a result, the YCrCb color space has been adopted in a number of international image storage standard, such as JPEG. The RGB to YCbCr color space conversion can be achieved by using the MATLAB command `rgb2ycbcr` and inverse conversion by `ycbcr2rgb`. The detail implementation will leave to the readers as an exercise in the problem section of this chapter. It should also be noted that each entry in the YCbCr color space only required to be an unsigned 8-bit integer to achieve the same resolution as that of an RGB color space with 8-bit per color component. In other words, the two color systems have a consisting color depth to describe the color image. However, the conversion between color space is a non-invertible transform, such that the true color information (RGB) will be lost in the conversion and cannot be readily recovered.

2.9 Noise

The main barrier to effective signal processing and thus image processing in general is noise. Noise is the variation of signal from its true value by a small (random) amount due to external or internal factors in image capturing, transmitting, and processing. These factors cannot be (easily) controlled, and thus introducing random elements into the processing results, which may be dependent on, or independent of, the image content. Noise is the key problem in 99% of cases where image processing techniques either fail or further image processing is required to achieve the required result. As a result, a large part of image processing algorithm, and thus image interpolation algorithm development, is dedicated to increase the robustness of the algorithm toward noise. To cope with noise, we shall have to understand that the noise in digital images can originate from a variety of sources:

1. *Capture noise* can be the result of variations in lighting, sensor temperature, electrical sensor noise, sensor nonuniformity, dust in the environment, vibration, lens distortion, focus limitations, sensor saturation (too much light), and underexposure (too little light).
2. *Sampling noise* originates from the limitations in sampling and intensity quantization that are a source of noise in the form of representational aliasing. It should be noted that the sampled digital image is not a true representation of the analog image, but an alias of the original.
3. *Processing noise* originates from the limitations in numerical precision (floating point numbers), potential integer overflow, and mathematical approximations (e.g. $\pi = 3.142\ldots$) that are all potential sources of noise in the processing itself.
4. *Image-encoding noise* originates from the loss in lossy compression. Many modern image compression techniques (e.g. JPEG used intrinsically by modern digital cameras) are lossy compression techniques. By lossy we mean that they compress the image by removing visual information that represents detail not general perceivable to the human viewer. The problem is that this loss of information due to compression undermines image processing techniques that rely on this information. This loss of detail is often referred to the appearance of compression artifacts in the image. In general, loss, compression loss, and noise are considered to be equivalent. Besides the lossy compression format, there is lossless compression in image formats, such as PNG, which offer lossless compression to counter this issue.

Besides classifying the noise in the above systematic ways, noise in images can also be roughly characterized into two major classes: *additive* and *multiplicative*. An example of multiplicative noise is variable illumination, where the visual artifact of the image caused by uneven illumination can be considered as a form of multiplicative noise. The additive noise is often assumed to be *impulse* noise (also known as *"salt and pepper"* noise) or *Gaussian* noise:

1. *Impulse noise* alters at random the value of some pixels. As a result, the impulse noise-corrupted binary image will have some pixels that become white in black image area and black in white image area. This is why this noise is also called *"salt and pepper"* noise. This noise is a very common problem in digital image acquisition, where the randomness appears from hardware elements because the behavior of electronic device (in particular image capturing device) can be random on account of thermal conditions; such behavior is inherently a charge flow phenomenon and is highly dependent on the temperature. Shown in Figure 2.29a is the *Cat* image corrupted by the additive impulse noise with signal-to-noise ratio (SNR) of 4.18 dB (a formal definition of SNR will be given in Chapter 3).
2. *Gaussian noise* adds an intensity drawn from a zero mean Gaussian probability density function to the true value of every pixel. Unlike impulse noise that only affects a portion of randomly selected pixels in the image, additive Gaussian noise affects all pixels in the whole image. Shown in Figure 2.29b is the *Cat* image corrupted by the additive white noise with the same noise power as that in Figure 2.29a. It can be observed that the impulse noise is visually more annoying than that of the additive Gaussian noise.

The salt and pepper noise and Gaussian noise can be easily generated by using the MATLAB function `imnoise(f,type,param)`. `imnoise` adds specific type of noise

(a)

(b)

(c)

(d)

(e)

(f)

Figure 2.29 Image noise and denoising: (a) impulse noise-corrupted (also known as "Salt & Pepper Noise") *Cat* image with $SNR = 4.18$ dB, (b) additive Gaussian noise-corrupted *Cat* image with $SNR = 4.18$ dB, (c) denoised image (a) recovered by median filter of window size of 5×5, (d) denoised image (a) recovered by Gaussian smoothing filter of size 5×5 and $\sigma = 2$ (refer to Section 2.5.2.2), (e) denoised image (b) recovered by median filter of window size 5×5, and (f) denoised image (b) recovered by Gaussian smoothing filter of size 5×5 and $\sigma = 2$, where the filters used for denoising can be referred to Section 2.5.2.2.

to the image, where the input parameters `type` defines the type of noise source to be added and `param` defines additional specification to the noise source. Listing 2.9.1 shows the example of adding salt and pepper noise and Gaussian noise to the input image `f` to generate corrupted images `s` and `g`, respectively. The identifier of salt and pepper noise is `'salt & pepper'`, and only one additional specification parameter that defines the noise density is allowed (noise density is 0.05 in default). Figure 2.29a shows the salt and pepper noise-corrupted *Cat* image with noise density equals 0.1 (and hence 10% of the pixels in `f` will be corrupted with salt & pepper noise). To obtain image with Gaussian noise added, the identifier `'gaussian'` should be applied. There are two additional specification parameters that define the mean and variance of the Gaussian noise probability density function. In the following example, the Gaussian noise is generated with zero mean and variance equals 0.1 and added to the image `f`. The Gaussian noise-corrupted image `g` is shown in Figure 2.29b.

MATLAB 2.9.1—Noisy image.

```
>> s = imnoise(f,'salt & pepper',0.1);
>> g = imnoise(f,'gaussian',0,0.1);
```

Ultimately, no digital image is a perfect representation of the original scene: it is limited in resolution by sampling and contains noise. One of the major goals of image processing is to limit the effects of these aspects in image visualization and analysis. An effective way to counteract noise-corrupted image is to perform *rank order filtering* to remove impulse noise and *smoothing* to reduce Gaussian noise.

2.9.1 Rank Order Filtering

The output of a rank order filter depends on the ranking of the pixel intensities inside the filter window. The most common rank order filter is the *median* filter. Consider the case of a median filter with window size 5×5. The median of the gray level of the pixels within these windows will be the output of the filter, which will replace the original intensity of the pixel situated at the middle of the window. This has the effect of forcing pixels with distinct intensities to be more alike with their neighbors, thus eliminating intensity spikes that appear with isolated gray level. The impulse noise in Figure 2.29a can be effectively removed by median filter as shown in Figure 2.29c. Listing 2.9.2 shows the usage of MATLAB built-in function of median filtering `medfilt2`. `medfilt2` returns the denoised image `d`, where the pixels in `d` are the median values of the corresponding 5-by-5 neighboring pixels in the image `s`.

MATLAB 2.9.2—Median filter.

```
>> s = imnoise(f,'salt & pepper',0.1);
>> d = medfilt2(s, [5 5]);
```

2.9.2 Smoothing Filtering

A smoothing filter is a low-pass filter, where the Gaussian smoothing filter discussed in Section 2.5.2.2 is an example. Considering applying the Gaussian smoothing filter with kernel size 5×5 to the additive Gaussian noise-corrupted image in Figure 2.29b, the filtered image is shown in Figure 2.29d. It is vivid that the filter effectively suppressed the Gaussian noise. The MATLAB implementation of Gaussian filter image filtering is shown in Listing 2.9.3, where the function f special creates a 2D filter specified by the filter identifier, and in our example gaussian is supplied to define the required filter. For Gaussian filter, the second and the third input parameters specify the filter size and the value of the σ in the Gaussian filter. In our example, the filter size is chosen to be 5×5 and $\sigma = 5$. h is the Gaussian smoothing filter, and it is applied to the noisy image g by the function imfilter to filter the noise-corrupted image g and give the recovered image d.

MATLAB 2.9.3—Gaussian filter.

```
>> g = imnoise(f,'gaussian',0,0.1);
>> h = fspecial('gaussian',5,5);
>> d = imfilter(g,h);
```

Figure 2.29e,f shows the recovered images of the Gaussian noise-corrupted *Cat* image (Figure 2.29b) by the 5×5 median filter and the Gaussian smoothing filter with size of 5 and σ of 5, respectively. It can be observed from Figure 2.29c–f that the median filter is more effective to remove impulse noise, while Gaussian smoothing filter is more effective in removing additive Gaussian noise. The poor median filter performance on Gaussian noise-corrupted image is easy to understand because additive Gaussian noise does not create pixels with isolated intensities within localized region. Applying the Gaussian smoothing filter to remove impulse noise (see Figure 2.29d), the recovered image will be blurred because part of the high frequency components in the corrupted image is removed, but there is still trace of impulse noise in the filtered image.

To understand why the Gaussian smoothing filter is more effective to remove Gaussian noise, we need to consider the spectrum of the noise-corrupted image and the Gaussian noise. Assuming the Gaussian noise is uncorrelated with the image, and has a flat spectrum, and the spectrum of the image has high value in low frequencies and is gradually reducing values as frequency increases, the two spectra are plotted in Figure 2.30.

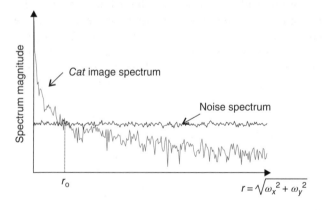

Figure 2.30 The average spectral power at radian frequency $r = \sqrt{\omega_x^2 + \omega_y^2}$ of the *Cat* image and additive Gaussian noise. At radian frequency r_0 and larger, the noise power will dominate spectrum.

The Gaussian smoothing filter is a low-pass filter with cutoff frequency at r_o. Generally, r_o will be chosen at a particular frequency where the noise power dominates the spectrum beyond that particular frequency. As a result, if a low-pass filter at r_o is applied to the Gaussian noise-corrupted image, all noise-dominated high frequency component of the corrupted image will be removed. However, the low-pass filter will also remove the high frequency component of the original image, and hence the recovered image will be blurred.

2.10 Summary

In this chapter, we have experienced a digital image capturing system that captures, processes, and represents a physical scene into a digital image, which involves a series of hardware and software operations. To prepare for the discussion in later chapters, we have unified the convention used for representing a digital image in this chapter. We have also reviewed the mathematics of fundamental image processing and image features representation.

2.11 Exercises

2.1 MATLAB experiment: Import image and data type conversion.
1. Imports the grayscale image "grasssea.jpg," and stores it using with the variable f.
2. View the data type and size of f.
3. Convert the data type of f to double.

2.2 The ITU-R recommendation BT.601 [10] defines $k_b = 0.114$ and $k_r = 0.299$ and further constrains Y in the range of [0,255] with the RGB in the same range. Derive the equations that convert RGB to YCbCr, and from YCbCr to RGB, and implement the conversion function in MATLAB.

2.3 There are two main group of methods to convert color images to grayscale image: luminosity methods and color-altering methods. Luminosity method is based on the brightness of the color, while color-altering method is according to the color contrast of the image. Develop MATLAB procedures that perform color to grayscale image conversion for the color *Cat* image to grayscale image by:
1. Luminosity method with the following conversion formulas
   (a) Green weighted
   $$Y = 0.21R + 0.62G + 0.17B. \tag{2.75}$$
   (b) Red weighted
   $$Y = 0.62R + 0.21G + 0.17B. \tag{2.76}$$
   (c) Blue weighted
   $$Y = 0.62R + 0.17G + 0.21B. \tag{2.77}$$

2. Averaging method

$$Y = \frac{R + G + B}{3}.$$ (2.78)

3. Lightness method

$$Y = \frac{1}{2}(\max(R, G, B) + \min(R, G, B)).$$ (2.79)

Compare and comment on the obtained grayscale images from the above five methods.

2.4 MATLAB experiment: Reduce the spatial resolution of image "grasssea.jpg" from 1024-by-1024 to 512-by-512 by implementing the following decimation methods in MATLAB:
1. Direct subsampling.
2. Block averaging.
3. Sinc filtering.

2.5 Construct first-order derivative edge detector that can detect edges with angle of 45°, implement the corresponding MATLAB function, and apply it to the *Cat* image. Select an appropriate detection threshold, and plot the detection result.

2.6 Given the *Prewitt* filter in horizontal and vertical direction, P_x and P_y, respectively,

$$P_h = \begin{bmatrix} -1 & 0 & 1 \\ -1 & 0 & 1 \\ -1 & 0 & 1 \end{bmatrix},$$ (2.80)

$$P_v = \begin{bmatrix} -1 & -1 & -1 \\ 0 & 0 & 0 \\ 1 & 1 & 1 \end{bmatrix}.$$ (2.81)

Apply the given *Prewitt* filter to image letter A, and display the corresponding filtered image in MATLAB. [*Hint*: MATLAB built-in function imshow and filter2 can be used.]
1. Apply *Prewitt* filter in horizontal direction, P_h, to show the filtered image p_h (i.e. edge image showing horizontal edges).
2. Apply *Prewitt* filter in horizontal direction, P_v, to show the filtered image p_v (i.e. edge image showing vertical edges).
3. Combine results of (1) and (2) with the relation of $\sqrt{p_h^2 + p_v^2}$ to show the all horizontal edges and vertical edges in the edge image.

2.7 Given a 3×3 image block

$$f = \begin{bmatrix} 1 & 2 & 3 \\ 4 & 5 & 6 \\ 7 & 8 & 9 \end{bmatrix}.$$ (2.82)

Extend the image block to the dimension of 9×9 by:
1. Zero padding.
2. Periodic extension.
3. Symmetric extension.

2.8 Compute the memory space required to store 256×256 pixels of
1. a binary image,
2. a grayscale image with 8-bit shades, and
3. a color image with 8-bit per each primitive color.

2.9 Develop a MATLAB program to load the color *Cat* image, and convert the color image into grayscale image using:
1. MATLAB built-in function `rgb2gray`.
2. $y = \frac{r+g+b}{3}$.

Are the two images the same? Explain your observation.

2.10 Describe and explain the result of the magnitude of the matrix obtained from performing a Fourier transform on a Fourier transform of an image.

2.11 **Mask**
1. Explain how an averaging mask would affect the output of a Fourier transform.
2. Compare and describe the results of the Fourier transform of an image filtered with (a) a 3×3, (b) a 5×5, and (c) a 4×4 averaging mask. What is the effect of increasing the size of the averaging mask?

2.12 Consider the array below is a grayscale image.

$$
\begin{matrix}
40 & 40 & 40 & 20 & 20 & 20 & 20 & 20 & 20 \\
40 & 40 & 40 & 40 & 40 & 40 & 40 & 40 & 20 \\
40 & 40 & 40 & 20 & 20 & 20 & 20 & 40 & 20 \\
40 & 40 & 20 & 20 & 20 & 20 & 20 & 40 & 20 \\
40 & 20 & 20 & 20 & 20 & 20 & 20 & 40 & 20 \\
20 & 20 & 20 & 20 & 40 & 20 & 20 & 40 & 20 \\
20 & 20 & 20 & 20 & 20 & 20 & 20 & 20 & 20 \\
40 & 20 & 40 & 40 & 20 & 20 & 20 & 40 & 40 \\
40 & 20 & 20 & 40 & 20 & 20 & 40 & 20 & 40 \\
\end{matrix}
$$

1. Compute the output image by applying masks (a) to (h) to the grayscale image. Zero padding should be used for boundary extension in these cases.

(a) $\begin{bmatrix} -1 & -1 & 0 \\ -1 & 0 & 1 \\ 0 & 1 & 1 \end{bmatrix}$.

(b) $\begin{bmatrix} 0 & -1 & -1 \\ 1 & 0 & -1 \\ 1 & 1 & 0 \end{bmatrix}$.

(c) $\begin{bmatrix} -1 & -1 & -1 \\ 2 & 2 & 2 \\ -1 & -1 & -1 \end{bmatrix}$.

(d) $\begin{bmatrix} -1 & 2 & -1 \\ -1 & 2 & -1 \\ -1 & 2 & -1 \end{bmatrix}$.

(e) $\begin{bmatrix} -1 & -1 & -1 \\ -1 & 8 & -1 \\ -1 & -1 & -1 \end{bmatrix}$.

(f) $\begin{bmatrix} 1 & 1 & 1 \\ 1 & 1 & 1 \\ 1 & 1 & 1 \end{bmatrix}$.

(g) $\begin{bmatrix} -1 & 0 & 1 \\ -1 & 0 & 1 \\ -1 & 0 & 1 \end{bmatrix}$.

(h) $\begin{bmatrix} 0 & -1 & 0 \\ -1 & 4 & -1 \\ 0 & -1 & 0 \end{bmatrix}$.

2. Describe the effect of each of the masks on the image.

2.13 Derive a 3 × 3 mask that will cause no change to an image.

2.14 Apply larger and larger Gaussian filters to the image *Cat*. What is the smallest filter size for which the whiskers cannot be seen?

3

Image Quality

The performance assessment of image interpolation algorithms can be categorized into objective and subjective assessments, and they are just the two faces of the mirror. Since the interpolated images are to be perceived by human eyes, therefore, subjective analysis is considered to be the final quality assessment of the interpolated image. However, one's medicine is the other's poison. It is difficult if not impossible to provide a subjective analysis to the interpolated image as it requires time and money and is highly inconvenient. Not to mention that there is no commonly accepted subject quality measure or feature sets for all varieties of image interpolation problems. Researchers are devoting massive efforts in developing different objective quality assessment algorithms that take the *human vision system* (HVS) into consideration (to model and to approximate the behavior of human vision) such as to provide an objective mean to compare the visible artifacts generated throughout the interpolation process. These algorithms give objective quality score that mimic the subjective quality measure for the image under test, without going through the subjective quality analysis. The objective scores (which are sometimes referred to as index) of different quality assessment algorithms depend on how the visible artifacts are quantified and also the sources of the reference data for comparison. Therefore, it is important for the readers to understand the definition of visible artifacts in terms of their appearances and also the sources of the reference data, such that they can make appropriate choices of the objective quality assessment methods to be applied for their own purposes. In this chapter, we shall first introduce the different image features and also the image artifacts commonly observed in interpolated images in Section 3.1, while the following will discuss the classification of quality assessment algorithms according to the sources of reference images.

The source of the reference image adopted in different quality assessment algorithms categorizes the algorithms into three groups, including *full-reference image quality index* (FRIQ), *no-reference image quality index* (NRIQ), and *reduced-reference image quality index* (RRIQ). Among various image quality indices, the interest of this book is the FRIQ, because we have no difficulties to obtain the reference image in our analysis. The FRIQ scores the quality of the interpolated image by comparing it with a reference image, which is also known as the undistorted image. The algorithm makes use of certain parameters of the image to estimate the quality score of the interpolated image with reference to the undistorted image. A list of commonly applied FRIQ measures together with their analytic backgrounds will be discussed in Section 3.2, in which all

Digital Image Interpolation in MATLAB®, First Edition. Chi-Wah Kok and Wing-Shan Tam.
© 2019 John Wiley & Sons Singapore Pte. Ltd. Published 2019 by John Wiley & Sons Singapore Pte. Ltd.
Companion website: www.wiley.com/go/ditmatlab

the algorithms focus on the some kinds of measures of the absolute difference in pixel intensities between the interpolated image and the reference image.

In Section 3.3, we shall discuss a benchmark FRIQ, known as *structural similarity* (SSIM) index, which considers the HVS. The SSIM takes an in-depth look on the impact of image structure on the assessment of image quality. The readers should note that neither subjective nor objective assessments could be used alone. It is always more convincing when both quality measures are applied together or at least applied a limited subjective quality measure to assist the objective assessment of the interpolated image quality.

3.1 Image Features and Artifacts

The human eye interprets the information in an image by classifying the image into different feature zones and determines the image quality by looking for visible artifacts, which refers to the features that should not exist in the particular feature zones. A rough classification of the different feature zones of a natural image can be illustrated by the natural image *Cat* in Figure 3.1:

1. *Homogeneous*: The variations of the grayscales within these zones are small (or smaller than a predefined quantity), which makes interpolation artifacts (large pixel value variations) in these region to be easily detectable.
2. *Textured*: Regions with repetitive patterns and structures at various scales and orientations. The human eye is not very sensitive to pixel value variations within these zones, and thus interpolation artifacts are difficult to be detected in these regions.
3. *Edges*: The edges separate two homogeneous regions with different mean grayscales, which makes the interpolation artifacts in this zone readily noticeable.

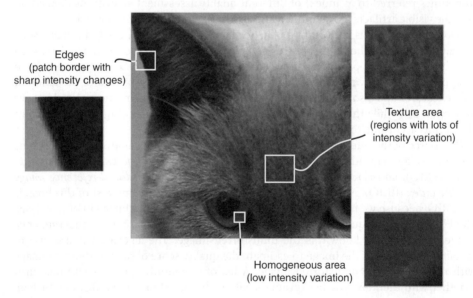

Figure 3.1 A natural image *Cat* showing three basic image features: homogeneous area, texture area, and edges.

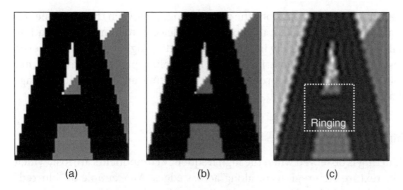

      (a)   (b)   (c)

Figure 3.2 Image interpolation artifacts of the synthetic image letter *A* demonstrating (a) aliasing (jaggy), (b) blurring, and (c) edge halo and ringing.

Subjective quality assessment assesses the image quality through human eye, which is often considered to be the only "*correct*" way to evaluate the image quality. The subjective *mean opinion score* (MOS) is a popular method to achieve statistical significance. To achieve a satisfactory assessment result, which can be considered to be general and reliable, the number of participants should be as large as possible. As a result, each assessment will require an adequate number of participants, and a series of tests are required, making the experiment extremely time-consuming and expensive. Therefore, a great deal of efforts has been made in recent years to develop objective image quality metrics that correlate with perceived quality measurement, which are the topics in Section 3.2, where a number of FRIQ metrics will be discussed. Before we move onto FRIQ metrics, the following subsections will list the commonly observed visual artifacts in an interpolated image, so we could have a better understanding on the nature and origin of different image artifacts and how they are perceived by human eyes. In order to clearly display each image artifact, the synthetic image letter *A*, a noise-free computer drawing with sharp edges will be used for illustration, instead of the natural image *Cat* (see Figure 3.2).

3.1.1 Aliasing (Jaggy)

When the sampling frequency applied to generate the digital image is lower than the highest spatial frequency of the natural image under concern, sampling theorem (Section 1.1) tells us that the obtained digital image will be susceptible to aliasing noise. The aliasing distorted digital image is observed to have undesirable high frequency oscillation around the high spatial frequency region of the image. The aliasing noise is not only observed in the under-sampled digital image but also observed in the interpolated image. This is because the frequency response of the interpolation kernel will almost likely not to be an ideal low-pass filter, and hence the high frequency components of the aliasing component in the up-sampling process will remain in the interpolated image. These high frequency noises will have the same effect in the interpolation process as that of the high frequency noises in the down-sampling operation. An example of aliasing distorted image is shown in Figure 3.2a, where the aliasing noise is observed as staircase-like features and is therefore also known as "jaggy" artifact. This observation closely resembles the effect of aliasing noise in the down-sampling process.

Transitional pixels are required to smooth the sharp changes between the grayscales on the two sides of a sharp edge to make it to appear to be pleasant to human observation. Such transitional pixels occur naturally in images captured by digital camera. However, when such transitional pixels are lost in the down-sampling process, they may not be reproduced in the interpolation process, thus generating an interpolated image corrupted by aliasing noise.

3.1.2 Smoothing (Blurring)

Smoothing or blurring is observed when the high frequency components are lost, which can happen in the texture-rich regions or along/across edges. An example of "blurred" image is shown in Figure 3.2b, where the letter *A* has a "washed-out" appearance. In some cases, the smoothing is localized, thus producing undesirable piecewise constant or blocky regions in the interpolated image as shown in Figure 3.2b. In particular, when the edges of the interpolated image are over-smoothed, the interpolated image will appear to be out of focus, which can also be observed in Figure 3.2b. While the smoothing problem can be the result of a number of operations, the most common cause is due to the application of an interpolation kernel that is low-pass in nature. Such high frequency lossy interpolation process is vivid from the linear interpolation process of a sampled 1D step curve by linear interpolation as shown in Figure 3.3, where the details will be discussed in Chapter 4. Figure 3.3b shows the interpolation of a low-resolution step function. The linear interpolation result obtained by averaging the two nearest-neighbor pixels is shown in Figure 3.3c, which shows the step is dispersed and becomes a ramp function when compared with the high-resolution step function in Figure 3.3a. We can easily conjecture from the linear interpolation process shown in Figure 3.3 that smoothing/blurring will occur in any interpolation process, which involves the estimation of unknown pixel by averaging the neighboring known pixels. The blurring problem worsens with increased interpolation kernel size, which will cause the averaging effect spans over a larger number of pixels.

3.1.3 Edge Halo

The edge halo can be considered as a visual artifact that is opposite to smoothing. An image corrupted with edge halo artifact is shown in Figure 3.2c. It is vivid from Figure 3.2c that the edges are observed to be over-sharpened where white tracks are formed around the edges of the images, which creates an impression of an additional false edge and hence its name "halo." The halo is more apparent than the contrast

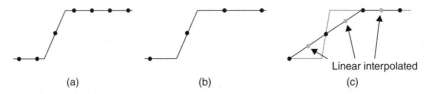

Linear interpolated

(a)   (b)   (c)

Figure 3.3 Blurring effect of linear interpolation in one-dimensional case: (a) original high-resolution data points, (b) low-resolution data obtained by subsampling, and (c) recovered data by linear interpolation.

between the two sides of the edges, which creates the illusion of enhanced sharpness. But edge halos are undesirable in natural image interpolation, especially in the case where it creates ghost images around natural objects.

3.1.4 Ringing

Besides the artifacts caused by nonideal frequency response of the interpolation kernel, the visual quality of the interpolated image is also affected by the spatial properties of the interpolation kernel. Ringing or oscillating wavelike artifacts can be observed in the interpolated image because most good interpolation kernels are functions of oscillating waves (see Figure 3.2c). The extent of the ringing artifact is proportional to the length of the interpolation kernel. Furthermore, ringing often happens around step edges, where the oscillating waves are the natural results of the Gibbs phenomenon (both intensity and spatial occupancy) [43]. Note that the discontinuity at the image block edges is also considered to be a kind of step edges and hence will cause ringing noise too. An appropriate interpolation kernel (smooth and non-oscillating spatial function) or high sampling rate can help to reduce the ringing artifacts.

3.1.5 Blocking

Besides the aforementioned artifacts, there is another artifact known as blocking artifact (also known as *"zigzag"*), which has a similar outlook as that of jaggies, where there are discontinuities within or along the image features. However, the discontinuity looks more like that of a repetitive block of image feature copied from nearby regions, and this kind of artifacts is also known as the *blocking effect*. Moreover, the origin of the blocking artifact, in the frequency response aspect, is different from that forming the jaggy artifacts. The blocking artifact is strengthened by the finite kernel size in spatial domain interpolation where the size of the kernel is smaller than the entire feature size. It can also be caused by cropping the high frequency components of the image due to finite block size of signal processing tool (also known as the kernel size). It becomes severe when the interpolation magnifies the image for several times. More details will be discussed in Chapter 5.

3.2 Objective Quality Measure

Objective quality measures are the alternative ways to assess the interpolated image quality other than the subjective quality measures. They provide automatic evaluation through quantifying metrics known as the objective image quality metrics. Unlike subjective quality measure, which has to be performed as a blind quality assessment for fair comparison, objective quality measure could be performed without human interaction, and the output of such assessment is almost identical (the variations are the results of accuracy of the computing system and any variations induced are systematic and consistent for all test images). As discussed in the introduction of this chapter, objective quality measures can be classified into three groups depending on how much the original (high resolution) image information is available. In this book, we shall only focus on the FRIQ.

The FRIQ metric $Q(g, \Upsilon)$ correlates the perceived difference (quality) between the interpolated image g and the high-resolution reference image Υ, which also satisfies the following conditions:

1. *Symmetric*: $Q(g, \Upsilon) = Q(\Upsilon, g)$.
2. *Boundedness*: $Q(g, \Upsilon) \leqslant B$ for a constant B.
3. *Unique maximum*: $Q(g, \Upsilon) = B$ if and only if $g = \Upsilon$ (no distortion between the two images).

Among various FRIQ metrics, the *mean squares error* (MSE) and the *peak signal-to-noise ratio* (PSNR) are two commonly used metrics. These metrics are convenient in their simplicity to compute, and their physical meanings as similarity measurement metrics by comparing the intensity of the two images in a pixel-by-pixel fashion, where neither the structure of the image nor human perception to the image features is considered. Therefore, they may not match well with the subjective quality measure and may lead to undesirable results in some cases.

To improve the assessment accuracy, the similarity measures have to be modified to make it compatible with the HVS. *Edge peak signal-to-noise ratio* (EPSNR) discussed in Section 3.2.3 is a modified PSNR, which considers the image edges by applying different weighting factors onto the edge and non-edge pixels. EPSNR can be considered as our first step to perform objective similarity measure in response to the HVS. A more sophisticated and widely applied HVS modified similarity measures, the SSIM [63], will be presented in Section 3.3.

Once an objective quality metric is chosen, it can be applied to evaluate the performance of an image interpolation algorithm through a scheme as shown in Figure 3.4.

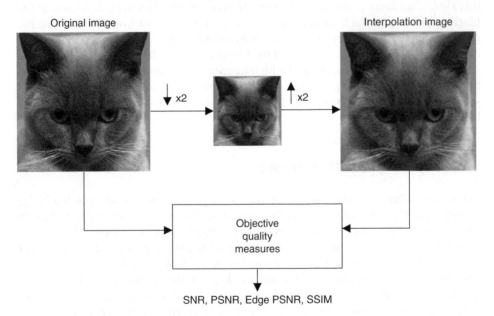

Figure 3.4 Image interpolation quality computation.

This scheme considers a high-resolution reference image, which is first down-sampled by a factor of two horizontally and vertically and then interpolated back to its original image size by the interpolation algorithm under test. The difference between the original high-resolution image and the interpolated image is compared by means of the chosen FRIQ metric. It should be noted that the degree of degradation of the interpolated image is content-dependent. Therefore, it is a common practice to evaluate the image interpolation method using multiple reference images that have different image details and cover a wide class of image features that are important for the applications with the applied image interpolation algorithm under concern. For simplicity, and clarity of discussions in this book, we shall concentrate on the case of using the *Cat* and letter *A* as reference images.

3.2.1 Mean Squares Error

Intuitively, the interpolated image can be regarded as the sum of the high-resolution reference image and an error signal (also known as error image). Therefore, the MSE is one of the most traditional similarity measures. Starting with the computation of the error image e (also known as the difference image) between the interpolated image array g and the high-resolution reference image array Υ, both of size $M \times N$ by

$$e[m, n] = \Upsilon[m, n] - g[m, n]. \tag{3.1}$$

The MATLAB source code in MATLAB 3.2.1 implements the function to compute the error image.

MATLAB 3.2.1—Error image.

```
function e=imageerr(g,r)
  e = (double(r)-double(g));
```

With the availability of the error image, the total error between the two images is given by $\sum_{m=0}^{M-1} \sum_{n=0}^{N-1} e[m, n]$. However, the elements in $e[m, n]$ have both positive and negative values. Therefore, it is more reasonable to consider the magnitude of $e[m, n]$. The *mean absolute error* (MAE) (also known as mean absolute difference) provides such a quality factor between the interpolated image array g and the high-resolution reference image array Υ, both of size $M \times N$.

$$\text{MAE} = \frac{1}{M \times N} \sum_{m=0}^{M-1} \sum_{n=0}^{N-1} \text{abs}(e[m, n]). \tag{3.2}$$

The MATLAB source code in MATLAB 3.2.2 implements the function to compute the error image.

MATLAB 3.2.2—MAE.

```
function mae_value=mae(g,r)
  e = imageerr(g,r);
  mae_value = mean(mean(abs(e)));
```

In particular, the most popular quality factor is the MSE, which is equivalent to the computation of the square power of the error signal $e[m, n]$. The MSE is defined as

$$MSE = \frac{1}{M \times N} \sum_{m=0}^{M-1} \sum_{n=0}^{N-1} (e[m, n])^2. \tag{3.3}$$

The MATLAB source code listed in MATLAB 3.2.3 implements the MSE function.

MATLAB 3.2.3—MSE.

```
function mse_value=mse(g,r)
  e = imageerr(g,r);
  mse_value = mean(mean(e.^2));
```

It is also common to give the MSE, mse_value, through the square root operation to generate a value that resembles the meaning of average pixel error of the two images, which is known as the *root mean squares error* (RMSE).

$$RMSE = \sqrt{(MSE)}. \tag{3.4}$$

The MATLAB source code listed in MATLAB 3.2.4 computes the RMSE by means of the function mse.

MATLAB 3.2.4—RMSE.

```
function rmse_value=rmse(g,r)
  rmse_value = sqrt(mse(g,r));
```

It should be noted that g and r should have the same array size to avoid runtime error.

3.2.2 Peak Signal-to-Noise Ratio

The MSE does not consider the dynamic range of the image but only the absolute error in between two images and is therefore biased. Such bias can be removed by normalization. The PSNR is the most commonly used normalized objective quality metric for interpolated image quality assessment. The denominator of the PSNR is the MSE, while the numerator is the highest dynamic range achievable by the image function under consideration, which is also known as the ratio between the maximal power of the reference image and the noise power of interpolated image. It is represented in the logarithmic domain in decibels (dB) because the powers of signals usually have a wide dynamic range. An example for PSNR computed for an n-bit grayscale image is given by

$$PSNR = 10 \log_{10} \left(\frac{(2^n - 1)^2}{MSE} \right). \tag{3.5}$$

For example, an 8-bit/pixel grayscale image will have $(2^n - 1)^2 = 255^2 = 65\,025$ as the numerator of the PSNR. The MATLAB code 3.2.5 will compute the PSNR with the assumption that the input image array in "uint8" datatype and thus $n = 8$.

MATLAB 3.2.5—PSNR.

```
function psnr_value=psnr(g,r)
    psnr_value = 10*log10((255^2)/mse(g,r)).
```

The above discussed quality metrics can be easily extended to color images by treating each color channel independently as a grayscale image. In the case of color images in RGB domain, the PSNR of the three color channels are first computed and then recombined to give the final PSNR by averaging as

$$\text{PSNR}_{\text{RGB}} = (\text{PSNR}_{\text{red}} + \text{PSNR}_{\text{green}} + \text{PSNR}_{\text{blue}})/3, \tag{3.6}$$

where PSNR_{red}, $\text{PSNR}_{\text{green}}$, and $\text{PSNR}_{\text{blue}}$ are the PSNR values for the red, green, and blue channels of the color image computed with Eq. (3.5), respectively. Without loss of generality, the rest of the book will use PSNR to imply both the PSNR in Eq. (3.5) for grayscale images and PSNR_{RGB} in Eq. (3.6) for color images depending on the context.

The PSNR is widely used because it is simple to calculate, has clear physical meanings, and is mathematically easy to deal with for optimization purposes. High PSNR value of the interpolated image is more favorable because it implies less distortion. However, the PSNR measure is not ideal. Its main shortcoming is that the signal strength is estimated by the highest dynamic range of the image that can be possibly achieved, which is $2^n - 1$, rather than the actual signal strength of the image. Furthermore, PSNR does not take the HVS into consideration. It has been widely criticized for not correlating well with subjective quality measurement. One of such quality is the preservation of edges in the interpolated image. Otherwise, the PSNR is considered to be able to provide an acceptable measure for comparing interpolation results.

3.2.3   Edge PSNR

A critical shortcoming of MSE and PSNR is that they are not compliant to HVS. This problem is vivid in the interpolated images in Figure 3.5. In this example, the down-sampled *Cat* image is interpolated by two different algorithms to produce (a) and (b). It is vivid that the image (a) has better visual quality, while (b) is visually observed to be seriously degraded; however, the PSNR of the image in (a) and (b) are both close to 23.04 dB. This is because the HVS perceives pixels differently and depends on their visual features, while PSNR considers all pixels to be the same. As a result, although being an objective and simple measure, the PSNR might lead to a totally wrong quality measurement result.

A simple step to improve the correlation between PSNR and visual quality of the interpolated image is to incorporate the differentiation of pixels perceived by the HVS. This can be achieved by assigning different weights to the edge and non-edge pixels in the error image when computing the PSNR to simulate the relative importance of different pixels perceived by the HVS. The edge pixels can be located by the edge extraction algorithm presented in Section 2.5. It should be noted that applying different edge detection algorithms will lead to minor differences in the result. The Sobel edge detector is being adopted by the International Telecommunication Union (ITU) [1] for the EPSNR.

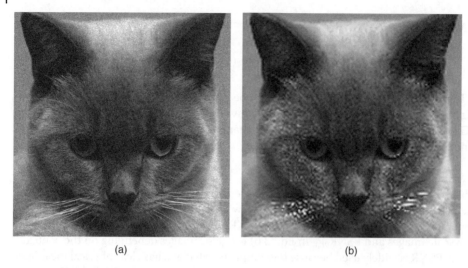

(a)   (b)

Figure 3.5 The *Cat* image is down-sampled by a scaling factor of 2 and then restored to its original size by the same scaling factor by different algorithms to produce (a) and (b) with the PSNR of both images close to 23.04 dB.

Without loss of generality, assume the weight w is assigned to the edge pixels and $1 - w$ to the non-edge pixels. The error image should be modified as

$$e_{edge}[m, n] = e[m, n](s[m, n](1 - 2w) + w), \tag{3.7}$$

where $s[m, n]$ is the edge map of the interpolated image with 0 being the value assigned to edge pixels and 1 be assigned to non-edge pixels.

Besides the consideration of the HVS sensitivity differences toward edge and non-edge pixels in the interpolated image, the actual contrast of the interpolated image should also be addressed by applying the peak intensity pixel value in the computation of the objective metric instead of the highest possible pixel value as in Eq. (3.5). The MATLAB source code 3.2.6 computes the EPSNR.

MATLAB 3.2.6—EPSNR.

```
function epsnr_value=epsnr(g,r,w,t)
  P = max(g(:));
  e = imageerr(g,r);
  s = edge(g,'Sobel',t);
  eedge = e.*((s)*(1-2*w)+w);
  msee = sum(eedge(:))/sum(s(:));
  epsnr_value = 10*log10(double(P^2/msee));
```

where `edge` is a MATLAB built-in function that returns the binary edge map of the input image. The `Sobel` filter and the sensitivity threshold `t` have been chosen as the input parameters for `edge` in Listing 3.2.6. The matrix `eedge` is the error image e_{edge}. As you may have noticed from the MATLAB function `epsnr`, the mean squares edge error is normalized not by the image size, but by the number of pixels that are declared as edge pixels in $s[m, n]$. Similar to PSNR, the higher the EPSNR, the less the distortion will be observed on the image edges, and thus the better in perceived image quality. Finally, it must be pointed out that the EPSNR result is deeply affected by the threshold t, which is the threshold value applied to the gradient results obtained by the Sobel filter to decide each pixel locations to be edge or non-edge pixels. The threshold value should be determined by the local contrast of the image, and therefore, a global threshold might not produce good edge detection results as discussed in Section 2.5 and hence biased the EPSNR. The following will discuss the structure similarity metric that applies localized analysis to evaluate the difference between the two images.

3.3 Structural Similarity

The EPSNR is a good start to apply HVS to objective quality measure, but it will suffer from several problems. First, it is a point-wise measure. Although the edge map is generated with Sobel filter, which has a detector kernel size larger than a single pixel, the actual computation of the error image is still a point-wise routine. Knowing the luminance and contrast of the image observed by HVS is not a point-wise process, but through a small localized region. Therefore, it will be critical to convert the point-wise operation to a localized small image region in the objective quality metric. Second, the point-wise operation of EPSNR is basically a luminance comparison operation. The contrast and the structure of the localized image region are being ignored in the computation of EPSNR.

To render the perception of luminance, contrast, and structure by human vision in the quality measurement, a variety of HVS compatible objective quality metrics are proposed for interpolation image quality evaluation [26, 64]. Among those reported metrics, the SSIM index proposed by Wang et al. [63] is a benchmark metric in literature, which correlates well with the perceptual image quality. The SSIM is obtained as the product of the luminance, contrast, and structural factors between the interpolated image (g) and the reference image (Y). These factors are obtained with the use of basic statistical parameters like mean, variance, and covariance as

$$\text{SSIM}(g, Y) = \frac{(2\mu_g\mu_Y + C_1)(2\sigma_{gY} + C_2)}{(\mu_g^2 + \mu_Y^2 + C_1)(\sigma_g^2 + \sigma_Y^2 + C_2)}, \tag{3.8}$$

where C_1 and C_2 are added to provide stability to each factors, such as to prevent the denominator becoming zero and at the same time bounding the metric to be within a predetermined range (in the case of Eq. (3.8), the fraction will be in the range of $[-1, 1]$ but not equal to 0), and μ_x and σ_x are the mean and variance of the random variable x, respectively. Note that the statistical features are computed locally in Eq. (3.8). However, the images are generally nonstationary with space-variant image structures, as shown in Section 3.1. Therefore, the localized regions applied to compute Eq. (3.8) are extracted by sliding window w to adapt to the space-variant image structure. Starting from the top-left corner of the image, a sliding window of size $w_L \times w_L$ moves pixel by pixel horizontally and vertically through all the rows and columns of the image until the bottom-right corner is reached. At the kth step, the local quality index $Q_k = \text{SSIM}$ is computed within the sliding window. As a result, each processed window will assign an SSIM value at the corresponding pixel coordinate located at the center of the processing window. This forms an SSIM map of the SSIM value for each pixel of the interpolated image under concern. If there are a total of K steps, then the overall quality index Q is the mean SSIM (MSSIM) given by averaging all the results obtained in the K steps.

$$\text{MSSIM}(g, Y) = \frac{1}{K} \sum_{k=1}^{K} \text{SSIM}_k(g, Y). \tag{3.9}$$

It is vivid that the dynamic range of both SSIM and MSSIM are $[-1, 1]$. The best value 1 can be achieved if and only if $\Upsilon = g$ for every pixel. The lowest value -1 occurs when $\Upsilon = 2\mu_g - g$ for every pixel. The following subsections will discuss the mathematical formulation of SSIM in Eq. (3.8) in terms of the three HVS components, namely, the luminance, contrast, and structural components.

MATLAB 3.3.1—MSSIM.

```
function [Q,map]=mssim(g,r)
  w = fspecial('gaussian', 11, 1.5);
  w = w/sum(sum(w));                    % normalize the filter DC gain
  K = [0.01 0.03];                      % default settings
  L = 255;                              % 8 bit grayscale image
  C1 = (K(1)*L)^2; C2 = (K(2)*L)^2;
  g = double(g); r = double(r);

  mg   = filter2(w,g,'valid');          % localized mean by Gaussian
       filtering
  mr   = filter2(w,r,'valid');
  mgs = mg.^2;                          %g^2
  mrs = mr.^2;                          %r^2
  mgr = mg.*mr;                         %gr
  sgs = filter2(w,g.^2,'valid')-mgs;    %sigma_g^2 = w(g^2)-g^2
  srs = filter2(w,r.^2,'valid')-mrs;    %sigma_r^2 = w(r^2)-g^2
  sgr = filter2(w,g.*r,'valid')-mgr;    %sigma_gr = w(gr)-gr

  num1 = 2*mgr + C1;                    % 2gr + C1
  den1 = mgs + mrs + C1;                % g^2 + r^2 +C1
  num2 = 2*sgr + C2;                    % 2*sigma_gr +C2
  den2 = sgs + srs + C2;               % sigma_g^2 + sigma_r^2 + C2

  map = (num1.*num2)./(den1.*den2);
  Q = mean2(map);
```

The MATLAB Listing 3.3.1 implements Eq. (3.8) with the sliding window of a 11×11 Gaussian window with unit gain and $\sigma = 1.5$, $C_1 = (K_1 L)^2$, and $C_2 = (K_2 L)^2$, where $L = 255$ is the dynamic range of the pixel intensity for an 8-bit grayscale image. The Gaussian window is chosen instead of other window functions because it can avoid blocking effect, which is predominant in windowed local spatial analysis. To understand how mssim works, let us rewrite SSIM in Eq. (3.8) as

$$\text{SSIM} = \frac{num}{den} = \frac{num1 \times num2}{den1 \times den2}, \tag{3.10}$$

where

$$num1 = 2\mu_g \mu_\Upsilon + C_1, \tag{3.11}$$

$$num2 = 2\sigma_{g\Upsilon} + C_2. \tag{3.12}$$

The denominators $den1$ and $den2$ are given by

$$den1 = \mu_g^2 + \mu_\Upsilon^2 + C_1, \tag{3.13}$$

$$den2 = \sigma_g^2 + \sigma_\Upsilon^2 + C_2. \tag{3.14}$$

Table 3.1 MSSIM value of Figure 3.5a with different K_1 and K_2 values.

K_1	K_2	SSIM
0.01	0.03	0.4184
0.05	0.05	0.5259
0.01	0.01	0.3411

From Eqs. (3.11) to (3.14), MATLAB Listing 3.3.1 implements them equation by equation. In particular, the implementation chooses $K_1 = 0.01$ and $K_2 = 0.03$, which is also the particular choice in [63]. Note that the mean values of all the small localized blocks (for mg, mr, sgs, srs, and sgr) are implemented with Gaussian smoothing, which captures the nonstationarity of the image structure in the localized regions.

To investigate the effect of K_1 and K_2, let us consider an original image and its distorted version by additive Gaussian noise ($\sigma = 0.005$ and $\mu = 0.01$) as shown in Figure 3.5a. The calculated MSSIM for these two images under different K_1 and K_2 are tabulated in Table 3.1. The percentage difference of the MSSIM for $K_1 = 0.05$ and $K_2 = 0.05$ is almost 25% and for values $K_1 = 0.01$ and $K_2 = 0.01$ is almost 44% compared with the nominal MSSIM value computed with $K_1 = 0.01$ and $K_2 = 0.03$. These errors in estimation of the quality of the image can lead to faulty decisions, and we shall discuss the effect of these two parameters in terms of luminance, contrast, and structure in the following sections.

3.3.1 Luminance

The mean luminance μ can be used to compare the luminance of two images. A simple comparison metric can be formed by considering the ratio between the geometric means and the arithmetic means of the two luminance means as

$$\tau_\ell(g, Y) = \frac{2\mu_g \mu_Y + C_1}{\mu_g^2 + \mu_Y^2 + C_1},$$

(3.15)

such that $0 \leqslant \tau_\ell(g, Y) \leqslant 1$ and equals to 1 if and only if $\mu_g = \mu_Y$. The factor C_1 is added to the computation of τ_ℓ to ensure the robustness of τ_ℓ. Otherwise, with $C_1 = 0$ and both $\mu_g = \mu_Y = 0$, the metric will be undefined with $\tau_\ell = \frac{0}{0}$. Among all the possible C_1 values, SSIM selected

$$C_1 = (K_1 L)^2,$$

(3.16)

where L is the dynamic range of the pixel intensity. In an 8-bit grayscale image, $L = 255$ and the squares are the result of considering a two-dimensional image. As a result, C_1 is totally controlled by K_1 and should be chosen to avoid the luminance component to dominate SSIM. $K_1 = 0.01$ has been suggested in [63], which has shown to provide a useful SSIM metric. Incidentally, this definition is also compatible with the Weber's law of just-noticeable luminance change, which states that the just-noticeable luminance change within a local area in an image depends on the relative change R in mean luminance with the localized area under concern with $\mu_g = (1 + R)\mu_Y$. The equivalent between Weber's luminance quality index and τ_ℓ can be established by

$$Q_{weber} = \frac{2(1+R)}{1+(1+R)^2} = \frac{2\mu_g}{\mu_\Upsilon} \frac{1}{1+\left(\frac{\mu_g}{\mu_\Upsilon}\right)^2} = \frac{2\mu_g\mu_\Upsilon}{\mu_g^2 + \mu_\Upsilon^2} = \tau_\ell(g,\Upsilon)\Big|_{C_1=0}. \qquad (3.17)$$

To incorporate the local statistical property of the nonstationary image signal into the metric, a window function is applied to preprocess a localized image block. The applied window function has to have unit gain and be circular symmetric to avoid spatial bias. One of such windows is the Gaussian window. In this book, a Gaussian window of size 11×11 with standard deviation of 1.5 will be applied to preprocess the image signal. The mean μ_x of the image block x will be replaced with the Gaussian weighted mean, which can be conveniently implemented by convolution operation as

$$\mu_x = w \otimes x. \qquad (3.18)$$

In MATLAB, this can be implemented with the `filter2` operation as

MATLAB 3.3.2—Gaussian window weight local mean computation.

```
>> w = fspecial('gaussian', 11, 1.5);
>> w = w/sum(sum(w));           % normalize the filter DC gain
>> mg = filter2(w,g,'valid');   % localized mean by Gaussian filtering
```

which is implemented in MATLAB Listing 3.3.1 to generate a map of localized mean weighted by a Gaussian window.

3.3.2 Contrast

The contrast component in SSIM is computed in a similar manner as that of the luminance component with μ being replaced by σ as

$$\tau_c(g,\Upsilon) = \frac{2\sigma_g\sigma_\Upsilon + C_2}{\sigma_g^2 + \sigma_\Upsilon^2 + C_2}, \qquad (3.19)$$

such that $0 \leqslant \tau_c(g,\Upsilon) \leqslant 1$ and it equals to 1 if and only if $\sigma_g = \sigma_\Upsilon$. The factor C_2 has a similar function as that of C_1, and thus it is also chosen to be equal to

$$C_2 = (K_2 L)^2. \qquad (3.20)$$

Similar to C_1, C_2 is totally controlled by K_2^2 and should be chosen to avoid the luminance component to dominate the SSIM. $K_2 = 0.03$ has been suggested in [63], which has shown to provide useful SSIM metric for interpolation algorithm performance comparison. Eq. (3.19) has shown that the metric τ_c depends on the relative contrast changes, which is consistent with the contrast masking property of the HVS.

3.3.3 Structural

The structural similarity between two random variables is best investigated by the Pearson correlation [35], and thus the structure component in SSIM is given by

$$\tau_s(g,\Upsilon) = \frac{2\sigma_{g\Upsilon} + C_3}{\sigma_g\sigma_\Upsilon + C_3}, \qquad (3.21)$$

such that $-1 \leqslant \tau_s(g,\Upsilon) \leqslant 1$. If we discard C_3, the Pearson correlation factor $|\tau_s| = 0$ when the two images g and Υ are not related. If the two images are associated with each other, $|\tau| > 0$. In particular $|\tau_s| = 1$ when g and Υ can form a linear relationship, $g = a \times \Upsilon + b$ with constants a and b. This relationship implies that the two images are an exact copy of each other structurally with difference in lighting condition only. The factor C_3 is similar to C_1 and C_2. The overall SSIM is given by the product of these three metrics, τ_ℓ, τ_c, and τ_s as

$$\text{SSIM}(g, \Upsilon) = (\tau_\ell \cdot \tau_c \cdot \tau_s)\circ(g, \Upsilon). \tag{3.22}$$

It is vivid from Eqs. (3.19) and (3.21) that the numerator of τ_c and the denominator of τ_s share the same factor except the constants C_2 and C_3. Therefore, there are two factors that can be eliminated from SSIM. Furthermore, C_2 and C_3 are unified to form a single constant and hence obtained the SSIM in Eq. (3.8).

Readers should also take note that when C_1 and C_2 are both equal to zero, the metric will be the same as the *universal quality index* (UQI).

3.3.4   Sensitivity of SSIM

In the above sections, we have discussed how the luminance, contrast, and structure of an image are considered in the SSIM. Eq. (3.8) tells us that SSIM is a function of image parameters (μ_Υ, μ_g, σ_Υ, σ_g, and L) and user-defined functions (C_1 and C_2). These two user-defined functions adjust the impact of luminance, contrast, and structure of a natural image toward the SSIM computation. The values of C_1 and C_2 are controlled by two user input parameters, K_1 and K_2, respectively. In the following sections, we shall explore the sensitivity of SSIM toward the parameters K_1 and K_2 ($\partial SSIM/\partial K_1$ and $\partial SSIM/\partial K_2$) and find out the appropriate range of K_1 and K_2 that should be chosen such that a fair SSIM index could be generated that provides meaningful comparison among wide range of natural images.

3.3.4.1 K_1 Sensitivity
To understand the sensitivity of SSIM toward K_1, a sensitivity analysis can be performed by rewriting the SSIM function as depicted in Eq. (3.8) as

$$\text{SSIM}(g, \Upsilon) = \frac{(2\mu_g\mu_\Upsilon + (K_1L)^2)(2\sigma_{g\Upsilon} + (K_2L)^2)}{(\mu_g^2 + \mu_\Upsilon^2 + (K_1L)^2)(\sigma_g^2 + \sigma_\Upsilon^2 + (K_2L)^2)}$$

$$= C \frac{2\mu_g\mu_\Upsilon + (K_1L)^2}{\mu_g^2 + \mu_\Upsilon^2 + (K_1L)^2}. \tag{3.23}$$

The sensitivity of SSIM toward K_1 is the first derivative of Eq. (3.6) with respect to K_1 with K_2, μ_Υ, μ_g, σ_Υ, σ_g, and L considered to be constant, such that we have

$$\frac{\partial SSIM}{\partial K_1} = C \frac{(2K_1L^2)(\mu_g - \mu_\Upsilon)^2}{(\mu_g^2 + \mu_\Upsilon^2 + (K_1L)^2)^2} = C' \frac{K_1}{\left(1 + K_1^2\left(\frac{L^2}{\mu_g^2 + \mu_\Upsilon^2}\right)\right)^2}, \tag{3.24}$$

with $C = \frac{2\sigma_{g\Upsilon} + (K_2L)^2}{\sigma_g^2 + \sigma_\Upsilon^2 + (K_2L)^2}$, and $C' = C \frac{2L^2(\mu_g - \mu_\Upsilon)^2}{(\mu_g^2 + \mu_\Upsilon^2)^2}$. It is vivid that the sensitivity of SSIM toward K_1 depends on L, μ_g, and μ_Υ, but to what extent?

It should be noted that for a given image, L has to be a constant depending on the data type of the image. For example, an image in uint8, $L = 255$. To simplify and without affecting the discussions, we generalize to use μ to represent μ_g and μ_r, unless otherwise specified. With μ being the mean intensity of an image, it is vivid that the dynamic

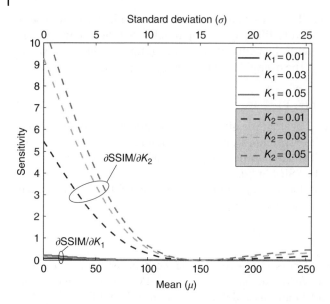

Figure 3.6 The sensitivity of SSIM toward K_1 with varying $\mu \in [0,255]$ at different K_1 (the solid lines) and the sensitivity of SSIM toward K_2 with varying $\sigma \in [0, 25]$ at different K_2 (the dashed lines). (*See insert for color representation of this figure.*)

range of μ is 0–255. In other words, no matter which interpolation method has been applied to the interpolated image, $\mu_r \in [0,255]$. To focus our study to the impact of the choice of K_1 toward the SSIM sensitivity to K_1, we consider $\mu_g = 128$, $\sigma_r = \sigma_g = 15$, and $K_2 = 0.03$, and the SSIM sensitivity to K_1 as a function of μ_Y at $K_1 = 0.01$, 0.03, and 0.05 are plotted in Figure 3.6 (solid lines). It should be noted that it is rare in natural image to have μ equal 0 or 255, as $\mu = 0$ implies that all pixels within the localized image block to be 0, while $\mu = 255$ implies all pixels within the localized image block to be 255. It is because there is always a background noise generated from the capture device, and hence a large region of pure color seldom happens in the captured images. Therefore, we can ignore the part of the SSIM sensitivity to K_1 curves at the two ends. In this case, the remaining curves are all fairly flat and close to zero, which allows us to conclude that the SSIM sensitivity to K_1 is independent to the choice K_1. We can further conclude that the SSIM of a natural image is insensitive to K_1 for a fixed K_2. Figure 3.7 shows the sensitivity of SSIM as a function of K_1 (see the solid line), where the curve is obtained by considering μ_g and σ_g to be 10% greater than μ_Y and σ_Y, respectively. The curve is almost independent to K_1, which further confirms the above conjecture.

3.3.4.2 K_2 Sensitivity
Similar to Section 3.3.4.1, the sensitivity of SSIM toward K_2 can be analyzed by rewriting Eq. (3.8) as

$$\text{SSIM}(g, Y) = C \frac{2\mu_g \mu_Y + (K_2 L)^2}{\mu_g^2 + \mu_Y^2 + (K_2 L)^2}. \tag{3.25}$$

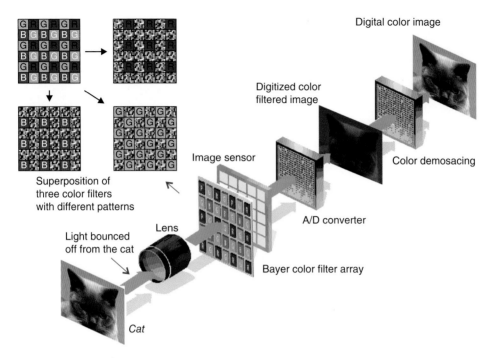

Figure 2.1 Illustration of capturing an image by digital camera.

Figure 2.27 Three separate RED, GREEN, and BLUE channels are combined to create a final, full-color image.

Digital Image Interpolation in MATLAB®, First Edition. Chi-Wah Kok and Wing-Shan Tam.
© 2019 John Wiley & Sons Singapore Pte. Ltd. Published 2019 by John Wiley & Sons Singapore Pte. Ltd.
Companion website: www.wiley.com/go/ditmatlab

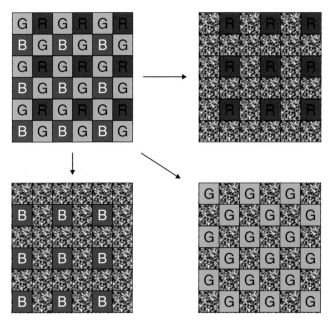

Figure 2.28 Red, green, and blue samples obtained from *Bayer pattern* color filter.

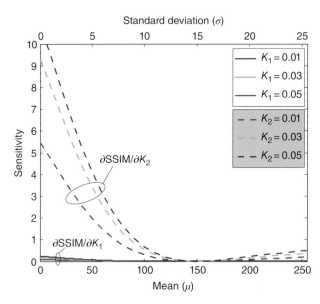

Figure 3.6 The sensitivity of SSIM toward K_1 with varying $\mu \in [0,255]$ at different K_1 (the solid lines) and the sensitivity of SSIM toward K_2 with varying $\sigma \in [0, 25]$ at different K_2 (the dashed lines).

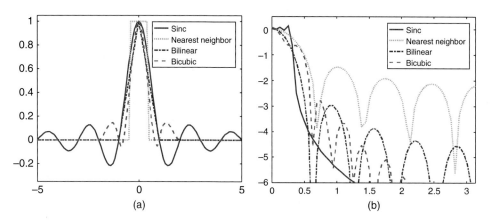

Figure 4.16 The spatial (a) and frequency response (b) of the nearest neighbor, bilinear, and bicubic interpolation kernels.

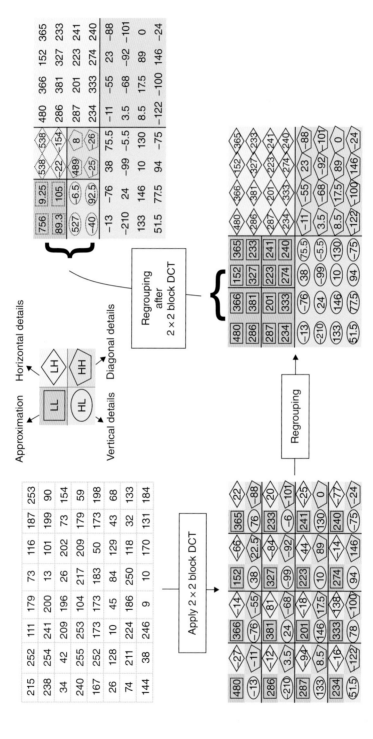

Figure 6.20 Example of reordering of DCT coefficient to form multi-resolution image representation.

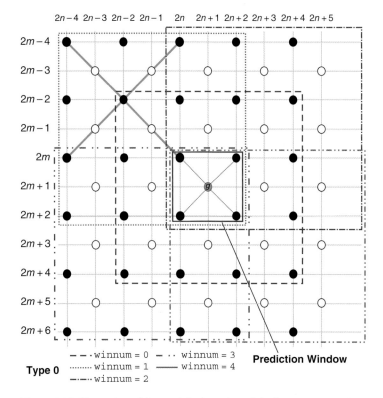

Figure 8.20 Illustration of the spatial adaptation of the five mean covariance windows adopted in the EMEDI for type 0 pixel. Noted the window `winnum=0` is same as that in the original NEDI.

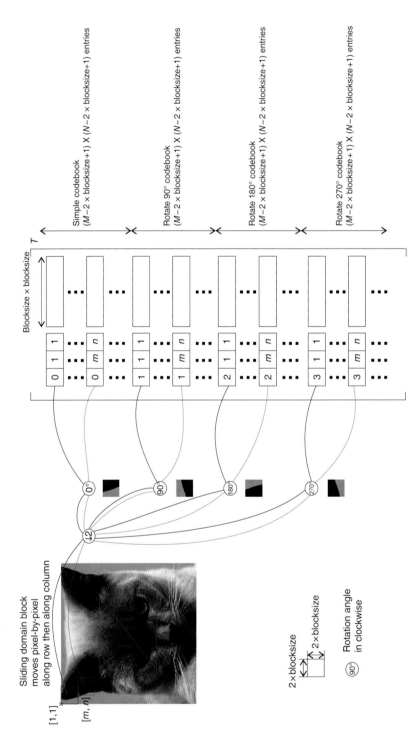

Figure 9.3 Generation of `codebook` that contains the four rotation affine transform down-sampled domain blocks extracted from the original image.

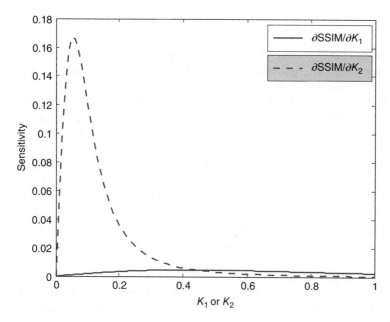

Figure 3.7 The sensitivity of SSIM toward K_1 with varying K_1 (solid lines) and the sensitivity of SSIM toward K_2 with varying K_2 (dashed lines).

The sensitivity of SSIM to K_2 is the first derivative of SSIM with respect to K_2 and is given by

$$\frac{\partial \text{SSIM}}{\partial K_2} = C\frac{(2K_2 L^2)(\sigma_g - \sigma_Y)^2}{(\sigma_g^2 + \sigma_Y^2 + (K_2 L)^2)^2} = C'\frac{K_2}{\left(1 + K_2^2\left(\frac{L^2}{\sigma_g^2 + \sigma_Y^2}\right)\right)^2}, \tag{3.26}$$

with $C = \frac{2\mu_g \mu_Y + (K_1 L)^2}{\mu_g^2 + \mu_Y^2 + (K_1 L)^2}$ and $C' = C\frac{2L^2(\sigma_g - \sigma_Y)^2}{(\sigma_g^2 + \sigma_Y^2)^2}$. It is vivid from Eq. (3.26) that the sensitivity of SSIM toward K_2 depends on L, σ_g, and σ_Y. To simplify and without affecting the discussions, we decided to use σ to represent σ_g and σ_Y, unless otherwise specified. To focus our study to the impact of the choice of K_2 toward the SSIM sensitivity to K_2, we consider $\sigma_Y = 15$, $\mu_Y = \mu_g = 128$, and $K_1 = 0.01$. The SSIM sensitivity to K_2 as a function of σ_Y at $K_2 = 0.01$, 0.03, and 0.05 is plotted in Figure 3.6 (dashed lines) with $\sigma_Y \in [0, 25]$. It is vivid from Figure 3.6 that the SSIM sensitivity to K_2 with respect to σ is sensitive to K_2. The $\partial \text{SSIM}/\partial K_2$ is more sensitive to K_2 when σ is small (less than $\sigma < 13$). It can also observe from Figure 3.6 that the sensitivity increases with large K_2. Figure 3.7 shows the sensitivity of SSIM toward K_2 as a function of K_2 (see the dashed line), where the curve is obtained by considering μ_g and σ_g to be 10% greater than μ_Y and σ_Y, respectively. Both σ_Y and σ_g have chosen to be below 15, such that $\partial \text{SSIM}/\partial K_2$ is the most sensitive with respect to σ, but the curve in Figure 3.7 exhibits a much less magnitude when compared with that shown in Figure 3.6. It shows that $\partial \text{SSIM}/\partial K_2$ is also not sensitive to the variation in K_2. In conclusion, it is more appropriate to choose both K_1 and K_2 to be small such that both the sensitivity of K_1 and K_2 are kept to minimal. Therefore, Wang et al. [63] proposed to use $K_1 = 0.01$ and $K_2 = 0.03$ in the SSIM analysis, which is generally suitable for wide range of natural images.

3.4 Summary

In this chapter, we have introduced the idea of image quality measurement, which computes the performance of an interpolation algorithm. In our discussions, we have particularly chose full-reference quality measurement, where the original (distortion free) high-resolution image is considered to be available prior to comparison. Both objective and subjective image quality measurements have been discussed. The objective quality measurement, in contrast to the subjective measurement, is conducted by the image quality metric that counts the difference between the original image and the distorted image. MSE is the most common objective quality measurement metrics that is widely used in literature, and it forms the basis of other objective quality metrics, such as the PSNR and EPSNR. Objective quality measure plays an important role in a variety of image interpolation applications. Firstly, it can dynamically control and adjust image quality in real time. Secondly, it can be used to optimize algorithms and parametric settings of image interpolation systems. Thirdly, it can be used to benchmark image interpolation systems.

However, human vision perceives and interprets different image features differently, and the distortion on the image contents perceived by different people may be different. It is difficult if not impossible to quantify such subject perception because it will require a large amount of data collected from a large number of interviewees to generate fair comparison results, which is very complicated and time-consuming. A series of image quality metrics have been developed to model the HVS in the perception of different image features and image structures, which form tools to quantify the subjective measures in a general way, and without any tedious data collection process. In this chapter, a benchmark subjective measurement known as SSIM has been chosen to illustrate the idea of subjective quality measurement. SSIM considers the image distortion through three aspects: luminance variation, contrast variation, and image structure variation. These three image features are the most sensitive information that the human visual system would consider. To analyze the generality of the SSIM, its sensitivity toward image contents, through varying the intensity means (μ), intensity variances (σ), and user-defined parameters (K_1 and K_2),is discussed. Although SSIM is generally image dependent, with a particular range of K_1 to K_2 (in our case, we set $K_1 = 0.01$ and $K_2 = 0.03$), the results will be valid for a wide range of natural images. The reasons behind the performance robustness of SSIM are discussed by considering the sensitivity analysis of SSIM toward the variation of K_1 and K_2.

The MATLAB implementations of the objective and subjective quality measurements are listed for the readers to understand and to provide practical implementations of our discussions and applications in later chapters.

3.5 Exercises

3.1 Modify the MATLAB function mse such that it will verify the size of the input images matrices to have the same size. Otherwise, it will output an error message of images are not the same size and set mse=NaN.

3.2 Besides the image interpolation quality computation method shown in Figure 3.4, it has been proposed in literature that the objective quality measures can be obtained by computing the quality metrics between the original image and an image obtained by:

1. First interpolating the original image and then down-sample it back to the original image size.
2. Twelve successive rotation of 30° of the original image.

Please comment on the applicability of the above quality metric evaluation methods.

3.3 Down-sample the *Cat* image by `directds` in Section 2.7.2.1 to generate `f`. Interpolate the down-sampled *Cat* image by bilinear interpolation method using MATLAB built-in function `interp2(f,2)`.

a. Compute the error image `e` of the interpolated image `f` and the original image. Rescale the error image to make it span the numerical range of [0, 255]. Plot the scaled error image.

b. Compute the SSIM of `f` with the default K_1 and K_2 used in Section 3.3. Rescale the SSIM map to span the numerical range of [0, 255]. Plot the scaled SSIM map.

c. Compute the edge image of `f` of the interpolated image using MATLAB built-in Sobel edge detection function `edge(f,'Sobel',t)` with several different threshold value `t`. Rescale the obtained Sobel edge map to make it span the numerical range of [0, 255]. Plot the scaled edge map.

Observe and comment the following:

1. The similarity and disagreement between the three plotted images.
2. Derive a method to combine the obtained edge maps under different threshold values to generate an image that looks more similar to the
   (a) Error image.
   (b) SSIM map.

4

Nonadaptive Interpolation

There are a number of treatments for the interpolation process in literature. In this book, we adopt the oldest and most widely accepted definition for interpolation that you can find in modern science:

> "*to insert (an intermediate term) into a series by estimating or calculating it from surrounding known values*"

Such a definition of "interpolation" can be found in the Oxford dictionary and can be fulfilled using model-based signal processing technique. As a result, in digital signal processing, interpolation is also referred to as model-based recovery of continuous data from discrete samples within a given range of abscissa [61]. In the context of digital image, interpolation is further refined to describe the process that estimates the grayscale values of pixels in a particular high density sampling grid with a given set of pixels at a less dense grid, such that the interpolated image is close to the actual analog image sampled with the high density grid. We have discussed the meaning of having two images being "close," where the closeness can be measured by any objective and subjective metrics as described in Chapter 3. An example of image interpolation method known as nearest neighbor has been presented in Section 2.7.3, which follows the algorithm shown in Figure 4.1 to generate an image with twice the size (sampling grid with twice the density) as that of the original image. The size expansion is achieved by first increasing the sampling density, such that every 2×2 block in the resolution-expanded image is considered as a local block (with one known pixel at the upper left corner and the rest of pixels with unknown values). The nearest neighbor interpolation method fills up the unknown pixels by replicating the pixels with known values in the local block as shown in Figure 2.26c. This pixel replication method usually results in poor image quality for most natural images, where both peak signal-to-noise ratio (PSNR) and Structural SIMilarity (SSIM) are poor, and the interpolated images usually contain visually annoying artifacts, mostly jaggy edges. The pro is its simplicity, which has virtually the lowest computational complexity. Because of this particular advantage, it is still used in a number of imaging equipment. In fact, the trade-off between interpolation quality and computational complexity is one of the major design considerations in selecting an appropriate image interpolation algorithm for a particular application.

Digital Image Interpolation in MATLAB®, First Edition. Chi-Wah Kok and Wing-Shan Tam.
© 2019 John Wiley & Sons Singapore Pte. Ltd. Published 2019 by John Wiley & Sons Singapore Pte. Ltd.
Companion website: www.wiley.com/go/ditmatlab

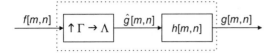

Figure 4.1 General framework of image interpolation.

This book is dedicated to the discussion of advanced image interpolation algorithms. Before opening the front curtain of advanced image interpolation algorithms, an overture of classical image interpolation methods based on convolution will be first reviewed in this chapter. While our discussions are general for interpolation ratio $r \in \mathbb{R}^+$, we shall demonstrate various image interpolation algorithms with an interpolation ratio of 2 whenever we consider appropriate to simplify our discussions.

4.1 Image Interpolation: Overture

Mere resizing of the image does not increase the image resolution. In fact, resizing should be accompanied by approximations for components with frequencies higher than those representable in the original image and at the same time to obtain higher signal-to-noise ratio after the approximations. We may call the process of resizing for the purpose of "increasing the resolution" as *up-sampling* or image interpolation. The traditional method of up-sampling consists of two steps: signal approximation and resampling. Signal approximation is a process to construct a continuous function to represent the original data wherein the original data has to be perfectly coincided with the approximated continuous function. Resampling is a process to map the approximated continuous function with a finer sampling grid by inserting additional sampling points to the approximated curve surface to increase the sample density. In the case of image up-sampling, all newly added samples are interleaving within the original data and will never be out of the boundary of the original image, while the original data has to be preserved; hence, *image up-sampling* is also called *image interpolation* (not super-resolution wherein original data may not even exist). In actual implementation, image interpolation of digital image can be considered as a two-step process: resampling followed by reconstruction, as illustrated in the framework in Figure 4.1. The former process (resampling) expands the resolution of the original image, $f[m, n]$, by mapping it to an expanded image lattice to generate the intermediate image $\hat{g}[m, n]$. The later process (reconstruction) applies a low-pass filter to the intermediate image to filter out unwanted high frequency signals or to synthesize the high frequency components, due to lattice expansion to generate a final high-resolution image $g[m, n]$.

The "resampling" process can be mathematically represented by

$$\hat{g}[m, n] = \begin{cases} f[m, n], & [m, n] \in \Gamma \uplus \Lambda, \\ 0, & [m, n], \in \Gamma \notin \Lambda, \end{cases} \tag{4.1}$$

where Γ and Λ are the low-resolution and high-resolution sampling grids, respectively. The MATLAB implementation of the resampling processing is given by the function `directus` listed in Listing 4.1.1.

MATLAB 4.1.1—Low-resolution to high-resolution image 2× resampling.

```
function g = directus(f)
    [M,N]=size(f);
    g=zeros(2*M,2*N);
    g(1:2:end,1:2:end)=f;
return;
```

Increasing the sampling grid density in spatial domain will generate undesired spectral replicas that have to be filtered out with a low-pass filter $h[m, n]$. As discussed in Section 1.1, in the ideal case, the optimal filter $h[m, n]$ is a discrete sinc function. The practical sinc function cannot have an infinite number of coefficients, but the underlying image $g[m, n]$ is suffering from aliasing and resulting terrible ringing and undesirable artifacts due to distortion at high frequency components after filtering. Therefore, interpolation using sinc filter is not recommended in image up-sampling. Different practical choices for the filter $h[m, n]$ are adopted in practice, such as the zero-order hold (ZOH), linear and cubic interpolators, etc. These filters try to minimize the spectral leakage at the expense of a wider main lobe. The large main lobe will compromise the resolution of the filtered image and results in blurred image. The design of a good filter $h[m, n]$ is always a trade-off between blur and ringing in the up-sampled image $g[m, n]$. This blur is acceptable if the goal is just to increase the size of the image. Nevertheless, when a better perceived resolution is also required, better approaches that are capable of synthesizing high frequency contents are needed.

The reconstruction process can be considered as a 2D filtering process discussed in Section 2.4, where the resampled image $\hat{g}[m, n]$ is convolved with the low-pass filter $h[m, n]$. Recalling Eq. (2.17), the reconstruction process in Figure 4.1 is formulated as

$$g[m, n] = (\hat{g} \otimes h)[m, n] = \sum_{k=M_1}^{M_2} \sum_{\ell=N_1}^{N_2} \hat{g}[m - k, n - \ell]h[k, \ell], \tag{4.2}$$

where the range of the convolution is determined by both the data array size and the kernel size of the filter. The pixel values of the newly added samples via resampling will be obtained through convolution. Therefore, the low-pass filter $h[m, n]$ is also known as the *interpolation kernel*. The interpolation kernel is a major factor that affects the quality of the reconstructed image. Many interpolation kernels have been proposed and analyzed in literature, which have different interpolation quality and computational complexity, such that certain trade-off between the processing time and reconstruction quality will have to be made to select the best interpolation kernel for your application. As an example, more satisfactory interpolation results can be obtained by using interpolation kernel that can smooth the jaggedness of the interpolated image when compared with that obtained by nearest neighbor interpolation method. In this section we describe some of the most well-known convolution-based interpolation techniques. Although the convolution kernels of each technique are different, they do share some common characteristics, which shall also be reviewed in Section 4.1.1. We shall also review the implementation of different interpolation kernels in practice, which applies MATLAB built-in matrix manipulation functions to ease the entire interpolation process and possibly accomplish the resampling and reconstruction in one single step.

4.1.1 Interpolation Kernel Characteristics

Before we step into the details of different interpolation kernels, let us take a look of their general characteristics. To accommodate the needs of different image applications, different interpolation kernels can be adopted. However, to minimize the undesirable distortion on the final image, a good convolution kernel, h, should process the following properties to achieve the desired interpolation results:

- *Translation invariance*: Given a translation operator τ, where $\tau(f[m,n],p,q) = f[m+p,n+q]$ with $p,q \in \mathbb{Z}$, the interpolation kernel h should satisfy

$$h \circ \tau(f,p,q) = \tau(h \circ f,p,q). \tag{4.3}$$

- *Rotation invariance*: Given a rotation operator r, where $r(f[m,n],\theta) = f[\hat{m},\hat{n}]$ with rotation angle $\theta \in [0,2\pi]$,

$$\begin{bmatrix} \hat{m} \\ \hat{n} \end{bmatrix} = \begin{bmatrix} \cos\theta & -\sin\theta \\ \sin\theta & \cos\theta \end{bmatrix} \begin{bmatrix} m \\ n \end{bmatrix}. \tag{4.4}$$

The interpolation kernel h should satisfy

$$h \circ r(f,\theta) = r(h \circ f,\theta). \tag{4.5}$$

- *Grayscale shift invariance*: Given any integer α, the grayscale intensity shifting is given by $\alpha + f[m,n]$. The interpolation kernel h should satisfy

$$h \circ (\alpha + f) = h \circ f + \alpha. \tag{4.6}$$

- *Grayscale scale invariance*: Given any integer α, the grayscale intensity scaling is given by $\alpha \cdot f[m,n]$. The interpolation kernel h should satisfy

$$h \circ (\alpha \cdot f) = \alpha \cdot h \circ f. \tag{4.7}$$

Obviously the above requirements are fulfilled by the linear convolution operator with a symmetric convolution kernel. Further discussions in this book will reveal that the type, size, and shape of the interpolation kernel (either convolution or other types of interpolation methods) will also be major factors that contribute to the quality of the interpolation results. We shall also discuss how these characteristics are adopted in image processing application. In the following sections, we shall introduce a number of traditional and yet still very popular convolution kernels used in image interpolation. They have been shown to be very effective and produce high quality interpolation results for certain types of input images. To simplify the discussion, the interpolation ratio is limited to 2 in the following sections ($r = 2$).

4.1.2 Nearest Neighbor

Nearest neighbor technique uses the grayscale value from the nearest pixel, which is also known as *pixel replication* technique. The nearest neighbor kernel can be expressed as

$$h[m,n] = \begin{cases} 1, & 0 \leqslant |n| < r-1, \quad 0 \leqslant |m| < r-1, \\ 0, & \text{elsewhere.} \end{cases} \tag{4.8}$$

In the case of $r = 2$, the kernel size is 2×2 rectangular function. It should be noted that the kernel size is interpolation ratio dependent.

The nearest neighbor interpolation begins with spatial domain resampling to map the original image from the image lattice (Γ) to an expanded lattice (Λ) as depicted in Eq. (4.1) and realized by padding zeros to the original image in every alternative row and column to generate an intermediate image $\hat{g}[m, n]$ (an example can be seen in Section 2.7.1). This kind of resampling is regarded to be resolution expansion in spatial domain, which will be adopted for other spatial domain image interpolations to be discussed in this book.

> **MATLAB 4.1.2—Image interpolation (×2) by nearest neighbor interpolation by 2D convolution.**
>
> ```
> function g = nnfilter(f)
>    h=[1 1; 1 1];
>    g = directus(f);
>    [M,N]=size(g);
>    hg=conv2(g,h);
>    g=hg(1:M,1:N);
> return;
> ```

The MATLAB function `nnfilter` listed in Listing 4.1.2 implements the nearest neighbor interpolation by 2D interpolation. The low-resolution image f is first zero padded by the function `directus`. Then the zero-padded pixels will be assigned with new grayscale values based on the results of the convolution of the intermediate image $\hat{g}[m, n]$ and the interpolation kernel $h[m, n]$ as depicted in Eq. (4.2), thus producing the final image $g[m, n]$. It is vivid that the convolution of $g[m, n]$ and h will suffer from boundary effect, and thus the size of the convolution result will be bigger than that of the desired 2× image size. The last row of command in `nnfilter` extracts the correctly interpolated image from the convolution result.

The implementation in Listing 4.1.2 is a direct implementation of the nearest neighbor interpolation through theoretical derivation of Eq. (4.2). However, for the sake of simple implementation, and also for computational efficiency, we shall also exploit the implementation of nearest neighbor interpolation in spatial domain with the application of the built-in array manipulation functions in MATLAB to accomplish the resampling and reconstruction in few lines of codes. Listing 4.1.3 shows the user-defined MATLAB function (nn) that implements the nearest neighbor interpolation for the up-sampling ratio $r = 2$.

> **MATLAB 4.1.3—Image interpolation (×2) by nearest neighbor interpolation by matrix repetition.**
>
> ```
> function g = nn(f)
>    [M,N]=size(f);
>    g = zeros(2*M,2*N);
>    for y=1:N for x=1:M
>       g([2*x-1 2*x],[2*y-1 2*y]) = repmat(f(x,y),2,2);
>    end;end;
> ```

The row and column dimensions of the low-resolution input image f are first retrieved by the built-in function `size` and stored in the variables M and N, respectively. The high-resolution image g is initiated as a zero matrix of the same size as that of the desired interpolated image $((r \times M) \times (r \times N))$ through g = zeros(2*M,2*N) with r being set to 2. The nested loops in the function is the core for the pixel replication, wherein the built-in function `repmat` replicates the pixel value in the coordinate [x,y] in the low-resolution image f to form a 2×2 block. The pixel replication can be illustrated mathematically by $f[m, n] \times \mathbf{H}$ with

$$\mathbf{H} = \begin{bmatrix} 1 & 1 \\ 1 & 1 \end{bmatrix}. \tag{4.9}$$

The corresponding block in the zero matrix (at location [2*x-1 2*x],[2*y-1 2*y]) will be overwritten with the replicated pixel block. It is vivid from Eq. (4.9) that the nearest neighbor is a zero-order polynomial interpolation scheme and is graphically illustrated in Figure 4.2. Figure 4.3 shows a numerical example to illustrate the implementation of the nearest neighbor interpolation, where a 2×2 image is considered to be the original image f. The image f has four pixels, and they are assigned with the values of "1"–"4" as shown in Figure 4.3. The MATLAB function first creates an empty expanded lattice with the same size as that of the final high-resolution image g. The grayscale values of the original pixels will be replicated in the nearest three pixels via the MATLAB built-in function `repmat` (the immediate left, upper left, and top pixels) to form the matrix BLK. In the example, the lower right pixel with coordinates [x,y] was chosen first, wherein the pixel value under investigation is "4." The same pixel values are replicated in the matrix BLK. The entire matrix BLK is then assigned to the corresponding blocks in the intermediate expanded lattice. In this example, BLK is written to the destination lattice starting from pixel [2x-1, 2y-1] and spanning 2×2 pixels to the right and to the bottom directions. By repeating the same procedures for all pixels, the final image g is generated as shown in Figure 4.3. The nearest neighbor interpolation is simple, and it consumes the least computation effort among all other interpolation algorithms because it is just pixel value replication. However, this method results in severe loss of quality in the interpolated image (mainly aliasing, or also known as jaggy), such that this method is not suitable for resizing images that are rich in continuous lines or edges.

Figure 4.4 shows the result of the nearest neighbor interpolation on the synthetic image letter A, where the intensity maps along the horizontal edge and diagonal edge are also shown in the same figure. The staircase-like artifact along the diagonal edge is the so-called jaggy artifact, which is the most severe artifact in the nearest neighbor

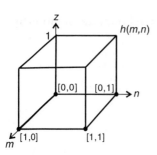

Figure 4.2 The nearest neighbor interpolation kernel in spatial domain.

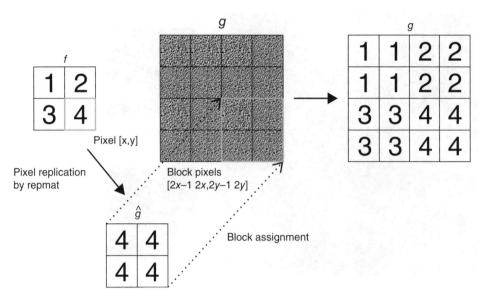

Figure 4.3 A 2 × 2 image block interpolated by nearest neighbor method with interpolation ratio of 2 to achieve a 4 × 4 interpolated image.

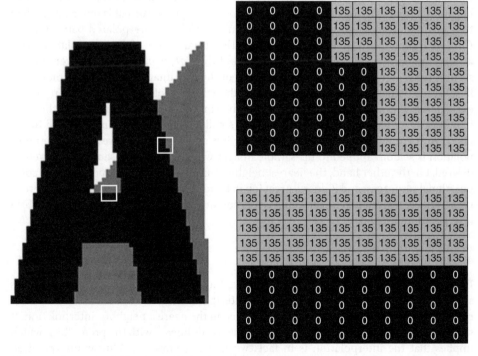

Figure 4.4 Nearest neighbor interpolation: interpolated image of "letter A" and intensity maps of the enclosed diagonal and vertical edges.

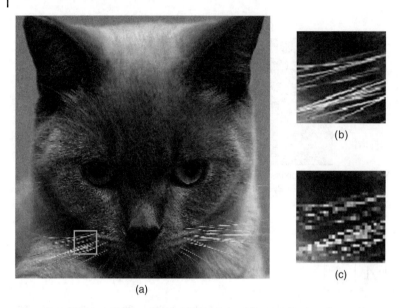

(b)

(c)

(a)

Figure 4.5 Nearest neighbor interpolation of natural image *Cat* by a factor of 2 (PSNR = 25.98 dB): (a) the full interpolated image, (b) zoom-in portion of cat's whiskers in original image, and (c) zoom-in portion of cat's whiskers in interpolated image.

interpolation. Although the same artifact is also observed in natural images, this artifact becomes more annoying in the interpolated image simply because it is much larger than the original image. Figure 4.5 shows the nearest neighbor interpolated natural image *Cat* (see Figure 4.5a) with PSNR of 25.98 dB. The visual quality of the interpolated image around the texture-rich region (the forehead of the *Cat*) is pleasant. However, there is serious jaggy along the long edges (whiskers of the *Cat* image). The jaggy is more easily observed when the zoom-in portion of the whiskers of the *Cat* image (in box) is extracted for comparison. We can see that the smooth and solid whiskers in the original image (see Figure 4.5b) are broken into small segments in the interpolated image (see Figure 4.5c). This distortion is truly annoying, and hence the nearest neighbor interpolation is seldom applied to up-sample images when visually pleasant enlargement is desired. On the other hand, the nearest neighbor interpolation consumes the least computational resources, and it does a great job in handling the smooth regions; therefore, it is still widely chosen for up-sampling operation on smooth regions in variety of hybrid interpolation methods.

4.1.3 Bilinear

Bilinear interpolation is another well-received interpolation technique because of its simplicity while it applies a better low-pass filtering operation in the reconstruction that reduces the awkward jaggy artifact as perceived in the nearest neighbor interpolation. It should be noted that "bilinear" comes from the word "linear" with the prefix "bi-," which implies that the interpolation is in fact two linear operations. Bilinear interpolation is equivalent to the approximation of a straight line (linear interpolation) along row, followed by approximating a straight line (another linear interpolation) along column.

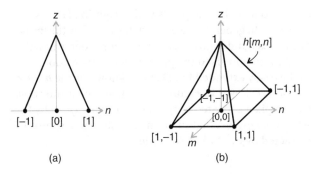

(a)   (b)

Figure 4.6 The plot of (a) linear interpolation kernel and (b) bilinear interpolation kernel in spatial domain.

Therefore, we can simplify our analytical discussion by considering the 1D linear interpolation kernel. Here shown is the interpolation kernel of the linear interpolation

$$h[n] = \begin{cases} 1 - |n|, & 0 \leqslant |n| < 1, \\ 0, & 1 \leqslant |n|. \end{cases} \tag{4.10}$$

The impulse response of this linear filter is shown in Figure 4.6a, which is a triangular function. It should be noted that this figure is plotted by considering the special case of even weighting from neighboring pixels due to the fixed spacing between neighboring pixels in the digital image, which will be further elaborated later. The triangular function has C^0 regularity (continuous but not differentiable). It corresponds to a modest low-pass filter in the frequency domain. Similar to all linear convolution image interpolation techniques, resampling operation comes first to generate the intermediate signal $\hat{g}[n]$

$$\hat{g}[q] = \begin{cases} f[n], & q = 2n - 1, \\ 0, & \text{otherwise.} \end{cases} \tag{4.11}$$

However the interpolation result $g[n]$ is obtained by convolving the filter in Eq. (4.10) to $\hat{g}[n]$. Hence, the interpolated result is given by

$$g[q] = (1 - \Delta n)\hat{g}[q - 1] + \Delta n\hat{g}[q + 1], \tag{4.12}$$

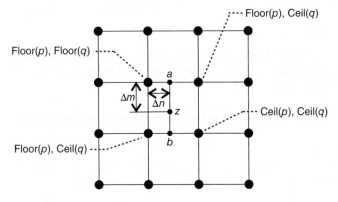

Figure 4.7 Spatial weighting map of the bilinear interpolation for the pixel z located at (p, q).

where $g[q]$ is a weighted sum of the two neighboring pixels with weighting factors $(1 - \Delta n)$ on pixel $\hat{g}[q - 1]$ and Δn on $\hat{g}[q + 1]$. In general case, Δn is determined by the impact of the neighboring pixels toward the pixel under investigation or simply determined by the relative spacing of the two neighboring pixels to the pixel under investigation.

The 1D linear interpolation can be easily extended to 2D and is known as the *bilinear interpolation* with the impulse response shown in Figure 4.6b. The bilinear interpolation computes the pixel intensity of a pixel z located at spatial coordinate (p, q) by first locating the four corner pixels of the smallest box that surround z as shown in Figure 4.7. These four coordinates can be extracted by the MATLAB code

```
>> z = [p,q];
>> C = ceil(z);
>> F = floor(z);
```

such that the four corner pixels are given by f (F(1):C(1), F(2):C(2)). The bilinear interpolation weighting to be assigned to each corner pixel is computed as the distance between (p, q) and each corner pixel as given by the MATLAB code

```
>> A = [...                     % bilinear weighting for all four corner pixels
        ((C(2)-z(2))*(C(1)-z(1))),...
        ((z(2)-F(2))*(z(1)-F(1)));
        ((C(2)-z(2))*(z(1)-F(1))),...
        ((z(2)-F(2))*(C(1)-z(1)))];
```

The interpolated pixel intensity b is given as the weighted sum of corner pixels:

```
>>     b = sum(sum(bsxfun(@times, A, double(f(F(1):C(1),F(2):C(2))))));
```

It should be noted that if either p or q is integer, the above matrix A will be a zero matrix. Therefore, the case of integer p or q should be treated separately. In fact, if both p and q are integers, the interpolated pixel b should be equal to the pixel f (p,q). If either p or q is integer, but not both, linear interpolation on the axis that contains the non-integer coordinate should replace the bilinear interpolation. In the case when q is not an integer,

```
>> A = [C(2)-z(2), z(2)-F(2)];    % linear interpolation along q
   coordinate
>> b = sum(bsxfun(@times, A, double(f(F(1),F(2):C(2)))));
```

If it is, p being not an integer,

```
>> A = [C(1)-z(1); z(1)-F(1)];    % linear interpolation along p
   coordinate
>> b = sum(bsxfun(@times, A, double(f(F(1):C(1),C(2)))));
```

The MATLAB function bi2x2 listed in Listing 4.1.4 implements the above per-pixel bilinear interpolation with a given image f and interpolated pixel location z=[p,q] and returns the intensity of the interpolated pixel.

MATLAB 4.1.4—Compute the intensity of pixel z= [p,q] from image f using bilinear interpolation.

```
function b = bi2x2(f,z)
  C = ceil(z);              % location of smallest bounding box contains
      the interpolated pixel
  F = floor(z);
```

```
if (C(1)==F(1))
   if (C(2)==F(2))      % location is integer for both m and n
      b = double(f(C(1),C(2)));     % copy the low-resolution pixel
   else                 % location is integer for m only
      A = [C(2)-z(2), z(2)-F(2)];   % linear interpolation along n
         axis
      b = sum(bsxfun(@times, A, double(f(F(1),F(2):C(2))))) ;
   end
elseif (C(2)==F(2))     % location is integer for n only
   A = [C(1)-z(1); z(1)-F(1)];      % linear interpolation along m
      axis
   b = sum(bsxfun(@times, A, double(f(F(1):C(1),C(2))))) ;
else                    % non-integer location for both m and n
   A = [...             % bilinear weighting for all four corner
      pixels
      ((C(2)-z(2))*(C(1)-z(1))),...
      ((z(2)-F(2))*(z(1)-F(1)));
      ((C(2)-z(2))*(z(1)-F(1))),...
      ((z(2)-F(2))*(C(1)-z(1)))];
   b = sum(sum(bsxfun(@times, A, double(f(F(1):C(1),F(2):C(2)))))) ;
end;
return;
```

The bilinear image interpolation with ratio r can be obtained by first generating the grid map of the interpolated image and then applying bi2x2 to compute the intensity of each pixel.

MATLAB 4.1.5—Bilinear image interpolation with interpolation ratio r and low-resolution image f.

```
function g = biinterp(f,r)
   [M,N] = size(f);
   nf = double(zeros(M+1,N+1));
   nf(1:M, 1:N)  = double(f);        % convert the input image to double
   nf(M+1,:) = nf(M,:); nf(:,N+1) = nf(:,N); % boundary extension
   P = r*M; Q=r*N;                   % interpolated image size
   g = double(zeros(P,Q));
   z = double([0,0]);                % initial interpolated pixel
      location
   for p = 1:P                       % iterate on each pixel in the
         interpolated image
      for q = 1:Q
         z(1) = (double(p-1)/double(r))+1; % interpolated pixel locations
         z(2) = (double(q-1)/double(r))+1;
         g(p,q) = bi2x2(nf,z);       % bilinear interpolation
   end; end;
```

Noted that the image f has to be boundary extended (by adding one column at the rightmost and one row at the bottom) to accommodate the bilinear interpolation around boundary pixels. Among various extension methods, Listing 4.1.5 has implemented the infinite extension (boundary pixel value repetition) as discussed in Section 2.4.1.4. The bilinear interpolation result of the synthetic image letter A with interpolation ratio equal to 2 obtained from the MATLAB function call g=biinterp(f,2) is shown in Figure 4.8 where the intensity map along the horizontal edge and diagonal edge is

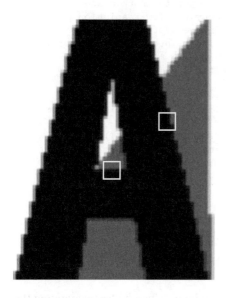

0	0	0	34	101	135	135	135	135	135
0	0	0	34	101	135	135	135	135	135
0	0	0	34	101	135	135	135	135	135
0	0	0	25	76	110	127	135	135	135
0	0	0	8	25	59	110	135	135	135
0	0	0	0	0	34	101	135	135	135
0	0	0	0	0	34	101	135	135	135
0	0	0	0	0	34	101	135	135	135
0	0	0	0	0	34	101	135	135	135
0	0	0	0	0	34	101	135	135	135

135	135	135	135	135	135	135	135	135	135
135	135	135	135	135	135	135	135	135	135
135	135	135	135	135	135	135	135	135	135
135	135	135	135	135	135	135	135	135	135
101	101	101	101	101	101	101	101	101	101
34	34	34	34	34	34	34	34	34	34
0	0	0	0	0	0	0	0	0	0
0	0	0	0	0	0	0	0	0	0
0	0	0	0	0	0	0	0	0	0
0	0	0	0	0	0	0	0	0	0

Figure 4.8 Bilinear interpolation: interpolated image of "letter *A*" and intensity map of the enclosed diagonal and vertical edges.

also shown in the same figure. The staircase-like artifact along the diagonal edge, which is also known as the jaggy artifact, is found to be the most severe artifact in nearest neighbor interpolation. The same artifact is also observed in bilinear interpolated natural image in Figure 4.8. However, almost all edges are blurred in the interpolated letter *A*. Besides blurring, there is a ghost edge surrounding all edges of the letter *A*. Figure 4.9 shows the bilinear interpolated natural image *Cat* (see Figure 4.9a). The interpolated image has a PSNR of 28.39 dB. The visual quality is pleasant around the texture-rich region (*Cat*'s forehead) of the interpolated image. However, there is serious jaggy along long edges (*Cat*'s whiskers and hairs). The jaggy can be easily observed when compared with the zoom-in (enclosed in boxes) of both the original image (see Figure 4.9b,d) and the bilinear interpolated image (see Figure 4.9c,e).

The averaging operation of the bilinear interpolation results in a smooth interpolated image when compared with that obtained from the nearest neighbor interpolation. The visual quality of the bilinear interpolated image is better than that of the nearest neighbor interpolated image with less jaggies, which are smoothed out by the averaging operation of the bilinear interpolation. In addition to the better visual quality, there is a substantially better objective quality obtained by the bilinear interpolated image. The PSNR of bilinear interpolated image is better than that of the nearest neighbor interpolated image. However, bilinear interpolated images suffer from severe blurring artifacts when compared with that of the nearest neighbor interpolated images. Furthermore, bilinear interpolation requires relatively higher computations when compared with that of the nearest neighbor interpolation algorithm.

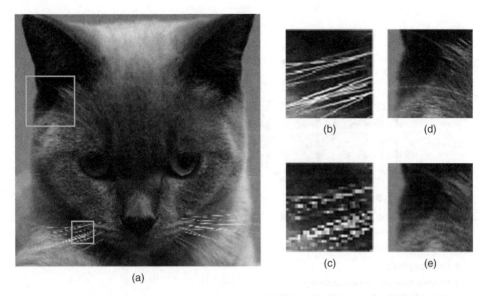

Figure 4.9 Bilinear interpolation of natural image *Cat* by a factor of 2 (PSNR = 28.39 dB): (a) the full interpolated image, (b) zoom-in portion of cat's whiskers in original image, (c) zoom-in portion of cat's whiskers in interpolated image, (d) zoom-in portion of cat's ear in original image, and (e) zoom-in portion of cat's ear in interpolated image.

4.1.4 Bicubic

Bicubic interpolation improves the bilinear interpolation by using a bigger interpolation kernel. The kernel size of the bicubic interpolation is 4×4 as shown in Figure 4.10, compared with the 2×2 kernel of bilinear interpolation. As a result, bicubic interpolation is a third-order interpolation, compared with the first-order interpolation of bilinear interpolation and zero-order interpolation of the nearest neighbor interpolation. The higher-order interpolation can achieve interpolated image with sharper edges than that produced by bilinear interpolation, and at the same time it provides better suppression on jaggy artifacts when compared with that produced by nearest neighbor interpolation. However, the bicubic interpolation requires very complicated calculations. After all, the interpolation kernel is four times larger than that of bilinear interpolation.

Similar to bilinear interpolation, the prefix "bi-" of bicubic interpolation reveals its separability nature, where bicubic image interpolation can be implemented by sequential application of the 1D cubic spline interpolations along the row and then the column of the image. Consider the example in Figure 4.10, where the original image lattice is expanded with up-sampling ratio of 2. The black dots in Figure 4.10 illustrate the pixels preserved from the original image. The unknown pixels in between the original pixels have to be interpolated. We shall make use of the separable property of bicubic interpolation to compute the interpolated pixel value at $[m, n]$ from its neighboring original pixels. Therefore, we shall first compute four 1D cubic spline interpolations (the F_0, F_1, F_2, and F_3 functions plotted as dashed/red splines in the figure) to obtain the intermediate pixels $[m, n - 3]$, $[m, n - 1]$, $[m, n + 1]$, and $[m, n + 3]$ (the white dots). These four intermediate pixels will be applied to another 1D cubic spline interpolation (the solid/blue splines in the figure) to produce the intensity of the unknown pixel $[m, n]$.

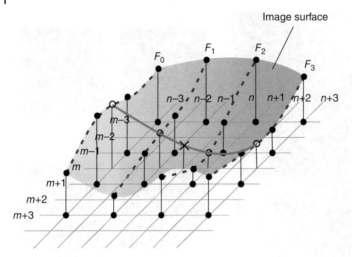

● Original pixels

○ Intermediate pixels produced by
cubic spline interpolation in row direction

x Unknown pixel under interpolation

Figure 4.10 Bicubic interpolation: estimation of unknown pixels lying on the exact surface defined by the neighboring 16 pixels. (*For color interpretation please refer the digital version of this figure.*)

As a result, we can complete the bicubic interpolation with a given 1D cubic spline interpolation kernel, which is generally defined as a combination of the piecewise cubic polynomials for the sake of simple implementation. Among various definitions of 1D cubic spline interpolation kernel, this book chooses the cubic spline interpolation given by Reichenbach and Geng [55] as shown in the following.

$$
h[n] = \begin{cases} (a+2)|n|^3 - (a+3)|n|^2 + 1, & |n| \leqslant 1, \\ a|n|^3 - 5a|n|^2 + 8a|n| - 4a, & 1 < |n| < 2, \\ 0, & \text{otherwise}, \end{cases}
\tag{4.13}
$$

where a is usually set in between the range of -0.5 and -0.75. The piecewise cubic polynomials are nonzero with $n \leqslant 2$ whatever the values of a, and this set of polynomials is also known as the basic function of cubic spline. The basic functions with $a = -0.5, -1$, and -2 are plotted in Figure 4.11.

The basic functions with different choices of a show us that the smaller values of a will result in an interpolation kernel with wider lobe, which is more helpful in preserving the image structure with greater feature size. The con is that its legs will go into more negative values that will result in more severe ringing artifacts in the interpolated image. Therefore, the quality of the interpolated image is highly dependent on the choice of a. The best compromise is to choose a to be -0.5, which forms the third-degree cubic kernel [36]. Similar to the bilinear interpolation, the 1D cubic interpolation kernel can be extended to 2D version by convolution of the 1D filter to its transpose. Figure 4.12 shows the 2D plot of the impulse response of the bicubic interpolation kernel with $a = -0.5$ in spatial domain. Though the bicubic interpolation can be realized by the convolution of

Figure 4.11 Basic function of cubic convolution.

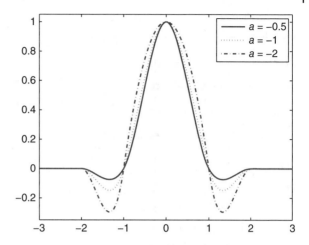

Figure 4.12 The 2D bicubic interpolation kernel in spatial domain.

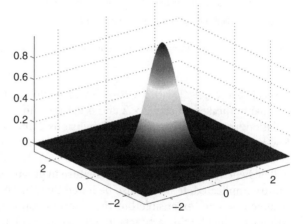

the 2D filter to the neighboring pixels for all pixels in the image, the computation is very exhaustive. Therefore, the practical implementation will usually make use of the separable property of the kernel and perform the interpolation as illustrated in Figure 4.10 with the 1D cubic spline interpolation kernel given by Eq. (4.13).

Before we go into the MATLAB implementation of the bicubic interpolation, it will be easier for the readers to get an idea on the collection of the neighboring pixels for bicubic interpolation and the major difference of such collection when compared with that of bilinear interpolation. Figure 4.13 shows part of the high-resolution grid with pixel $[m, n]$ being the pixel under estimation (the white dot) to illustrate the relative location of the neighboring pixels to $[m, n]$. As described in Section 4.1.3, we need four closest known pixels surrounding the pixel under estimation (the black dots at $[m - 1, n - 1]$, $[m - 1, n + 1]$, $[m + 1, n - 1]$, and $[m + 1, n + 1]$), where the known pixels are those pixels taken from the low-resolution image. The unknown pixel $[m, n]$ is estimated as the weighted sum of the four neighboring pixels in bilinear interpolation. For bicubic interpolation, 12 additional numbers of neighboring pixels will be considered (the gray dots), such that the collection will contain both the black and gray

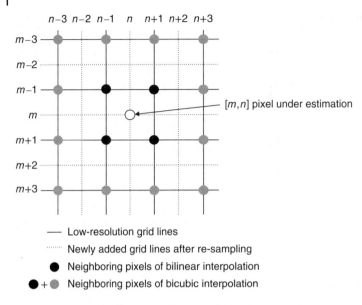

Figure 4.13 Neighboring pixels of bilinear and bicubic interpolation.

pixels ($[m + k, n + \ell]$ with $k \in [-3, -1, 1, 3]$ and $\ell \in [-3, -1, 1, 3]$). In other words, we can name the kernel size 2×2 and 4×4 for bilinear interpolation and bicubic interpolation, respectively, where the dimensions 2 and 4 are equivalent to the number of low-resolution pixels in row–column direction counted toward to the interpolation. It is vivid that the bicubic interpolation works with a bigger interpolation kernel, which will be beneficial to preserve image feature in greater size; however, the computation is more complicated. It should also be noted that the kernel size for both the bilinear and bicubic cases are extensible but the computation complexity will inevitably increase. Moreover, the blurring artifacts in bilinear interpolation with larger kernel size will be more significant.

Listing 4.1.6 is the MATLAB bicubic interpolation function (`bicubic(f,r)`) that up-samples an image f with interpolation ratio r. The parameter `gridSize` is an array containing the relative position of the neighboring pixels (in the input image f) to be considered in the interpolation with reference to the position of the unknown pixel in the final image g. The `gridSize` further combines with the parameters di and dj to provide sufficient information to define all the required neighboring pixels, where di and dj are the distances of the unknown pixel relative to corresponding neighboring pixels in row and column directions, respectively. For the case of $r = 2$ and with the grid size in digital image being even, the values of di and dj are equal and are given by $1/r = 0.5$. Based on `gridSize`, di, and dj, the neighboring pixels aX, bX, cX, dX, aY, bY, cY, and dY are obtained. This pixel location computation is essential in image interpolation because the operation involves resampling. The parameter `afact` defines the weighting factor a in Eq. (4.13), which will be used to estimate the unknown pixel.

MATLAB 4.1.6—Image interpolation (×2) by bicubic interpolation.

```
function g= bicubic(f,r)
[M,N] = size(f);
M0 = M*r; N0 = N*r;
gridSize = [r,0;0,r];
afact = -0.5;
for m = 1:M0
        for n = 1:N0
    temp = [m n]*inv(gridSize);
    di=temp(1)-floor(temp(1));
    dj=temp(2)-floor(temp(2));
    y = floor(temp(1));
    x = floor(temp(2));
    aX=max(x-1,1);
    bX=max(x,1);
    cX=min(x+1,N);
    dX=min(x+2,N);
    aY=max(y-1,1);
    bY=max(y,1);
    cY=min(y+1,M);
    dY=min(y+2,M);
    F0=bicubic4x4([f(aY,aX),f(aY,bX),f(aY,cX),f(aY,dX)],dj,afact);
    F1=bicubic4x4([f(bY,aX),f(bY,bX),f(bY,cX),f(bY,dX)],dj,afact);
    F2=bicubic4x4([f(cY,aX),f(cY,bX),f(cY,cX),f(cY,dX)],dj,afact);
    F3=bicubic4x4([f(dY,aX),f(dY,bX),f(dY,cX),f(dY,dX)],dj,afact);
    g(m,n)=bicubic4x4([F0,F1,F2,F3],di,afact);
end end
return;
```

The program then calls another function `bicubic4x4` given by MATLAB Listing 4.1.7, which is the realization of Eq. (4.13) with the first parameter defining the v matrix containing the pixel intensities of the required pixels required in forming the bicubic function as shown in Eq. (4.13), the second parameter defining the relative position to be estimated, and the third parameter defining the variable a. It should be noted that the bicubic interpolation problem is also separable, such that the computation can be achieved by computing the 1D estimation along row and then along column. Hence, we can obtain F0, F1, F2, and F3 (F_0, F_1, F_2, and F_3 as shown in Figure 4.10) and further apply these four functions to another `bicubic4x4` to give the value of the pixel in the final image `g(i,j)` (the unknown pixel in Figure 4.10).

MATLAB 4.1.7—MATLAB implementation of the bicubic interpolation function depicted in Eq. (4.13).

```
function [X] = bicubic4x4(v,fact,afact)
  X = 0;
  if fact==0 X = v(2); return end
  Y = [1 0 1 2];
  Z = [1 1 -1 -1];
  a = afact;
```

```
A=(2+a);
B=-(3+a);
C=1;
D=a;
E=-5*a;
F=8*a;
G=-4*a;
for i = 1:4
  if v(i)~=0
    Fi = Y(i)+fact*Z(i);
    if Fi<1
       X = X + v(i)*(1 + Fi*Fi*(B + Fi*A));
    elseif Fi<2
       X = X + v(i)*(G + Fi*(F + Fi*(E + Fi*D)));
    end
  end
end
```

Figure 4.14 shows the bicubic interpolation results on the synthetic image letter *A* with 2× interpolation ratio by the MATLAB function call g=bicubic(f,2), where the intensity maps along the horizontal edge and diagonal edge are also shown in the same figure. It is vivid that there are overshoots in pixel intensities when the interpolation is along two regions with extreme intensities (across edges). This artifact is known as *overshooting* and is observed to be multiple inverted paths parallel to edges. The same artifact is also observed in bicubic interpolated natural image, and this artifact distorts the image in the form of *ringing* as shown in the result of the bicubic interpolated

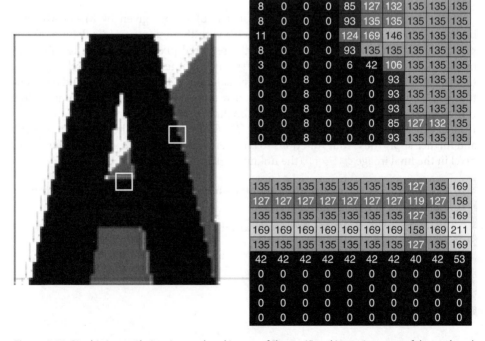

Figure 4.14 Bicubic interpolation: interpolated image of "letter *A*" and intensity maps of the enclosed diagonal and vertical edges.

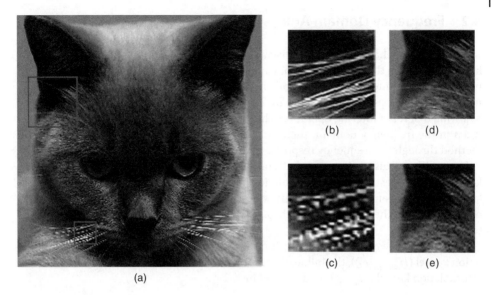

(b)　　　　　　(d)

(c)　　　　　　(e)

(a)

Figure 4.15 Bicubic interpolation of natural image *Cat* by a factor of 2 (PSNR = 24.9 dB): (a) the full interpolated image, (b) zoom-in portion of *Cat's* whiskers in original image, (c) zoom-in portion of *Cat's* whiskers in interpolated image, (d) zoom-in portion of *Cat's* ear in original image, and (e) zoom-in portion of *Cat's* ear in interpolated image.

natural image *Cat* (see Figure 4.15a) with PSNR of 24.9 dB. To facilitate the discussion, the zoom-in portions of the whiskers and ear of the original *Cat* image are shown in Figure 4.15b,d, respectively, while the corresponding portions of the bicubic interpolated image are shown in Figure 4.15c,e, respectively. It shows consistent performance at the texture-rich region (forehead of the *Cat* image) as that of nearest neighbor interpolation and bilinear interpolation. The bicubic interpolation achieves better interpolation results along long edges (as shown in the whiskers of the *Cat* image in Figure 4.15b,c) in order to preserve the edge sharpness when compared with that of bilinear interpolation. Moreover, the bicubic interpolation results in less blurred image around the ear of the *Cat* (see Figure 4.15d,e) when compared with that of bilinear interpolation. These observations show that bicubic interpolation is able to preserve the image features due to the use of higher-order function in the interpolation and also the use of larger interpolation kernel. However, the whiskers are turned to be *zigzag*-like structure in the bicubic interpolated image that is attributed to the ringing artifacts and also because of the overshoot at the boundary of the 4 × 4 kernels. Large intensity changes along sharp edges with overshoots generate unnatural appearance of bright and dark pixels along the two adjacent bicubic surfaces. Once such pattern repeats across several surfaces, it will be observed as the *zigzag* artifact. Nonetheless, bicubic interpolation results in the lowest PSNR value among nearest neighbor interpolation and bilinear interpolation due to the higher noise level encountered in the large kernel.

In general, bicubic interpolation generates better visual quality than bilinear interpolation. For smooth regions, bicubic interpolation generates smoother outputs because the derivatives across source pixels on a surface generated by bicubic polynomials are continuous but the ones by bilinear polynomials are not. For edges, bicubic polynomials generate overshoots that enhance contrast and are visually favorable because most high quality natural images contain visually sharp edges.

4.2 Frequency Domain Analysis

In Section 4.1, we have focused our discussions on the three basic nonadaptive interpolation methods in the spatial domain, where their interpolation kernels have also been introduced. The interpolation methods in Section 4.1 can be interpreted as 2D filtering zero-padded up-sampled images by 2D filters formed by the interpolation kernels. Knowing that it is a filtering operation, the interpolation problem can therefore be analyzed in the frequency domain, such as to reveal the properties of each interpolation method through the frequency response of the interpolation kernels.

To simplify the discussions, we shall state the frequency response of the interpolation kernel of the nearest neighbor interpolation, bilinear interpolation, and bicubic interpolation below, without going through the step-by-step computation of Fourier transform of these kernels. The readers can go through the derivation on their own with reference to Section 2.3.

The frequency responses of the sinc function ($H_{sinc}(\omega)$), the nearest neighbor interpolation kernel ($H_{nearest}(\omega)$), the bilinear interpolation kernel ($H_{bilinear}(\omega)$), and the bicubic interpolation kernel ($H_{bicubic}(\omega)$) are given by

$$H_{sinc}(\omega) = \begin{cases} 1, & \omega \leqslant \omega_s, \\ 0, & \omega > \omega_s, \end{cases} \tag{4.14}$$

$$H_{nearest}(\omega) = \text{sinc}\left(\frac{\omega}{2}\right), \tag{4.15}$$

$$H_{bilinear}(\omega) = \text{sinc}\left(\frac{\omega}{2}\right), \tag{4.16}$$

$$H_{bicubic}(\omega) = \frac{12}{\omega^2}\left(\text{sinc}^2\left(\frac{\omega}{2}\right)\right) + a\frac{8}{\omega^2}(3\text{sinc}^2(\omega) - 2\text{sinc}(2\omega)), \tag{4.17}$$

where ω_s is the bandwidth of the sinc function. It should be noted that due to the separable property of these four interpolation filters, only the 1D frequency responses will be presented and discussed. The spatial and frequency responses of the above four filters are plotted in Figure 4.16.

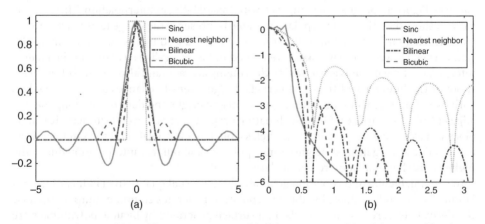

Figure 4.16 The spatial (a) and frequency response (b) of the nearest neighbor, bilinear, and bicubic interpolation kernels. (*See insert for color representation of this figure.*)

There are two things of interest for the design of reconstruction filter: the passband and the stopband. The passband governs which portion of the frequency components can be retained after the reconstruction, while the stopband suppresses the unwanted frequency components so they will not be appeared in the reconstructed signal. In ideal case, perfect reconstruction requires a low-pass filter with passband greater than all the frequency components that needed to be preserved. Therefore, as shown in Figure 4.16, only the sinc filter is the most appropriate candidate for perfect reconstruction as it has a sharp cutoff at ω_s. However, it is not practical to implement this filter in real application because it is not possible to implement infinite number of samples in spatial domain to preserve the perfect sinc function. The nearest neighbor filter, bilinear filter, and bicubic filter that have the same cutoff frequency at ω_s are shown in the same figure. The nearest neighbor filter has a relatively steeper falloff, and it can achieve better reconstruction, where more high frequency components (close to ω_s) can be preserved, such that the final image will be sharper. However, it has many subharmonic lobes such that the high frequency components falling in those lobes will appear in the reconstructed image. As a result, severe jaggy artifacts are observed in the interpolation results. The bilinear filter has a degraded passband that suppresses some of the high frequency components in the image, thus resulting in a blurred image. However, its subharmonic lobes have lower magnitudes; thus the jaggy artifacts are less severe when compared with that of nearest neighbor filter. The con is that the bilinear filter interpolated images show more severe ringing artifacts. The bicubic filter has a similar passband as that of bilinear filter, while it has even weaker subharmonic lobes that help to further suppress the effect of unwanted high frequency components in the interpolated images. The interpolated images are observed to be similar to that obtained with the application of bilinear filter but with improvement in the suppression of ringing artifacts.

4.3 Mystery of Order

We have discussed first-order, second-order, and third-order polynomial interpolation methods with the nearest neighbor interpolation, bilinear interpolation, and bicubic interpolation, respectively. It is possible to further increase the interpolation filter kernel to higher order to improve the interpolation quality. Mathematically, a 1D nth-order polynomial interpolation kernel can be applied to perfectly interpolate $n + 1$ data points, such that the interpolated curve is smooth and it passes through all the data points. However, the application of higher-order polynomial interpolation kernel to the entire dataset with unlimited bandwidth will lead to unwanted artifacts, including overshoot and oscillation around pixels with abrupt intensity changes as illustrated in Figure 4.17.

The number of data points considered in the interpolation is increased from 4 in Figure 4.17a to 8 in Figure 4.17c, which improves the approximation. The increase in the data points considered is actually increasing the order of the polynomial interpolation kernel. However, increasing the polynomial order will result in overshoot and oscillation around pixels (as shown in Figure 4.17c), which degrades the interpolation performance. To reduce the overshoot and oscillation artifacts in image interpolation, practical image interpolation makes use of piecewise continuous interpolation (as shown in Figure 4.17d). Consider the case of piecewise continuous interpolation by spline functions with various orders. The lowest-order spline function is the first-order

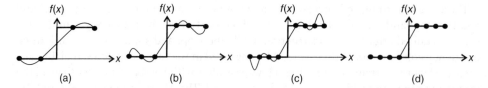

Figure 4.17 A visual representation of a situation where linear interpolation is superior to higher-order interpolating polynomials. The function to be fit (an edge) undergoes an abrupt change at $x = 0$. Parts (a)–(c) indicate that the abrupt change induces oscillations in interpolating polynomials. In contrast, because it is limited to third-order curves with smooth transitions, a linear interpolation (d) provides a much more acceptable approximation.

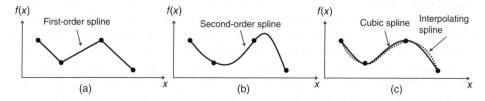

Figure 4.18 Illustration of different spline functions: (a) first-order spline, (b) second-order spline, and (c) cubic spline.

spline, which is also known as the *linear spline*. The linear spline connects all data points using a series of linear lines. The linear spline itself is continuous, but its first derivative is not continuous (see Figure 4.18a). It is vivid that the interpolation result is not satisfactory, where the first-order approximation is not detailed enough to estimate the smooth curve. When we increase the spline function order to 2, where the spline function is known as the *spline of degree 2* or *second-order spline*, the spline function itself and its first derivatives are continuous throughout all data points under consideration. Moreover, the spline function has to be a polynomial of degree at most 2 on each subinterval formed by two consecutive points inside the entire interval under consideration. In other words, the second-order spline is a quadratic spline that is continuously differentiable piecewise quadratic function. The second-order spline interpolation result is shown in Figure 4.18b. We can observe that the second-order spline generates a more pleasant interpolation result when compared with that of linear spline. If we further increase the order of the spline function to 3, which is known as *spline of degree 3* or *third-order spline*, the third-order spline has continuous first derivative and second-order derivatives over the entire interval under consideration. Moreover, the functions in the subintervals formed by two consecutive data points also described by a polynomial of degree at most 3 over the entire data set. It can be observed from Figure 4.18c that the third-order spline generates the best interpolation result among that obtained by interpolation using the linear and quadratic spline functions. The third-order spline is known as the *cubic spline*, which overcomes the problem of "overshoot," and it is easier to deal with when compared with that of higher-order polynomials. Extensive research works have showed that further increasing the spline function order does not provide further improvement in the quality of the interpolated image, while the complexity of the interpolation using high-order kernel is exponentially increasing with respect to the kernel size, which is defined by the spline function order. In other words, the high-order spline functions have prohibitively high computational complexity to prevent them from applying in practical cases. At the same time, we should also note that the spline function has improved smoothness with increasing spline function order. This is caused by both the large kernel size and the continuity of high-order derivative. Therefore, application of high-order spline function for image interpolation with spline function order higher than 3 can seldom be found in real-world applications. Extensive research works have shown that the *cubic spline* is almost the best one to obtain the best interpolation among all spline function orders.

4.4 Application: Affine Transformation

The above nonparametric interpolation techniques are commonly used in image processing applications, either being invoked alone or being applied with other image processing techniques. In this section, we shall discuss one of the applications of image interpolation to *affine transformation*, which we have briefly introduced in Section 2.6. *Affine transformation* of an object is the general form of all geometric transformations, which is the operation of series of geometric transformation, including translation, rotation, and scaling. Affine transformation maps an object from one coordinate system to another system, where the shape of the object may not be maintained, but the transformation will maintain:

- Straight line to be straight.
- Parallel lines to be parallel.
- Midpoint of a line to be the midpoint of the transformed line.

Affine transformation is a particular form of the geometric transformation. Let us recall the general geometric transformation formula depicted in Eq. (2.55).

$$\hat{S} = T_1 S + T_2,$$ (4.18)

where T_1 and T_2 can be the concatenation or multiplication of the transformation matrices discussed in Section 2.6. In other words, *translation*, *rotation*, and *scaling* are the three most simple and independent cases of the *affine transformation*, and the sequence of transformations would affect the structure of T_1 and T_2 due to the concatenation or multiplication of matrix operations. Figure 4.19 shows one of the practical application

Figure 4.19 Example of affine transformation: (a) input image and (b) transformed image.

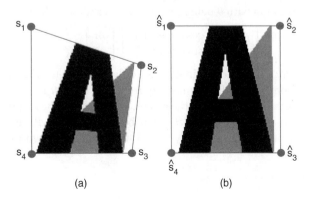

(a) (b)

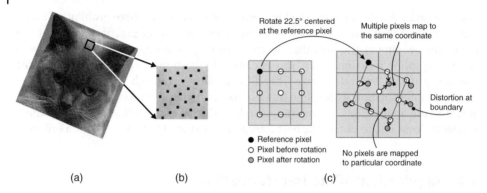

Figure 4.20 Image rotation through pixel mapping from original coordinate grid to a rotated grid: (a) rotated *Cat* image, (b) missing pixel after rotation, and (c) illustration of pixel mapping in image rotation.

of *affine transform*, which rectifies an alphabet to regular alignment for the ease of reading. The tilted alphabet (shown in Figure 4.19a) can be due to the misalignment of the object to the capturing device, commonly seen in document scanning application. The four vertices in Figure 4.19a forms $\mathbf{S} = [\mathbf{s}_1, \mathbf{s}_2, \mathbf{s}_3, \mathbf{s}_4]$ in Eq. (4.18). The matrices $\mathbf{T}_1$ and $\mathbf{T}_2$ map the points in $\mathbf{S}$ to give $\hat{\mathbf{S}} = [\hat{\mathbf{s}}_1, \hat{\mathbf{s}}_2, \hat{\mathbf{s}}_3, \hat{\mathbf{s}}_4]$ in Figure 4.19b. It is vivid that the irregular image has been rotated and scaled such that the entire image can be fully fitted onto the predefined rectangular frame, where the shape of the original image and final image are different but all straight lines remain straight and parallel lines remain in parallel. Unfortunately, the mapping of pixel coordinates may not necessarily produce output coordinates in integer. Hence, round off on the output coordinates is inevitable. On the other hand, the display system, printing system, and standard image storage system can only handle images defined in an integer Cartesian coordinate system. As a result, there will be missing pixels in the final image, where image interpolation steps in to estimate the unknown pixel values. The importance of image interpolation in *affine transformation* can be more easily observed by considering one of its special case, *image rotation*, as illustrated in Figure 4.20.

Rotating an image is a simple affine mapping that remaps the image pixels from one position (the original image Cartesian coordinate (m, n)) to a new position (the rotated coordinate (p, q)). They are related by affine transform equation with the rotation angle θ as parameter with the geometric transformation matrix given by Eq. (2.69) for clockwise rotation with θ being positive and restated in the following again.

$$\begin{bmatrix} p \\ q \end{bmatrix} = \begin{bmatrix} \cos\theta & -\sin\theta \\ \sin\theta & \cos\theta \end{bmatrix} \begin{bmatrix} m \\ n \end{bmatrix}. \tag{4.19}$$

Since image coordinates can only be discrete values, some transformations resulting from integer $[p, q]$ may require either m or n in $[m, n]$ to be non-integer. As a result, some of the pixels of the rotated image cannot be mapped to a pixel in the original image. An example of the *Cat* image being rotated by 40° is shown in Figure 4.20a. When we zoom into a small box within the image as shown in Figure 4.20b, there are numbers of missing pixels that correspond to the coordinates $[p, q]$ that maps to a non-integer coordinate (m, n). To demonstrate this remapping problem graphically, let us consider Figure 4.20c. The rotation makes reference to a chosen origin, the reference pixel, which in our case is the black dot. Rotation moves the pixels to new locations by mapping the original pixels to a new coordinate system. However, the mapping is determinative, and there will be overlapping or skipping in the new system. As a result, the remapping will sometimes result with pixels having no value assigned to them in the new system and sometimes with more than one pixel from the original image to be contributed to the rotated image. The artifacts are more severe along the image boundary.

To avoid and suppress the artifacts aroused after the coordinate transformation, interpolation technique is applied to estimate and assign pixel values to the rotated image. As discussed in this chapter, there are a number of interpolation techniques that we can make use of. First, let us consider the nearest neighbor interpolation, such as to introduce the detailed implementation on how to rotate a digital image in the most simple manner. The following Listing 4.4.1 implements `rotatenn` that rotates the image f with radian angle a using nearest neighbor interpolation.

MATLAB 4.4.1—Image rotation by nearest neighbor interpolation.

```
function g = rotatenn(f,a)
T = [+cos(a) +sin(a); -sin(a) +cos(a)]; % transform matrix
[M,N] = size(f);
pq = round( [1 1; 1 N; M 1; M N]*T );    % rotated image size
pq = bsxfun(@minus, pq, min(pq)) + 1;
g = 255*ones([max(pq)]);
for p = 1:size(g,1)
  for q = 1:size(g,2)
    mn = ([p q]-pq(1,:))*T.';             % coordinate transform
    mn = round(mn);                       % nearest neighbor
    if all(mn>= 1) && all(mn<= [M,N]) % original image bounding box
      g(p,q)=f(mn(1),mn(2));              % pixel value assignment
end end end end
```

To obtain the 40° rotated *Cat* image, we shall invoke `rotatenn` as

```
>> f = imread('cat256.png');
>> degree = 40;
>> a = degree*pi/180;    % convert to radian
>> g = rotatenn(f,a);
>> imshow(mat2gray(g));
```

The nearest neighbor interpolation is being performed by substituting the pixels that map to non-integer spatial coordinates in the original image with pixel values in the location obtained by rounding of the pixel coordinates, which in strict sense is not nearest neighbor, but this implementation gives a close enough nearest neighbor interpolation result to demonstrate the mapping of pixel values in two coordinate systems. This algorithm can be easily improved to use bilinear interpolation for improved image quality as demonstrated by Listing 4.4.2.

MATLAB 4.4.2—Image interpolation by bilinear interpolation.

```
function g = rotatebi(f,a)
T = [+cos(a) +sin(a); -sin(a) +cos(a)];  % transform matrix
[M,N] = size(f);
pq = round( [1 1; 1 N; M 1; M N]*T );     % rotated image size
pq = bsxfun(@minus, pq, min(pq)) + 1;
g = uint8(255*ones([max(pq)]));
for p = 1:size(g,1)
  for q = 1:size(g,2)
    mn = ([p q]-pq(1,:))*T.';              % coordinate transform
    if all(mn>= 1) && all(mn<= [M N])
       g(p,q) = bi2x2(f,mn);   % bilinear interpolation
end end end end
```

A 40° rotated *Cat* image using `rotatebi` is shown in Figure 4.21b. Shown in the same Figure 4.21a is the *Cat* image obtained from `rotatenn` by nearest neighbor interpolation. It can be observed that the rotated image obtained from nearest neighbor interpolation is blocky, just like that of the interpolated image obtained from nearest neighbor interpolation. But the rotated image obtained from bilinear interpolation has better image quality. It can be conjectured that for better image interpolation algorithm can produce rotated image with better image quality.

4.4.1 Structural Integrity

There is no accident for us to discuss the application of image interpolation to image rotation in this chapter. It is our intention to use image rotation to demonstrate the importance of the structural quality factor to image interpolation algorithm, which is

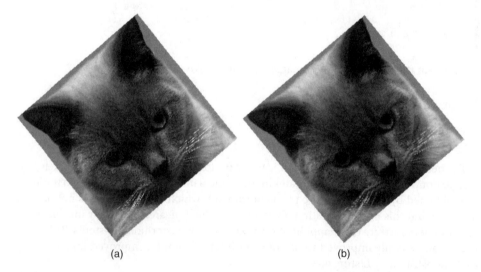

(a)   (b)

Figure 4.21 *Cat* image rotated with 40° obtained from (a) nearest neighbor interpolation by `rotatenn(f,a)` with f being the *Cat* image matrix and $a = 40\pi/180$ and (b) bilinear interpolation by `rotatebi(f,a)`.

something that cannot be measured by PSNR or SSIM. As discussed in previous section, image rotation requires to resample an image from a square lattice to another lattice grid that describes the rotated image. This is a lossy operation except for some special angle of rotation. The amount and quality of information loss will depend on the image interpolation method being applied in the resampling process since information lost in the rotation operation is accumulative. As a result, it can be expected that the image will be largely distorted after the image goes through successive rotations. The image interpolation method that obtains the best rotated image is also known as the one that can best preserve the structure of the image. It is not scientific to use the word "best" without an analytical metric to define the quality of the rotation, because the only information that we have is the original image f before rotation. We can therefore define a rotation quality metric using the PSNR quantity between the given image f and the image obtained by nine successive rotations of $40°$ or radian angle of $2\pi/9$ on the image f. It is understood that the intermediate rotated image will have larger support and the final rotated image will be cropped to the initial image size. Figure 4.22 shows the above described procedure.

Besides the rotation functions implemented in previous section, MATLAB image processing toolbox has a built-in image rotation function `imrotate(f,a,method)`, where `method` specifies the interpolation method to be applied to recover the pixels

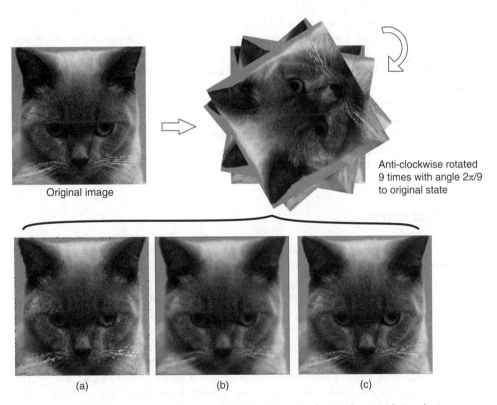

Original image

Anti-clockwise rotated
9 times with angle $2\pi/9$
to original state

(a)　　　　(b)　　　　(c)

Figure 4.22 Image interpolation algorithm structural integrity evaluation by considering the image rotated 9 times with angle $2\pi/9$ for (a) nearest neighbor, (b) bilinear, and (c) bicubic.

Table 4.1 PSNR and SSIM of *Cat* image down-sampled to 64 × 64 and rotated 9 times with angle $2\pi/9$.

	Nearest neighbor	Bilinear	Bicubic
PSNR (dB)	22.7552	25.5519	28.0559
SSIM	0.6305	0.7280	0.8501

mapped to non-integer coordinates during rotation. The available interpolation methods include `nearest` for nearest neighbor interpolation discussed in Section 4.1.2, `bilinear` for bilinear interpolation discussed in Section 4.1.3, and `bicubic` for bicubic interpolation discussed in Section 4.1.4. The rotated images using `imrotate` after nine successive rotations of 40° as shown in Figure 4.22 are shown at the bottom of Figure 4.22, with the PSNR and SSIM of the resulting images obtained by different interpolation methods listed in Table 4.1.

Performing the rotation using nearest neighbor interpolation clearly provides a poor quality as shown in Figure 4.22a. The bilinear interpolation-based rotation provides blurred images in Figure 4.22b. The bicubic interpolation-based rotation outperformed the other two, and the generated image closely resembles the image structure of the original image as shown in Figure 4.22c. Readers may argue that the performance of different interpolation methods can be compared through studying of the PSNR and SSIM of the interpolated images as presented in previous sections. It may be true that the PSNR and SSIM can provide us some insight on the structural integrity of the interpolation algorithm. However, the small differences in the numeric values of PSNR and SSIM between various interpolation methods do not translate to such a large structural integrity difference as that revealed through image rotations as shown in Figure 4.22 and Table 4.1. The ability to demonstrate the preservation of structural integrity is the reason why image rotations have been adapted in some literature to investigate and compare the performance of image interpolation methods.

4.5 Summary

In this chapter, we have started our journey in the exploration of different image interpolation methods by first investigating the nonparametric image interpolation methods. Down to the application level, image interpolation is the process of enlarging or expanding the size of an image. The size of the image can be enlarged due to the resample and reconstruction of the image by a particular image interpolation process. The resample step expands the resolution of the original images by increasing the sampling rate of the image in both the row and column directions, which is usually accomplished by inserting new zeros in between the pixels in the original image in spatial domain or duplicating the image spectrum in frequency domain (as will be discussed in Chapter 5). The reconstruction step estimates the intensities of pixels located at those newly inserted zero value spatial locations during the resampling step, where the estimation can also be completed by a convolution operation with the interpolation kernel. Most practical interpolation kernels are low-pass in nature. It is vivid in frequency domain that such resampling and reconstruction do not introduce new information to the final image; however, the quality of the low-pass filter does affect the quality of the final image. The nature of the low-pass filter is therefore the key topic to be considered in this chapter and also in the later chapters. We have reviewed the properties of the interpolation kernel in spatial domain, and the reason why we have been focused in the spatial domain is because most of the implementation of image interpolation algorithms is in spatial domain. Among the many interpolation kernels, we have gone through the three most basic linear spatially invariant interpolation kernels, also known as the nonparametric interpolation kernels (because the filter does not depend on the image nature). The three interpolation methods are the nearest neighbor interpolation, bilinear interpolation, and bicubic interpolation. The discussions on each interpolation method cover the description of the interpolation filters of each method in both spatial and frequency domains. To facilitate analysis and implementation, their spatial matrix representations are also discussed. MATLAB source codes of each method are presented with detailed discussions to connect the source codes to the mathematical derivations. The performance of each method is compared with both the subjective (mainly concerns about the visual artifacts: blurring, jaggy, blocking, etc.) and objective (PSNR and SSIM) measures. The nearest neighbor interpolation is the replication of neighboring known pixel value to the unknown pixels, which makes use of a box-shaped filter. This method has the simplest computation, but it suffers from severe staircase-like artifacts (jaggies) along the region with sharp contrast changes (edges). Bilinear interpolation tends to produce interpolated images that appear softer, where the contrast is reduced because of the averaging of neighboring pixel values through the convolution of a triangular-shaped filter in spatial domain. Improved quality interpolated image can be obtained from bicubic interpolation when compared with that of the nearest neighbor interpolation and bilinear interpolation. Bicubic interpolation makes use of third-order approximation to achieve better reconstruction, especially along regions with sharp contrast changes. Therefore, the interpolated image obtained by bicubic interpolation preserves the advantage of bilinear interpolation and also provides more visually pleasant results along the high contrast region. However, the kernel of bicubic filter is a high-order filter kernel that may result in overshooting (also known as ringing), thus degrading the PSNR performance.

Besides spatial domain analysis, in-depth comparison of these three filters is also performed in the frequency domain, where the frequency response of each filter is presented. The passband and the stopband of the filter govern which frequency components can be preserved and which to be discarded during the reconstruction process. We also investigate the effect of estimation order. Though increasing the estimation order can reduce the estimation error, however, the interpolated image will suffer from overshooting and undergoing artifacts near the abrupt change regions. As a result, the optimal order of the interpolation filter kernel will be 3 for most practical image interpolation applications with natural images. Finally, we conclude this chapter's discussion on nonparametric interpolation filter by applying the interpolation in affine transformation and pointing out the importance of preserving the structure properties of the interpolated image. In the following chapters, we shall go through more advanced interpolation methods, where the image nature will be considered during the interpolation to achieve better interpolated image quality.

4.6 Exercises

4.1 Derive a causal interpolation filter kernel for the nearest neighbor and bilinear interpolations and implement the filter kernels in MATLAB. Analyze and discuss the following.

1. The consequence of implementing the filter kernel in MATLAB when compared with the corresponding filter kernel discussed in this chapter
2. The difference in the boundary extension required for the noncausal filters and that of the corresponding filter kernel discussed in this chapter to achieve signal interpolation

4.2 Given the following pixel values $f[m, n]$, use bilinear interpolation to estimate the pixel value at location $(5.25, 4.8)$.

$$f(2, 1) = 60, \quad f(9, 1) = 57.5, \quad f(2, 6) = 55, \quad f(9, 6) = 70. \tag{4.20}$$

4.3 With reference to Listing 4.1.3, develop a MATLAB function $nn(f, k)$, that will return a nearest neighbor interpolated image of ratio k, where $k \in \mathbb{Z}^+$.

4.4 With reference to Listing 4.1.6, develop a MATLAB function cubic-spline6(f,k), that will return an order 3 (with kernel size 6×6) cubic spline interpolated image of ratio k, where $k \in \mathbb{Z}^+$.

4.5 [**Affine transformation**] Write a MATLAB code for computing an affine transform with a given image. The inputs to your program are (i) image, (ii) parameters of the affine transform, and (iii) interpolation method. Your report should include:

1. M-file with a well-commented code.
2. The result, namely, F, when the input image is spatially transformed using the matrix T and the bilinear interpolation, where T is specified as

$$T = \begin{bmatrix} 0.3 & 0.1 & 0 \\ 0.5 & 1.9 & 1 \\ 0 & 0 & 1 \end{bmatrix}. \tag{4.21}$$

3. The difference between the input image and the image that has been obtained by applying the inverse spatial transform T^{-1} to F (apply zero padding if the images have different sizes). Explain the meaning of bright and dark pixels. (*Hint*: MATLAB commands: "maketform," "imtransform.")

4.6 [**Frequency domain image rotation and shear**] Rotation and shear are just special cases of affine transformation. As the component shears can be chosen to be purely in the m and n directions, a rotation can be split into three one-dimensional operations. The process is most clearly defined in terms of a matrix equation as

$$\begin{bmatrix} \hat{m} \\ \hat{n} \end{bmatrix} = \begin{bmatrix} \cos\theta & \sin\theta \\ -\sin\theta & \cos\theta \end{bmatrix} \begin{bmatrix} m \\ n \end{bmatrix} = \mathbf{M}_\theta \begin{bmatrix} m \\ n \end{bmatrix}, \tag{4.22}$$

where (m, n) is the original image coordinate and $(\hat{m}, \hat{n})$ is the mapped coordinate of the rotated image with clockwise rotation angle θ. The three component shears are as follows

$$\mathbf{M}_\theta = \mathbf{M}_m \mathbf{M}_n \mathbf{M}_m, \tag{4.23}$$

with the shearing transforms

$$\mathbf{M}_m = \begin{bmatrix} 1 & \tan(\theta/2) \\ 0 & 1 \end{bmatrix}, \tag{4.24}$$

$$\mathbf{M}_n = \begin{bmatrix} 1 & 0 \\ -\sin\theta & 1 \end{bmatrix}. \tag{4.25}$$

A simple application of the Fourier shift theorem will be equivalent to a one-dimensional B-spline interpolation. The following is a particular implementation to perform shearing of image f in m direction with $\theta = \pi/8$:

```
>> [M, N] = size(f);
>> M2=2*M; N2=2*N;
>> g = ones(M2,N2);
>> g(floor(M/2):floor(M/2)+M-1,floor(N/2):floor(N/2)+N-1)=f(:,:);
     % enlarge the image bounding box
>> theta=pi/8;   % define the rotation angle theta
>> a = tan(theta/2); b=-sin(theta);
>> Nn = ifftshift(-floor(NN/2):ceil(NN/2)-1); % compute the fft
     shift indices
>> fm = zeros(MM,NN);    % prepare the sheared output image
>> for k=1:MM
     fm(k,:)=(ifft(fft(g(k,:)).*exp(-2*i*pi*(k-floor(MM/2))*Nn*a/NN)
        ));
   end
>> fm=abs(fm);
>> figure; imshow(mat2gray(fm));
```

Performing the above operation will generate a sheared image fm. Complete the rest of the MATLAB source to perform Eq. (4.23) and generate a rotated image of f with clockwise rotation of $\pi/8$.

4.7 [Color demosaic]

1. Develop a MATLAB function that read in full-color image matrices, such as that of the full-color *Cat* image, and output a Bayer pattern encoded color image matrix as shown in Figure 2.28. Plot the overlay image.
2. Develop an image interpolation function that will read in the Bayer pattern encoded image matrix, and interpolate the matrix to obtain three separate full-color image matrices. Plot the demosaic color image.
3. Explain your choice of interpolation method in the above demosaic function. What are the pros and cons of using the selected interpolation method. Use demosaic image result to sustain your discussions.

4.8 Expand the sequence below to lengths of (i) 9, (ii) 11, and (iii) 15 pixels using nearest neighbor and bilinear interpolation. [1 4 7 4 3 6]

4.9 Consider the grayscale image array below.

$$
\begin{matrix}
8 & 8 & 13 & 9 \\
1 & 13 & 1 & 15 \\
5 & 4 & 7 & 7 \\
5 & 10 & 3 & 7
\end{matrix}
$$

Resize the array sizes of (i) 7 × 7, (ii) 8 × 8, and (iii) 10 × 10 by hand using nearest neighbor and bilinear interpolation.

4.10 Suppose an image is up-sampled in size by a factor r and followed by a down-sampling in size by the same factor. Is the final image exactly the same as the original image? If not, why not? What if the resizing sequence is reversed with down-sampling followed by up-sampling in size?

4.11 Rotate the image *Cat* by an angle of 45° clockwise and then rotate back by the same angle using (i) nearest neighbor or (ii) bilinear interpolation. Is the final image exactly the same as the original image? If not, why not?

5

Transform Domain

We have discussed in Chapter 2 that an image can be represented by the function $f[m, n]$ with two indexing variables $[m, n]$ that specify the spatial location, while the magnitude of the function at $[m, n]$ is the light intensity of the image at that spatial location. In this case, the function $f[m, n]$ is said to be defined in the *spatial* domain. Besides the spatial domain, image can also be represented in other domains. The operation that converts the image representation from one domain to another is known as "transformation." According to the Oxford dictionary, *transform* means "change in form or nature." Mathematically, the word *transform* has been adopted to mean "to change to different form while having the same value." A more vigorous definition of image transformation can be given to describe the mathematical process of converting and representing an image into its alternative form that usually means representing the image using an equivalent set of functions in a different domain. For example, an image can be represented as sums of series of 2D sinusoids with varying degree of frequencies specified by u and v and magnitude given by $F[u, v]$. Such representation can be obtained by the discrete Fourier transform (DFT) of the function $f[m, n]$ (as discussed in Section 2.3). The domain that contains $F[u, v]$, the DFT result of $f[m, n]$, is known as the *frequency* (Fourier) domain. An important question that must be pondered upon is: Why do we want to perform image transformation when the information content is the same in all domains? A simple answer to this question is that the transform domain image representation helps to provide a different view of the image that can reveal important features that are of particular interest to the application in concern. As an example, certain transformation helps to organize the image features in a way that aligns with the human visual system (HVS). Such properties have been exploited in image and video compression to achieve image data compaction with high visual fidelity. In fact, because of the storage efficiency, it is not surprising to find that the transform domain representation of images has already suppressed the spatial domain image representation to become the most common format for image storage since the millennium.

Transform domain image processing can be applied in image interpolation for both algorithmic efficiency and quality improvement. To visualize how transform domain processing can be applied in image interpolation, we shall first consider a simpler problem of interpolating a 1D sampled signal in the Fourier domain. A continuous bandlimited waveform $f(x)$ with bandwidth $\pm B/2$ Hz, as shown in Figure 5.1, is sampled with sampling frequency ω_s to obtain the sampled signal sequence $f[n]$. It should be noticed that the Fourier spectrum of $f(x)$ is the envelope of the discrete time Fourier transform

Digital Image Interpolation in MATLAB®, First Edition. Chi-Wah Kok and Wing-Shan Tam.
© 2019 John Wiley & Sons Singapore Pte. Ltd. Published 2019 by John Wiley & Sons Singapore Pte. Ltd.
Companion website: www.wiley.com/go/ditmatlab

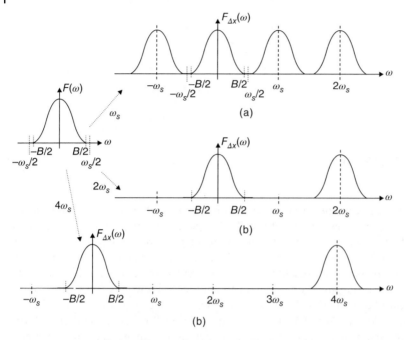

Figure 5.1 Spectra of a bandlimited signal $f(x)$ with bandwidth $\pm B/2$ sampled at sampling rate of (a) ω_s, (b) $2 \times \omega_s$, and (c) $4 \times \omega_s$.

(DTFT) spectrum of $f[n]$ and is periodic with period 2π, where the angular frequency 2π is mapped to the analog frequency ω_s as shown in Figure 5.1a. When the same signal $f(x)$ is sampled with sampling frequency $2\omega_s$, the angular frequency 2π in the DTFT spectrum is mapped to the analog frequency $2\omega_s$ as shown in Figure 5.1b, and the spectrum of the sample sequence is periodic with period $2\omega_s$. If the same signal is sampled with sampling frequency $4\omega_s$, the spectrum of the new sample sequence is distributed on the frequency axis with period $4\omega_s$ as shown in Figure 5.1c. When $|\omega_s| \geqslant B/2$, the spectrum of the sampled signal $f[n]$ outside $\pm B/2$ is zero. This suggests a method of getting new sample sequence that mimics the sampled sequence of $f(x)$ with sampling frequency $2\omega_s$ from a given sampled sequence $f[n]$ of $f(x)$ at sampling frequency ω_s. The method will consist of (i) calculating a length N spectrum sequence $F[\nu]$ of a length N sequence $f[n]$ and (ii) adding $N/2$ zeros on both sides of the baseband (at both sides of the sequence $F(\nu)$, outside the frequency range $\pm B/2$). Finally, (iii) inverse discrete Fourier transform (IDFT) is applied on the zero-padded spectral sequence with length $2N$ to obtain a length $2N$ signal sequence $g[n]$, which should be the same as the signal sequence obtained from sampling $f(x)$ with sampling frequency $2\omega_s$. In other words, $g[n]$ is a 2× interpolated signal sequence of $f[n]$.

The above sampled signal sequence interpolation method in the frequency domain is feasible, only if the sampled signal satisfies the Nyquist sampling theorem, which will require the sampled signal $f[n]$ to be free from aliasing noise. If this is the case, interpolating the signal in frequency domain will be trivial because the additional high frequency samples are zeros. On the other hand, it is very unlikely that the sampled signal is sampled with a sampling frequency that satisfies the Nyquist sampling theorem.

Therefore, the above zero padding method will most likely to produce a corrupted interpolated signal with aliasing artifacts. The following sections will analytically analyze the transform domain zero padding interpolation method and discuss the associated artifacts and various remedies that help to alleviate the unpleasant visual artifacts observed in the interpolated images.

5.1 DFT Zero Padding Interpolation

Previous section has shown us how to interpolate a discrete signal sequence by taking the Fourier transform, padding zeros to the spectral signal sequence to create the pseudo-high frequency components, and then inverse Fourier transforming the zero-padded sequence to obtain the spatial interpolation result. To analytically understand the interpolation process, let us consider a 1D DFT sequence $F[v]$ of an even length real-valued 1D sequence $f[n]$. The DFT sequence is zero padded to obtain $G[v]$ as

$$
G[v] = \begin{cases}
r \cdot F[v], & 0 \leqslant v \leqslant \frac{N}{2} - 1, \\
\frac{1}{2} r \cdot F\left[\frac{N}{2}\right], & v = \frac{N}{2}, \\
0, & \frac{N}{2} + 1 \leqslant v \leqslant K - \frac{N}{2} - 1, \\
\frac{1}{2} r \cdot F\left[\frac{N}{2}\right], & v = K - \frac{N}{2}, \\
r \cdot F[v - (K - N)], & K - \frac{N}{2} + 1 \leqslant v \leqslant K - 1,
\end{cases}
\tag{5.1}
$$

where r is the interpolation ratio, N is the length of the sequence $f[n]$ and is assumed to be even, and $K = r \cdot N$ is the length of the interpolated sequence $g[n]$. The Fourier domain representation of $g[n]$ has zero values in the high frequency range and satisfies the following conjugate symmetry condition

$$
G[K - v] = G[K - v]^*, \quad 1 \leqslant v \leqslant \frac{N}{2},
\tag{5.2}
$$

where $*$ is the complex conjugate operator. Maintaining the conjugate symmetry of $G[v]$ will enable us to obtain a real value sequence after performing IDFT on $G[v]$. This is very important, as image pixel values are the light intensity that by definition are real value numbers. It is because we need to ensure $G[v]$ to satisfy the conjugate symmetry condition and at the same time preserve the total power of the signal; therefore, the spectral sequence $G[v]$ contains two half-valued $F\left[\frac{N}{2}\right]$ samples. Now, let us examine the IDFT of $G[v]$, which yields

$$
\begin{aligned}
g[n] &= \frac{1}{K} \sum_{v=0}^{K-1} G[v] W_K^{-vn} \\
&= \frac{1}{N} \left(\sum_{v=0}^{\frac{N}{2}-1} F[v] W_K^{-vn} + \sum_{v=K-\frac{N}{2}+1}^{K-1} F[v] W_K^{-vn} \right) \\
&\quad + \frac{1}{2N} \left(F\left[\frac{N}{2}\right] W_K^{-\frac{N}{2}v} + F\left[\frac{N}{2}\right] W_N^{-(K-\frac{N}{2})v} \right).
\end{aligned}
\tag{5.3}
$$

Since $f[n]$ is a real value sequence, therefore, the related Fourier function $F[v]$ will satisfy Eq. (5.2). By defining $\hat{v} = K - v$, we shall obtain

$$\sum_{v=K-\frac{N}{2}+1}^{K-1} F[v]W_K^{-vn} = \sum_{\hat{v}=1}^{\frac{N}{2}-1} F[K-\hat{v}]W_K^{-(K-\hat{v})n} = \sum_{\hat{v}=1}^{\frac{N}{2}-1} F[\hat{v}]^* W_K^{\hat{v}n}, \tag{5.4}$$

where we make use of the fact that $W_K^{-vK} = 1$ for all integer v. Substituting Eq. (5.4) into (5.3) and using the equality $W_K^{-(K-\frac{N}{2})v} = W_K^{\frac{N}{2}v}$ will yield

$$g[n] = \frac{1}{N}\left(F[0] + \sum_{v=1}^{\frac{N}{2}-1}(F[v]W_K^{-vn} + F[v]^* W_K^{vn})\right) + \frac{1}{2N}F\left[\frac{N}{2}\right]\left(W_K^{-\frac{N}{2}n} + W_K^{\frac{N}{2}n}\right). \tag{5.5}$$

With reference to the formal definition of DFT in Eq. (1.10), the first term in Eq. (5.5) can be written as

$$z_1[n] = \frac{1}{N}\sum_{k=0}^{N-1}f[k]\left(1 + \sum_{v=1}^{\frac{N}{2}-1}(W_N^{kv}W_K^{-vn} + W_N^{-kv}W_K^{vn})\right)$$

$$= \frac{1}{N}\sum_{k=0}^{N-1}f[k]\left(1 + 2\sum_{v=1}^{\frac{N}{2}-1}\cos\left(\frac{2\pi nv}{K} - \frac{2\pi kv}{N}\right)\right). \tag{5.6}$$

Moreover, $W_N^{\frac{N}{2}} = -1$ with an even N. The second term in Eq. (5.5) can be written as

$$z_2[n] = \frac{1}{2N}F\left[\frac{N}{2}\right]\left(W_K^{-\frac{N}{2}n} + W_K^{\frac{N}{2}n}\right)$$

$$= \frac{1}{2N}\sum_{k=0}^{N-1}f[k]W_N^{-\frac{N}{2}k}2\cos\left(\frac{\pi nN}{K}\right)$$

$$= \frac{1}{N}\sum_{k=0}^{N-1}(-1)^k f[k]\cos\left(\frac{\pi nN}{K}\right). \tag{5.7}$$

The spatial sequence $g[n]$ is obtained by summing $z_1[n]$ and $z_2[n]$.

$$g[n] = z_1[n] + z_2[n]$$

$$= \frac{1}{N}\sum_{k=0}^{N-1}f[k]\left(1 + 2\sum_{v=1}^{\frac{N}{2}-1}\left(\cos\left(\frac{2\pi vn}{K} - \frac{2\pi kv}{N}\right) + (-1)^k\cos\left(\frac{\pi nN}{K}\right)\right)\right). \tag{5.8}$$

Using the identities $\cos(\theta_1 - \theta_2) = \cos(\theta_1)\cos(\theta_2) + \sin(\theta_1)\sin(\theta_2)$, $\cos(k\pi) = (-1)^k$, and $\sin(k\pi) = 0$, we are ready to derive the identity

$$(-1)^k\cos\left(\frac{\pi nN}{K}\right) = \cos(k\pi)\cos\left(\frac{2\pi n\frac{N}{2}}{K}\right) = \cos\left(\frac{2\pi n\frac{N}{2}}{K} - \frac{2\pi k\frac{N}{2}}{N}\right). \tag{5.9}$$

Substituting the above identity into Eq. (5.8) together with the fact that $\cos(0) = 1$ yields

$$g[n] = \sum_{k=0}^{N-1} f[k] \sum_{v=0}^{\frac{N}{2}} \beta_v \cos\left(\frac{2\pi n v}{K} - \frac{2\pi k v}{N}\right), \qquad \beta_v = \begin{cases} \frac{1}{N}, & v = 0, \frac{N}{2}, \\ \frac{2}{N}, & v = 1, 2, \ldots, \frac{N}{2} - 1. \end{cases}$$

(5.10)

Considering a shifted interpolated sequence with $n = \ell r + \rho$, and the fact that $K = rN$, Eq. (5.10) can be rewritten as

$$g[\ell r + \rho] = \sum_{k=0}^{N-1} f[k] \left(\sum_{v=0}^{\frac{N}{2}} \beta_v \cos\left(\frac{2\pi(\ell r + \rho)v}{K} - \frac{2\pi k v}{N}\right) \right)$$

$$= \sum_{k=0}^{N-1} f[k] b_1\left(\ell + \frac{\rho}{r} - k\right),$$

(5.11)

where

$$b_1(x) = \sum_{v=0}^{\frac{N}{2}} \beta_v \cos\left(\frac{2\pi x v}{N}\right).$$

(5.12)

Let $\tau = \ell + \frac{\rho}{r}$, such that τ can be any real number within $[0, N)$ for all interpolation factors r between 1 and ∞. Substituting τ into Eq. (5.11) yields

$$g(r\tau) = \sum_{k=0}^{N-1} f[k] b_1(\tau - k),$$

(5.13)

which has the same form as Eq. (1.2) with the interpolation kernel given by

$$b_1(\tau) = \sum_{k=0}^{\frac{N}{2}} \beta_k \cos\left(\frac{2\pi k \tau}{N}\right).$$

(5.14)

This function looks different from the sinc function in Theorem 1.1. However, when we plot the function $b_1(\tau)$ in Eq. (5.14) (i.e. the solid line) on the same graph with $\text{sinc}(\tau)$ (i.e. the dashed line), as shown in Figure 5.2 (where $N = 30$), it is vivid that $b_1(\tau)$ does provide a good approximation to the sinc function. As a result, even though the DFT zero padding interpolation is not analytically equivalent to sinc interpolation, it does provide an almost identical solution as that obtained from the sinc interpolation, and hence it has been treated as equivalent to sinc interpolation in many applications.

5.1.1 Implementation

The implementation of image interpolation algorithm by zero padding in Fourier domain will first consider the dimension separability property of the 2D Fourier kernel, such that zero padding will be applied to the rows and columns of the transformed image separately. Consider the case of interpolating a length N 1D signal $f[n]$ with an interpolation ratio r. To preserve the symmetry of the zero-padded DFT sequence, we shall discuss the even and odd N cases separately. When N is odd, there will be $(r - 1)N$

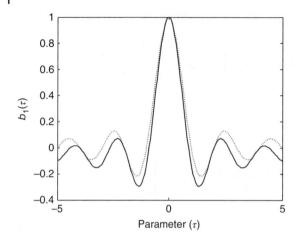

Figure 5.2 The interpolation kernel $b_1(\tau)$ in Eq. (5.14) with $N = 30$ is plotted using solid line, while the sinc function sinc(τ) is plotted with dashed line.

zeros inserted in between the $(N-1)/2$th and $(N+1)/2$th samples of the length N DFT sequence of $F[v]$ to obtain the zero-padded sequence $G[v]$ as

$$G = \left[F \left[0 : \frac{N-1}{2} \right] \quad \mathbf{0}_{1\times(r-1)N} \quad F \left[\frac{N+1}{2} : N-1 \right] \right], \tag{5.15}$$

where the matrix $\mathbf{0}_{1\times(r-1)N}$ is the zero matrix with size $1 \times (r-1)N$. The subscript $1 \times (r-1)N$ represents the size of the matrix. The same convention will be adopted to describe the same matrices throughout this chapter. When N is even, the zero insertion will be performed either by

1. Placing $(r-1)N+1$ zeros in between the $(N/2-1)$th and $(N/2+1)$th samples of the N-point DFT sequence of $f[n]$, and the $N/2$th sample of $F[v]$ is discarded, or
2. Placing $(r-1)N$ zeros after the $N/2$th sample of the N-point DFT sequence of $f[n]$, and then the sequence will be repeated with the first $N/2$ components of $F[v]$, or
3. Placing $(r-1)N$ zeros after the $N/2$th sample and before the $1 + N/2$th sample of the sequence $F[v]$, where both the $N/2$th and the $1 + N/2$th samples of $F[v]$ are halved.

Although these three zero padding interpolation methods will yield different interpolation results, the third method is commonly used because of the ease to handle the symmetry of the zero-padded sequence. The 2D interpolation is achieved by applying the above 1D interpolation to both the row and column dimensions separately. The MATLAB function `dftinterp` carries out the zero-padded 1D signal interpolation with an even number of samples using method 3.

MATLAB 5.1.1—Fourier interpolation of a length N sequence to a length K sequence by method 3.

```
function g=dftinterp(f,K)
  N = length(f);
  freqf=fft(f);
  zp=zeros(K,1);
  zp(1:N/2)=freqf(1:N/2);
  zp(N/2+1)=freqf(N/2+1)/2;
  zp(K-N/2+2)=freqf(N/2+1)/2;
```

```
   zp(K-N/2+3:K)=freqf(N/2+3:N);
   g=real(ifft(zp))*(K/N);
return;
```

Considering the data sequence shown in Figure 1.6, it can be Fourier interpolated to a sequence with length of $K = 100$ by calling the function `dftinterp([4 8 12 16 16 12 12 8 8 8],100)`. A few comments on the code are in order. The goal is to apply a length N `fft` followed by a length K `ifft` and then multiply the spatial sequence by $r = K/N$, with N being the length of `f` and K being the length of the interpolated sequence `g`. The first $N/2$ coefficients of the `fft` transformed coefficients of `f`, `freqf`, are moved to the first part of the vector `zp`, and the last $N/2 - 2$ coefficients to the last section of the vector `zp`. The coefficient `freqf(N/2+1)` is split into two halves (a simple division by 2) and stored in `zp(N/2+1)` and `zp(K-N/2+2)`. The rest of the `zp` sequence are filled with zeros (from positions $N/2 + 2$ to $K - N/2 + 1$). The zero-padded DFT sequence `zp` is inversely transformed by the `ifft` command. Although the transformed signal sequence should be real valued theoretically, computational rounding error might produce small imaginary part in some of the spatial coefficients obtained from `ifft`. This is removed by applying the `real` command. Notice that a constant $r = K/N$ is multiplied to the inverse transformed sequence. This operation helps to maintain the mean value of the interpolated signal sequence to be the same as that of the low-resolution sampled signal sequence. This is equivalent to maintain the brightness of the interpolated image to be the same as that of the original image when applying the function into image interpolation.

The function `dftinterp` can be applied twice on the row and the column to interpolate an image as the following MATLAB program does.

MATLAB 5.1.2—2× Image interpolation by DFT zero padding.

```
function outf=zpfft(f)
   [M N] = size(f);
   OUTM = 2*M;
   OUTN = 2*N;
   zero_pad = zeros(OUTM,OUTN);
   F = fftshift(fft2(f));
   xstart = floor(OUTM/2)-floor(M/2)-1;
   xend = xstart+M-1;
   ystart = floor(OUTN/2)-floor(N/2)-1;
   yend = ystart+N-1;
   zero_pad(xstart:xend,ystart:yend) = F;
   outf = 4*ifft2(ifftshift(zero_pad));
   outf = abs(outf);
```

Shown in Figure 5.3a is the 2D spectral figure of the *Cat* image (with `fftshift` and `log(real(·))` to compress the dynamic range of the 2D spectral signal to make it easy to be observed visually). To achieve 2× interpolation, the $M \times N$ spectral image of *Cat* in Figure 5.3a is zero padded to $2M \times 2N$ as shown in Figure 5.3b. The 2× image interpolation result of the *Cat* image is shown in Figure 5.4a. As simple and elegant as the method is, the result is often not good enough. The spatial regions of the interpolated *Cat* that contain the high frequency components, such as in the edges of the *Cat* whiskers, are

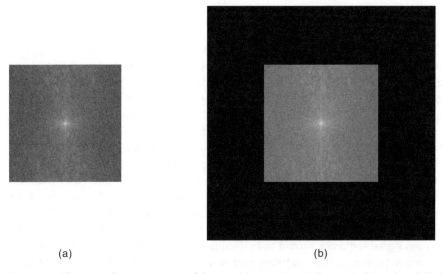

(a)   (b)

Figure 5.3 The spectral representation of the natural image *Cat*: (a) the original image and (b) the zero-padded spectral representation of a 2× image interpolation. (*Note*: `fftshift` is applied to obtain this spectral plot. Readers may want to review Example 2.1.)

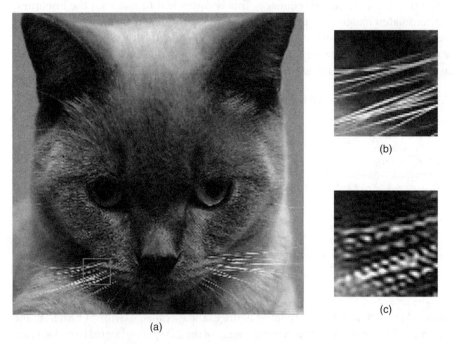

(b)

(c)

(a)

Figure 5.4 A 2× interpolated *Cat* image obtained by zero-padded DFT (PSNR = 26.9 dB, SSIM = 0.8053 dB): (a) the full interpolated image, (b) the zoom-in portion of cat's whiskers in original image, and (c) zoom-in portion of cat's whiskers in interpolated image. Note that the heavy oscillations (ringing) around the cat's whiskers shown in the zoom-in image (c) are the result of *Gibbs phenomenon*.

observed to have non-smooth transitions as shown in Figure 5.4c when compared with that of the high-resolution *Cat* image in Figure 5.4b. These nonstationary high frequency ripples propagate far from image edges to the smooth areas, which make them fairly easy to be detected by human eyes, and in particular around the image boundaries. This interpolation artifact is the result of the Fourier transform treating the spatial image as being virtually periodic. As a result, the pixels at the left and right image borders and the upper and bottom image borders should be, virtually, the immediate neighbors in the interpolation process. Any discontinuity between opposite border samples will suffer from Gibbs phenomenon and cause heavy discrete oscillations that propagate far away from the borders.

An example of the heavy oscillation (which is also known as the ringing artifact in image interpolation) in the vicinity of image border discontinuity is vivid from the interpolated 1D ramp signal example in Figure 5.5b, when compared with the low-resolution 1D ramp signal in Figure 5.5a. The 1D ramp signal in Figure 5.5a is obtained from uniform time domain sampling between [0, 31] with 32 samples. The 8× interpolated sequence is obtained by MATLAB Listing 5.1.3. In this MATLAB example, `fftshift` is applied to shift the spectrum (as explained in Section 1.2.1), such that zero padding is equivalent to prepend and append zeros to the shifted spectral sequence. `fftshift` is then applied to obtain a sequence that can be inverse transformed by `ifft` to get back the interpolated spatial sequence. The MATLAB Listing 5.1.3 demonstrates an alternative way to implement the Fourier domain zero padding interpolation algorithm, which, with the readers' imagination, will soon discover that there exist a lot of different algorithmic implementations for the Fourier domain zero padding interpolation method. Coming back to the DFT zero padding interpolation artifacts, the high frequency ripples due to boundary mismatch. There are a few ways to alleviate this prob-

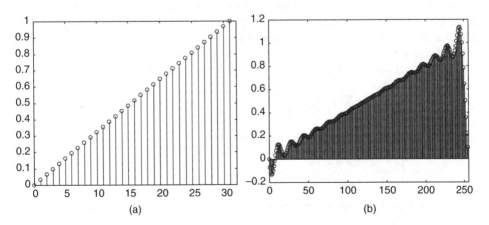

Figure 5.5 Illustration of heavy oscillations (ringing) at the borders of the DFT zero-padded interpolated signal: (a) the original ramp signal with 32 uniformly sampled samples and (b) the 8× interpolated ramp signal.

lem, and the most fundamental solution is to eliminate the boundary mismatch through boundary extension method as discussed in Section 2.4.1.

MATLAB 5.1.3—An 8× interpolation of a discrete ramp by DFT zero padding.

```
>> N=32; K=8*N;
>> t=linspace(0,N-1,N);         % low-resolution indices
>> t1=linspace(0,K-1,K);        % high-resolution indices
>> x=t./(N-1);                  % discrete ramp
>> y=fftshift(fft(x));
>> xstart = floor(K/2)-floor(N/2)+1;
>> xend = floor(K/2)+floor(N/2);
>> out_pad=zeros(1,K);          % create a length K zero vector
>> out_pad(xstart:xend)=y;      % embed the low-resolution DFT vector
>> out=8*ifft(ifftshift(out_pad));
>> figure(1);stem(t,x);         % Figure 5.5(a)
>> figure(2),stem(t1,out);      % Figure 5.5(b)
```

5.2 Discrete Cosine Transform

In Section 2.4.1, we have discussed a number of methods to alleviate the boundary effect in image filtering through boundary extension. The boundary extension by mirror reflection is considered to be the most efficient way. The DFT of signal sequence that has been extended to double its length by mirror reflection will reduce to be the *discrete cosine transform* (DCT) signal sequence. The mirroring operation will eliminate all signal boundary discontinuities, and thus the nonstationary high frequency noise propagation problem is alleviated. Depending on the type of extensions (symmetrical or antisymmetrical; whole-point or half-point symmetric), there are four different types of DCTs. In this book, we shall consider the *type II DCT*, which can be computed using only real arithmetic instead of complex arithmetic as required by DFT. Without causing any ambiguity, we shall refer the *type II DCT* as DCT in the rest of this book. The 1D DCT of a signal with N samples as defined by Ahmed et al. [2] is given by

$$F[v] = \sqrt{\frac{2}{N}}c[v] \sum_{\ell=0}^{N-1} f[\ell] \cos\left(\frac{\pi(2\ell+1)v}{2N}\right), \quad 0 \leqslant v \leqslant N-1, \tag{5.16}$$

where c is the normalization factor and is given by

$$c[v] = \begin{cases} \frac{1}{\sqrt{2}}, & \text{for } v = 0, \\ 1, & \text{otherwise.} \end{cases} \tag{5.17}$$

It is easy to extract the transform kernel of the 1D DCT from Eq. (5.16) as

$$C[v, \ell] = \begin{cases} \frac{1}{\sqrt{N}}, & \text{for } v = 0, \ 0 \leqslant \ell \leqslant N-1, \\ \sqrt{\frac{2}{N}} \cos\left(\frac{\pi(2\ell+1)v}{2N}\right), & \text{for } 1 \leqslant v \leqslant N-1, \ 0 \leqslant \ell \leqslant N-1. \end{cases} \tag{5.18}$$

The MATLAB Listing 5.2.1 listed the source code that constructs the DCT transform kernel matrix $C = [C[v, \ell]]$, or simply known as the DCT matrix, where the forward and backward transforms can be obtained by performing matrix multiplications between C and C^{-1} to the input signal vectors.

MATLAB 5.2.1—Length N DCT kernel.

```
function c=dctkernel(N)
  for v=0:N-1 for l=0:N-1
    if (v==0) c(v+1,l+1)=sqrt(1/N);
    else c(v+1,l+1)=sqrt(2/N)*cos(((2*l+1)*pi*v)/(2*N));
end; end; end; return;
```

The MATLAB has a built-in fast DCT function, dct, with complexity $N \log_2 N$ for length N 1D signal sequence [37]. The $N \times N$ DCT matrix C can also be obtained through MATLAB built-in functions, such as dct(eye(N)) or dctmtx(N). Consider the vector set $\phi_C[v] = C[v, :]$ with $0 \leqslant v \leqslant N - 1$, such that the DCT matrix C can be written as

$$C = \left[\begin{array}{ccc} \phi_C[0] & \cdots & \phi_C[N-1] \end{array} \right]^T. \tag{5.19}$$

It is easy to show that the vector set ϕ_C forms an *orthonormal set*, that is, the dot product, or inner product, of any pair of the transform kernel vectors equals 1 if and only if $v_1 = v_2$. Otherwise, the dot product equals zero.

$$\phi_C[v_1]^T \cdot \phi_C[v_2] = \sum_{n=0}^{N-1} C[v_1, n]C[v_2, n] = \left\{ \begin{array}{ll} 1, & \text{when } v_1 = v_2, \\ 0, & \text{otherwise.} \end{array} \right. \tag{5.20}$$

In other words,

$$\phi_C[v_1]^T \cdot \phi_C[v_2] = \delta(v_1, v_2). \tag{5.21}$$

Since the 1D DCT is orthogonal, the signal vector $f[n]$ can be recovered by multiplying the transform vector $F[v]$ to the transpose of C, which is equivalent to

$$f[n] = \sum_{v=0}^{N-1} c[v]F[v] \cos\left(\frac{\pi(2n+1)v}{2N}\right), \quad 0 \leqslant n \leqslant N - 1. \tag{5.22}$$

The DCT can be extended to 2D in a similar manner as that of 2D DFT. The mathematical formula to obtain the 2D forward DCT $F[u, v]$ from $f[m, n]$ with block size $M \times N$ is given by

$$F[u, v] = \frac{2}{\sqrt{MN}} c[u]c[v] \sum_{n=0}^{N-1} \sum_{m=0}^{M-1} f[m, n] \cos\left(\frac{\pi(2n+1)v}{2N}\right) \cos\left(\frac{\pi(2m+1)u}{2M}\right), \tag{5.23}$$

for $u = 0, 1, \ldots, M - 1$ and $v = 0, 1, \ldots, N - 1$. It is vivid from Eq. (5.23) that the 2D DCT is dimensional separable and can be written as

$$F[u, v] = \sqrt{\frac{2}{M}} c[u] \sum_{m=0}^{M-1} \left\{ \sqrt{\frac{2}{N}} c(v) \sum_{n=0}^{N-1} f[m, n] \cos\left(\frac{\pi(2n+1)v}{2N}\right) \right\}$$
$$\times \cos\left(\frac{\pi(2m+1)u}{2M}\right). \tag{5.24}$$

The 2D *inverse discrete cosine transform* (IDCT) is computed in a similar fashion as

$$f[m, n] = \sqrt{\frac{2}{N}} \sum_{v=0}^{N-1} c[v] \left\{ \frac{2}{\sqrt{M}} \sum_{u=0}^{M-1} c(u) F[u, v] \cos \left(\frac{\pi(2m + 1)u}{2M} \right) \right\}$$
$$\times \cos \left(\frac{\pi(2n + 1)v}{2N} \right). \tag{5.25}$$

In matrix computation, the 2D DCT transformed signal array $\mathbf{F}$ can be obtained by applying the 1D DCT independently to the two directions of the signal array f with appropriate transposition of the intermediate result as

$$\mathbf{F} = C(Cf^T)^T = CfC^T. \tag{5.26}$$

When implemented in MATLAB, the 2D DCT can be obtained via F=dct (dct (f')'), which will return the 2D DCT signal matrix F from the 2D signal matrix f.

Besides free from boundary distortion, and the availability of fast algorithm, there is one more reason why we choose to discuss DCT in this book. This is because natural image signals process high correlations among neighboring pixels, allowing them to be accurately modeled as first-order Markov sources [51]. The DCT is well known to be a nearly optimal representation of such signals in which most of the transform coefficients have magnitude close to zero, demonstrating the property of high energy compaction. Consequently, the DCT is commonly used in many image and video compression algorithms, including many international standards, such as JPEG, MPEG, ITU/T H.261, H.263, etc. The better energy compaction property of the DCT does allow us to develop better image interpolation algorithm than that of other orthogonal transform algorithm.

5.2.1 DCT Zero Padding Interpolation

Since the DCT is a type of DFT with a special preprocessing step, it is not surprising to make a wild guess that the spatial signal can be interpolated by considering the IDCT of a zero-padded DCT signal sequence. To understand how zero padding in DCT domain can interpolate a discrete signal sequence, we first present the DCT signal interpolation Theorem 5.1.

Theorem 5.1 *The function*

$$g_N(x) = \frac{1}{\sqrt{N}} F[0] + \sqrt{\frac{2}{N}} \sum_{k=1}^{N-1} F[k] \cos \frac{k(2x + 1)\pi}{2N}, \tag{5.27}$$

with $x \in \mathbb{R}$ and $F = Cf$ where $f \in \mathbb{R}_{N,1}$ and $F \in \mathbb{R}_{N,1}$, satisfies

$$g_N(n) = f[n], \quad \text{for } n = 0, \dots, N - 1. \tag{5.28}$$

Theorem 5.1 implies $g_N(x)$ is the analog function that interpolates the data set $(0, f[0])$, $(1, f[1])$, ..., $(N - 1, f[N - 1])$, such that $g_N(x)$ passes through all N points $(\ell, f[\ell])$, $\forall \ell \in [0, N - 1]$. This observation can be easily proven by considering

$$g_N(0) = \frac{1}{\sqrt{N}}F[0] + \sqrt{\frac{2}{N}}\sum_{k=1}^{N-1}F[k]\cos\frac{k\pi}{2N}, \qquad (5.29)$$

$$g_N(1) = \frac{1}{\sqrt{N}}F[0] + \sqrt{\frac{2}{N}}\sum_{k=1}^{N-1}F[k]\cos\frac{3k\pi}{2N}, \qquad (5.30)$$

$$\vdots \quad \vdots \qquad \vdots$$

$$g_N(N-1) = \frac{1}{\sqrt{N}}F[0] + \sqrt{\frac{2}{N}}\sum_{k=1}^{N-1}F[k]\cos\frac{k(2N-1)\pi}{2N}, \qquad (5.31)$$

which are exactly the same as the equation that defines $g_N(x)$ in Eq. (5.27). Furthermore, the above system of equations can be written as

$$\begin{bmatrix} g_N(0) \\ \vdots \\ g_N(N-1) \end{bmatrix} = C^T \begin{bmatrix} F[0] \\ \vdots \\ F([N-1]) \end{bmatrix} = C^T F = f = \begin{bmatrix} f[0] \\ \vdots \\ f[N-1] \end{bmatrix}, \qquad (5.32)$$

where we use the orthogonality property of $F = Cf$, which implies $f = C^T F$. An application of Theorem 5.1 is shown in Example 5.1, which demonstrates how to construct a 1D continuous function from the given discrete signal pairs.

Example 5.1 Consider the DCT interpolation of the following points in the $X - Y$ plane.

$$(0, 2), \ (1, 0), \ (2, -1), \ (3, 0), \ (4, 0.25), \ (5, -1.5), \ (6, -2).$$

The DCT transform with $N = 7$ of the vector

$$f = [2, \ 0, -1, \ 0, \ 0.25, -1.5, -2]^T \qquad (5.33)$$

yields the transform coefficient vector

$$F = Cf = [-0.8504, \ 2.4214, \ 0.0715, \ 1.9751, \ 0.8116, -0.3764, \ 0.1387]^T. \qquad (5.34)$$

Theorem 5.1 provides a particular interpolated function of f as

$$g_7(x) = \frac{1}{\sqrt{7}}(-0.8504) + \sqrt{\frac{2}{7}}\left[2.4214\cos\frac{(2x+1)\pi}{14} + 0.0715\cos\frac{2(2x+1)\pi}{14}\right.$$

$$+1.9751\cos\frac{3(2x+1)\pi}{14} + 0.8116\cos\frac{4(2x+1)\pi}{14}$$

$$\left.-0.3764\cos\frac{5(2x+1)\pi}{14} + 0.1387\cos\frac{6(2x+1)\pi}{14}\right]. \qquad (5.35)$$

The interpolated function $g_7(x)$ is a combination of seven cosine basis functions.

In terms of linear algebra, the DCT interpolation is nothing else but expressing $g_N(x)$ as a unique linear combination of N cosine basis functions of increasing frequencies (the first term $\frac{1}{\sqrt{N}}F[0]$ corresponds to cosine of zero frequency (or the DC term)), weighted

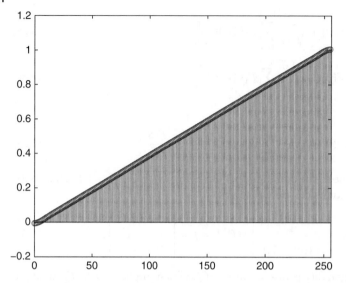

Figure 5.6 The 8× interpolated signal of the ramp signal shown in Figure 5.5a by zero-padded DCT. Note the missing high frequency oscillations at the borders in the interpolated ramp signal compared with the one shown in Figure 5.5b.

by appropriate transform coefficients. On the other hand, the DCT kernel is so special that the zero-padded DCT interpolation processes some nice properties that cannot be found in its revival, zero-padded DFT. Shown in Figure 5.6 is the IDCT result of the zero-padded DCT signal sequence obtained by MATLAB Listing 5.2.2.

MATLAB 5.2.2—An 8× interpolation of a discrete ramp by DCT zero padding.

```
>> N=32; K=8*N;
>> t=linspace(0,N-1,N);      % low-resolution indices
>> t1=linspace(0,K-1,K);     % high-resolution indices
>> x=t./(N-1);
>> y=dct(x);
>> out=8*idct([y zeros(1,K-N)]); %idct of a zero-padded low-
   resolution sequence
>> figure(2),stem(t1,out);   % Figure 5.6
```

It is vivid from Figure 5.6 that the signal oscillation (ringing) problem around the boundaries of the interpolated ramp signal, as observed in Figure 5.5b obtained from DFT zero padding interpolation, has been alleviated. This very nice signal boundary handling capability, together with the availability of fast DCT, and many other properties made DCT to be the most frequently used transform in image processing applications, such as JPEG image compression standard. The existence of the JPEG image storage format is also a vivid demonstration that there are more images stored in your computer in their transform domain representation than that in spatial domain.

The 1D DCT interpolation is readily extendible to 2D by the following 2D DCT interpolation theorem for a 2D signal with size $M \times N$.

Theorem 5.2 *The function*

$$g_N(x,y) = \frac{2}{\sqrt{M \times N}} \sum_{k=0}^{M-1} \sum_{\ell=1}^{N-1} F[k,\ell] a_k a_\ell \cos \frac{k(2x+1)\pi}{2M} \cos \frac{\ell(2y+1)\pi}{2N}, \quad (5.36)$$

with

$$a_k = \begin{cases} 1/\sqrt{2}, & k = 0, \\ 1, & k > 0, \end{cases} \quad (5.37)$$

and $F = CfC^T$, satisfies

$$g_N(m,n) = f[m,n], \quad \text{for } m = 0,\ldots,M-1, \text{ and } n = 0,\ldots,N-1. \quad (5.38)$$

Theorem 5.2 implies that $g_N(x,y)$ is an analog function that interpolates the data $(f[m,n])$, for $m = 0,1,\ldots,M-1$, and $n = 0,1,\ldots,N-1$. An application of this theorem is shown in Example 5.2, which demonstrates how to construct a continuous 2D function from the given discrete signal array f.

Example 5.2 Consider the 2D DCT transform of the data

$$f = \begin{bmatrix} 1.0 & 0.8 & 1.0 & 1.0 & 0.8 & 1.0 \\ 1.0 & 0.5 & 0.3 & 0.0 & 0.5 & 1.0 \\ 1.0 & 0.3 & 0.2 & 0.0 & 0.3 & 1.0 \\ 1.0 & 0.2 & 0.0 & 0.0 & 0.2 & 1.0 \\ 1.0 & 0.3 & 0.2 & 0.0 & 0.3 & 1.0 \\ 1.0 & 0.8 & 1.0 & 1.0 & 0.8 & 1.0 \end{bmatrix}, \quad (5.39)$$

which yields

$$F = \begin{bmatrix} 3.7500 & 0.0427 & 1.4901 & -0.1167 & 0.6010 & 0.1594 \\ 0.1077 & 0.0106 & -0.0354 & -0.0289 & -0.0911 & 0.0394 \\ 1.2247 & -0.0149 & -0.9500 & 0.0408 & -0.0866 & -0.0558 \\ -0.1500 & -0.0183 & 0.0612 & 0.0500 & 0.1061 & -0.0683 \\ 0.4950 & -0.0345 & -0.4619 & 0.0943 & 0.100 & -0.1288 \\ 0.0077 & 0.0106 & -0.0354 & -0.0289 & 0.0503 & 0.0394 \end{bmatrix}. \quad (5.40)$$

Theorem 5.2 implies that the interpolated function $g_6(x,y)$ is given by

$$g_6(x,y) = \frac{2}{6} \left[\frac{1}{2}(3.75) + \frac{1}{\sqrt{2}}(0.0427) \cos \frac{(2x+1)\pi}{12} + \frac{1}{\sqrt{2}}(1.4901) \right.$$

$$\times \cos \frac{2(2x+1)\pi}{12} + \cdots + \frac{1}{\sqrt{2}}(0.0503) \cos \frac{5(2x+1)\pi}{16} \cos \frac{4(2y+1)\pi}{16}$$

$$\left. + \frac{1}{\sqrt{2}}(0.0394) \cos \frac{5(2x+1)\pi}{16} \cos \frac{5(2y+1)\pi}{16} \right]. \quad (5.41)$$

5.3 DCT Zero Padding Image Interpolation

The 2D DCT interpolation Theorem 5.2 suggested the application of zero padding in DCT domain to perform image interpolation. Besides the reduced computational complexity of being a real value transformation, unlike the DFT zero padding interpolation, image interpolation by means of DCT spectral zero padding does not need to worry about signal symmetry. As a result, the interpolation of a $M \times N$ image f is just as simple as inversely transform the DCT transformed image $F = C_{M \times M} f_{M \times N} C_{N \times N}^T$ with zero padding.

$$g_{2M \times 2N} = C_{2M \times 2M}^T G_{2M \times 2N} C_{2N \times 2N},$$

$$= C_{2M \times 2M}^T \begin{pmatrix} 2C_{M \times M} f_{M \times N} C_{N \times N}^T & \mathbf{0} \\ \mathbf{0} & \mathbf{0} \end{pmatrix} C_{2N \times 2N}. \qquad (5.42)$$

A MATLAB source that zero pads a matrix F from size of $M \times N$ to the matrix G with size of $2M \times 2N$ is given in Listing 5.3.1 (i.e. the MATLAB implementation of the formation of $G_{2M \times 2N}$ from $f_{M \times N}$ in Eq. (5.42)). Note that the multiplication of 2 in Eq. (5.42) and in Listing 5.3.1 helps to preserve the DC values of the low-resolution and the high-resolution images, which is equivalent to the preservation of the average brightness of the two images.

> **MATLAB 5.3.1—Zero padding a [M,N] block F to a [2M,2N] block G.**
>
> ```
> function G=zeropad2(F)
>   [M,N]=size(F);
>   G=[2*F zeros(M,N); zeros(M,2*N)];
> return;
> ```

There are several advantages of the DCT-based zero padding image interpolation. Firstly, the low frequency components of the low-resolution image are preserved in the interpolated image, thus preserving the smoothness of the image. Secondly, this technique can be naturally used when images are represented in a compressed form, which is in the DCT domain, such as in the case of JPEG. In this case, interpolation can be carried out without the need to decompress the images. However, even with fast DCT algorithm, performing image interpolation by whole image transformation is prohibitively time consuming. This is the same reason why the image compression standard JPEG does not perform whole image transformation. Instead, JPEG resorts to process the image by subdividing it into many non-overlapping small 8×8 blocks and process each block separately. This block-based image processing not only achieves an affordable computational complexity, but it also poses a lot of nice features that alleviate various image processing difficulties. The block-based image processing and the related interpolation methods will be discussed in the sequel.

5.3.1 Blocked Transform

Discrete orthogonal transforms, such as DFT and DCT, can be applied to signal either globally to all available signal samples at once or block-wise (locally) through

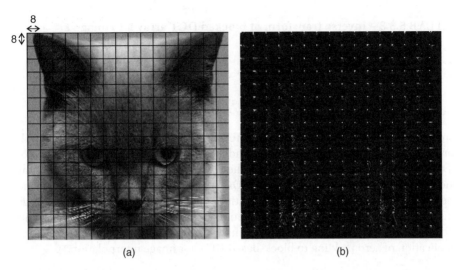

8 ↔

8 ↕

(a)   (b)

Figure 5.7 (a) Subdividing the cat image into non-overlapping 8 × 8 blocks. (b) Plots of the DCT coefficients of each 8 × 8 transformation.

non-overlap sliding window. The block-based transform subdivides the input image into blocks, and the corresponding transform is applied to individual blocks as shown in Figure 5.7. Among all available block sizes, the eight-point DCT is typically used in practice. This is because the 8 × 8 points DCT can achieve a balance between computational complexity and overall image quality performance. Having said that it does not mean other block sizes should not be used, nor cannot achieve good interpolation results. Actually the block size problem will be investigated in Section 5.3.2.1. In the meantime, an example of a size 128 × 128 *Cat* image (smaller size is chosen in the example to allow more clear image partitioning to be plotted in the book figures) is being divided into non-overlapping blocks with size of 8 × 8 as shown in Figure 5.7a. When the 8 × 8 DCT is applied to each block in Figure 5.7a by Listing 5.3.2 with the MATLAB command `blockproc`, the transformed image is shown in Figure 5.7b. Unlike Listing 5.1.2 that makes use of `for` loop to compute the DFT of the image, the vectorization of operations brought forward by `blockproc` will result in 3× to 6× speedup in computation (depending on the capability of the processor running MATLAB).

MATLAB 5.3.2—Forward 8 × 8 DCT block processing of image array f.

```
function F = blockdct(f,L)
   dct = @(x) dct2(x.data);
   F = blockproc(double(f),[L L],dct);
return;
```

It should be noted that L is the block size and f is the input image. The image in Figure 5.7b is obtained with F=blockdct(f,8). The original image can be obtained from the forward DCT block-transformed image matrix F by the IDCT transform MATLAB code in Listing 5.3.3.

> **MATLAB 5.3.3—Inverse transform of blocked DCT array F to image f.**
>
> ```
> >> L = 8;
> >> c = dctkernel(L);
> >> F = blockdct(f,L);
> >> idct = @(x) (c')*x.data*(c);
> >> f = blockproc(double(F),[L L],idct);
> ```

Noted that there are built-in 2D IDCT, idct2, function in MATLAB. However, the vector-matrix multiplication methods are adopted in Listing 5.3.3 to illustrate how the IDCT coefficients can be derived from the DCT coefficients matrix, further showing the block-based operation nature of the DCT. This provides the necessary interface for the implementation of the later interpolation functions. One of the best advantages of block-based transformation is the reduction in computational complexity, which enables the widespread of transform-based image processing. The next section presents the application of zero padding to block-based DCT for image interpolation.

5.3.2 Block-Based DCT Zero Padding Interpolation

In this section, we shall discuss interpolation based on block transformation following the computation steps depicted in Figure 5.8. In this example, the *Cat* image is block transformed with block size 8×8. Each block is zero padded to a size of 16×16 before inverse block transformed to the spatial domain. The MATLAB code Listing 5.3.4 makes use of Listing 5.3.2 to obtain the DCT block-transformed image array and applies the zero padding function zeropad2 in Listing 5.3.1 to perform the zero padding block-based DCT image interpolation with block size L.

> **MATLAB 5.3.4—Interpolating image f by subdividing into $L \times L$ blocks and DCT zero padding.**
>
> ```
> function g=dctx2(f,L)
>   L2 = L*2;
>   dctL = @(x) dct2(x.data);
>   F = blockproc(double(f), [L L], dctL);
>   zp = @(x) zeropad2(x.data);
>   G = blockproc(F, [L L], zp);
>   idctL2 = @(x) idct2(x.data);
>   g = blockproc(G, [L2 L2], idctL2);
> return;
> ```

The dctx2 function makes use of the MATLAB fast 2D DCT commands dct2 and idct2 to achieve forward and IDCT. Furthermore, it also makes use of the blockproc vectorization operation to speed up the computation. The image g obtained from the interpolation function g=dctx2(f,8) (MATLAB Listing 5.3.4) is an array with double entries. It will have to be quantized to uint8 before it can be displayed and be called as a digital image. At the same time, we should also note that the dct2 and zero-padded idct2 operations cannot achieve perfect interpolation results due to numerical errors in the course of computation. Such numerical errors can be corrected by post-processing, which includes converting all negative values in g to zero, and normalizing the interpolated image to have the same dynamic range as

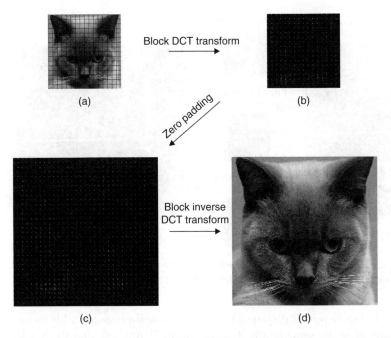

Figure 5.8 Framework of the zero-padded DCT interpolation of an image: (a) subdividing the *Cat* image into 8 × 8 blocks, (b) applying 2D DCT to each of the 8 × 8 block, (c) zero-padded 2D DCT spectral image each block from size of 16 × 16 to form the interpolated image in spectral domain, and (d) converting the spectral image in (c) back into a 2× interpolated image in spatial domain by inverse DCT with block size 16 × 16.

that of the low-resolution image f, and hence the MATLAB brightness normalization function brightnorm as listed Listing 5.3.5 is developed. The interpolated image g after the application of g=brightnorm(f,g) is displayed in Figure 5.8d with the MATLAB command imshow(uint8(g)).

MATLAB 5.3.5—Normalizing the dynamic range of the 2× interpolated image g to be the same as that of the low-resolution image f.

```
function ng =  brightnorm(f,g)
  [Lmax MaxInd] = max(f(:));
  [mmax, nmax] = ind2sub(size(f),MaxInd);
  [Lmin MinInd] = min(f(:));
  [mmin, nmin] = ind2sub(size(f),MinInd);
  fmax = Lmax;
  fmin = Lmin;
  gmax = max(max(g(1:2:end,1:2:end)));
  gmin = min(min(g(1:2:end,1:2:end)));
  if gmin<0
    gmin =0;
  end;
  g(g<0)=0;
  scale = (fmax-fmin)/(gmax-gmin);
  ng = (g-gmin)*scale+fmin;
  ng = ng*(mean(mean(f))/(mean(mean(ng))));
end
```

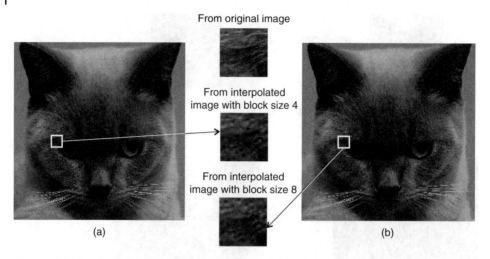

Figure 5.9 (a) Image doubling by zero padding 4×4 and (b) with 8×8 DCT block *Cat* image; the zoom-in sub-images are displayed in the middle together with that from the original high-resolution image.

The same image in Figure 5.8d is displayed in Figure 5.9b again together with zoom-in sub-image displayed in the same figure. It is vivid from Figure 5.9b that the block-processed interpolated image has the blocking artifacts as discussed in Section 3.1.5. This artifact is the result of the independent treatment of individual image block in block transformation, hence causing pixel intensity differences along the borders of adjacent image blocks. It is vivid to observe the blocking artifacts in the zoom-in sub-image shown in Figure 5.9. This is a huge drawback of the block-based transform domain image interpolation algorithm, despite the fact that it is also an effective way to achieve stationary for better transform domain-based image interpolation results. Radical solution to the blocking artifact problem will be discussed in the sequel, while image interpolation method that completely alleviates the blocking artifact problem will be discussed in Chapter 6 with the application of wavelet transform.

Besides the blocking artifacts, the interpolated image in Figure 5.9b is observed to be blurred in texture-rich area or should we say lack of high frequency components. This is the direct results of using zero values to estimate the high frequency DCT coefficients of the interpolated image. The interpolated image quality can only be rescued by adopting methods that provide better high frequency DCT coefficients estimation or at least generate some pseudo-high frequency DCT coefficients for the interpolated image.

5.3.2.1 Does Kernel Size Matter

Transform analysis based on global information is not adequate for the study of compact or local patterns. A windowed transform, such as the short-time Fourier transform introduced by Gabor (1946) using a sliding Gaussian window, has shown to be an effective tool for investigating the spatial and frequency relation of signal. Since stationary is assumed within the window, therefore, the smaller the window size, the better is the spatial resolution; however, the smaller the window size, the less the discrete frequencies that can be represented, thus weakening the discrimination potential among frequencies. The choice of window is thus leading to an uncertain trade-off. The same discussions also apply to the block size in other block-based transform domain image interpolation methods.

Let us consider the interpolation result of zero-padded DCT with 4×4 block obtained from g=dctx2(f,4), which is shown in Figure 5.9a. The zoom-in sub-image of Figure 5.9a is also shown in the same figure together with that obtained from 8×8 block-based zero-padded DCT interpolated image in Figure 5.9b. It is vivid that more details can be observed from the zoom-in part of the corner of the eye of the *Cat* image in Figure 5.9a; the interpolated image obtained from 4×4 block-based DCT interpolation is less blocky when compared with that in Figure 5.9b obtained from 8×8 block-based DCT interpolation. Analytically this can be understood by considering four adjacent 4×4 DCT blocks interpolated by zero padding to four 8×8 blocks, such that the four blocks will form a 16×16 spatial block of the interpolated *Cat* image and are given by

$$
g_{16\times16} = \begin{bmatrix} C_{8\times8}^T \begin{pmatrix} 2C_{4\times4}f_{1,4\times4}C_{4\times4}^T & \mathbf{0}_{4\times4} \\ \mathbf{0}_{4\times4} & \mathbf{0}_{4\times4} \end{pmatrix} C_{8\times8} & C_{8\times8}^T \begin{pmatrix} 2C_{4\times4}f_{2,4\times4}C_{4\times4}^T & \mathbf{0}_{4\times4} \\ \mathbf{0}_{4\times4} & \mathbf{0}_{4\times4} \end{pmatrix} C_{8\times8} \\ C_{8\times8}^T \begin{pmatrix} 2C_{4\times4}f_{3,4\times4}C_{4\times4}^T & \mathbf{0}_{4\times4} \\ \mathbf{0}_{4\times4} & \mathbf{0}_{4\times4} \end{pmatrix} C_{8\times8} & C_{8\times8}^T \begin{pmatrix} 2C_{4\times4}f_{4,4\times4}C_{4\times4}^T & \mathbf{0}_{4\times4} \\ \mathbf{0}_{4\times4} & \mathbf{0}_{4\times4} \end{pmatrix} C_{8\times8} \end{bmatrix}
$$

$$
= \begin{bmatrix} g_{00} & g_{01} \\ g_{10} & g_{11} \end{bmatrix}. \tag{5.43}
$$

A 16×16 DCT transformed block can be easily obtained by multiplication of $C_{16\times16}$ and its transpose on both sides of $g_{16\times16}$ because of the dimension separable property. If we further partition $C_{16\times16} = \left[\begin{array}{c|c} A & B \\ \hline C & D \end{array} \right]$, we shall obtain

$$
G_{16\times16} = C_{16\times16} \begin{bmatrix} g_{00} & g_{01} \\ g_{10} & g_{11} \end{bmatrix} C_{16\times16}^T
$$

$$
= \begin{bmatrix} A & B \\ C & D \end{bmatrix} \begin{bmatrix} g_{00} & g_{01} \\ g_{10} & g_{11} \end{bmatrix} \begin{bmatrix} A^T & C^T \\ B^T & D^T \end{bmatrix}
$$

$$
= \begin{bmatrix} Ag_{00}A^T + Bg_{10}A^T + Ag_{01}B^T + Bg_{11}B^T \\ Cg_{00}A^T + Dg_{10}A^T + Cg_{01}B^T + Dg_{11}B^T \end{bmatrix}
$$

$$
\begin{bmatrix} Ag_{00}C^T + Bg_{10}C^T + Ag_{01}D^T + Bg_{11}D^T \\ Cg_{00}C^T + Dg_{10}C^T + Cg_{01}D^T + Dg_{11}D^T \end{bmatrix}.
$$

It is vivid from the above derivation that the high frequency components in the 16×16 DCT block obtained from zero padding DCT with 4×4 blocks are not exactly zeros as opposed to that obtained from the zero padding of an 8×8 DCT block-transformed image [25]. This makes marginal improvement in the quality of the interpolated image as observed in the high frequency areas (the whiskers) of the *Cat* image. On the other hand, the texture-rich area of the interpolated *Cat* image obtained from the zero-padded DCT with block size 4×4 is shown to be blurred when compared with that obtained by the zero-padded 8×8 blocked DCT interpolation as shown in Figure 5.9b. This is because the small block size DCT has limited spectral resolution and hence does not interpolate middle frequency components that well, which will lead to blurring as observed in Figure 5.9a.

At this point, the readers may also consider the fact that most images are stored in the transform domain using DCT with block size 8×8. As a result, it is natural to use zero padding DCT interpolation with block size 8×8. However, we should point out that when there is a need, new algorithm will be invented. It has been shown in [48] that there exists fast algorithm to compute the 4×4 DCT blocks, directly from the 8×8

block-transformed JPEG images. As a result, the computational complexity is not the major consideration; it should be the quality of the interpolated image being the major issue in determining the transformation block size.

5.4 Overlapping

When using zero-padded block-based transformation to interpolate images, the main problem is the blocking artifacts. The blocking artifact is observed to behave like random white noise in nature but is translation variant. In other words, the blocking error depends on where the blocks are extracted from the image to perform the transformation and then the interpolation (through zero padding in transform domain). This space-variant property suggests a method to alleviate the blocking artifacts through averaging interpolated images obtained from blocks that do not have aligned block boundaries. To illustrate how to make use of the space-variant property of the block transformation, Figure 5.10 shows four different partitioning methods that can be applied to the *Cat* image.

The first partition in Figure 5.10a is the same as that studied in previous section, which we shall call "non-shifted image" f. The other three images in Figure 5.10 are obtained with the partition boundary shifted horizontally, vertically, and diagonally, as shown in Figure 5.10b–d. They are known as the "horizontal shift" (F_1), "vertical shift" (F_2), and "diagonal shift" (F_3), respectively. The horizontally shifted image is obtained by discarding the first $\frac{L}{2}$ and the last $\frac{L}{2}$ columns by the MATLAB function npart, where $L \times L$ is the block size for the transform under concern.

> **MATLAB 5.4.1—Return an image with the first L/2 and last L/2 columns discarded.**
>
> ```
> function nf=npart(f,L)
>   [M,N]=size(f);
>   n=L/2;
>   nf = f(1:M,n+1:N-n);
> return;
> ```

Similarly, the vertically shifted image F_2 as shown in Figure 5.10c is obtained with the MATLAB function mpart.

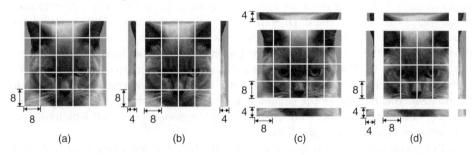

(a) (b) (c) (d)

Figure 5.10 Illustration of different block partition methods: (a) the original "non-shifted" image f, (b) the "horizontal shifted" image F_1, (c) the "vertical shifted" image F_2, and (d) the "diagonal shifted" image F_3.

MATLAB 5.4.2—Return an image with the first L/2 and last L/2 rows discarded.

```
function mf=mpart(f,L)
  [M,N]=size(f);
  n=L/2;
  mf = f(n+1:M-n,1:N);
return;
```

Finally, the diagonally shifted image F_3 as shown in Figure 5.10d is obtained with the MATLAB function dpart.

MATLAB 5.4.3—Return an image with the first L/2 and last L/2 columns and the first L/2 and last L/2 rows discarded.

```
function df=dpart(f,L)
  [M,N]=size(f);
  n=L/2;
  df = f(n+1:M-n,n+1:N-n);
return;
```

The images shown in Figure 5.10 can be obtained by invoking the functions npart, mpart, and dpart with L=8 for the 8 × 8 blocked transform. To properly display the shifted image and to facilitate the subsequent operations in the overlap and average strategy, the final size of the shifted image is rectified to be the same as that of the non-shifted image F_0 with the missing pixel values being padded with pixel values of 255 to give the final shifted images ngp, mgp, and dgp in Figure 5.10b–d, respectively. The MATLAB implementation is shown in Listing 5.4.4.

MATLAB 5.4.4—Generation of final shifted images ngp, mgp, and dgp in Figure 5.10b–d.

```
>> L=8;
>> n=L/2;
>> [M N] = size(f);

>> g = 255.*(M,N);
>> F1 = npart(f,L);    % prepare images
>> F2 = mpart(f,L);
>> F3 = dpart(f,L);

>> ngp = [g(1:M,1:n) F1 g(1:M,N-n+1:N)];    % render to be the same
     size as f
>> mgp = [g(1:n,1:N); F2; g(M-n+1:M,1:N)];
>> dgp = [g(1:n,1:N); g(n+1:M-n,1:n) F3 g(n:M-n-1,N-n+1:N);
     g(M-n+1:M,1:N)];
```

All images f, F_1, F_2, and F_3 will be interpolated by zero-padded DCT interpolation to give gF0, gF1, gF2, and gF3 through the MATLAB operation shown in Listing 5.4.5, and Figure 5.11a–d displays a portion of the zoom-in interpolated images of gF0, gF1, gF2, and gF3, respectively. It should be noted that the zoom-in region is the same region as investigated in Figure 5.9. The interpolated images gF1, gF2, and gF3 are rendered to be the same size as that of the interpolated "non-shifted" images gF0 by replacing the missing pixels in gF1, gF2, and gF3 with that from gF0 to generate the padded images gF1p, gF2p, and gF3p, respectively. The following MATLAB source performs the above operations to obtain each padded interpolated image from the four images obtained with different partitioning schemes. Noted that the final image of the shifted images is rectified by defining those missing pixels by direct copying the pixel values from the corresponding pixel locations in the non-shifted image.

MATLAB 5.4.5—Generation of 2× zero-padded DCT interpolated images gF0p, gF1p, gF2p, and gF3p, where all images are rectified to have same final image size.

```
% Initialize baseline image and parameters
>> L=8; blksize = 8;

>> F1 = npart(f,L);          % prepare images
>> F2 = mpart(f,L);
>> F3 = dpart(f,L);

>> gF0 = dctx2(f,blksize);   % zero padded DCT interpolation
>> gF1 = dctx2(F1,blksize);
>> gF2 = dctx2(F2,blksize);

>> gF3 = dctx2(F3,blksize);
>> gF0p = gF0;
>> gF1p = [gF0(1:M,1:L) gF1 gF0(1:M, N-L+1:N)]; % pad to be the same
   size
>> gF2p = [gF0(1:L,1:N); gF2; gF0(M-L+1:M,1:N)];
>> gF3p = [gF0(1:L,1:N); gF0(L+1:M-L,1:L) gF3 gF0(L:M-L-1,N-L+1:N);
   gF0(M-L+1:M,1:N)];
```

It can be observed in Figure 5.11 that all the interpolated image, whether the low-resolution image is "non-shifted" (Figure 5.11a) or is "shifted" (Figure 5.11b–d),

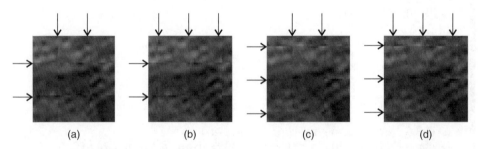

| (a) | (b) | (c) | (d) |

Figure 5.11 The zoom-in portion of the eye of the *Cat* image extracted from the zero-padded DCT interpolated images gF0p, gF1p, gF2p, and gF3p, where the same region is studied in Figure 5.9: (a) the non-shifted interpolated image gF0p, (b) the horizontally shifted interpolated image gF1p, (c) the vertically shifted interpolated image gF2p, and (d) the diagonally shifted interpolated image gF3p.

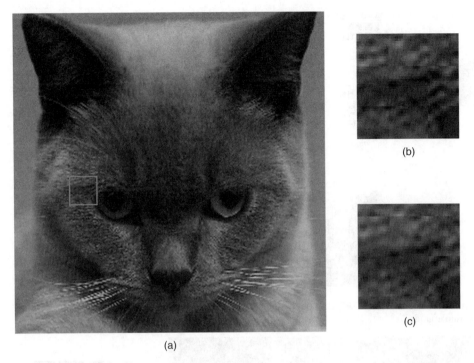

(b)

(c)

(a)

Figure 5.12 Interpolated image obtained from averaging the zero-padded 8 × 8 block DCT interpolation with non-shift and vertically shifted (by four pixels) images: (a) the interpolated image with averaging, (b) the zoom-in image of the interpolated image obtained from the interpolated image of "non-shifted" image, and (c) the zoom-in image of the interpolated image with averaging.

suffered from the blocking artifacts that are common in zero-padded DCT interpolation. However, it is easy to observe that the blocking artifacts are in different spatial locations in all the four images (where the boundaries of the blocks are addressed by the arrows). As a result, if gF2p is padded to the same size as that of gF0p, we can average the vertically shifted one with the non-shifted image by the following MATLAB code:

```
>> g = (gF0p+gF2p)/2;
```

Figure 5.12a shows the averaging result of the non-shifted gF0p and the vertically shifted gF2p, which confirms that the melted image with block boundaries of the two images overlapping one another will greatly improve the image quality. The zoom-in portion of the eye of the *Cat* image extracted from the gF0p (see Figure 5.12b) and that from the averaging result (see Figure 5.12c) is shown for comparison. It can be observed that the blocking artifacts in Figure 5.12c have been reduced and the zoom-in image has shown less blockiness vertically. However, the horizontal blockiness remains the same. This is due to the block locations between the non-shifted and the vertically shifted images that do not align vertically, but do align horizontally. Therefore, the blockiness along the horizontal axis does not improve through this averaging operation. Knowing that implies we shall perform the averaging operation on all four interpolated images

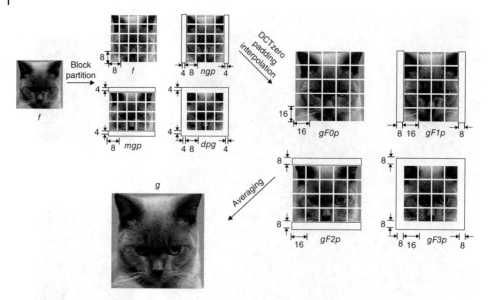

Figure 5.13 Framework of DCT zero padding image interpolation with mean filter applied to multiple overlap images.

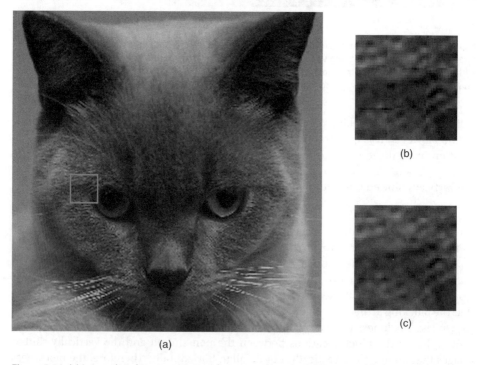

Figure 5.14 (a) Interpolated image obtained from averaging the DCT zero-padded 8×8 block DCT interpolation between non-shifted, vertically shifted, horizontally shifted, and diagonally shifted (by four pixels) images: (a) the interpolated image, (b) the zoom-in image of the selected region taken from the interpolated image of "non-shifted" image, and (c) the same zoom-in image of the selected region taken from the interpolated image shown in (a).

obtained with different shifts as shown in the framework illustrated in Figure 5.13. This operation is also known as applying mean filter between the "non-shifted" and "shifted" images. We shall expect the blocking artifacts , and thus the image quality can be further improved. The following MATLAB code will do the job:

```
>> g = (gF0p+gF1p+gF2p+gF3p)/4;
```

The interpolated images are shown in Figure 5.14, with the zoom-in portion of the same region in Figure 5.9b. It can be observed that the blockiness of the interpolated image has largely suppressed, and the details of the texture-rich regions of the *Cat* image can be maintained. A lot of variations of these schemes can be found in literature. In particular, the lapped transform [33, 45], has widely adopted in various image processing applications. The transform blocks overlap with the neighboring blocks in lapped transform, and thus guaranteed the block boundaries will meet at the same point and alleviated all block boundary discontinuity problems. Before we move to the next section, it should also be noted that the multi-block overlapped interpolation technique is also known as *cyclic-spinning* interpolation in literature, where each different shift of the low-resolution image is considered to be one spin of the original low-resolution image. The cyclic-spinning method will be discussed again in Section 6.3.

5.5 Multi-Kernels

Previous   section has shown the application of mean filtering among multiple interpolated images (averaging among multiple images) with different noise characteristics (in the case of Section 5.4, it is the blocking noise in different spatial locations) that can help to suppress the interpolation artifacts. Can we perform the same trick on groups of interpolated images obtained from other means? The answer to this question is affirmative. We have discussed that the transform domain zero padding image interpolation is applicable to all DFT variants. In this section, we shall discuss extendible IDCT [29], which performs interpolated IDFT over DCT transformed signal. We shall then perform mean filtering on the two interpolated images (zero-padded DCT interpolation and zero-padded DFT interpolation) to enhance the image interpolation results.

5.5.1 Extendible Inverse DCT

The extendible inverse discrete cosine transform (EIDCT) is first proposed in [29] to perform zero-padded DFT interpolation from the DCT coefficients (not from the DFT coefficients). There are several advantages. Firstly, it becomes computationally efficient when the DCT coefficients of the image are available, which is the case in images stored in JPEG file format. Secondly, and also the most important reason, EIDCT can perform zero-padded DFT interpolation with real arithmetic compared with the complex arithmetic required to compute DFT and IDFT. To understand how to derive EIDCT, let us consider the case of interpolating an even length signal sequence $f[k]$ with length L to a length K signal sequence $g[k]$. The interpolation ratio is $r = K/L \in \mathbb{Z}$. The interpolation is to be performed by zero padding in the DFT domain, with the zero-padded DFT signal sequence $G[k]$ given by

$$G[k] = \begin{cases} \frac{K}{L}F[k], & 0 \leqslant k < \frac{L}{2}, \\ 0, & \frac{L}{2} \leqslant k \leqslant K - \frac{L}{2}, \\ \frac{P}{L}F[k+L-K], & K - \frac{L}{2} < k \leqslant K - 1. \end{cases} \tag{5.44}$$

The FFT coefficient $F[k]$ can be represented by its related DCT coefficient $F_C[k]$ as

$$F[k] = \begin{cases} a_k W_{2L}^{-k/2} F_C[k], & 0 \leqslant k \leqslant L-1, \\ 0, & k = L, \\ -a_k W_{2L}^{-k/2} F_C[2L-k], & L+1 \leqslant k \leqslant 2L-1, \end{cases} \quad \text{with} \quad a_k = \begin{cases} 2\sqrt{L}, & k = 0, \\ \sqrt{2L}, & k \neq 0. \end{cases}$$
$$W_{2L} = e^{-j(2\pi/2L)}. \tag{5.45}$$

Substituting $F[k]$ into $G[k]$ derived in Eq. (5.44) will obtain a K-point extension FFT coefficients $G[k]$ with the DCT coefficients $F_C[k]$.

$$G[k] = \begin{cases} \frac{K}{L}a_k W_{2L}^{-k/2} F_C[k], & 0 \leqslant k \leqslant L-1, \\ 0, & L \leqslant k < 2K-L, \\ -\frac{K}{L}a_k W_{2L}^{\frac{-k+2K-2L}{2}} F_C[2K-L-k], & 2K-L+1 \leqslant k \leqslant 2K-1. \end{cases} \tag{5.46}$$

The K-point interpolated signal $g[n]$ can be obtained from the IDFT of $F[k]$.

$$g[n] = \frac{1}{\sqrt{L}}\sum_{k=0}^{L-1} a_k F_C[k] \cos\left(\left(\frac{n}{K} + \frac{1}{2L}\right)\pi k\right), \quad \text{with} \quad a_k = \begin{cases} 1, & k = 0, \\ \sqrt{2}, & 1 \leqslant k \leqslant L-1. \end{cases}$$
$$0 \leqslant n \leqslant K-1. \tag{5.47}$$

Performing the DFT interpolation in this way has several advantages. Firstly, it only requires real value operations. We do not need to worry about signal symmetry, where the zero-padded inverse transformed signal will always be real value. Secondly, the computational complexity of the last equation and that of a length N IDCT is the same.

In particular, when $K = L$, Eq. (5.47) becomes

$$g[n] = \frac{1}{\sqrt{L}}\sum_{k=0}^{L-1} a_k F_C[k] \cos\left(\left(\frac{2n+1}{2L}\right)\pi k\right), \tag{5.48}$$

which is the same as the IDCT in Eq. (5.22).

The EIDCT can be implemented with the same matrix multiplication between the EIDCT kernel and the transform coefficient matrix in row–column form. An example of the implementation of the EIDCT kernel is listed in MATLAB Listing 5.5.1.

MATLAB 5.5.1—Return the EIDCT kernel matrix with size K×N.

```
function c=eidctkernel(K,N)
   for u=0:N-1
      for v=0:K-1
         if (u==0) c(u+1,v+1)=1;
         else c(u+1,v+1)=sqrt(2/N)*cos((v/K+1/(2*N))*pi*u);
   end; end; end; return;
```

With the function generating the EIDCT kernel, a $L \times L$ block-based EIDCT interpolation for a transformed image F in the ratio of r can be implemented by the MATLAB function eidct as shown in MATLAB Listing 5.5.2. Given an 8×8 block DCT transformed image F, a $r\times$ interpolated image can be obtained by the MATLAB function eidct as eidct(F,8,r).

MATLAB 5.5.2—Return the DFT $r \times$ interpolated image of a LxL transformed image F (i.e. the EIDCT).

```
function g = eidct(F,L,r)
   eidct = eidctkernel(r*L,L);
   gblock = @(x) eidct'*x.data*eidct
   g = blockproc(F, [L L], gblock);
return;
```

For example, we can apply an EIDCT to an 8×8 block DCT transformed image F in ratio of 2 by invoking

```
>> g = eidct(F,8,2);
```

Note that the DCT transformed image F is assumed to be transformed with block size [L L]. Furthermore, the interpolated image g through eidct is of type double and is needed to be normalized by brightnorm to make it to have the same dynamic range as that of the input image. The obtained interpolated image is almost the same as that obtained by zero-padded DFT interpolation function, zpfft (Listing 5.1.2). The difference is due to numerical error in MATLAB because of the minor implementation difference.

When both blocked zero-padded DCT interpolated image and EIDCT-based blocked zero-padded DFT interpolated image are available, a better image can be obtained by computing the average image from these two images as shown Figure 5.15a, which is obtained by the following MATLAB source.

MATLAB 5.5.3—Averaging of zero-padded DCT interpolated image and EIDCT interpolated image.

```
>> L=8;
>> F = blockdct(f,L);
>> gdct = dctx2(f,L);
>> geidct = eidct(F,L,2);
>> gdct = brightnorm(f,gdct);
>> geidct = brightnorm(f,geidct);
>> g = uint8((gdct+geidct)/2);
```

It can be observed that the image has better details when compared with interpolated images obtained by either DCT or EIDCT alone. Figure 5.15b shows the zoom-in image of the whiskers of the *Cat* image taken from the enclosed portion in Figure 5.15b. It is vivid that the continuity of the whiskers is degraded by the blocking artifacts. The blocking artifacts are the result of the block-based operation in both the zero-padded DCT interpolation and the EIDCT interpolation. It is more vivid when we consider the same zoom-in image taken from the interpolated image obtained by averaging the zero-padded DCT interpolation and EIDCT interpolation, both using block size 16×16 as

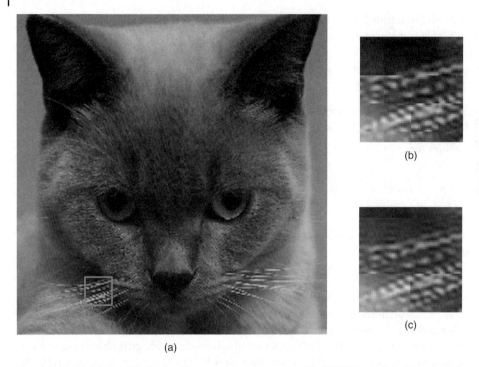

(a)

(b)

(c)

Figure 5.15 (a) A 512 × 512 obtained by averaging the zero-padded DCT interpolated image and EIDCT interpolated image with block size 8 × 8 in both interpolation methods. (b) The zoom-in image of the portion enclosed in (a). (c) The zoom-in image obtained from the portion enclosed in (a) with interpolated image obtained from zero-padded DCT and EIDCT using 16 × 16 block size.

shown in Figure 5.15c. The blocking artifacts still exist, but the block boundaries are comparatively more separated because the block size adopted is 16 × 16 in both interpolations. However, the blocking artifacts cannot be alleviated by this approach, as the spatial locations of the blocking boundaries in both interpolations are exactly the same. As a result, a combination of the multi-overlap image interpolation presented in Section 5.4 and multi-kernel image interpolation presented in this section programmed in a nested iterative interpolation process will be the key to obtain a better image interpolation result. The implementation of such nested application of two interpolation artifact alleviation schemes is obvious and will be left as exercise for the readers.

5.6 Iterative Error Correction

The block-based transform domain interpolation has demonstrated how to breakdown an image interpolation problem into a series of simpler interpolation problems. Under the same framework, the interpolation problem can be broken down into a series of rough interpolation problems in an iterative manner. At every iteration step, a small interpolation problem will aim at an optimal solution found within the current image. At the end of each iteration, the interpolated images will be summed with previous interpolation results to obtain a better interpolated image. Such an iterative and successive

Figure 5.16 Gradually fitting a metal sheet to a given surface.

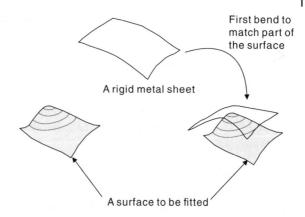

First bend to match part of the surface

A rigid metal sheet

A surface to be fitted

optimization technique exists naturally in real world. Imagine that we have a metal sheet with which we want to clad a curved surface as shown in Figure 5.16. The formation process is divided into roughing and finishing operations. In the roughing operation, the sheet is roughly formed in shape by a sequence of hammering. Then the roughly formed shape is corrected by hammering at the locations with large differences of shape in the finishing operation.

The above operation when applied to the zero-padded block-based DCT domain image interpolation method can improve the quality of the interpolated image by adding a residual image to compensate the error generated in the interpolation operation. The question is: What constitutes to an "*error*" in the interpolated image, and why does it exist in the interpolated image? The easy definition of interpolation error has been provided in Section 1.4, where the error is defined as the difference between the low-resolution image pixel intensities and that of the corresponding pixels in the high-resolution interpolated image. The interpolation by zero padding in DCT domain should preserve the pixel intensities of the low-resolution image as discussed in Section 5.2.1. However, due to the quantization of transform coefficients of the low-resolution image, the zero-padded block-based DCT image interpolation result seldom preserves the pixel intensities that correspond to that of the given low-resolution image. As a result, the error image is computed as

$$e = f - (g)\!\downarrow_r, \tag{5.49}$$

where the operation $\downarrow_r$ is the down-sampling by a ratio of r operator (where r should be the same as the interpolation ratio under concern) as discussed in Section 2.7.2.1 and r is nonzero. This operation will be adopted in the entire iterative error compensation process.

This iterative error compensation process is shown in Figure 5.17. For simplicity, let us consider $r = 2$. The low-resolution f_k to be considered in the kth iteration is actually the direct down-sampled image of the high-resolution image, g_{k-1}, in the previous iteration, such that

$$f_k = g_{k-1}\!\downarrow_2. \tag{5.50}$$

Then f_k is up-sampled by the desired interpolation method to give an intermediate high-resolution image $\hat{g}_k$. To generate the error image, $\hat{g}_k$ is directly down-sampled to give

$\hat{g}_k\downarrow_2$, such that the error image at the kth iteration is obtained by

$$e_k = f_k - \hat{g}_k\downarrow_2. \tag{5.51}$$

The corresponding MATLAB implementation is given as

```
>> e = f - directds(g,2);
```

where the usage of the function `directds` can be referred to Section 2.7.2.1 (MATLAB Listing 2.7.1). The residual image of the kth iteration, i_k, is obtained by up-sampling the error image by a factor of 2, which is

$$i_k = e_k\uparrow_2, \tag{5.52}$$

where the operator $\uparrow_2$ is the opposite of the $\downarrow_2$. The up-sampling operation is achieved by block-based zero-padded DCT interpolation with the same block size being applied in the previous iteration. For example, when 8×8 block is used, the MATLAB implementation is given as

```
>> i = dctx2(e,8);
```

The error-compensated image is generated by adding the residual image to the interpolated image as

```
>> g = hat_g + i;
```

The above sequence of operations can be repeated again and again to improve the quality of the interpolated image until a predefined norm (usually $\mathcal{L}_2$ or $\mathcal{L}_\infty$ norm is being applied in image interpolation) of the components of the error image e is close to zero or smaller than a given threshold t. Such interpolation image improvement scheme is also known as *back propagation* and is summarized in Figure 5.17 with an implementation using MATLAB by the function `dctx2bp` in Listing 5.6.1. In this particular implementation, the stopping criterion is the $\mathcal{L}_2$ norm of the error image to be smaller than predefined threshold t.

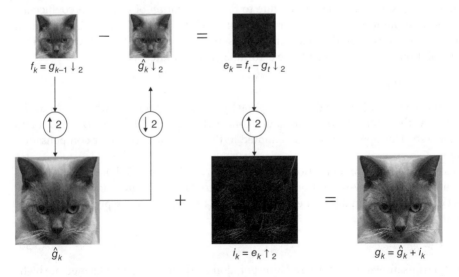

Figure 5.17 Error compensation signal flow block diagram.

MATLAB 5.6.1—Block-based zero-padded DCT interpolation with back propagation, where the block size is $L \times L$ and error threshold is t.

```
function g=dctx2bp(f,L,t)
   index=0;
   t = (double(t));
   g = double(zeros(2*size(f)));
   while 1
     e = double(f) - double(directds(g,2));
     mm = mean(mean(e.^2));
     if t > mm
       break
     end
     g = g + double(dctx2(e,L));
     g = brightnorm(double(f),g);
     index=index+1;
end; return;
```

The MATLAB Listing 5.6.1 is the MATLAB function implementing the block-based zero-padded DCT interpolation with back propagation on image f, where the adopted block size is $L \times L$ and the error threshold is t. This function returns the interpolated image g. The readers should notice the application of double to convert the intermediate image results to floating point before computing the error image and the application of brightnorm to convert the intermediate image to have the same dynamic range as that of the low-resolution image in each iteration. The back propagation algorithm is shown to be able to achieve very efficient improvement in minimizing the difference between the low-resolution image and the corresponding pixels in the interpolated image. Use the *Cat* image as an example. Shown in Figure 5.18a is the zero-padded DCT interpolated image with block size 8×8. The mean squares difference between the low-resolution *Cat* image and the down-sampled image of the interpolated *Cat* image is 44.1049. After one back propagation iteration, this difference reduces to 17.6107. In fact the decrementation is almost exponential. The image obtained with 1 back propagation iteration is shown in Figure 5.18b. It can be observed that the subjective quality of the texture-rich region of the *Cat* image has improved. However, the long edges in the image have minor artifacts. To investigate the edge area quality degradation, and the convergence of the back propagation algorithm, we considered the case with $t = 1$. Shown in Figure 5.18c are the interpolated images generated by dctx2bp with $t = 1$, which converges at the 46th iterations. The texture-rich area of the image in Figure 5.18c has excellent subjective quality, while the edges are suffering from artifacts similar to the chessboard effect, which is most obvious along strong edges. At the same time it is also observed that the PSNR of the interpolated image drops from 26.0916 to 25.9732 dB. This is because the back propagation method considered in dctx2bp only considers the low-resolution pixels and does not consider the underlying structure of the image. As a result, the interpolation for error correction is not guided by edges, and hence random error in error-corrected image will be observed. On the other hand, the algorithm aims to correct the intensities of the pixels corresponding to the low-resolution image, and hence all the error will be clustered to interpolated pixels. Such error clustering effect will not be visible in texture-rich area, and hence with the improvement of the intensities of the pixels corresponding to the low-resolution image, a general improvement

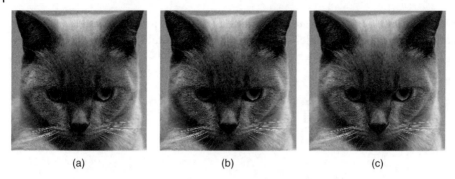

Figure 5.18 Zero-padded DCT interpolation with block size 8 × 8 and error compensation at the (a) 0th iteration (PSNR = 26.0916 dB and mean absolute difference with low-resolution image 6.4421). (b) 1st iteration (PSNR = 25.4664 dB and mean absolute difference with low-resolution image 6.5636). (c) 46th iteration (PSNR = 25.9732 dB and mean absolute difference with low-resolution image 5.6423).

on the subjective visual quality of the texture-rich area of the error-corrected image is perceived. On the other hand, the error clustering effect on edges of the image will cause broken edges in the error-corrected image, which are perceived as chessboard or ringing artifacts in the interpolated image. Furthermore, the dctx2 interpolated image has interpolation errors randomly distributed all over the whole image. After the error correction, all the interpolated errors are clustered to the interpolated pixels. Due to the power amplification effect of the squares within the PSNR computation, the results will be biased, and the PSNR is observed to fluctuate after each error correction iteration. This argument can be easily checked by considering both the PSNR and the mean absolute difference between the high-resolution *Cat* image and the interpolated images, which are 25.4664, 26.0011, and 25.9732 dB and 6.5636, 5.6729, and 5.6423 for interpolated images obtained from dctx2, subject to 1st, 25th, and 46th iterations, respectively. It can be observed that the mean absolute difference is decreasing with increasing number of back propagation. Together with the fact that the PSNR fluctuates with the back propagation iterations, it can be confirmed that the errors are clustered to the interpolated pixels.

As you can see, no single tricks can alleviate all interpolation artifacts. In reality, a number of these tricks have to be applied iteratively in a nested format to achieve the best image interpolation results. In the meantime, we have to point out that the back propagation algorithm dctx2bp does help to change the enlarged image from zooming to interpolation, which are important to some specific applications. In general, in order to tackle the PSNR reduction problem of the error-compensated image, we should apply a method that will spread the interpolation error evenly when performing error compensation, and the nested application of the multi-kernel transform domain image interpolation does show to be an appropriate choice. The development of such an image interpolation algorithm will be left as an exercise for the readers.

5.7 Summary

Image resizing in the transform domain has drawn considerable attention in recent years because of the increasing popularity of storing image information in the transform domain such as JPEG, MPEG, and ITU/T multimedia standards. The image interpolation algorithm that can directly perform interpolation in the transform domain without decoding the compressed image into the spatial domain will help to reduce the computational complexity. Furthermore, the transform domain image interpolation algorithm also appears to be simpler. Up-sampling in the transform domain is as simple as adjoint $K \times L - M \times N$ zeros to the transformed image. To obtain the interpolated image in spatial domain, the zero-padded transform image is inverse transformed to obtain the up-sampled approximation to the original image. As an example, the sinc interpolation discussed in Section 4.1 has high computational complexity, while when it is implemented in the transform domain, it will be a simple zero padding and inverse FFT. Further computation saving can be achieved with the application of pruned FFT algorithm [67]. In the dimension separated implementation of transform domain interpolation, to interpolate an $M \times N$ image to a $K \times L$ image would require $O(KMN \log M)$ operations (K times M-point FFTs for each of N image rows) for interpolation along the m-axis plus $O(KLMN \log N)$ operations ($L \times N$-point FFTs for each KM 1D interpolated image rows) for interpolating along the n-axis. Therefore, the per-output pixel computational complexity of the dimension separated transform domain interpolation for image of size $K \times L$ can be estimated as being $O(\log N + \log M / LM)$. This means the computational complexity of the dimension separated transform domain image interpolation using FFT is determined mainly by the lowest dimensionality of the image, while the dimension inseparable implementation requires performing $KL \times MN$-point FFTs. Therefore, the per-output pixel computational complexity will be $O(\log MN)$ operations, which is much higher. To further lower the computational complexity and also localize the image features for better interpolation results, blocked transform should be applied. The computational complexity is further reduced with the application of DCT, which is a real value transform. Furthermore, DCT has better boundary pixel performance and hence is the chosen transform kernel for image interpolation. The main drawback of the blocked transform-based interpolation algorithms is the discontinuities between blocks. Yet these discontinuities can be avoided by using overlapped blocks. Chapter 6 will present the wavelet transform-based image interpolation method, an ultimate solution to alleviate the blocking artifact problem. Besides the blocking artifact, there are ringing and other types of artifacts that are related to the choice of transform kernel (both the function and the length) used in the interpolation process. Various methods are discussed in this chapter to overcome these interpolation artifacts for which the authors will find that similar techniques can also be applied in other interpolation methods to achieve better image interpolation results, as will be presented in subsequent chapters.

5.8 Exercises

5.1 Implement the `dct` and `idct` function image MATLAB for a given image with user-defined block size in using `blockproc` operation.

5.2 If N is odd, show that Eq. (5.1) has to be revised as

$$Y(k) = \begin{cases} X(k), & k = 0, \dots, \frac{N-1}{2}, \\ 0, & k = \frac{N+1}{2}, \dots, \frac{3N-1}{2}, \\ X(k-N), & k = \frac{3N+1}{2}, \dots, 2N-1. \end{cases} \tag{5.53}$$

5.3 Construct a 2×2 DCT matrix, and use it to compute the 1D DCT for the data vector (a) $[3, 3]$, (b) $[2, -2]$.

5.4 1. Find the transform coefficients of the following eight pixels

$$35, \quad 81, \quad 190, \quad 250, \quad 200, \quad 150, \quad 100, \quad 21 \tag{5.54}$$

using a length 8 DCT.
2. Why is there only one significant AC coefficient?
3. Interpolate the 8 pixels with a ratio of 2 by zero padding the transform results in (1); comment on the interpolated pixel values.

5.5 Interpolate the following 1D data in the form of (x,y)

$$(0, 3), \quad (1, 1), \quad (2, 01), \quad (3, 3), \quad (4, 1.5), \quad (5, -0.5), \quad (6, -2)$$

using the DCT. Plot the data and the interpolating function together.

5.6 Let $x = [1, 0, -1, 0]^T$. Compute its DFT, and use the result to construct a continuous function that gives the x when sampled appropriately.

5.7 The FFT-based interpolation can be performed at any integer scaling factor no less than 2. Modify Eq. (5.1) to perform the interpolation with the factor $w = \lfloor \frac{N}{r} \rfloor$. The integer division in w serves the purpose that the original index sequences are now segmented into w pieces of an equal length w and a final index sequence of length $N - (r - 1) \times w$ while still holding the relationship Eq. (5.1).

5.8 Interpolate the following data matrix

$$f = \begin{bmatrix} -3.50 & -1.50 & -0.75 & -0.70 & -0.75 & -1.50 & -3.50 \\ -3.50 & -1.25 & -0.65 & -0.60 & -0.65 & -1.25 & -3.50 \\ -3.50 & -1.50 & -1.00 & -0.50 & -1.00 & -1.50 & -3.50 \\ -3.50 & -1.00 & -0.40 & 0.60 & -0.40 & -1.00 & -3.50 \\ -3.50 & -1.25 & -0.25 & -0.10 & -0.25 & -1.25 & -3.50 \\ -3.50 & -2.00 & -0.25 & 0.00 & -0.25 & -2.00 & -3.50 \\ -3.50 & -3.00 & -2.50 & -2.00 & -2.50 & -3.00 & -3.50 \end{bmatrix}$$

using the 2D DCT. Plot the data and the interpolating function together using 3D mesh in MATLAB.

5.9 (DCT Interpolation Property) Consider a 1D sequence $x[n]$ with length $N/2$ where N is even. Consider the zero-padded DCT transform sequence $Y[u]$ given by

$$V[u] = \begin{cases} C\{x[n]\}, & u = 0, 1, \ldots, N/2 - 1, \\ 0, & u = N/2, \ldots, N. \end{cases} \tag{5.55}$$

Consider another transform domain sequence constructed by $V[u]$ as

$$Y[u] = \frac{V[u] - V[N - u]}{\sqrt{2}}, \quad u = 0, 1, \ldots, N. \tag{5.56}$$

1. Show that if we apply the inverse DCT-I transform on $Y[u]$ where the forward transform is given by

$$Y[u] = w[u] \frac{1}{\sqrt{N}} \sum_{n=0}^{N-1} w[n]y[n] \cos \frac{un\pi}{N},$$ (5.57)

with

$$w[k] = \begin{cases} \frac{1}{\sqrt{2}}, & k = 0, N, \\ 1, & 1 \leqslant k \leqslant N - 1. \end{cases}$$ (5.58)

The obtained sequence $y[n]$ is given by

$$y[n] = \begin{cases} 0, & \text{if } n \text{ is even}, \\ x\left[\frac{n-1}{2}\right], & \text{if } n \text{ is odd}. \end{cases}$$ (5.59)

2. Implement a MATLAB procedure that performs zero insertion into the input sequence using the method in (1) to double the length of the sequence.

5.10 Implement a MATLAB function g=mkernoverlap(f,L) to perform nested application of the overlap and multi-kernel zero-padded blocked DCT-based image interpolation with DCT block size $L \times L$, where f is the input image and g is the output image. Note that this function does not require iterative application of overlap-based, nor multi-kernel-based zero-padded blocked DCT image interpolation.

5.11 Implement a MATLAB function g=nestdct(f,L,t) to perform an iterative back propagation-based overlap and multi-kernel zero-padded blocked DCT-based image interpolation with DCT block size $L \times L$, where f is the input image and g is the output image. The stopping criterion is the $\mathcal{L}_2$ norm of the error image between successive iterations to be smaller than the threshold t.

6

Wavelet

In contrast to the Fourier analysis that decomposes the image into spectral components with infinite precision, *wavelet transform* represents the image by a set of analysis functions that are dilation and translations of a few functions with finite support. Conceptually, we can consider that the wavelet cuts up the image into different frequency components and studies each component with a resolution matched to its scale, also known as multi-resolution analysis. The word *"wavelet"* that is used to describe such signal analysis and representation process as it captures the essence of the finite support (small kernel size) analysis functions has its root as "small wave" in Latin.

Unlike the blocked transform-based image processing, the wavelet transform operates on the image as a whole but still has the same computational complexity. As a result, wavelet image processing is free from blocking artifacts as that observed in blocked transform (however, it will be shown in a sequel that blocking artifacts by other means can still be observed in wavelet-based interpolated images). The forward dyadic wavelet transform (also known as analysis or decomposition) will decompose the signal into two components (and hence the word dyadic), known as the approximation and detail wavelet coefficients (which are also known as the subband signals). Such decomposition can be performed by the analysis multirate filter banks that are formed by subband filters followed by decimation processes. The decomposed signals are the level 1 analysis signals, while the original signal is the level 0 signal. Higher-level analysis signals can be obtained by iterative filtering and decimation of the approximation subband signals. In case the signal is 2D in nature, such as digital image, the multirate filtering operations and decimations can be performed in a dimension separated row–column form (as discussed in Section 2.3). An example is shown in Figure 6.4, where the dyadic decomposition of the *Cat* image generates four subband images in level 1 (after both row and column level 1 decompositions). Further decomposition can be performed in the low-pass subband image (the approximation image). A finite number of iterations will lead to discrete time multi-resolution analysis, also known as the *discrete wavelet transform* (DWT), of the *Cat* image. The application of wavelet to image processing, and in particular for image interpolation, can be found in [11, 18, 49, 50]. Actually, in a very vague definition, the discrete cosine transform (DCT) can also be considered as a particular kind of wavelet transform (even though the corresponding subband filters do not satisfy the regularity property that will be discussed in a sequel). Besides the very special subband filters, there are other differences between the DCT and the DWT, which include

Digital Image Interpolation in MATLAB®, First Edition. Chi-Wah Kok and Wing-Shan Tam.
© 2019 John Wiley & Sons Singapore Pte. Ltd. Published 2019 by John Wiley & Sons Singapore Pte. Ltd.
Companion website: www.wiley.com/go/ditmatlab

the kernel overlap and the variation of window sizes (DCT has a fixed block size). This very vague relationship between DCT and the DWT will be investigated by the readers as an exercise in the exercise section.

If we examine the subband images in Figure 6.4, it is vivid that the approximation subband image shows the general trend of pixel values and the three detail subband images show the vertical, horizontal, and diagonal details or *"changes"* in the original image. If these details are very small, then they can be set to zero without significantly changing the image. This is the key feature on the application of DWT to image compression and in particular image interpolation. However, before we jump into the wavelet interpolation topic, we shall develop the basic mathematical tools to perform the DWT, such that we have common mathematical notations and theorems to work with. Readers who are interested in a detailed study on the wavelet theory should refer to [58].

6.1 Wavelet Analysis

The implementation of 1D wavelet transform by means of multirate filter banks has been developed since the late 1980s. The forward dyadic wavelet transform is formed by a pair of analysis filters $\{h_0, h_1\}$ followed by down-sampling the filtered signals with decimation factor of 2. To reconstruct the signal from the wavelet coefficients (that is, the subband signals), the inverse wavelet transform is performed with zero insertion at every other signal of the subband signals and then filtering the zero-inserted subband signals with a pair of synthesis filters $\{p_0, p_1\}$.[1] These set of filters are also known as the subband filters, and the filter system together with the down- and up-samplers will form a multirate filter system. Subband filters with different cutoff frequencies can be employed to analyze the input signal. In the case of wavelet signal interpolation, a half-band low-pass filter h_0 (with passband $0 \sim \pi/2$ radians) is usually applied to remove all the frequency components that are above half of the highest frequency in the signal. The low-pass filter h_0 is reducing the signal resolution by half but leaving the scale unchanged. According to Nyquist theorem (Theorem 1.1), the subband signal that has the highest frequency of $\pi/2$ radians instead of π will only require half of the original samples to represent the signal without loss. As a result, the filtered output is down-sampled by a factor of 2, simply by discarding every other sample, and the scale of the subband signal is now doubled. The resolution and scale of the approximation subband signal can be further doubled by putting it through the multirate filter bank again. The approximation signal is now filtered with the low-pass subband filter h_0, whose passband is just half of the previous filter bandwidth, and the subsequent down-sampling by a factor of 2 will change the scale once again. As a result, the signal is being decomposed into subband signals with descending resolutions (as the detail subbands keep down-sampling). Such decrease in resolution and increase in scale will be repeated as shown in Figure 6.1 until

---

1 The authors are sorry for using the symbol p as the synthesis subband filters, despite the custom of using g, which in this book is being used to represent the reconstructed image. The corresponding transform domain synthesis filter will be represented as $P(\cdot)$. This is one of the difficulties faced by the authors when putting different topics into a single book, where each topic already has its familiar set of symbols.

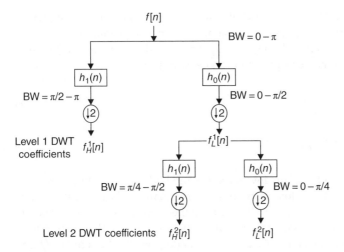

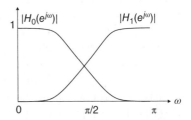

Figure 6.1 Illustration of 1D DWT decomposition. The bandwidth of the resulting signal is marked with "BW."

Figure 6.2 Spectral response of a typical perfect reconstruction two-channel subband filter bank.

a coarse description of the signal is achieved at a desired level. Note that the spectral responses of the analysis subband filters have finite transition regions and will overlap with one another, as shown in Figure 6.2, which means that the down-sampling and up-sampling processes will introduce aliasing distortion into the subband signals and the reconstructed signal. To eliminate the aliasing distortion in the reconstructed signal, the synthesis and analysis filters need to have certain relationships such that the aliased components in the transition regions will be canceled by the synthesis filters. While the perfect reconstruction condition will be discussed in Section 6.1.1, the subband filters must also satisfy other conditions before a multi-resolution analysis (wavelet analysis) can be achieved, which will be discussed in Section 6.1.2.

6.1.1 Perfect Reconstruction

To understand how to achieve an aliasing free reconstruction of the signal from the subband signals obtained by nonideal analysis subband filters, let us consider a two-band filter bank, as shown in Figure 6.1. To simplify our discussions, let us consider the 1D signal $f[n]$ being processed by subband filters shown in Figure 6.1. The signal $f[n]$ is filtered in parallel by a low-pass filter h_0 and a high-pass filter h_1 at each level of the wavelet decomposition. The two output subband signals are then down-sampled by dropping the alternate output samples in each signal sequence to produce the low-pass subband f_L (approximate signal) and high-pass subband f_H (detail signal) as shown in Figure 6.1. The above arithmetic computation can be expressed as

$$f_L[n] = \sum_{k=0}^{L_{h_0}-1} h_0[k]f[2n-k],$$
(6.1)

$$f_H[n] = \sum_{k=0}^{L_{h_1}-1} h_1[k]f[2n-k],$$
(6.2)

where L_{h_0} and L_{h_1} are the lengths of the low-pass (h_0) and high-pass (h_1) filters, respectively. The low-pass subband f_L is low-resolution approximation of the input signal f. As a result, applying the above analysis to decompose the signal f_L, which will generate f_L^2 and f_H^2. Note that we have expanded the subband signals to include the superscript 2 to indicate the level of decomposition. As a result, f_L and f_H will be the same as f_L^1 and f_H^1. This multi-resolution decomposition approach is shown in Figure 6.1 for two-level decomposition. This decomposition can be iteratively applied to all the low-pass subband signal until the k level low-pass subband signal f_L^k is obtained. During the inverse transform, both f_L^k and f_H^k in the lowest level (the highest k of the subband signals in concern) are up-sampled by inserting zeros between every two samples and then filtering the zero-inserted subband signal sequences by the synthesis low-pass filter p_0 and high-pass filter p_1. The two output signal sequences are added together to obtain the subband signal $\hat{f}_L^{k-1}$ at a higher level as shown in Figure 6.1. This process will continue until level 0 to obtain the reconstructed signal $\hat{f}$, which has the same resolution/scale as that of f. It should be noted that the hat in the symbol $\hat{f}$ indicates it is a reconstructed signal for the ease of discussion without ambiguity. The multirate filter bank is said to be a perfect reconstruction system if and only if $\hat{f}$ is a shifted version of f, which in turn requires the subband filters to satisfy the power complementary condition.

$$|H_0(e^{j\omega})|^2 + |H_1(e^{j\omega})|^2 = 1.$$
(6.3)

There are infinitely many subband filters that form perfect reconstruction filter banks. The built-in perfect reconstruction filter bank families in MATLAB include Daubechies (db), Coiflets (coif), Symlets (sym), Discrete Meyer (dmey), and Reverse Biorthogonal (rbio). In MATLAB's convention, the number that follows the mother wavelet family name is the subband filter length. As an example, db1 is the length 1 Daubechies subband filter, which is also known as the Haar wavelet. In this chapter, we choose the Haar wavelet, because it is the simplest and yet works just as good as other wavelets.

6.1.2 Multi-resolution Analysis

Not all perfect reconstruction subband filter banks can form wavelet transform. The analysis low-pass subband filter has to satisfy the orthonormality constraint, such that $\sum_k h_0[k] = \frac{1}{\sqrt{2}}$. Furthermore, it must have at least one vanishing moment, which implies $\sum_k k h_0[k] = 0$. The infinite product of such subband filter, $\lim_{J\to\infty} \prod_{k=1}^{J} H_0(\frac{\omega}{2^k})$, will converge to a function $\phi(\omega)$ whose inverse Fourier transform is the continuous time function $\phi(x)$ known as the scaling function. The scaling function $\phi(x)$ is the solution to the dilation equation.

$$\phi(x) = 2 \sum_k h_0[k]\phi(2x - k), \tag{6.4}$$

and it is orthogonal to its integer translates. The scaling function determines the wavelet function $w(x)$ by means of the analysis high-pass subband filter h_1 with

$$w(x) = 2 \sum_k h_1[k]\phi(2x - k). \tag{6.5}$$

The set of functions obtained from the dilation and translation of $w(t)$ as $\{w(2^k x - \ell)\}_{k,\ell \in \mathbb{Z}}$ forms a tight frame in $\mathcal{L}^2(\mathbb{R})$. In other words, the span of dilates and translates of the scaling function $\phi(x)$ forms a series of subspace V^k in $\mathcal{L}^2(\mathbb{R})$.

$$V^k = \operatorname*{span}_{k,\ell} \phi(2^k x - \ell), \quad \forall k, \ell \in \mathbb{Z}^+. \tag{6.6}$$

Since V^0 spans $\mathcal{L}^2(\mathbb{R})$, therefore, any continuous time function $f(x)$ can be expanded as a linear combination of the scaling function as

$$f(x) = \sum_n v^0[n]\phi(x - n), \tag{6.7}$$

where the superscript "0" denotes the expansion coefficient $v^0[n]$ obtained with the scaling function at scale 0. In dyadic decomposition, the function $f(x)$ will be subsequently decomposed into coarse-scale components with the functions in subspace V^J and details at several intermediate scales (from 1 to J). A coarse approximation of the function $f(x)$ at scale k is given by

$$v^k[n] = ((v^{k-1} \otimes h_0) \downarrow_2)[n], \tag{6.8}$$

which is implemented as low-pass filtering followed by down-sampling in the two-channel subband filter bank. The details are provided by the wavelet function and are computed with the high-pass filter $h_1[n]$. These subspaces have the relation of

$$\begin{aligned} V^0 = V^1 \oplus W^1 &= (V^2 \oplus W^2) \oplus W^1 \\ &= ((V^3 \oplus W^3) \oplus W^2) \oplus W^1 \\ &\quad \vdots \\ &= (\cdots (V^J \oplus W^J) \oplus \cdots) \oplus W^1, \end{aligned} \tag{6.9}$$

as shown in Figure 6.3.

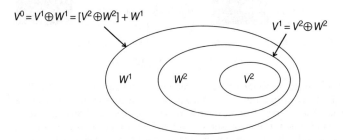

Figure 6.3 Multi-resolution space representation.

Besides the orthonormality constraint and the vanishing moment constraint, the wavelet transform usually forms an orthogonal transform, such that the analysis subband filters and synthesis subband filters are the same set of filters. Except the very special Haar wavelet, there do not exist any other subband filters that can form a perfect reconstruction orthogonal filter bank, while the subband filters also have linear phase. On the other hand, the human visual system has shown to be very sensitive to signal phase distortion. Therefore, it is very important to use linear phase subband filters. A way to achieve perfect reconstruction with linear phase subband filters is to allow the analysis subband filters and the synthesis subband filters to be different. Such multirate filter bank system will form a biorthogonal wavelet transform. The extra freedom in the design of biorthogonal subband filters will allow more accurate design of the low-pass filter to suit for particular image processing problem. On the other hand, departure from orthogonality generally has a negative impact on the signal representation efficiency. It has found that biorthogonal bases that closely resemble orthonormal bases are suitable for image processing application. The wavelet filters chosen for image compression in JPEG2000 are the biorthogonal 9/7 and 5/3 subband filters that are nearly orthogonal [4]. A filter bank with the two subband filters' length of 7 and 9 can have 6 and 2 vanishing moments or 4 and 4 vanishing moments as in the case of JPEG2000 wavelet. The same wavelet is also known as the Daubechies 9/7 (based on filter size) or biorthogonal 4.4 (based on vanishing moments). Nevertheless, this chapter will concentrate on the application of Haar wavelet for image interpolation, as it is the easiest to work with and can still provide very good interpolation results. Furthermore, it helps to explain the concepts clearly without messing with the forward and backward DWT transformation programming difficulties.

6.1.3 2D Wavelet Transform

The 2D DWT on the image f can be computed by first performing 1D DWT (horizontally) on the rows. Then we perform the same 1D DWT on the columns (vertically) for both the low-pass and high-pass subband signals obtained in the horizontal analysis as shown in Figure 6.4 with the *Cat* image as an example. As a result, there will be four subband images $f_{LL}^1, f_{LH}^1, f_{HL}^1$, and f_{HH}^1, where the L and H follow the same notations as that in

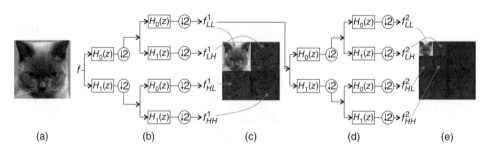

(a)   (b)   (c)   (d)   (e)

Figure 6.4 Illustration of 2D wavelet decomposition of the *Cat* image. (a) Filter bank structure for 2D wavelet image transformation, (b) the corresponding second-level wavelet decomposition, and (c) the subband stitched together to show the invariance of the overall spatial size, (d) second-level dyadic decomposition, with (e) the subband images from first- and second-level decomposition stitched together (the subband images look darker because brightness scaling has been applied to squeeze the dynamic range of all subband images to be displayed in the same figure).

1D DWT with the superscript indicating wavelet decomposition, where the superscript "1" refers to 1-level wavelet decomposition. Needless to say, we assume that the subband filter kernels of the 2D DWT are separable so that the wavelet decomposition can be carried out along the rows and columns separately. The decomposed subband images have a total size equal to that of the original image, which can be observed from Figure 6.4c with all the subband images that are stitched together to form one image. The multi-resolution analysis will repeat the operation on the f_{LL}^1 subband image as the input image for further decomposition. A 2-level wavelet decomposition of the *Cat* image is illustrated in Figure 6.4d using the MATLAB wavelet toolbox function dwt2 as in Listing 6.1.1, and the stitched image from all the subband images obtained from the two levels of decompositions is shown in Figure 6.4e. Note that in order to display all the subband images with the same dynamic range, the pixels of all the subband images, except f_{LL}^2, have been scaled by performing log10 and multiplying the result with 50 for those in the first-level decomposition and 100 for those in the second level of decomposition, as shown in Listing 6.1.1. It should be noted that the superscript "2" of f_{LL}^2 indicates it is a 2-level wavelet decomposed low-pass subband image. Similarly, the superscript convention can be applied to the symbols of the other 2-level subband images.

MATLAB 6.1.1—Discrete wavelet transform.

```
>>[LL1,LH1,HL1,HH1] = dwt2(f,'db1');
>>[LL2,LH2,HL2,HH2] = dwt2(LL1,'db1');
>>gLL1 = [LL2 log10(0.1+abs(LH2))*100; log10(0.1+abs(HL2))*100 log10
    (0.1+abs(HH2))*100];
>>g = [gLL1 log10(0.1+abs(LH1))*50; log10(0.1+abs(HL1))*100 log10(0.1+
    abs(HH1))*100];
>>figure; imshow(uint8(g));
>>figure; imshow(mat2gray(gLL1));
```

The dwt2 performs one-level wavelet decomposition of the image f using the wavelet defined by the second input parameter, which in this case is db1, the Haar wavelet. The function dwt2 is then applied to LL1 (where LL1 is the subband image f_{LL}^1) again to obtain the second-level decomposition. Note that the pixels in subband image LL2 (where LL2 is the subband image f_{LL}^2) have the same dynamic range as that of the original image f, while all other subband images have small and sparse pixel values. It is vivid from Figure 6.4e that the 2-level decomposed subband images f_{HLL}^2 (LH2 in MATLAB), f_{HL}^2 (HL in MATLAB), and f_{HH}^2 (HH in MATLAB), contains the horizontal, vertical, and diagonal details of the original image f, respectively. The last line of the codes in Listing 6.1.1 makes use of the mat2gray function to normalize the pixel intensity of gLL1 for display purpose. To reconstruct the image from the subband images, we shall make use of idwt2 as in Listing 6.1.2. To simplify the discussion without losing generality, in the rest of the discussions, the superscript on the 1-level decomposed subband images will be omitted, but that of the 2-level decomposed subband images would be remained. The same idea would be applied to the MATLAB symbols, e.g. LL and LL1 are both referring to the 1-level decomposed subband image.

MATLAB 6.1.2—Inverse discrete wavelet transform.

```
>>f = idwt2(idwt2(LL2,LH2,HL2,HH2,'db1'),LH1,HL1,HH1,'db1');
```

The output of the IDWT function `idwt2` is of class `double` and contains negative and other pixel values outside the dynamic range of the original image `f`. As a result, some mappings will have to be performed before you can display them as that in Figure 6.4, where the MATLAB function `brightnorm` will be used (see Listing 5.3.5).

6.2 Wavelet Image Interpolation

Consider the DWT of a 1D high-resolution signal $\hat{g}[n]$ with a bandwidth support of $[0, \pi]$ as shown in Figure 6.5. This high-resolution signal $\hat{g}$ is decomposed into the low frequency component $\hat{g}_L = f$ and high frequency component $\hat{g}_H$ as shown in the figure. However, only the low frequency subband signal $\hat{g}_L$ is available, while the high frequency subband signal $\hat{g}_H$ is missing. A high-resolution signal g that approximates $\hat{g}$ can be obtained by computing the inverse discrete wavelet transform (IDWT) of $\hat{g}_L$ together with an estimation of the high frequency subband component $\hat{g}_H$ using f as shown in Figure 6.5. In a similar manner, the 2D DWT of a high-resolution image $\hat{g}$ with missing high frequency subband images ($\hat{g}_{LH}$, $\hat{g}_{HL}$, and $\hat{g}_{HH}$) can be approximated by computing the 2D IDWT using the low-resolution subband image $\hat{g}_{LL}$ and the estimation of the missing subband images. Readers should be able to understand that this is the same as recasting the interpolation problem to a subband image estimation problem, where the given low-resolution image f enumerates $\hat{g}_{LL}$, with the unknown $\hat{g}_{LH}$, $\hat{g}_{HL}$, and $\hat{g}_{HH}$ being estimated. As a result, the IDWT of f together with the estimated $\hat{g}_{LH}$, $\hat{g}_{HL}$, and $\hat{g}_{HH}$ will construct g, an approximation to the high-resolution image $\hat{g}$, which in turn is the interpolated image of the low-resolution image f. In the following discussion, we shall denote the $\hat{g}_L$, $\hat{g}_{LH}$, $\hat{g}_{HL}$, and $\hat{g}_{HH}$ as *LL*, *LH*, *HL*, and *HH* subband images for simplicity in this section. It should be noted that the two sets of symbols would be interchangeably used.

6.2.1 Zero Padding

The simplest DWT interpolation method is discrete wavelet transform zero padding (DWT-ZP), where the low-resolution image will enumerate the *LL* subband image, while the other three subband images (*LH*, *HL*, and *HH*) are padded with zeros. This kind of high frequency subband image estimation method hits off with the observation that the pixel values of the high frequency subband images are usually very small, which hints that replacing the high frequency subband images with zero matrices will not cause much information loss. The IDWT of the zero-padded subband images will have to be multiplied with a scaling factor to restore the brightness of the reconstructed

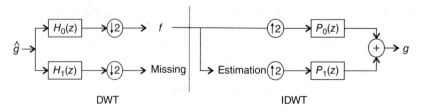

Figure 6.5 Image interpolation by wavelet coefficient estimation.

image to be compatible with that of the given low-resolution image. Depending upon the implementation of the DWT, the system will have a different DC gain for the low-pass filter and Nyquist gain for the high-pass filter, which will result in different scaling factors. In our example, we choose to use db1, the Haar wavelet, where the subband filters with both DC and Nyquist gain equal to $\sqrt{2}$ (the orthonormality constraint as discussed in Section 6.1.2). This will help to maintain all four subband images to have the same dynamic range. Consequently, the scaling factor will be 2, which is the multiplication of the squares of the DC gain. The MATLAB source Listing 6.2.1 implements the DWT zero padding image interpolation with db1 wavelet. Note that the scaling factor of 2 is applied to the idwt function to obtain the interpolated image ng. Further note that all pixels with negative intensity values will be substituted with zero intensity and the final image array is cast to unit8 to obtain the final interpolated image *g*.

MATLAB 6.2.1—WZP: DWT zero padding wavelet image interpolation.

```
function g = wzp(f)
  z = zeros(size(f));
  LL = double(f);
  ng = 2*idwt2(LL,z,z,z,'db1');
  ng(ng<0) = 0;
  g = uint8(ng);
return;
```

The interpolation result of the *Cat* image shown in Figure 6.6 can be obtained by the following MATLAB function call:

```
>> figure; imshow(uint8(wzp(f)));
```

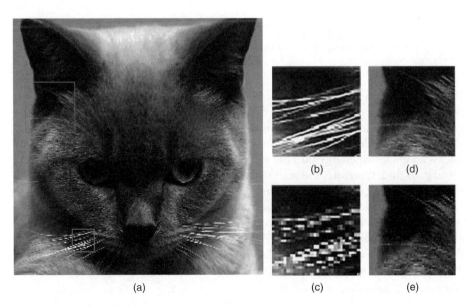

(a) (b) (d) (c) (e)

Figure 6.6 *Cat* image interpolated with Haar wavelet zero padding and the zoom-in sub-images of the *Cat* whiskers in (c) and ear in (e), while shown in (b) and (d) are the sub-images of the same area extracted from the original high-resolution *Cat* image.

Readers may have already noticed that with all the high frequency subband images (*LH*, *HL*, and *HH*) being constrained with zero values, the DWT-ZP interpolation is essentially the same as the linear interpolation method described in Figure 4.1 with the interpolation kernel given by the subband synthesis filter $p_0(z)$. Similar image interpolation performance as that discussed in Chapter 4 is therefore expected, and no advantages of the wavelet multi-resolution analysis have been made use of.

6.2.2 Multi-resolution Subband Image Estimation

A natural way to exploit the DWT multi-resolution analysis property is to make use of the multi-resolution dependency between different levels of wavelet decomposition to estimate the high frequency subband images required for the inverse transform to create the interpolated image. In other words, the high frequency subband images of f (i.e. f_{LH}, f_{HL}, and f_{HH}) can be estimated from the subband images obtained in higher-level decomposition. As an example, the bilinear interpolation of the high frequency subband images obtained from the second-level DWT decomposition of f (i.e. dwt(LL,'db1')) is applied to estimate the high frequency subband images of the interpolated image g, i.e. g_{LH}, g_{HL}, and g_{HH} in the MATLAB source Listing 6.2.2, where the bilinear interpolation is implemented with the function biinterp listed in MATLAB Listing 4.1.5 discussed in Chapter 4.

> **MATLAB 6.2.2—WBP: Wavelet image interpolation by bilinear interpolating subband images.**
>
> ```
> function g=wbp(f)
>     LL = double(f);
>     [fLL1,fLH1,fHL1,fHH1] = dwt2(LL,'db1');
>     gLH1 = biinterp(fLH1,2);
>     gHL1 = biinterp(fHL1,2);
>     gHH1 = biinterp(fHH1,2);
>     g = brightnorm(LL,2*idwt2(LL,gLH1,gHL1,gHH1,'db1'));
> return;
> ```

The brightnorm function in Listing 6.2.2 has been discussed in Chapter 5 and is applied to normalize the pixel intensity dynamic range of the interpolated image g to be the same as that in image f. The reason why a fixed scaling factor 2 cannot be applied to do the job in wavelet based image interpolation is because we have injected subband images with unknown energy into the estimated high frequency subband images (g_{LH}, g_{HL}, and g_{HH}), and, therefore, the scaling factor is most probably not equal to 2. As one of the interpolation constraints is the interpolated image pixels that correspond to the low-resolution image should be the same, therefore, we shall normalize the interpolated image to have the same dynamic range as that of the low-resolution image and hence the brightness normalization function.

The interpolated *Cat* image using MATLAB source Listing 6.2.2 with the following MATLAB function call is shown in Figure 6.7:

```
>> figure; imshow(uint8(wbp(f)));
```

There are some improvement on the high frequency regions of the interpolated image when compared with that of Figure 6.6, such that the edges of the interpolated image are not as blur as that in Figure 6.6. On the other hand, it is not difficult to notice that

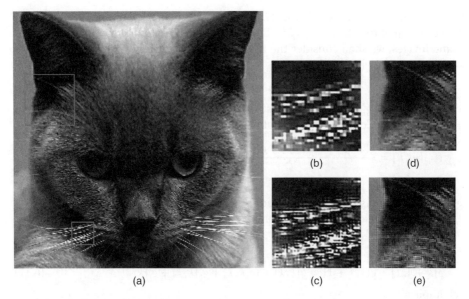

Figure 6.7 (a) *Cat* image interpolated with Haar wavelet with high frequency subband images obtained from bilinear interpolation of lower-level high frequency subband images and the zoom-in sub-images of the *Cat* whiskers in (c) and ear in (e), while shown in (b) and (d) are the sub-images of the same area extracted from the interpolated image obtained by Haar wavelet zero padding.

there is high frequency noise, similar to impulsive noise, in the texture-rich region of the interpolated image. Heavy ringing artifacts and salt and pepper noises can also be observed in the texture-rich region of Figure 6.7. To understand why interpolating the high frequency subband images does not work well in the overall interpolated image, we shall consider the pixel relationship between a given high-resolution image g and its four subband images obtained by Haar wavelet first-level DWT analysis.

$$f = g_{LL}[m,n] = \frac{1}{4} \sum_{[k,\ell]=[0,0]}^{[1,1]} g[2m-1+k, 2n-1+\ell], \tag{6.10}$$

$$g_{LH}[m,n] = \frac{1}{2} \sum_{\ell=0}^{1} (g[2m-1, 2n-1+\ell] - g[2m, 2n-1+\ell]), \tag{6.11}$$

$$g_{HL}[m,n] = \frac{1}{2} \sum_{k=0}^{1} (g[2m-1+k, 2n-1] - g[2m-1+k, 2n]), \tag{6.12}$$

$$g_{HH}[m,n] = \frac{1}{2} \sum_{k=0}^{1} (g[2m-1+k, 2n-1+k] - g[2m-k, 2n-1+k]). \tag{6.13}$$

It is vivid that the low-resolution subband image is the average of the pixels in the high-resolution image, while the coefficients of high-resolution subband images are the pixel difference of the high-resolution image. If we correlate the similarity between the low-resolution images f and these subband images, their relationship can be represented by Taylor series. A good approximation of the high frequency subband images will assist us to reconstruct a high-resolution image that approximates the actual high-resolution image well.

As discussed in Section 6.2.1, the *LL* subband image of the high-resolution image *g* should be equal to *f* (i.e. $f = g_{LL}$ in Eq. (6.10)). To approximate the high frequency subband images, we shall consider the first-order Taylor series expansion of the high-resolution image *g*, which yields

$$g[m + \delta m, n + \delta n] \approx g[m, n] + \Delta m \cdot g'_m[m, n] + \Delta n \cdot g'_n[m, n], \tag{6.14}$$

where $g'_m[m, n]$ and $g'_n[m, n]$ are the first-order derivatives along *m* and *n*, respectively, and $\Delta m = \Delta n = 2$. Consider the *HH* subband image

$$g_{HH}[m, n] = \frac{g[2m - 1, 2n - 1] + g[2m, 2n] - (g[2m, 2n - 1] + g[2m - 1, 2n])}{2}, \tag{6.15}$$

where similar analysis is also considered in [17]. Rewriting $k = 2m - 1$ and $\ell = 2n - 1$ and applying the Taylor series expansion on *g* in Eq. (6.14) yields

$$g[k, \ell] + g[k + 1, \ell + 1] \approx g[k, \ell] + (g[k, \ell] + g'_k[k, \ell] + g'_\ell[k, \ell]), \tag{6.16}$$

$$g[k + 1, \ell] + g[k, \ell + 1] \approx g[k, \ell] + (g[k, \ell] + g'_k[k, \ell] + g'_\ell[k, \ell]), \tag{6.17}$$

which implies

$$g[2k - 1, 2\ell - 1] + g[2k, 2\ell - 1] \approx g[2k, 2\ell - 1] + g[2k, 2\ell]. \tag{6.18}$$

As a result, we shall approximate

$$g_{HH}[m, n] \approx 0. \tag{6.19}$$

In similar manner, the *LH* subband image is given by

$$g_{LH}[m, n] = \frac{g[2m - 1, 2n - 1] - g[2m, 2n - 1]}{2} + \frac{g[2m - 1, 2n] - g[2m, 2n]}{2}. \tag{6.20}$$

Again, considering $k = 2m - 1$ and $\ell = 2n - 1$, the *LH* subband image can be rewritten as

$$g_{LH}[m, n] = \frac{g[k, \ell] - g[k + 1, \ell]}{2} + \frac{g[k, \ell + 1] - g[k + 1, \ell + 1]}{2}. \tag{6.21}$$

The Taylor series expansion of *g* in Eq. (6.14) yields

$$g[k, \ell] - g[k + 1, \ell] \approx g[k, \ell] - (g[k, \ell] + g'_k[k, \ell])$$
$$= -g'_k[k, \ell]. \tag{6.22}$$

Further note that

$$g[k, \ell] - g[k + 2, \ell] \approx -\Delta k g_k[k, \ell] = -2g_k[k, \ell], \tag{6.23}$$

where $\Delta k = 2$. The above equation implies

$$g[k, \ell] - g[k + 1, \ell] \approx \frac{g[k, \ell] - g[k + 2, \ell]}{2}, \tag{6.24}$$

or equivalently

$$g[2m - 1, 2n - 1] - g[2m, 2n - 1] \approx \frac{g[2m - 1, 2n - 1] - g[2m + 1, 2n - 1]}{2}. \tag{6.25}$$

This relationship is invariant with shifting by 2 along both m and n. Therefore,

$$g[2m-1,2n]-g[2m,2n] \approx \frac{g[2m-1,2n]-g[2m+1,2n]}{2}. \tag{6.26}$$

Substituting Eqs. (6.25) and (6.26) into (6.20) yields

$$\begin{aligned}
g_{LH}[m,n] &\approx \frac{1}{2}\left(\frac{g[2m-1,2n-1]-g[2m+1,2n-1]}{2}\right.\\
&\quad\left.+\frac{g[2m-1,2n]-g[2m+1,2n]}{2}\right)\\
&= \frac{1}{2}\left(\frac{g[2m-1,2n-1]+g[2m-1,2n]}{2}\right.\\
&\quad\left.-\frac{g[2m+1,2n-1]+g[2m+1,2n]}{2}\right),
\end{aligned} \tag{6.27}$$

which is the difference between the means of two column pixels separated by one column apart, and each column has two components. Consider that the decimation of the means of the pixels will yield $f[m,n]$. As a result, Eq. (6.27) is equivalent to the computation of the horizontal difference (along m direction) between adjacent $f[m]$, which is equivalent to f_{LH} of the first-level Haar wavelet decomposition of f. In other words, the g_{LH}^2 from the 2-level wavelet decomposition of g is a good approximation of g_{LH}^1. With $g_{LH}^1[m,n] = g_{LH}^2[m/2,n/2] = f_{LH}^1[m/2,n/2]$ with even m and n, the missing $g_{LH}^1[m,n]$ with either m or n or both being odd has to be estimated. There exists a lot of estimation method for these missing LH subband image pixels, and we have tried the bilinear interpolation in MATLAB Listing 6.2.2, which does not give good result in general. As a result, the most straight forward method has been proposed in [62], which padded the unknown pixels in $g_{LH}^1[m,n]$ with zero for either m or n or both being odd. Similar relationship is derived for the g_{HL}^1 subband image. This forms the alternate zero padding wavelet image interpolation method. Shown in Figure 6.8 is a synthetic figure that shows the two subband images g_{LH}^1 and g_{HL}^1 obtained from alternate zero padding wavelet image interpolation method, while $g_{HH}^1 = [0]$. Together with $g_{LL} = f$, the IDWT result of these four subband images of g^1 will yield the interpolated image.

MATLAB 6.2.3—WAZP: Alternate zero wavelet image interpolation.

```
function g = wazp(f)
   LL = double(f);
   [fLL1,fLH1,fHL1,fHH1] = dwt2(LL,'db1');
   [M N] = size(f);
   gHH1 = zeros(M,N); gLH1 = gHH1; gHL1 = gHH1;
   gLH1(1:2:M,1:2:N)=fLH1;
   gHL1(1:2:M,1:2:N)=fHL1;
   ng = brightnorm(LL,2*idwt2(LL,gLH1,gHL1,gHH1,'db1'));
   g = uint8(ng);
end
```

The alternate zero padding wavelet interpolation method is implemented in MATLAB Listing 6.2.3 with function name `wazp`. Similar to the bilinear subband

Figure 6.8 Wavelet zero padding image interpolation with alternate zero wavelet coefficient insertion.

image interpolation-based wavelet interpolation method (i.e. wbp), the interpolated image normalization factor is affected by the energy of the estimated subband images that we have injected into the IDWT process. In this case, it is image dependent, and, therefore, the brightness normalization function brightnorm is applied to normalize the interpolated image to have the same dynamic range as that of the given low-resolution image.

The interpolated *Cat* image obtained from MATLAB source Listing 6.2.3 with the following function call is shown in Figure 6.9:

```
>> figure; imshow(uint8(wazp(f)));
```

It is vivid that the image edges are not as blur nor noisy as that in Figures 6.6 and 6.7 of wavelet zero padding (WZP) interpolation and wavelet with bilinear interpolated subband images interpolation. The most obvious artifacts in Figure 6.9 are the sudden brightness of the interpolated pixels near the edges of the image, which are perceived as impulsive noise or shot noise.

The unpleasant shot noise is mostly observed to be near the edges of the interpolated image that is caused by excess signal power of the high frequency subband images. A simple test of decreasing the high frequency subband image energy by dividing the subband coefficients by 1.5 as the following MATLAB function wazp15 will confirm the conjecture on the origin of the shot noise.

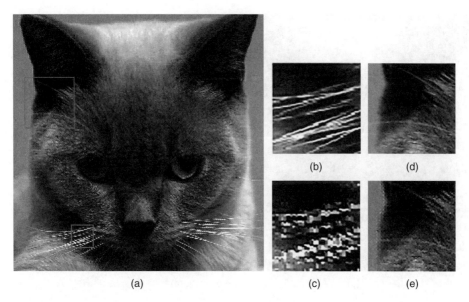

Figure 6.9 (a) *Cat* image interpolated with alternate zero padding wavelet interpolation and the zoom-in sub-images of the *Cat* whiskers in (c) and ear in (e), while shown in (b) and (d) are the sub-images of the same area extracted from the original high-resolution *Cat* image.

MATLAB 6.2.4—WAZP15: Alternate zero wavelet image interpolation with LL band divided by 1.5.

```
function g = wazp15(f)
   LL = double(f);
   [fLL1,fLH1,fHL1,fHH1] = dwt2(LL,'db1');
   [M N] = size(f);
   gHH1 = zeros(M,N); gLH1 = gHH1; gHL1 = gHH1;
   gLH1(1:2:M,1:2:N)=fLH1/1.5;
   gHL1(1:2:M,1:2:N)=fHL1/1.5;
   ng = brightnorm(LL,2*idwt2(LL,gLH1,gHL1,gHH1,'db1'));
   g = uint8(ng);
end
```

The interpolated *Cat* image using MATLAB source Listing 6.2.4 with the following function call is shown in Figure 6.10:

```
>> figure; imshow(uint8(wazp15(f)));
```

It can be observed that most of the shot noise is suppressed when compared with that in Figure 6.9. At the same time, the edge sharpness is preserved. This result prompted us to investigate the correct scaling of the energy of the estimated high frequency subband images to be applied in the wavelet image interpolation problem. To learn how to scale the estimated high frequency subband images, we have to understand some basic functional analysis using wavelet.

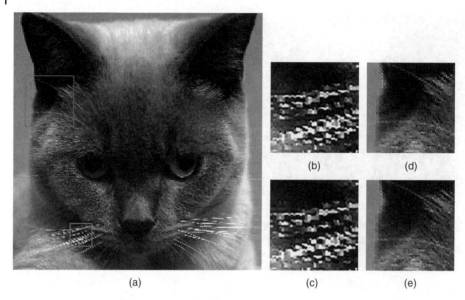

(b)   (d)

(a)   (c)   (e)

Figure 6.10 (a) *Cat* image interpolated with alternate zero padding wavelet interpolation and subband images divided by 1.5 and the zoom-in sub-images of the *Cat* whiskers in (c) and ear in (e), while shown in (b) and (d) are the sub-images of the same area extracted from the interpolated image obtained by alternate zero padding wavelet without scaling the subband images.

6.2.3 Hölder Regularity

In order to bring a spatial coherence between the spatial image and the wavelet coefficients, the basis of the applied wavelet transform must satisfy a smoothness constraint. A smooth wavelet transform of high-resolution image will render regions that do not have much high frequency components to have the corresponding wavelet coefficients with very small magnitudes, which can be ignored without affecting the overall quality of the wavelet image representation. However, if a region has edges, the corresponding wavelet coefficients are usually significant, and they cannot be neglected while obtaining the high-resolution image.

The smoothness of an image can be defined in terms of Hölder regularity of the wavelet transform [22]. Functions with a large Hölder exponent will be both mathematically and visually smooth. Locally, an interval with high regularity will be a smooth region, and an interval with low regularity will correspond to roughness, such as at an edge in an image. To extend this concept to image interpolation, the smoothness constraints should be enforced while up-sampling at relatively smooth regions and enhancing the edges of the interpolated high-resolution image. Since this chapter is about the application of wavelet to interpolate images, we are trying our best to avoid the functional analysis discussion of wavelet, which we considered to be out of the scope of this book. On the other hand, we do have to bring in the Lipschitz property on functional analysis. The Lipschitz property let us know that the wavelet coefficients for pixels near sharp edges decay exponentially over scale [44]. The wavelet analysis of the interpolated image should preserve the regularity during analysis. There are two schools of regularity preservation in wavelet image interpolation.

The first method preserves the energy ratio of the high frequency subband image across scale. In other words, among 1-level, 2-level, and 3-level DWT decomposed *LH* images, their energy, computed as variance of the coefficients in the subband images, should satisfy

$$\frac{\text{var}(g_{LH}^1)}{\text{var}(g_{LH}^2)} = \frac{\text{var}(g_{LH}^2)}{\text{var}(g_{LH}^3)}. \tag{6.28}$$

To put this into implementation, the *LH* subband image should be scaled by the variance ratio of the 1-level and 2-level *LH* subband images as $\frac{\text{var}(f_{LH}^1)}{\text{var}(f_{LH}^2)}$. The following MATLAB source modified from Listing 6.2.4 applied the regularity-preserving property in Eq. (6.28) to interpolate image.

> **MATLAB 6.2.5—WRAZP: Alternate zero padding with regularity-preserving subband scaling wavelet image interpolation.**
>
> ```
> function g = wrazp(f)
>   LL = double(f);
>   [fLL1,fLH1,fHL1,fHH1] = dwt2(LL,'db1');
>   [M N] = size(f);
>   gHH1 = zeros(M,N); gLH1 = gHH1; gHL1 = gHH1;
>   [fLL2,fLH2,fHL2,fHH2] = dwt2(fLL1,'db1');
>   sLH = (var(reshape(fLH1,[],1)))/(var(reshape(fLH2,[],1)));
>   sHL = (var(reshape(fHL1,[],1)))/(var(reshape(fHL2,[],1)));
>   gLH1(1:2:M,1:2:N) = fLH1*sLH;
>   gHL1(1:2:M,1:2:N) = fHL1*sHL;
>   ng = brightnorm(LL,2*idwt2(LL,gLH1,gHL1,gHH1,'db1'));
>   g = uint8(ng);
> return;
> ```

The interpolated *Cat* image obtained by `wrazp` with the function call

```
>> figure; imshow(uint8(wrazp(f)));
```

is shown in Figure 6.11. It can be observed that almost all shot noise are suppressed in the interpolated image when compared with Figures 6.9 and 6.10. At the same time, the edge sharpness is preserved.

6.2.3.1   Local Regularity-Preserving Problems

To improve the image interpolation result, the subband image coefficient scaling should be adaptive, such that for those subband coefficients that are identified as strong edges, the energy ratio of the corresponding subband coefficients across scales (where the energy in this case will be the squares of the subband coefficients) will be used to scale the corresponding subband coefficients or even estimate the subband coefficients. This property is first proposed in Mallat's wavelet modulus maxima theory [44] that extrapolates wavelet transform extrema across scales and then the regularity-preserving image interpolation methods in [11] and [14].

The regularity-preserving interpolation technique synthesizes a new wavelet subband based on the decay of known wavelet transform coefficients [11]. The creation of the high frequency subband image is separated into two separate steps. In the first step, row edges with significant correlation across scales are identified. Then near these edges the rate

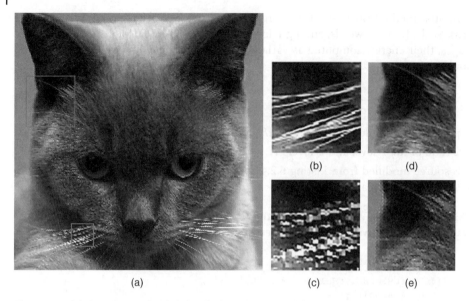

Figure 6.11 (a) *Cat* image interpolated with alternate zero padding with regularity-preserving subband scaling wavelet image interpolation and subband images scaled to satisfy across scale subband image energy ratio and the zoom-in sub-images of the *Cat* whiskers in (c) and ear in (e), while shown in (b) and (d) are the sub-images of the same area extracted from the original high-resolution *Cat* image.

of decay of the wavelet coefficients is extrapolated to approximate the high frequency subband required to resynthesize a row of twice the original size. In the second step, the same procedure as in the first step is applied to each column of the row interpolated image. There are a number of problems associated with this local regularity-preserving interpolation method.

Firstly, we shall assume symmetric wavelets are applied to the local regularity-preserving image interpolation problem. This is because the nonsymmetric wavelets will cause incoherent in the signs and/or locations of the wavelet transform extrema. Let us consider the spatial coherent problem of an edge across three levels of symmetric wavelet decomposition. Consider the case where we try to locate a pixel which has maximum intensity in the third level decomposed subband image. The actual maximum intensity pixel will either locate exactly on the pixel under consideration, or it will locate on the inter-pixel location between either one of the two neighboring pixels to the pixel under consideration. On the 2 level, there should have corresponding zero crossings. However, due to the down-sampling operation, the localization of the zero crossing will have four possible pixel locations and also the inter-pixel locations of these four pixels. Similarly, after up-sampling, the 1-level edge location will have a localization of eight possible pixel locations and the nine possible inter-pixel locations of these eight pixels. As a result, using low-level wavelet coefficient maxima to determine the edge location at the high-resolution spatial domain will have very wide ambiguity. Therefore, preserving the regularity through wavelet maxima will cause edge localization problem.

In other words, there will be mismatch between the edge locations between the estimated high frequency subband images by lower-scale subband images and that of the given low-resolution image. In other words, the generated high-resolution image will be subjected to artifacts caused by edge mismatch between the low frequency subband image and high frequency subband images, which will be observed as ringing and zigzag noises in the interpolated image.

6.3   Cycle Spinning

Although wavelet interpolation algorithm is not block-based interpolation algorithm, blocking-like artifacts (the zigzag artifacts) are observed in the interpolated image. This is caused by the incomparability between the low frequency subband image (the low-resolution image) and the high frequency subband images. The wavelet transform is shift invariant. However, the forward transform alone and hence the generation of subband images are not. As a result, by making use of the shift variant property, a scheme similar to that in Section 5.4 that averages shifted interpolated images could be developed to suppress zigzag noise. This forms the basis of the cycle spinning wavelet interpolation method presented in [60].

There are a number of ways to generate *"shifted"* high-resolution images. It can be obtained from removing some rows and columns of an intermediate interpolated image similar to that in Section 5.4. These shifted images are applied with 2D DWT to obtain the subband images of each shifted image. Now we have to decide if we are going to replace the high frequency subband images or the low frequency subband images. The following two sections will discuss the algorithm of each method and their interpolation results.

6.3.1   Zero Padding (WZP-CS)

The easiest way to generate the shifted high-resolution images is to perform 2D DWT on the spatially shifted intermediate interpolated image (say, obtained by WRAZP) and then replace the high frequency subband images with zeros. Reconstruct the zero-padded 2D DWT images (which are equivalent to WZP), and average the result as shown in Figure 6.12. This is the original cycle spinning method in [60], which is the first to consider this approach. A MATLAB implementation of this wavelet zero padding cyclic spinning (WZP-CS) image interpolation scheme is shown in Listing 6.3.1.

Readers might have observed several interesting implementation details in Listing 6.3.1. First, the spatial shifting of the intermediate images is achieved by `npart`, `mpart`, and `dpart` as in Section 5.4. A pseudo block size of four pixels is applied in shifting the high-resolution image, such that the actual spatial shift is half of the block size and is therefore equal to two pixels. A spatial shift of two pixels in the high-resolution image is applied because after the decimation process, the low-resolution subband images of the shifted high-resolution images will be equivalent to shift the low-resolution image f by one pixel, which is achieved by `npart`, `mpart`, and `dpart` with pseudo block size of two pixels.

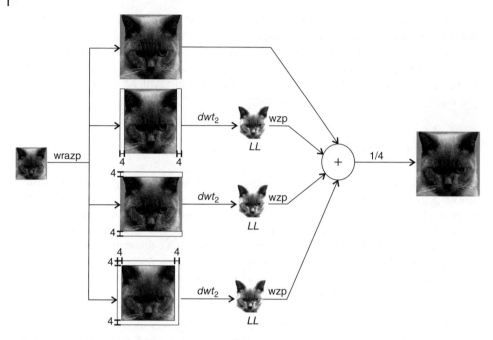

Figure 6.12 WZP-CS image interpolation signal flow diagram.

MATLAB 6.3.1—WZPCS: Wavelet zero padding cyclic spinning image interpolation using intermediate image generated by WRAZP image interpolation.

```
function gcp = wzpcs(f)
  grazp = wrazp(f);
  [M N] =size(grazp);
  F1 = npart(grazp,4); ff1 = npart(f,2);
  F2 = mpart(grazp,4); ff2 = mpart(f,2);
  F3 = dpart(grazp,4); ff3 = dpart(f,2);
  [F1LL1,F1LH1,F1HL1,F1HH1] = dwt2(F1,'db1');
  [F2LL1,F2LH1,F2HL1,F2HH1] = dwt2(F2,'db1');
  [F3LL1,F3LH1,F3HL1,F3HH1] = dwt2(F3,'db1');
  gzpF1 = double([grazp(1:M,1:2) wzp(F1LL1/2) grazp(1:M,N-2+1:N)]);
  gzpF2 = double([grazp(1:2,1:N); wzp(F2LL1/2); grazp(M-2+1:M,1:N)]);
  gzpF3 = double([grazp(1:2,1:N);grazp(2+1:M-2,1:2) wzp(F3LL1/2) grazp
     (2:M-2-1,N-2+1:N); grazp(M-2+1:M,1:N)]);
  ngcp = brightnorm(double(f),(double(grazp)+gzpF1+gzpF2+gzpF3)/4);
  gcp = uint8(ngcp);
return;
```

It can also be noticed that the magnitude of the low frequency subband images is reduced by a factor of 2. This is because the wzp interpolation algorithm will scale the interpolated image with the gain of the subband filter (which is 2). However, the gain of the subband filter is intrinsic to the low-pass subband image of the 2D DWT images, and, therefore, the extra scaling of 2 has to be taken out from wzp, and hence the division of 2 in the input to the algorithm. The interpolated shifted images are padded with rows and columns of the intermediate subband image to make it the same size as that of the high-resolution image.

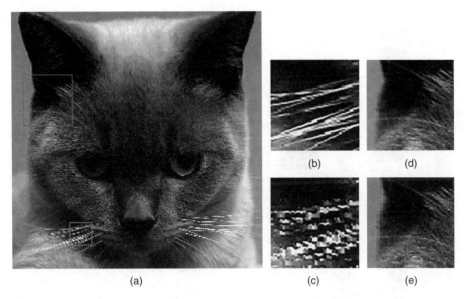

Figure 6.13 (a) *Cat* image interpolated with wavelet zero padding cyclic spinning image interpolation with intermediate image generated by WRAZP image interpolation through MATLAB function `wzpcs` and the zoom-in sub-images of the *Cat* whiskers in (c) and ear in (e), while shown in (b) and (d) are the sub-images of the same area extracted from the original high-resolution *Cat* image.

The interpolated image obtained with the function call `wzpcs(f)` as

```
>> figure; imshow(uint8(wzpcs(f)));
```

is shown in Figure 6.13. It can be observed that the zigzag noise around the texture-rich area of the *Cat* image has been alleviated, especially around the cheek of the *Cat*. The edges are sharp and with better continuity when compared with all other wavelet image interpolation results discussed so far in this chapter.

6.3.2 High Frequency Subband Estimation (WLR-CS)

Another way to generate the spatially shifted high-resolution images is to perform 2D DWT on the spatially shifted intermediate interpolated image (say, obtained by WRAZP) and then replace the low frequency subband image with the given low-resolution image *f* with appropriate spatial shift. The fused DWT subband images will be IDWT to generate the spatially shifted high-resolution images, which are averaged to obtain the final image. The algorithm is summarized in Figure 6.14. In this way, the high frequency subband images are preserved, and a better and sharper interpolated image is expected. We shall call this as the wavelet low-resolution image cyclic spinning (WLR-CS) image interpolation, because we have fused the spatially shifted (cyclic-spinned) low-resolution images to the DWT results of the intermediate image. A MATLAB implementation of the WLR-CS image interpolation scheme is shown in Listing 6.3.2. It can be observed that the spatial shifting in `wlrcs` is basically the same as that in `wzpcs`, where the high-resolution image is shifted horizontally, vertically, and diagonally by two pixels, while the low-resolution image is shifted similarly by one pixel because of the decimation by a factor of 2 when generating the subband image. It can also be noticed that the magnitude of the low frequency subband images is replaced

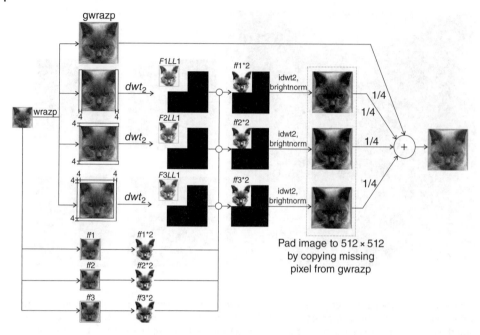

Figure 6.14 Wavelet low-resolution image cyclic spinning image interpolation signal flow diagram.

with the spatially shifted low-resolution image after scaled by a factor of 2, which is equal to the analysis subband filter gain as discussed in Section 5.1.

MATLAB 6.3.2—WLRCS: Wavelet low-resolution image cyclic spinning image interpolation using intermediate image generated by WRAZP image interpolation.

```
function gcp = wlrcs(f)
  grazp = wrazp(f);
  [M N] =size(grazp);
  F1 = npart(grazp,4); ff1 = double(npart(f,2));
  F2 = mpart(grazp,4); ff2 = double(mpart(f,2));
  F3 = dpart(grazp,4); ff3 = double(dpart(f,2));
  [F1LL1,F1LH1,F1HL1,F1HH1] = dwt2(F1,'db1');
  [F2LL1,F2LH1,F2HL1,F2HH1] = dwt2(F2,'db1');
  [F3LL1,F3LH1,F3HL1,F3HH1] = dwt2(F3,'db1');
  ngf1 = brightnorm(double(ff1),idwt2(ff1*2,F1LH1,F1HL1,F1HH1,'db1'));
  ngf2 = brightnorm(double(ff2),idwt2(ff2*2,F2LH1,F2HL1,F2HH1,'db1'));
  ngf3 = brightnorm(double(ff3),idwt2(ff3*2,F3LH1,F3HL1,F3HH1,'db1'));
  pgF1 = double([grazp(1:M,1:2) ngf1 grazp(1:M,N-2+1:N)]);
  pgF2 = double([grazp(1:2,1:N); ngf2; grazp(M-2+1:M,1:N)]);
  pgF3 = double([grazp(1:2,1:N);grazp(2+1:M-2,1:2) ngf3 grazp(2:M-2-1,
      N-2+1:N); grazp(M-2+1:M,1:N)]);
  gczp= (double(grazp)+pgF1+pgF2+pgF3)/4;
  gcp = uint8(gczp);
return;
```

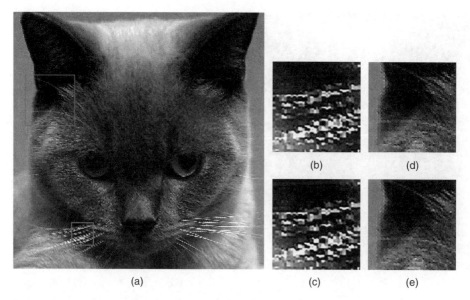

(b)   (d)

(a)   (c)   (e)

Figure 6.15 (a) *Cat* image interpolated with wavelet low-resolution subband cyclic spinning with intermediate image generated by `wrazp` image interpolation through MATLAB function `wlrcs` and the zoom-in sub-images of the *Cat* whiskers in (c) and ear in (e), while shown in (b) and (d) are the sub-images of the same area extracted from the high-resolution *Cat* image obtained from `wzpcs`.

The interpolated image obtained from the function call of `wlrcs(f)` as

```
>> figure; imshow(uint8(wlrcs(f)));
```

is shown in Figure 6.15. It can be observed that the zigzag noise around the texture-rich area of the *Cat* image has been alleviated, but is not as good as that in Figure 6.13 obtained by `wzpcs`, especially around the cheek of the *Cat*. However, the edges are sharper and with better continuity when compared with that of `wzpcs`. This is because the preservation of high frequency subband images in `wlrcs` will better preserve the edges not to be blurred by the averaging action in the algorithm. However, preserving the high frequency subband images also means the preservation of the mismatch between the high frequency subband images and the low frequency subband images, and hence the zigzag noise is also preserved in some extent in the interpolated image.

As a compromise, we can also consider averaging the two images obtained from `wzpcs` and `wlrcs` as

```
>> g = (double(wzpcs(f))+double(wlrcs(f)))/2;
>> figure; imshow(uint8(g));
```

It can be observed from the averaged interpolated image in Figure 6.16 that the edges of the image are well defined, without blurring and ringing noise. The texture-rich area of the image has almost unobservable zigzag noise. The result is almost perfect. Except one thing, this is a fitted high-resolution image, but not an interpolated high-resolution image. This is because the low-resolution image pixel values are not preserved in the high-resolution image. To correct the fitted high-resolution image to an interpolated image, we shall turn to iterative error correction technique similar to Section 5.6

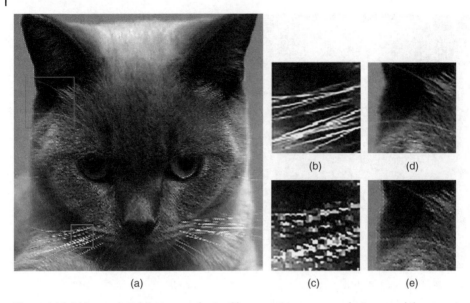

Figure 6.16 (a) Interpolated *Cat* image obtained by averaging `wzpcs` and `wlrcs` and the zoom-in sub-images of the *Cat* whiskers in (c) and ear in (e), while shown in (b) and (d) are the sub-images of the same area extracted from the original high-resolution *Cat* image.

6.4 Error Correction

The wavelet-based image interpolation methods discussed in previous sections (except WZP) interpolate the missing pixels in some way that is consistent with the frequency content of the rest of the signal, which are obtained a priori from the low-resolution image. As a result, the preservation of the low-resolution pixel values in the corresponding location of the high-resolution interpolated image is not guaranteed. In other words, when the high-resolution interpolated image is directly down-sampled, the result will be almost sure not to be the same as the given low-resolution image. This result does not fulfill the low-resolution pixel value preservation requirement in image interpolation. To make up the differences, we shall perform the error correction method discussed in Section 5.6. The overall error correction method based on WZP is summarized in Figure 6.17. Readers may have already noticed that we have dropped the word iterative as compared with that in Section 5.6. This is because the WZP that we have applied in the

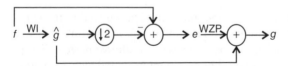

Figure 6.17 Image interpolation by wavelet multi-resolution synthesis with error correction. (*Note:* WI can be any wavelet interpolation methods except `wzp`.)

error correction routine is an interpolation method. In other words, the low-resolution pixel errors will be exactly the same in the corresponding high-resolution error pixels. In other words, only one iteration will suffice to correct the errors. An implementation of the method that makes use of WZP to interpolate image is shown in MATLAB Listing 6.4.1, where the input to the function `wecor` is a wavelet fitted high-resolution image and the original low-resolution image f. The input image ag can be generated by other wavelet-based interpolation methods other than WZP. The choice of the generation of the ag using other methods will be left as exercises for the readers.

> **MATLAB 6.4.1—WECOR: Iterative error correction through wavelet zero padding.**
>
> ```
> function g = wecor(f,ag)
>    wg = double(ag);
>    [M N] =size(ag); z = zeros(M/2,N/2);
>    err = double(f) - wg(1:2:M,1:2:N);
>    ge = idwt2(err*2,z,z,z,'db1');
>    wg = double(wg)+ge;
>    g = uint8(wg);
> return;
> ```

If we consider the differences between the fitted high-resolution *Cat* image ag obtained from `ag=wlrcs(f)` and the low-resolution *Cat* image f, the maximum absolute difference between the down-sample fitted high-resolution image `ag(1:2:M,1:2:N)`, where `[M N]=size(ag)`, is 74:

```
>> err = double(f)-ag(1:2:M,1:2:N);
>> max(max(err))
ans =
     74
```

This big difference in the fitted high-resolution image and the corresponding low-resolution image can be alleviated by executing

```
>> g = wecor(f,ag);
```

which will bring the difference down to nil. The resulting image is shown in Figure 6.18. It can be observed that the blocking artifacts are almost gone, and the edges are sharp. However, new artifacts of small size blocks with alternating brightness are observed in the texture-rich areas. This is caused by the error image-induced false edge information. In conclusion, it is nice to obtain an interpolated image using `wecor`. However, that does come with the scarification of a new type of high frequency noises observable in the texture-rich area. This makes the engineers to ponder if it is good enough to use the fitted high-resolution image. The same question will resurface in Chapter 9 when we discuss the fractal image interpolation, which makes use of fractal object to approximate high-resolution images and is therefore intrinsically a fitting algorithm, not an interpolation algorithm. On the other hand, the fractal object-based high-resolution image generation method does show high visual fidelity that cannot be achieved by most methods in literature.

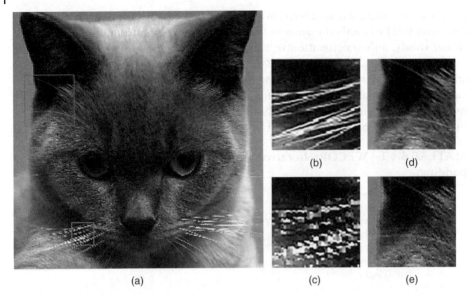

(a)   (b)   (c)   (d)   (e)

Figure 6.18 (a) Interpolated *Cat* image obtained by error correcting (`wecor`) the (`wlrcs`) wavelet low-resolution image cyclic spinning high-resolution image using intermediate image generated by WRAZP image interpolation (`wlrcs`) and the zoom-in sub-images of the *Cat* whiskers in (c) and ear in (e), while shown in (b) and (d) are the sub-images of the same area extracted from the original high-resolution *Cat* image.

6.5 Which Wavelets to Use

Only the Haar wavelet `'db1'` is considered in this chapter. Readers may ask if other wavelets give better results to generate a high-resolution approximation to the given low-resolution image. To answer this question, we shall have to understand that in wavelet signal analysis, the signal is represented in terms of its coarse approximation at scale J (with basis function $\phi(2^K x - n)$) and the J details (with basis function $\omega(2^j x - n)$, $1 \leqslant j \leqslant J$). The key to efficient multi-resolution signal representation by wavelet depends on the properties of the wavelet basis. The three key properties of the wavelet bases are:

Regularity: The regularity of scaling function ϕ has mostly a cosmetic influence on the error introduced by thresholding or quantizing the wavelet coefficients. If ϕ is smooth, then the generated error is a smooth error. For image interpolation applications, a smooth error is often less visible than an irregular error. Better quality images are obtained with wavelets that are continuously differentiable than those obtained from the discontinuous Haar wavelet. Wavelet regularity increases with the number of vanishing moments. As a result, choosing high regularity wavelet is the same as choosing wavelets with large vanishing moments.

Number of vanishing moments: This affects the amplitude of the wavelet coefficients at fine scale. For smooth regions, wavelet coefficients are small at fine scales if the wavelet has enough vanishing moments to take advantage of the image regularity. A wavelet has m vanishing moments if and only if its scaling function can generate polynomial of degree smaller than or equal to m. Both the number of vanishing moments and the regularity of orthogonal wavelets are related, but it is the number of vanishing moments and not the regularity that affects the amplitude of the wavelet coefficients at fine scales [43].

Kernel size: These need to be reduced to minimize the number of high amplitude coefficients. On the other hand, a large kernel size is required to provide enough vanishing moments. Therefore, the choice of optimal wavelet is a trade-off between the number of vanishing moments and kernel size.

Every function that satisfies the admissibility condition can be used in a wavelet transform and generates its own wavelets. The ability to approximate signals with a small number of non-zero coefficients is undoubtedly the key to the success of wavelets for image interpolation. An orthonormal function should also be used such that individual subband signals are independent of each other, and hence the interpolation errors will not propagate across subbands. As a result, orthonormal wavelet with the wavelet transform of an image producing few non-zero coefficients, which are independent with each subband, is the best wavelet for image interpolation. On the other hand, image interpolation should preserve phase information, as HVS is sensitive to phase error. However, orthogonal wavelets do not have linear phase, except Haar wavelet. Therefore, biorthogonal wavelets with linear phase transform kernel will be the best engineering choice for image interpolation.

In summary, the following listed are the important properties of wavelet functions in image interpolation:

1. Compact support (as compact kernel size, which minimizes the high frequency artifacts in the interpolated image and also provides efficient implementation).
2. Symmetry (useful in avoiding phase noise in image processing).
3. Orthogonality (reduces noise propagation across subbands).
4. Regularity and degree of smoothness (improve the smoothness of the interpolation error and hence less visible).

One should choose the wavelet filters based upon the characteristics of the image for suitable perceptual quality. However, the underlying operations in the algorithm are not image content dependent and hence nonadaptive in nature. As a result, should we spend time to choose a specific wavelet with the goal of finding the optimal wavelet for a given image and risking of losing generality? The readers may want to adapt the wavelet image interpolation algorithms discussed in this chapter for image interpolation. But the authors' trial showed that the use of "turnkey" resources provided by MATLAB, in particular the Haar wavelet, will provide just as good image interpolation results as other wavelet transformations.

6.6 Summary

Wavelet transform is an actively pursued area of research. There are many textbooks available for a comprehensive discussion on this topic. The readers are referred to [49] for further discussion on wavelet decomposition. The basic wavelet-based interpolation method is the WZP that interpolates images by zero padding the high frequency subbands (i.e. setting all elements of these subbands to zeros) followed by inverse wavelet transform. WZP has demonstrated to be able to achieve interpolated image with higher PSNR than that achieved by bilinear and bicubic methods. However, visually the method exhibits little difference with conventional convolution-based method discussed in Chapter 4. The wavelet-based method seems to sharpen the edges, but the texture-rich and smooth regions of the image are blurred. This effect is understood because the interpolation step is similar to 1D bilinear interpolation, except at strong edges. To make use of the benefits of wavelet image transformation, the information across wavelet scales should be considered in the interpolation method.

Unlike traditional transform-based image interpolation methods discussed in Chapter 5, the wavelet-based interpolation methods give us the flexibility to choose the analysis and synthesis functions. It further allows us to explore the structure of the interpolating image through local Hölder regularity. Wavelet-based interpolation methods that make use of across scale information and local Hölder regularity information can achieve interpolated images with better PSNR and visually sharpened edges. Having said that, wavelet transform can be performed with any one pair of wavelet transform kernel from an almost infinite number of wavelet transform basis. On the other hand, using wavelets with long kernel will result in interpolated image with image edges being not sharp and smoothed texture-rich areas. Therefore, most wavelet image interpolation methods make use of simple and short kernel analysis and synthesis basis functions.

Besides the across scale information, the shift variant property of wavelet transformation [15] can also be applied to achieve better interpolated image quality. The cycle spinning [60] and its variant methods that make use of the wavelet shift variant property have shown to be an effective method against blurring, brokening, and zigzag noise observed on edges.

The last but not the least, readers should understand that except WZP, it is very likely that wavelet-based image interpolation methods can only achieve a fitted enlarged image instead of an interpolated image. Error correction method has to be applied to constrain the pixels in the fitted high-resolution image that correspond to the low-resolution image to have the same pixel intensities. The pro is the increment of the PSNR of the interpolation image. The con is the blocking-like artifacts because of the brightness mismatch between the low-resolution image pixel values and the corresponding neighboring pixels in the wavelet interpolated image. Wavelet image fusion technique should be applied to fuse them nicely together to avoid the blocking-like artifacts, but the fusion technique will usually blur the edges of the interpolated image, and it is therefore required to be handled with care.

6.7 Exercises

6.1 Why is the complexity of the 1D discrete wavelet transform linear with N?

6.2 Write a function `greduce` that takes a square image, `img`, of size $M \times N$ as input, convolves the rows and columns of `img` with the filter kernel $\frac{1}{20}[1\ 5\ 8\ 5\ 1]^T$, and then down-samples the convolution results to produce an output image of size $\frac{M}{2} \times \frac{N}{2}$. Demonstrate your function on an image of your choice.

6.3 Write a function `gproject` that takes a square image, `img`, of size $M \times N$ as input, up-samples the image to $2M \times 2N$, and then convolves the rows and columns of the up-sampled image with the kernel $\frac{1}{10}[1\ 5\ 8\ 5\ 1]^T$. Demonstrate your function on an image of your choice.

6.4 Write a Laplacian pyramid function `[pyr]=lappry(img,k)` that takes a square image, `img`, as input, and returns a list of k images representing the k levels of a two-dimensional Laplacian pyramid transformed images. Demonstrate your function's ability by writing a function `disppyr(pyr,k)` that displays the k levels of the two-dimensional Laplacian pyramid using the recursive scheme shown in Figure 6.19. Demonstrate your function on the *Cat* image. *Note*: The image representing the Laplacian pyramid levels must each be normalized to the range [0–255] to construct the display.

Figure 6.19 Laplacian pyramid transform of the *Cat*.

6.5 Write a function `g = lappryrecon(pyr,k)` to invert a Laplacian pyramid you compute with `[pyr]=lappry(im,k)` in the above exercise with k images stored in the 3D matrix `pry`, and return the reconstructed image. Use the *Cat* image Laplacian pyramid image sequence in previous exercise, and display the reconstructed image.

6.6 Multi-resolution representation can be generated by DCT in a similar way as that of the wavelet transform through reordering the coefficients into subbands as shown in Figure 6.20. Construct a MATLAB algorithm that takes in an image `im`, generate a two-level multi-resolution representation of the image using DCT as the basis function, and display it on screen. *Note*: The HH, HL, and LH subband image levels should be normalized to the range [0–255] with mean gray level equals 128 prior to constructing the display.

6.7 Compute a three-level 1D Haar wavelet decomposition of the signal vector [9 7 3 5], and report your finding in the form [L_2 H_2 H_1].

6.8 Compare the performance of image interpolation by `wecor(f,ag)` for the low-resolution input image `f` and different fitted high-resolution image `ag` generated by (a) `wlrcs`, (b) `wzpcs`, (c) `wrazp`, and (d) `wazp`.

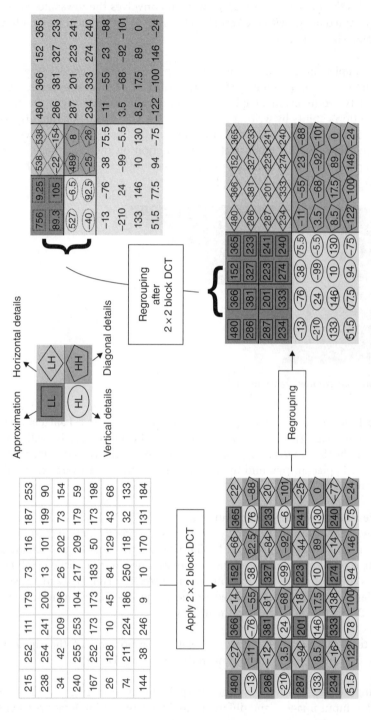

Figure 6.20 Example of reordering of DCT coefficient to form multi-resolution image representation. *(See insert for color representation of this figure.)*

7

Edge-Directed Interpolation

The image interpolation methods presented in previous chapters can deliver high visual quality interpolated images. However, no matter how the interpolation is performed in spatial domain or in transform domain, the interpolated images still have different levels of visual artifacts, particularly around the areas of image edges and high frequency texture-rich regions. The most obvious artifacts are usually observed in the form of blurred edges, blocky image, edge discontinuities, lack of fine details in texture-rich areas, etc. Different from the task of up-sampling a one-dimensional (1D) signal, up-sampling an image should exploit the fact that high frequency image features, such as edges and textures, are anisotropic in nature. The spectrum of the edges is also asymmetric since the frequency is low along the edge direction and high in the direction across the edge. As discussed in Chapter 4, the interpolation is mostly similar to a low-pass reconstruction process, which imposes technical difficulties to preserve all the frequency components in the interpolated images, in particularly in preserving the high frequency components of the anisotropic edge spectrum, which results in distorted edges and loss of fine details in the interpolated images.

If we further investigate the causes of interpolation artifacts, we shall notice that the *nonparametric interpolation* methods introduced in previous chapters interpolate all pixels in the same fashion, where a single interpolation filter is applied throughout the entire image and the filter structure is independent of the input image and also not affected by external control parameters; therefore they are known as "nonparametric." Such interpolation algorithms are also known as "nonadaptive" because of the invariance of interpolation filter being applied throughout the whole interpolation process. The advantage of using invariant filter is the low computational complexity. Among all *nonparametric* methods, polynomial interpolation functions, such as bilinear and bicubic interpolations, are known to be the simplest and the most efficient interpolation methods. On the other hand, the human visual system (HVS) is the most sensitive to image edges. As a result, the subject quality of the *nonparametric* interpolation algorithms should be judged by how well the interpolation methods can recover high frequency components. However, as there are limited numbers of coefficients in the polynomial interpolation functions, it is not able to provide good frequency resolution, and thus it cannot restore the high frequency components, such as the edges and texture, from the low-resolution image. As a result, the subjective quality of *nonparametric* interpolation methods, such as the polynomial interpolation methods, usually provide poor interpolation results, especially for natural image interpolation.

Digital Image Interpolation in MATLAB®, First Edition. Chi-Wah Kok and Wing-Shan Tam.
© 2019 John Wiley & Sons Singapore Pte. Ltd. Published 2019 by John Wiley & Sons Singapore Pte. Ltd.
Companion website: www.wiley.com/go/ditmatlab

In order to pursue better image interpolation visual quality, analytical model can be applied to adapt the interpolation kernel according to the image details. In other words, the interpolation method will be able to interpolate each pixel in the image in a different way according to the local image features. Such interpolation method can be computationally exhaustive. In order to strike a balance between computational complexity and the interpolation performance, we shall consider the most important HVS parameter to construct the analytical image model as discussed in Chapter 2. In Section 2.5, the image is modeled to be composed of a collection of texture patches. Pixels within the patch are homogeneous and carry the same texture property with similar intensity. The boundaries outline and distinguish different patches in the image. The adaptive image interpolation algorithm should preserve the boundary information and integrity to obtain an interpolated image that will be subjectively determined to be visually pleasant. Formally, the "adaptive interpolation" should interpolate the image according to the following rules [43]:

1. Image patch along edge direction to be smoothed.
2. Rate of intensity change across image patches (i.e. across edge direction) to be sharp.

In this chapter, we shall discuss a few selected *adaptive interpolation* methods known as the "*edge-directed interpolation*" (EDI), which are considered to be the class of image interpolation method that can preserve the edge structure with high visual quality. To understand the importance in the perseverance of image edges, let us consider an image sample in Figure 3.3. Figure 3.3 is a low-resolution solid edge image that will become a graded line pattern after nearest neighbor interpolation to form a high-resolution image. Such kind of interpolation artifacts is known as "jaggies," and "blurring" effects (more details can be found in Section 3.1). High quality image interpolation method should consider and utilize the edge information to produce interpolated image with unnoticeable artifacts by preserving the edge structures within the image. The EDI analyzes the image content and directs the interpolation by the edges (the boundaries of different patches) in the image.

The EDI is a very general family of image interpolation. We shall focus on the EDI methods that classify pixels into edge or non-edge type by comparing the relative intensity or frequency variation with its neighboring pixels. Notwithstanding which kind of EDI methods, all EDI methods aim to maintain "geometric regularity" by applying special interpolation method on pixel on edges or near edges and at the same time applying simple "nonparametric" interpolation to pixels within the smooth image patches to achieve the best interpolated image quality at a reasonable computational complexity. Interpolation along ideal step edges is not difficult since accurate edge direction information can be obtained explicitly from edge detectors. However, natural images have patch boundaries that appear to be spatially blurred edges due to sensor noise, focal blur, penumbral blur, shading, image compression, etc. When edges are blurred or noisy, it is difficult to explicitly specify their characteristics, which makes detection of natural edges difficult. In the following sections, we shall introduce the integration of different edge detection methods into image interpolation and the pros and cons of different interpolation methods in extracting edge attribute to generate satisfactory interpolation results. We shall also review how various EDI methods preserve geometric regularity and at what computational complexity.

7.1 Explicit Edge-Directed Interpolation

We shall start our discussions on EDI method with the algorithm proposed by Allebach and Wong [3] where the general framework is shown in Figure 7.1. This EDI framework is considered to be the mother framework for all EDI algorithms using explicit edge map, and we shall call it the general explicit EDI method in this chapter. This algorithm is a selective interpolation process guided by explicit edge detection result, which is also known as *explicit EDI*. A collection of edge information is presented in the form of a 2D image known as "edge map." The edge map has the same dimension as that of the high-resolution image, and the coordinate is consistent with that of the high-resolution image. A straightforward way to generate the edge map is to up-sample a low-resolution image edge map through interpolation. However, this straightforward method will complicate the image interpolation problem by introducing an extra interpolation step of the low-resolution to high-resolution edge map, which inevitably introduces interpolation errors in the form of false edges and hence degrades the quality of the EDI results. One of the possible way to generate a high accuracy edge map is to perform *sub-pixel edge estimation* from the low-resolution image.

Among all the sub-pixel edge map generation methods, the general explicit EDI method in [3] considers the *center-on-surround-off* (COCS) filter. The COCS filter has a constant positive center region embedded within a constant negative surround region, which is an approximation of the *Laplacian-of-Gaussian* (LoG) filter (readers can refer to Section 2.5.2.1 for details). The COCS filter is rotationally invariant and it has zero DC response. The filter coefficients are given by

$$
h_{COCS}[m, n] = \begin{cases} h_c, & |m|, |n| \leq R_c, \\ h_s, & \begin{cases} R_c < |m| \leq R_s \ \text{and} \ |n| \leq R_s, \\ R_c < |n| \leq R_s \ \text{and} \ |m| \leq R_s, \end{cases} \\ 0, & \text{otherwise}, \end{cases} \tag{7.1}
$$

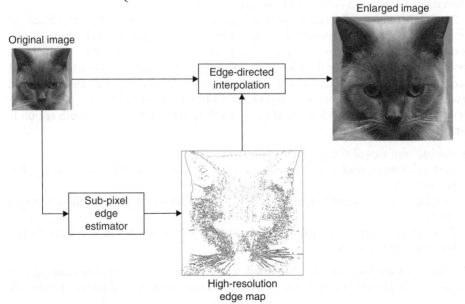

Figure 7.1 Framework of general explicit edge-directed interpolation [3].

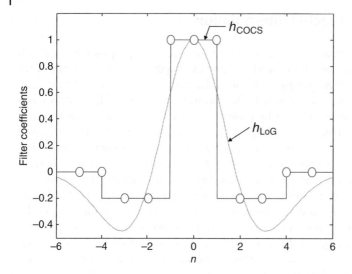

Figure 7.2 The center-on-surround-off filter and Laplacian-of-Gaussian filter.

where $[m, n]$ is the 2D index, R_c is the radius of the center-on region, and R_s is the outer boundary of the surround-off region. Figure 7.2 shows the 1D plot of COCS and LoG filters along $n = 0$ axis. It is vivid that the COCS filter closely approximates the LoG filter at the sampling incident. If we give up the rotational invariant property, the COCS filter can be implemented as a dimension separable filter. As a result, the 2D filtering process can be obtained by convolving the 1D filter in row–column fashion similar to that discussed in Section 2.4. However, even with a dimension separating implementation of the COCS filter, it is computationally expensive when compared with that of the LoG filter, where nine additions/subtractions and two multiplications are required to produce each output point with the dimension separated COCS filter being recursively applied in row–column (separable dimension) fashion.

The COCS filter has the same functional form as that of the LoG filter and is able to locate the edge at zero-crossing location, at which the pixel gradient exhibits the maximum rate of change. In summary, the sub-pixel edge detection is performed by first applying the COCS filter to the low-resolution image. This gradient map will be divided into rectangular blocks with each of the block corners containing the original filtered pixels (see Figure 7.3). A zero-crossing search within the sub-pixel location will be performed. The decision to determine the sub-pixels to be an edge or a smooth region is detailed in the following:

1) *Smooth regions*: All corners are in same sign.
2) *Vertical or horizontal edge*: Two adjacent corners have a different sign from the other two corners.
3) *Two intersecting edges*: Diagonal corners have a different sign from the other two corners.
4) *Edge separating one of the four corners*: One corner has a different sign from that of the other three corners.

The zero-crossing locations are estimated as the position where the lines joining two corners are of different signs. Let us consider an edge example as shown in Figure 7.3,

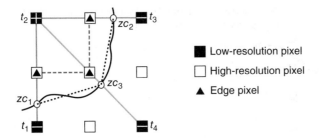

Figure 7.3 Lattices for edge-directed interpolation.

where the solid line denotes the edge in the low-resolution image. The dark pixels are the low-resolution corner pixels (denoted as "t_1," "t_2," "t_3," and "t_4") of the COCS filtered image block in concern. With scaling factor set to be 2, the white pixels are the sub-pixel location for which we shall determine if it is an edge pixel or pixel in a smooth region. The estimated edge map is therefore given by both the dark and white pixels in Figure 7.3. To determine the locations of the high-resolution edge pixels, all corner pixels of the COCS filtered gradient map will be compared and then linearly interpolated. In this example, only the corner "t_2" has a positive COCS filtered output gradient, while all the other three corner pixels, namely, "t_1," "t_3," and "t_4," have negative COCS filtered output gradients. A zero-crossing point exists when any two corners under comparison have different gradient signs. In this example, we shall be able to determine three zero-crossing points: zc_1 (between "t_1" and "t_2"), zc_2 (between "t_2" and "t_3"), and zc_3 (between "t_2" and "t_4"). The exact locations are determined by the linear interpolation between the COCS filtered output gradient intensities of the corresponding corner pixel pairs. The white pixel located midway of the pair or corner dark pixels with different polarity of COCS filtered output will be regarded as edge pixels. In this example, these sub-pixel edge pixels are marked with triangles. In analog image, the edge runs through all zero-crossing points (i.e. the dotted line in Figure 7.3). However, in the sub-pixel edge map, the edge is represented by piecewise linear line connecting those edge pixels (i.e. the dashed line in Figure 7.3).

The high-resolution edge map obtained by the sub-pixel edge estimation is applied to determine which interpolation strategy should be applied to interpolate the corresponding pixel. If the pixel to be interpolated is not an edge pixel, simple bilinear interpolation is performed with equal weighting factor from all the four low-resolution neighboring pixels. On the other hand, if the pixel to be interpolated is an edge, the weighting of the bilinear interpolation will be adjusted according to the distance between the zero-crossing points from the corresponding low-resolution neighboring pixels.

The sub-pixel edge estimation is a second-order edge estimation technique. As a result, weak edges and noise may get magnified during the edge interpolation process. A pre-processing step is required to suppress unwanted noise. Moreover, the zero-crossing points are estimated in a block of four corners, which is not enough to provide a precise estimation of the actual edge location. As an example, in the case where one of the corners has a relatively very small value (pixel "a" in Figure 7.4) than the others, the edge will be estimated to be located outside the block as shown in Figure 7.4 because of the interpolation error. This problem can be alleviated by considering the mean intensity of the neighboring pixels of each corner pixel [3].

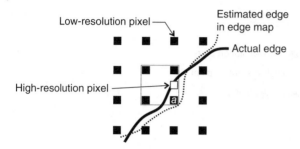

Figure 7.4 Estimation errors aroused by edge map.

Besides the general explicit EDI method [3], there are other EDI methods that utilize sub-pixel edge maps. This include the interpolation method presented by Wu and Zhang [65], which first finds the texture orientation map using directional Gabor filter with sub-pixel precision, and then a Fisher discriminant kernel is applied to refine the interpolation direction. The interpolation method presented by Carrato and Tenze [13] will first replicate the pixels and then correct their intensities by a rational operator designed to produce a least squares error average from some predefined edge patterns. This method is simple and suitable for hardware implementations. Dube and Hong [24] make use of a simple classification-based interpolation scheme to first classify the edges into some predetermined prototypes of directions and then to apply suitable directional filtering to sharpen the edges of the interpolated image. Jensen and Anastassiou [34] proposed an operator to fit detected edges with deterministic templates to improve the visual quality of the interpolated image. In some cases [34] the interpolation quality is better than that obtained from linear filtering, where the edges in the interpolated image are sharper. But the same algorithm [34] will sometimes result in an interpolated image that looks contrived and unnatural. This is because the large-scale context of edges is not considered and small variations in texture could be interpreted as an edge and mistakenly fitted with an edge template. Such mistakes result in distortion of textures. The computational complexity of the algorithm [34] is also too high for real-time implementation. All the above reviewed EDI methods are based on sub-pixel edge estimation aiming at producing interpolated images with improved quality. There are always additional steps that can be developed and implemented to improve the generation of the edge map, and to lower the edge estimation error. The following sections will discuss some of the popular *additional steps* in literature.

7.2 Implicit Edge-Directed Interpolation

The explicit EDI is intuitive and is easy to implement. However, the interpolation performance is highly dependent on the accuracy of the edge map. Moreover, as the edge map has to be extracted before the actual interpolation, it is not possible to apply the explicit EDI to streaming image or without the knowledge of the entire image. As a result, the implicit EDI, the counterpart of explicit EDI, is found to be very popular in vast image processing applications. As described by its name, implicit EDI does not require the use of edge map explicitly. The edge information is considered implicitly along with the interpolation. In the rest of this chapter, we shall review three implicit EDI methods.

7.2.1 Canny Edge Interpolation (CEI)

The *Canny edge interpolation* (CEI) [57] is well received as a simple and efficient image interpolation method. However it is not entirely an implicit EDI method. To understand why it is somewhere in between implicit and explicit EDI, we shall consider the CEI illustrated in Figure 7.5, which involves three steps. The CEI first up-samples the entire image by bilinear or bicubic interpolation as in Figure 7.5a, where the dark pixels are all the low-resolution pixels and the gray pixels are the newly added pixels with their intensity values estimated by bilinear or bicubic interpolation. Then the edge pixels of the up-sampled image are detected by Canny edge detector. This is also the reason why the interpolation method is named as *Canny* edge interpolation. Therefore, CEI does generate an edge map. However, the edge map is not generated from the low-resolution image through sub-pixel edge estimator as those considered in explicit EDI. Furthermore, the edge map is being generated on the fly when interpolating pixels. The pixels in the high-resolution image identified as edges by Canny detector will be estimated by linear interpolation function determined according to the spatial structure. As an example, let us consider the image block g in Figure 7.5b. The Sobel horizontal (SD_h) and the Sobel vertical (SD_v) derivatives of g are given by [57]

$$SD_h[m, n] = \frac{g[m-1, n-1] - g[m-1, n+1]}{4} + \frac{g[m, n-1] - g[m, n+1]}{2}$$
$$+ \frac{g[m+1, n-1] - g[m+1, n+1]}{4}, \tag{7.2}$$

$$\text{and} \quad SD_v(m, n) = \frac{g[m-1, n-1] - g[m+1, n+1]}{4} + \frac{g[m-1, n] - g[m+1, n]}{2}$$
$$+ \frac{g[m-1, n+1] - g[m+1, n+1]}{4}. \tag{7.3}$$

The gradients obtained by these two derivatives are compared, and the comparison result directs the appropriate low-resolution pixels to be applied in the interpolation process. When $|SD_h(m, n)| \geqslant |SD_v(m, n)|$, the horizontal edge dominates, such that the

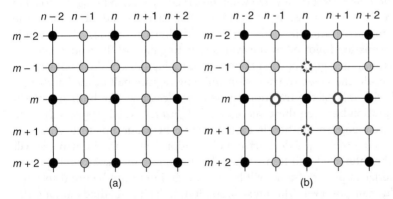

Figure 7.5 Illustration of Canny edge interpolation (CEI): (a) high-resolution image block obtained from up-sampling a low-resolution image block (the dark pixels are the original low-resolution pixels, and the gray pixels are newly added pixels with intensity estimated by bilinear interpolation) and (b) post-processing on edge pixels (white pixels): replacement of pixel intensity according to the edge orientation.

high-resolution pixels (the white pixels in solid outlines in Figure 7.5b) are estimated from the neighboring pixels in the same row given by

$$g[m, n - 1] = \frac{1}{2}(g[m, n - 1] + g[m, n - 2]), \tag{7.4}$$

$$g[m, n + 1] = \frac{1}{2}(g[m, n + 1] + g[m, n + 2]). \tag{7.5}$$

Similarly, when $|SD_h(m, n)| < |SD_v(m, n)|$, the vertical edge dominates, such that the high-resolution pixels (the white pixels in dotted outlines in Figure 7.5b) are estimated from the neighboring pixels in the same row given by

$$g[m - 1, n] = \frac{1}{2}(g[m - 1, n] + g[m - 2, n]), \tag{7.6}$$

$$g[m + 1, n] = \frac{1}{2}(g[m + 1, n] + g[m + 2, n]). \tag{7.7}$$

It should be noted that the edge pixels in Figure 7.5b are for illustration only, for which they may not be considered as edge pixels simultaneously in practice.

The CEI is able to improve the visual quality of the interpolated image by preserving the edge structure. However, the accuracy of the edge detection is limited by the threshold value set in the Canny edge detector. Moreover, only the horizontal and vertical edges are considered, thus limiting the edge structure to be preserved. Finally, CEI has a drawback that it requires the up-sampling of image before the edge detection, where estimation errors are inevitable in the up-sampling process, and irrevocably leads to falsely detected edge and hence wrong EDI result.

7.2.2 Edge-Based Line Averaging (ELA)

The implicit EDI reviewed in this section is developed to de-interlace images. Image interlace is a technique developed to reduce the bandwidth for video broadcasting. Traditional video broadcasting sends image sequence periodically known as frame, and thus the *motion pictures* form a video when observed by human being. Interlacing technique reduces the transmission bandwidth, such that instead of sending the complete image in each frame, it sends out the odd alternating lines of the whole image in one transmission followed by the even alternating lines of the whole image in the next transmission, then goes back to the odd alternating lines of the whole image, and so on. As a result, the video transmission will only require half of the bandwidth when compared with that of the traditional video broadcasting. The human eye will perform the integration between these successive *half frames*, which appears as if the complete image are being transmitted in each frame of the motion picture. However, this type of interlacing technique does have its limitation, where the human eye will fail to integrate the interlaced half frame when the frame rate or resolution is low. In this case, the interlaced picture frame will have to be de-interlaced before displaying in front of the human observer. The most basic de-interlacing methods among the many of its varieties is *edge-based line averaging* (ELA) [23], which considers the spatial correlation of the pixels in the vertical direction and the two diagonal directions within a 3×3 training window formed by pixels (the dark pixels) from the interlaced image together with the pixels (the white pixels) to be interpolated as shown in Figure 7.6.

The ELA can be divided into two steps: edge estimation and interpolation. The edges are located by spatial correlation measurement, which computes and compares the pixel intensity difference between a pair of oppositely located pixels in the training window. They are denoted as D_1, D_2, and D_3 in the example in Figure 7.6 and are given by

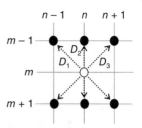

$$D_1 = |g[m-1, n-1] - g[m+1, n+1]|, \quad (7.8)$$

$$D_2 = |g[m-1, n] - g[m-1, n]|, \quad (7.9)$$

$$D_3 = |g[m+1, n+1] - g[m-1, n+1]|. \quad (7.10)$$

Figure 7.6 The 3×3 training window of ELA method.

Recall that the edge is defined as the location where an abrupt change in pixel intensity occurs. As a result, the larger the magnitude of D_1, D_2, and D_3, the more likely that the edge exists across the corresponding pair of pixels. In order to preserve the edge structure, the missing pixel should be estimated along the pixel pair that gives the minimum intensity difference, such that the edge structure would not be altered. Therefore, the ELA estimates the unknown pixel $g[m, n]$ as

$$g[m,n] = \begin{cases} (g[m-1, n-1] + g[m+1, n+1])/2, & \text{for } \min(D_1, D_2, D_3) = D_1, \\ (g[m-1, n] + g[m-1, n])/2, & \text{for } \min(D_1, D_2, D_3) = D_2, \\ (g[m+1, n-1] + g[m+1, n+1])/2, & \text{otherwise.} \end{cases}$$

$$(7.11)$$

The ELA achieves good performance in most of the cases. In particular it interpolates the unknown pixel in horizontal direction only (along the line only). Therefore it seldom suffers from jaggy problem. Nonetheless, this method considers only edges in three directions (vertical, 45°, and 135°), where the adopted edge information may not be able to accurately represent the actual edge orientation, thus resulting in interpolation errors that degrade the visual quality of the de-interlaced image. Moreover, only edge information within the training window will be considered for the estimation of the de-interlaced pixel, where the limited size of the window (the interpolation kernel size) that contains pixels to be involved in each interpolation process will result in severe visual artifacts for those image regions that contain high frequency intensity changes.

7.2.3 Directional-Orientation Interpolation (DOI)

The *directional-orientation interpolation* (DOI) is a variation of the ELA method aiming to achieve higher accuracy and finer resolution in edge detection by using sliding 3×3 training window instead of a fixed window as in ELA [69]. The training window slides through a predefined search area within the up-sampled image as illustrated in Figure 7.7, where the dark pixels mark the locations of the low-resolution interlaced image pixels. Let us denote the pixel to be interpolated as $g[m, n]$, and it is to be estimated from the "center training window." It should be noted that the center training window is exactly the same as that in ELA. With a search range equal to 3, the 3×3 window will be applied to 6 different locations (3 with centers around $m - 2$ and another 3 with centers around $m + 2$) as illustrated by the dotted square boxes in Figure 7.7, where the windows are shifted from 3 columns left of the center training window to 3 columns right of the

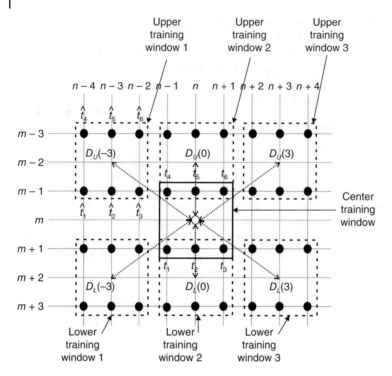

Figure 7.7 The sliding training window in directional-orientation interpolation (DOI), where the training window size is 3 × 3 and the search range is $k \in \{-3, 0, 3\}$.

center training window. As a result, the number of low-resolution pixels considered by all the training windows in DOI is 36 pixels compared with 6 pixels in ELA.

The spatial correlation measurement of all the pixels in all the sliding windows to the center window is computed by the upper region *spatial correlation vector* $D_U(k)$ and the lower region spatial correlation vector $D_L(k)$ based on squares error cost functions given by

$$D_U(k) = \sum_{\ell=-1}^{1} (|f(m+1, n+\ell) - f(m-1, n+\ell+k)|^2 + |f(m-1, n+\ell)$$

$$-f(m-3, n+\ell+k)|^2), \qquad \forall k \in [-3, 3], \tag{7.12}$$

$$D_L(k) = \sum_{\ell=-1}^{1} (|f(m+1, n+\ell) - f(m+3, n+\ell+k)|^2 + |f(m-1, n+\ell)$$

$$-f(m+1, n+\ell+k)|^2), \qquad \forall k \in [-3, 3], \tag{7.13}$$

where k is the index of the spatial correlation vector and the sliding window is exposed to the search range $[-R, R]$ (where $R = 3$ in the example shown in Figure 7.7). It should be noted that the step size of the sliding window moving in the image is defined by the size of the training window [69]. The subscripts U and L in the spatial correlation vectors denote the upper and the lower rows of the center training window being considered, respectively. $D_U(k)$ and $D_L(k)$ represent the sum of the squares pixel intensity difference between corresponding pixels in the center training window and that in the shifted training window under consideration. Considering the upper left training window in Figure 7.7, $D_U(-3)$ is computed as the summation of the squares intensity difference between the corresponding pixel pairs in the two windows. In this case, it is computed as the intensity difference between "t_1" and "$\hat{t}_1$" and then summed with the difference between "t_2" and "$\hat{t}_2$," and so on, for all six pairs of pixels. If the spatial correlation vectors have a high magnitude, it indicates a high likeliness of the existence of an edge. It also implies that the window structure is less correlated. To preserve the edge structure, the unknown pixel should be estimated with reference to the training window with similar structure. The training window that gives the spatial correlation vector with the minimum magnitude as

$$SDV_U = \arg\min\{D_U\}, \tag{7.14}$$

$$SDV_L = \arg\min\{D_L\}, \tag{7.15}$$

should be considered in the interpolation process, such that the unknown pixel is computed as

$$g[m, n] = \frac{f(m-1, n+i_U) + f(m+1, n+i_L)}{2}, \tag{7.16}$$

where $i_U = SDV_U/2$ and $i_L = SDV_L/2$. If i_U and i_L are not integers, $g[m, n]$ can be obtained by linear interpolation along the horizontal direction.

The use of sliding window makes DOI more robust and can preserve the integrity of the edge better. However, the use of sliding window suffers from the problem of generating periodic structural visual artifacts. Moreover, the edge orientation being considered is still restricted to three directions (vertical, 45°, and 135°), thus limiting the improvement on DOI over ELA.

7.2.4 Error-Amended Sharp Edge (EASE)

The error-amended sharp edge (EASE) [16] method extends the structural correlation measurement (from two directions in CEI and three directions in ELA and DOI) to four directions to obtain more accurate edge information for image interpolation (instead of de-interlacing). Furthermore, EASE utilizes two pixel pairs to estimate the unknown pixel, which can better preserve the edge structure than other methods that utilize single pixel pair. As a result, EASE can suppress staircase artifacts and achieve better interpolation results. EASE interpolates an image through two steps. The first step of EASE is a modified piecewise linear interpolation, where a coarse interpolated pixel $\hat{g}[n]$ (the square pixel in Figure 7.8) is first estimated from its neighboring pixels by linear interpolation. Then the interpolation error between $\hat{g}$ and the actual high-resolution signal g (the solid line in Figure 7.8) will be estimated. The intensity of the pixel $\hat{g}[n]$ will be amended with the estimated error to obtain the final interpolated pixel $g[n]$. It should be noted that although EASE-based image interpolation is not dimension separable, it is symmetric in both rows and columns. As a result, we shall first concentrate on the discussion of applying EASE in 1D interpolation (1D EASE) and then extend it to 2D.

The estimation problem of 1D EASE can be described by the example in Figure 7.8, where the solid line is the original continuous signal, while the dark dots indicate the locations of the pixels obtained with low-resolution sampling of the continuous

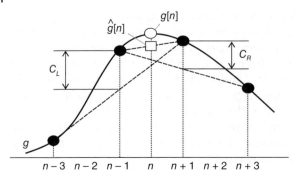

Figure 7.8 1D error-amended sharp edge (EASE).

signal. With an interpolation ratio of 2, linear interpolation will be applied to fill the low-resolution signal f to generate a coarse estimated signal $\hat{g}$ with the same resolution as that of the high-resolution signal, where $\hat{g}[n]$ is given by

$$\hat{g}[n] = \frac{g[n-1] + g[n+1]}{2}, \tag{7.17}$$

with n being odd, and $g[n-1]$ and $g[n+1]$ are obtained from the low-resolution signal $f[(n-1)/2]$ and $f[(n+1)/2]$ with the coordinates rounded to the nearest integer. In the estimation error-free case, the intensity of $\hat{g}[n]$ should overlap with the original continuous signal $g[n]$ (the white dot). However, when there is estimation error, as in the case of Figure 7.8, $\hat{g}[n]$ (the white square) will not overlap with $g[n]$ (the white dot). In this case, the 1D EASE will estimate an error correction factor $e_c[n]$ as

$$e_c[n] = \frac{\min \text{mod}(C_L, C_R)}{4}, \tag{7.18}$$

where C_L and C_R are shown in Figure 7.8, and the operator

$$\min \text{mod}(a, b) = \begin{cases} a, & \text{if } ab > 0 \text{ and } |a| \leqslant |b|, \\ b, & \text{if } ab > 0 \text{ and } |a| > |b|, \\ 0, & \text{if } ab \leqslant 0. \end{cases} \tag{7.19}$$

Compared with ELA and DOI, the estimation kernel size considered by EASE includes four neighboring pixels. The two terms in Eq. (7.19) measure the signal variation within this estimation kernel. In particular, C_L estimates the variation on the left-hand side of the estimated signal $\hat{g}[n]$, while C_R estimates the variation on the right-hand side of the estimated signal $\hat{g}[n]$.

$$C_L = g[n-1] - \frac{g[n-3] + g[n+1]}{2}, \tag{7.20}$$

$$C_R = g[n+1] - \frac{g[n-1] + g[n+3]}{2}. \tag{7.21}$$

Among C_L and C_R, the one with smaller magnitude should be chosen as estimation error between $\hat{g}$ and g. The final high-resolution pixel intensity should be given by the sum of this estimation error term $e_c[n]$ and the coarse estimation $\hat{g}[n]$ as

$$g[n] = \hat{g}[n] + e_c[n]. \tag{7.22}$$

For pixels located at the boundaries of $\hat{g}$ (the two ends of the signal $\hat{g}$), there will not be enough signals to estimate $e_c[n]$. In these cases, the 1D EASE simply lets $e_c[n]$ be zero. The MATLAB code in Listing 7.2.1 implemented the 1D EASE as the function easeld. The original low-resolution $1 \times N$ data f is the input to this function, and the function will return an up-sampled g with dimension $1 \times 2N$. When the interpolation rate increases from 2 to 4, the readers will only have to change all the 2* to 4*, and the program will run and generate the interpolation result with interpolation ratio equal to 4. The first four lines of code resample and zero pad the low-resolution signal. The interpolated signals at the boundaries are handled separately by the next three lines of the codes. The codes in the for loop will interpolate the signal one by one by implementing Eqs. (7.17)–(7.22).

MATLAB 7.2.1—1D EASE function.

```
function g = easeld(f)
   g=directusld(f);
   [M1 N1]=size(g);
   % settle end point data on both sides
   g(1,2)=(f(1,1)+f(1,2))/2; % 2nd column data
   g(1,N1-2)=(f(1,N1/2)+f(1,N1/2-1))/2; % last third column data
   g(1,N1)=f(1,N1/2); % last column data

   for n=4:2:N1-4
      CL=g(1,n-1)-(g(1,n+1)+g(1,n-3))/2; % Equation 7.20
      CR=g(1,n+1)-(g(1,n-1)+g(1,n+3))/2; % Equation 7.21
      % minmod operator
      if (CL*CR)>0
            if (abs(CL)>abs(CR))
                 minmod=CR;
            else
                 minmod=CL;
            end;
      else
            minmod=0;
      end;
      g(1,n)=(g(1,n-1)+g(1,n+1))/2+minmod/4; % Equation 7.22
   end;
return;
```

where the low-resolution vector f is first zero padded by directusld, a function similar to its 2D version directus in Eq. (4.1), and is formally defined by the following equation

$$g[2 \times n] = \begin{cases} f[n], & n \in [0, N-1], \\ 0, & \text{otherwise.} \end{cases} \tag{7.23}$$

MATLAB 7.2.2—directus1d: 1D direct up-sample by zero padding.

```
function g = directusld(f)
    [M,N]=size(f);
    g=zeros(1,2*N);
    g(1,1:2:end)=f;
return;
```

Interpolation will then be performed on the zero-padded signal according to Eqs. (7.20)–(7.22).

To extend the 1D EASE to 2D, we shall consider Figure 7.9, where the dark dots correspond to the low-resolution image pixels and the gray dots are the pixels to be interpolated. Similar to 1D EASE, a coarse estimation $\hat{g}[m, n]$ of the pixel to be interpolated will be obtained from applying 1D EASE to f by row and then by column. The difference between $\hat{g}$ and the actual high-resolution image will be estimated and used to correct $\hat{g}$. In the 1D EASE, the signal variation on the left- and right-hand sides of $\hat{g}[n]$ is computed and used as the error correction estimation. In 2D EASE, besides the left- and right-hand sides, there will also be the upper and lower sides of $\hat{g}[n]$ that need to be considered. The signal variation is measured by Sobel derivatives along these four orientations, which are obtained by positioning the Sobel derivative kernel on four different spatial locations around $\hat{g}[n]$ as indicated in Figure 7.9 and listed in the following.

$$D_1 = |g[m-1, n+1] + 2g[m, n+1] + g[m+1, n+1]$$
$$-g[m-1, n-1] - 2f[m, n-1] - f[m+1, n-1]|, \tag{7.24}$$

$$D_2 = \sqrt{2}|g[m-1, n] + g[m-1, n+1] + g[m, n+1]$$
$$-g[m, n-1] - g[m+1, n-1] - g[m+1, n]|, \tag{7.25}$$

$$D_3 = |g[m-1, n-1] + 2g[m-1, n] + g[m-1, n+1]$$
$$-g[m+1, n-1] - 2f[m+1, n] - f[m+1, n+1]|, \tag{7.26}$$

$$D_4 = \sqrt{2}|g[m, n-1] + g[m-1, n-1] + g[m-1, n]$$
$$-g[m, n+1] - g[m+1, n+1] - g[m+1, n]|, \tag{7.27}$$

where D_1, D_2, D_3, and D_4 measure the signal variation along vertical, 45°, horizontal, and 135° orientations. Note that a high signal variation actually indicates the existence of an edge perpendicular to the direction of variation. As a result, we can determine if the pixel $g[m, n]$ is located on a smooth region or be part of an edge by examining the magnitude of these four derivatives. By doing so, we have achieved EDI already. The 2D EASE takes a step further to consider two directions at the same time with appropriate weighting to

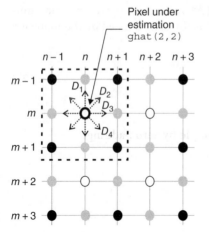

Figure 7.9 2D error-amended sharp edge (EASE).

determine if the pixel $g[m, n]$ is part of an edge or not. Consider two parameters D_p and D_q defined as

$$D_p = \min(D_1, D_3), \tag{7.28}$$
$$D_q = \min(D_2, D_4), \tag{7.29}$$

with $p = \{1, 3\}$ and $q = \{2, 4\}$ depending on the result of the min operation. When these two parameters are larger than a predefined threshold (which can be zero), the pixel $g[m, n]$ is in a smooth region, and no error correction is required. Otherwise, it will be either a horizontal or a diagonal edge, and the interpolated pixel should be given by

$$g[m, n] = \frac{\sqrt{2}D_p}{D_p + \sqrt{2}D_q} L_p + \frac{D_p}{D_p + \sqrt{2}D_1} L_q, \tag{7.30}$$

where L_p and L_q are given by

$$L_1 = (g[m, n-1] + g[m, n+1])/2, \tag{7.31}$$
$$L_2 = (g[m+1, n-1] + g[m-1, n+1])/2, \tag{7.32}$$
$$L_3 = (g[m-1, n] + g[m+1, n])/2, \tag{7.33}$$
$$L_4 = (g[m-1, n-1] + g[m+1, n+1])/2. \tag{7.34}$$

Listing 7.2.3 shows the MATLAB code of the function `ease2d` that implements the 2D EASE image interpolation with the input parameter `ghat` being the localized region to be considered in the 2D EASE for the estimation of $g[m, n]$. It should be noted that the mapping of the pixels in the function to that of Figure 7.9 is based on the reference points of `ghat(1,1)` and `ghat(1,2)`, which are actually $g[m-1, n-1] = \hat{g}[m-1, n-1]$ and $g[m, n-1] = \hat{g}[m, n-1]$ in the figure, respectively. To make it easy for the readers to understand the MATLAB implementation, the equation numbers are printed next to the corresponding MATLAB codes in Listing 7.2.3.

MATLAB 7.2.3—EASE 2D function.

```
function g = ease2d(ghat)

  % ghat(1,1) refers to ghat[m-1,n-1] in Figure 7.9,
  % ghat(1,2) refers to ghat[m,n-1] in Figure 7.9, and so on.
  D1=abs(ghat(3,3)+2*ghat(2,3)+ghat(1,3)-ghat(3,1)-2*ghat(2,1)-ghat
      (1,1));       % Equation 7.23
  D2=sqrt(2)*abs(ghat(1,2)+ghat(1,3)+ghat(2,3)-ghat(2,1)-ghat(3,1)-
      ghat(3,2));   % Equation 7.24
  D3=abs(ghat(1,1)+2*ghat(1,2)+ghat(1,3)-ghat(3,1)-2*ghat(3,2)-ghat
      (3,3));       % Equation 7.25
  D4=sqrt(2)*abs(ghat(2,1)+ghat(1,1)+ghat(1,2)-ghat(3,2)-ghat(3,3)-
      ghat(2,3));   % Equation 7.26
  L1=(ghat(2,1)+ghat(2,3))/2; % Equation 7.30
  L2=(ghat(3,1)+ghat(1,3))/2; % Equation 7.31
  L3=(ghat(3,2)+ghat(1,2))/2; % Equation 7.32
  L4=(ghat(3,3)+ghat(1,1))/2; % Equation 7.33

  if (D1>D3) Dp=D3; Lp=L3;    % Equation 7.27
  else Dp=D1; Lp=L1; end;
```

```
   if (D2>D4) Dq=D4; Lq=L4;      % Equation 7.28
   else Dq=D2; Lq=L2; end;

   g=ghat;                        % initialization of output matrix
   if (Dp+Dq==0)                  % when image data are flat
     g(2,2)=g(1,1);
   else                           % normal case and hence Equation 7.29
     g(2,2)=sqrt(2)*Dq/(Dp+sqrt(2)*Dq)*Lp+Dp/(Dp+sqrt(2)*Dq)*Lq;
   end;
 return
```

Finally the complete EASE image interpolation is implemented in MATLAB Listing 7.2.4 as the function ease. The input to ease is the low-resolution image f and will return a 2× interpolated high-resolution image g. The function will first resample the input low-resolution image by zero padding with directus. A coarse interpolation will be performed on the up-sampled signal by applying ease1d row wise and then apply column transpose before another 1D EASE to achieve the row–column application of 1D EASE to the 2D image. The high-resolution image interpolation error correction using ease2d will be applied to the coarse estimated interpolated image to yield the final high quality interpolated image.

MATLAB 7.2.4—EASE interpolation.

```
function g=ease(f)
  [M1 N1]=size(g);
  g=directus(f);   % lattice expansion
  for m=1:2:M1     % coarse estimation
    g(m,:)=ease1d(f((m+1)/2,:)); % interpolation on rows
    g(:,m)=(ease1d(f(:,(m+1)/2)'))'; % interpolation on columns
  end
  for m=1:2:(M1-3)  % 2D EASE error compensation
    for n=1:2:(N1-3)
        g(m:m+2,n:n+2)=ease2d(g(m:m+2,n:n+2));
  end end
  return;
```

The EASE interpolation results of the synthetic image letter *A* are shown in Figure 7.10. It can be observed from the intensity maps along the horizontal edge and diagonal edge shown in the same figure that there are staircase artifacts. However, it can also be observed that the edges are preserved better than that obtained by bilinear interpolation, where the edge is smooth along the edge direction in the EASE case. It can also be observed that the annoying ringing artifact is alleviated in the EASE interpolated image when compared with that of the bicubic interpolation. These show that the EASE image interpolation method is able to preserve the edge integrity and the edge-adaptive piecewise linear interpolation in EASE can alleviate the ringing artifact problem in the interpolated image.

The *Cat* image interpolation result using EASE has PSNR of 28.16 dB and SSIM of 0.8429 and is shown in Figure 7.11. If we compare the EASE *Cat* image interpolation result with that of the bicubic interpolation, such as the area around the whiskers of the *Cat* image, we can observed that the *Cat* image obtained by EASE has the whiskers of the *Cat* image to be observed as a continuous line along the edge direction with less staircase jaggy than that are observed in other nonparametric image interpolation results.

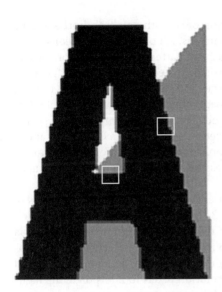

0	0	0	68	135	135	135	135	135
0	0	0	68	135	135	135	135	135
0	0	0	68	135	135	135	135	135
0	0	0	0	68	135	135	135	135
0	0	0	0	0	68	135	135	135
0	0	0	0	0	68	135	135	135
0	0	0	0	0	68	135	135	135
0	0	0	0	0	68	135	135	135
0	0	0	0	0	68	135	135	135
0	0	0	0	0	68	135	135	135

135	135	135	135	135	135	135	135	135
135	135	135	135	135	135	135	135	135
135	135	135	135	135	135	135	135	135
135	135	135	135	135	135	135	135	135
68	68	68	68	68	68	68	68	68
0	0	0	0	0	0	0	0	0
0	0	0	0	0	0	0	0	0
0	0	0	0	0	0	0	0	0
0	0	0	0	0	0	0	0	0
0	0	0	0	0	0	0	0	0

Figure 7.10 2× interpolated image of "letter A" using EASE and the associated intensity maps of the enclosed diagonal and vertical edges.

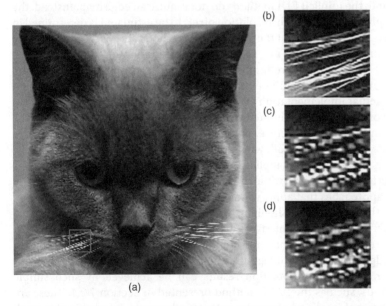

Figure 7.11 2× interpolated *Cat* image by EASE with PSNR = 28.16 dB and SSIM = 0.8429 and the associated zoom-in images of the whiskers of the *Cat* image taken from (b) the original image, (c) the bicubic interpolated image, and (d) the EASE interpolated image.

7.3   Summary

Natural image can be considered as a combination of smooth patches, short and long edges in different orientations, and mixture of patterns. All of these can be considered as image features. Among all these features, edges and patterns take the major stake in representing the image contents. To preserve the interpolated image integrity ("geometric regularity" [43]), the perseverance of image edges and patterns is prevailing. The EDI method is able to "adapt" to the "edges" of the image and obtain visually pleasant interpolation result. At the same time, the EDI method is simple as it only requires spatial domain operations when compared with those methods presented in Chapters 5 and 6. Therefore, the EDI is always an active research topic in image resolution enhancement. The EDI methods in literature can be roughly classified into two approaches: "explicit" EDI and "implicit" EDI.

The explicit EDI methods compute an explicit edge map that labels the locations of edge pixels in the image. The EDI method in [3] is considered as a general explicit EDI method with the edge map generated from the low-resolution image directly via "sub-pixel edge estimation." Once the edge map is available, the interpolation process is intuitive where different sets of weighting factors according to the nature of the pixel (edge or non-edge) will be applied to the low-resolution pixels to interpolate the high-resolution unknown pixels. Notwithstanding its effectiveness in preserving sharp edges, all explicit EDI methods suffer from the inherent problem that the interpolation result is very sensitive to the accuracy of the edge map. Furthermore, the explicit EDI methods are operated in a pixel-by-pixel basis based on the edge map information, which increases the computational complexity.

On the other hand, the implicit EDI methods do not require an edge map. Instead, the edge or non-edge property of the high-resolution pixels to be estimated is determined in the course of interpolation. As a result the implicit EDI methods are observed to be more computationally simple, as they do not require the computation of edge map before the interpolation. However, there are implicit EDI methods, such as the CEI method presented in Section 7.2.1, that require extra steps to post-process the low-resolution image before the actual implementation. Moreover, the edge model is constrained to a limited number of directions and limited training window sizes, which degrades the quality in preserving the edge structure. Nevertheless, the implicit EDI methods are able to demonstrate the flexibility of allowing interpolation without the complete image information, which are attractive to applications such as image streaming where interpolation can be performed on the fly while the images are being streamed in. To improve the performance, approaches that apply window overlapping and increased number of edge directions in the image model should be considered.

The implicit EDI methods presented in this chapter are simple and only involve correlation measurement (which does not require the use of statistical edge model, while statistical edge model-based image interpolation will be the topic of the next chapter). However, accurate interpolation results can be achieved by such simple implicit EDI methods, such as the EASE method presented in Section 7.2.4. There are many other variations of implicit EDI methods that we have not covered in this book but able to achieve pleasant interpolation results without scarifying the computation simplicity. During our discussions of the EASE method in Section 7.2.4, we introduced that the idea of the ultimate goal of image interpolation is to keep the interpolation error minimal. A simple approach that we can think of is minimizing the error through iterative error correction, similar to that in Sections 5.6 and 6.4. However, there are so many different kinds of edges (or so-called texture or features) in a natural image. Therefore, it is not possible for us to formulate the error correction problem as some simple first-order derivative of the objective function. As a result, in order to reach the ultimate goal, statistical model of image features is indispensable. In the next chapter, we shall introduce the "covariance-based interpolation" that incorporates a statistical model of the image edges to achieve excellent image interpolation results.

7.4   Exercises

7.1   Generate the sub-pixel edge map of the natural image *Cat* in MATLAB using the COCS filter with the following filter coefficients.
1. With $h_c = h_s = 1$ and $R_s = R_c = 3$
2. With $h_c = h_s = 1$ and $R_s = R_c = 5$
3. With $h_c = h_s = 1$ and $R_s = R_c = 7$
[*Hint*: The edge map is binary in nature, where a logic "1" will be assigned to edge pixel and a logic "0" will be assigned to non-edge pixel.]

7.2   Compare the visual difference on the sub-pixel edge maps generated in Exercise 7.1 (1), (2), and (3).

7.3   Canny edge interpolation (CEI) generates the edge map by considering a high-resolution image generated by nonparametric interpolation. Implement CEI in MATLAB by creating a function g=cei(f), but using different nonparametric interpolation methods as listed in the following to generate the high-resolution image for edge map extraction.
1. bilinear interpolation using MATLAB function biinterp.
2. bicubic interpolation using MATLAB function bicubic.

8

Covariance-Based Interpolation

The previous chapter has shown the importance of maintaining the image edges in image interpolation to obtain a natural-looking interpolated image. We have discussed the basic structure and model of image edges. The multi-resolution analysis presented in the chapter on wavelet (Chapter 6) has shown that an ideal step edge obeys the geometric regularity property [43], which refers to the correlation structure of an ideal step edge being independent of the scale of the image. In other words, the correlation structure of the local region that has enclosed an edge feature in the low-resolution image should have a similar correlation structure in the corresponding region in the high-resolution image. The edge-directed interpolated algorithms presented in the last chapter aim to preserve the correlation structures across scales by estimating the unknown pixels with the consideration of the locations and orientations of the image edges. The locations and the orientations of the image edges are specified by explicit edge map obtained through some kind of edge detection techniques. There are several problems associated with such approach. Firstly, the edge detection technique quantized the edge orientation in finite number of cases. As a result, the interpolation results can only preserve limited classes of correlation structures during the interpolation process. In other words, the geometric regularity cannot be fully preserved between the low-resolution image and the interpolated high-resolution image. Secondly, the edge detection algorithm has detection accuracy problems in both the spatial location of the edge pixel and the orientation of the associated edge. As a result, the edge-directed interpolation algorithm might falsely preserve a nonexisting edge structure and results in image artifacts with unnatural appearance and low in peak signal-to-noise ratio (PSNR).

To achieve good image interpolation result, the geometric regularity property should be fully exploited. Various algorithms have been proposed in literature that aim to preserve the geometric regularity between the low-resolution image and the interpolated high-resolution image, which include directly considering the geometric regularity in spatial domain [12, 38], reformulating the problem into a set of partial differential equations [6, 47], and constructing a convex set of geometric regularity [54], and proposed a projection-onto-convex-set algorithm to achieve an interpolated image with the best matched correlation structure between the low-resolution image and the interpolated high-resolution image.

Digital Image Interpolation in MATLAB®, First Edition. Chi-Wah Kok and Wing-Shan Tam.
© 2019 John Wiley & Sons Singapore Pte. Ltd. Published 2019 by John Wiley & Sons Singapore Pte. Ltd.
Companion website: www.wiley.com/go/ditmatlab

Among all the algorithms in literature, the new edge-directed interpolation (NEDI) [40] proposed by Li and Orchard in 2001 is regarded as the first edge-adaptive interpolation method that can fully exploit the geometric regularity problem between the original image and the interpolated image. Instead of considering an explicit edge map obtained from some edge detection techniques, the NEDI performs linear prediction to estimate the unknown pixel intensity to interpolate low-resolution image directly on the covariance of a local window across the low-resolution image and the interpolated high-resolution image. The covariance preservation between the low-resolution image and the interpolated high-resolution image is known as the preservation of "geometric duality," which indirectly maintains the geometric regularity. The formulation and accuracy of the linear prediction involves the statistical model of a natural image and the minimization of the prediction error by considering the "minimum mean squares error" (MMSE). In this chapter, the second-order statistical model of natural image and the basic of MMSE optimization-based image interpolation method will be discussed.

8.1 Modeling of Image Features

Among various interpretation of natural image, one of the interpretations considers natural image as combination of patches of smooth regions and texture-rich regions. Image structure within the same region should be homogeneous. A detailed discussion on how different regions in an image are classified has been presented in Chapter 2. It has been shown that the human visual system (HVS) is sensitive to the region boundaries, while the boundaries can be completely closed to enclose an object or formed by short segments with arbitrary length and open ends lying in arbitrary directions. These boundaries are known as the "edges." Figure 8.1 shows portion of the pixel intensity map extracted from the *Cat* image, where abrupt pixel intensity changes are observed across the boundary and two relatively uniform regions are observed on the two sides of the edge. However, it is vivid that the distribution of the pixel intensity in each region has a certain pattern but the patterns in the two regions may not be consistent. Though there are intensity changes, the HVS is only sensitive to those with significant changes – in

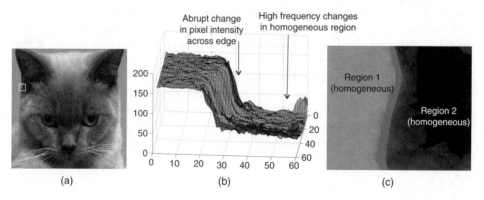

Figure 8.1 3D visualization of image containing edge: (a) original image with a selected portion under illustration, (b) the zoom-in 3D map, and (c) the intensity plot of the selected portion.

other words, more sensitive to the location where abrupt changes occur. To understand the importance on preserving edges in image interpolation, we can consider the geometric constraint in edge preservation for image interpolation through both psychological and information theoretical aspects. In the psychological point of view, HVS is sensitive to edge sharpness and artifacts appearing around edges instead of just the contrast of the homogeneous patches on the two sides of the edge. In the information theoretical aspect, estimating unknown pixel intensity along edge orientation will reduce the dimensionality of the estimation problem and render better estimation results. It has been shown in Section 2.5 that the edge property is the best analyzed by high-order statistics. In the next section, we shall discuss the modeling and analysis of edge features in digital image through second-order statistics. The presented statistical model will be applied in subsequent sections to develop image interpolation algorithms that preserve the geometric duality between low- and high-resolution images.

8.2   Interpolation by Autoregression

It has been discussed in Chapter 4 that the interpolation problem can be formulated as a weighted sum problem between the neighboring pixels surrounding the pixel to be interpolated. The bilinear interpolation makes use of the four neighboring pixels, and bicubic interpolation makes use of the 16 neighboring pixels. Let us consider the example of interpolating the missing pixel $g[2m + 1, 2n + 1]$ shown in Figure 8.2. When the image is modeled as random field, a fourth-order linear predictive image interpolation problem can be formulated as

$$g[2m + 1, 2n + 1] = \sum_{k=0}^{1} \sum_{\ell=0}^{1} \alpha[2k + \ell] g[2(m + k), 2(n + \ell)] + \eta[2m + 1, 2n + 1],$$

(8.1)

which is also known as a fourth-order autoregressive model with $\alpha[k]$ being the model parameters relating to the four neighbors of the interpolating pixel and η is the

Figure 8.2 Coefficients of linear prediction.

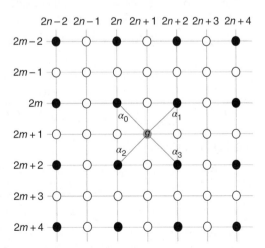

prediction error term. In particular, for 2× image interpolation, $g[2m, 2n] = f[m, n]$. As a result, Eq. (8.1) can be rewritten as

$$g[2m + 1, 2n + 1] = \sum_{k=0}^{1} \sum_{\ell=0}^{1} \alpha[2k + \ell] f[(m + k), (n + \ell)] + \eta[2m + 1, 2n + 1],$$

$$(8.2)$$

$$= \hat{g}[2m + 1, 2n + 1] + \eta[2m + 1, 2n + 1], \qquad (8.3)$$

which is an autoregressive model on f to produce g. In other words, Eq. (8.2) is a 2× image interpolation formulation with $\hat{g}$ in Eq. (8.3) as a pixel in the interpolated image. Unlike the nonparametric image interpolation methods discussed in Chapters 4–6, which use the same α all over the whole image (such as in the case of bilinear, bicubic, discrete cosine transform (DCT), etc. based image interpolation methods). It has been demonstrated in Chapter 7 that the model parameter α should adapt to the local image features, such that different α should be applied to interpolate pixels within the image with different features. There are a vast number of research works presented in literature discussing what is the best model to adapt the modeling coefficients α, including those presented in Chapter 7. In this section, we shall exploit the modeling coefficient α that minimizes the prediction error squares given by

$$\epsilon^2 = (g[2m + 1, 2n + 1] - \hat{g}[2m + 1, 2n + 1])^2$$

$$= \left(g[2m + 1, 2n + 1] - [\alpha[0] \ \alpha[1] \ \alpha[2] \ \alpha[3]] \begin{bmatrix} g[2m, 2n] \\ g[2m, 2n + 2] \\ g[2m + 2, 2n] \\ g[2m + 2, 2n + 2] \end{bmatrix} \right)^2$$

$$= (g[2m + 1, 2n + 1] - \boldsymbol{\alpha}^T \mathbf{g}_{2m+1, 2n+1})^2, \qquad (8.4)$$

where $\boldsymbol{\alpha}$ is the model coefficient vector and $\mathbf{g}_{2m+1, 2n+1}$ is the vector of the four neighboring pixels surrounding $g[2m + 1, 2n + 1]$. The vector $\mathbf{g}_{2m+1, 2n+1}$ is known as the pixel intensity vector of the prediction window, where the subscript $(2m + 1, 2n + 1)$ indicates the location of the vector in the image. This vector shall bear the variable xLR in the MATLAB implementation in later sections.

Without loss of generality, we shall consider the noise-free case, such that the image is a locally stationary Gaussian process and the optimal coefficient is given by

$$\frac{\partial E\{\epsilon^2\}}{\partial \boldsymbol{\alpha}} = \frac{\partial E((g[2m + 1, 2n + 1] - \boldsymbol{\alpha}^T \mathbf{g}_{2m+1, 2n+1})^2)}{\partial \boldsymbol{\alpha}}$$

$$= \frac{\partial E(g[2m + 1, 2n + 1]^2 - 2g[2m + 1, 2n + 1]\boldsymbol{\alpha}^T \mathbf{g}_{2m+1, 2n+1} + (\boldsymbol{\alpha}^T \mathbf{g}_{2m+1, 2n+1})^2)}{\partial \boldsymbol{\alpha}}$$

$$= 0.$$

Solving for $\boldsymbol{\alpha}$ yields

$$E(\mathbf{g}_{2m+1, 2n+1}^T \mathbf{g}_{2m+1, 2n+1})\boldsymbol{\alpha} = E(g[2m + 1, 2n + 1]\mathbf{g}_{2m+1, 2n+1})$$

$$\boldsymbol{\alpha} = E(\mathbf{g}_{2m+1, 2n+1}^T \mathbf{g}_{2m+1, 2n+1})^{-1} E(g[2m + 1, 2n + 1]\mathbf{g}_{2m+1, 2n+1})$$

$$\boldsymbol{\alpha} = \mathbf{R}^{-1}\mathbf{r}, \qquad (8.5)$$

where $\mathbf{R} = E(\mathbf{g}_{2m+1, 2n}^T \mathbf{g}_{2m+1, 2n+1})^{-1}$ and $\mathbf{r} = E(g[2m + 1, 2n + 1]|\mathbf{g}_{2m+1, 2n+1})$ are the correlation matrix and vector of the high-resolution image, respectively. It is however very sad to learn that the above solution to the problem of optimal prediction coefficients $\boldsymbol{\alpha}$ will not be readily available, because of the nonavailability of both correlation matrix and vector. Some kinds of assumptions are required to create these matrix and vector to obtain the optimal predication coefficients. This is where the NEDI comes into the picture, because with a very simple assumption that fits right into most of the real-world picture, these unavailable correlation matrix and vector will suddenly become available with the given low-resolution image alone.

8.3 New Edge-Directed Interpolation (NEDI)

NEDI is developed to remedy the interpolation problem in Eq. (8.5), such that the missing information required to compute the optimal prediction coefficient α will become available where the NEDI assumes the following image model assumptions:

1. Natural image is a locally stationary second-order Gaussian process.
2. Low-resolution and high-resolution images have similar second-order statistics in corresponding local patches.

As a result, the image is completely described by the second-order statistics, and hence the interpolated pixels can be obtained from the linear prediction (autoregression) model in Eq. (8.2) with the optimal prediction coefficients given by Eq. (8.5). In particular, the second assumption provided a method to obtain the correlation matrix and vector for Eq. (8.5) to compute the optimal prediction coefficients, where the correlation matrix and vector in the high-resolution image are the same as that obtained in a similar region of the low-resolution image. This property is known as the *geometric duality*.

In layman's terms, the interpolation making use of geometric duality assumes that the covariance matrices of a small local window associated with pixels within a small region are homogeneous. As a result, the optimal interpolation weighting α_k can be obtained as the average of the optimal interpolation weighting of its neighboring pixels:

$$\alpha_k = \frac{\sum_\ell^L \alpha_\ell}{L}, \tag{8.6}$$

where α_ℓ are the optimal prediction coefficients of the pixel with index with respect to a particular pixel p_ℓ. The summation is performed over all the pixels within a small region surrounding p_k, which we shall call the *mean covariance window* for the pixel p_k. All pixels in the mean covariance window and p_k are the local low-resolution pixels. The mean covariance window has L pixels that are associated with the low-resolution image pixels and are neighbors of p_k. Note that the optimal interpolation for each low-resolution pixel in the mean covariance window, which we denote them as p_ℓ is given by Eq. (8.5) as

$$\alpha_\ell = R_\ell^{-1} r_\ell, \tag{8.7}$$

where the correlation matrix and vector are given by

$$R_\ell = C_\ell^T C_\ell, \tag{8.8}$$

$$r_\ell = C_\ell p_\ell. \tag{8.9}$$

Consider a fourth-order autoregressive linear prediction problem. The C_ℓ is a 1×4 vector containing the four 8-connected neighbors of p_ℓ. The optimal α_k for the interpolation of pixel p_k is given by Eq. (8.6), which is the mean α_ℓ over all L mean covariance windows

$$\alpha_k = \left(\frac{1}{L}C^T C\right)^{-1} \left(\frac{1}{L}C^T p\right) = (C^T C)^{-1}(C^T p), \tag{8.10}$$

where $\mathbf{C} = [\mathbf{C}_0^T \ \mathbf{C}_1^T \ \cdots \ \mathbf{C}_{L-1}^T]^T$ is a $4 \times L$ matrix and $\mathbf{p} = [p_0 \ p_1 \ \cdots \ p_{L-1}]^T$ is a $1 \times L$ vector. The MATLAB function in Listing 8.3.1 implements the above optimal α_k estimation with a given $\mathbf{C}$ (in MATLAB C), local window pixel intensity vector $\mathbf{p}$ (in MATLAB win) within the mean covariance window (in MATLAB mwin), and a new parameter t (in MATLAB t), which will be discussed in a sequel. It should be noted that the dimension of C in MATLAB is the transpose of that presented in the mathematical formulation in (Eq. (8.10)), as a result, the reader might found that the transpose operations in the MATLAB program and that in the equations does not match well, unless the dimension of C is considered.

> **MATLAB 8.3.1—Weighted average interpolation weighting factors.**
>
> ```
> function [a] = nedi_weighting_factor(win,C,t)
>   num = size(C,1);
>   C2 = C*C';
>   if rank(C2)==num && var(win)>t
>     a = inv(C2)*(C*win); % Wiener filtering solution
>   else
>     a = ones(num,1)/num; % average filter
> end; return;
> ```

The output of the function nedi_weighting_factor is the linear interpolation weighting array a that contains the optimal α for the computation of the intensity for the interpolated pixel $g[m, n]$ with respect to the intensity vector xLR of the prediction window pwin as in Eq. (8.1) and is given by

$$g[m, n] = \alpha^T \text{xLR}. \tag{8.11}$$

The MATLAB implements this weighted sum as

```
>> g(m,n)=a'*xLR;
```

Readers may have also noticed that Listing 8.3.1 has an if-then-else clause associating with the rank of C2 and the intensity vector win. This is because there are cases where the inverse of $\mathbf{C}^T\mathbf{C}$ does not exist. In other words, the matrix $\mathbf{C}^T\mathbf{C}$ is rank deficient. This happens when the pixel g(m,n) is located at smooth region without much structures or within a region with multiple image features. In this case, Eq. (8.5) will not be applied to interpolate the pixel. Instead, the interpolation should be performed with the average of the neighboring pixels surrounding g(m,n). As a result, the linear prediction weighting factor is given by ones(num,1)/num, which is a num×1 vector with 1/num as the entries, where num is the row size of $\mathbf{C}$, which equals to the number of pixels in the prediction window. To determine if the covariance-based linear prediction or averaging should be applied, the rank of the covariance matrix $\mathbf{C}$ is tested against the full-rank, and the variance of the neighboring pixels surrounding g(m,n) (the mean covariance window pixel intensity $\mathbf{p}$, which is given by win in MATLAB implementation) should be larger than a given threshold t to avoid the case of applying a full-rank $\mathbf{C}$ due to noises over a smooth region to construct α. Analytically the conditions of going into covariance-based interpolation are

$$\text{rank}(\mathbf{C}) = \text{size}(\mathbf{C}, 1), \tag{8.12}$$

$$\text{var}(\mathbf{p}) = \text{var}(\text{win}) \geqslant t, \tag{8.13}$$

where t is the minimum pixel intensity variation of all the neighboring pixels surrounding $g(m,n)$. The operator rank(·) extracts the rank of the matrix. Covariance-based interpolation will be enforced when the rank of **C** equals to the number of row of **C**, which is `size(C,1)` in MATLAB. The second condition, var(**p**), computes the variance of the intensity vector **p** and further constrains that the covariance-based interpolation will be applied when the full-rank of **C** is not caused by noises in a smooth region.

To understand the importance of Eq. (8.13), Figure 8.3a plots the pixels (in white) where full-rank **C** is detected. It can be observed that almost all pixels have full-ranked **C**. This figure is obtained by applying Eq. (8.12) alone. When we apply Eqs. (8.12) and (8.13) together with $t = 8$, the number of pixels classified to be covariance-based interpolation reduced dramatically and is shown in Figure 8.3b. However, as observed in Figure 8.3b, not only the image edges but also part of the low gradient regions of the images is determined to be interpolated with covariance-based linear prediction. It can be foreseen that applying the covariance-based interpolation to smooth region will result in annoying visual artifacts (as will be discussed in Section 8.3.5). As a result, we shall have to increase t to avoid noisy smooth regions being classified to undergo covariance-based interpolation. Finally, when we increase $t = 48$, the pixels classified by Eqs. (8.12) and (8.13) to be covariance-based interpolation are shown in Figure 8.3c. It can be observed from Figure 8.3c that most of the pixels being classified as covariance-based interpolations are indeed regions of the edge image of the *Cat*, as those in Figures 2.14 and 2.17. This observation tells us that it is efficient to determine if the covariance-based image interpolation should be applied by considering Eqs. (8.12) and (8.13).

To complete the implementation of the NEDI image interpolation, what is left is the construction of the windows required by the above discussions. But before we jump into that, the readers will need to understand that the NEDI implementation will first resample the low-resolution image to a high-resolution image by zero padding using `directus` as shown in Figure 8.4, where the black pixels are the low-resolution pixels and the white pixels are the newly added high-resolution pixels, which are subject to interpolation. The NEDI will then consider the interpolation of each missing pixel in the high-resolution image in a pixel-by-pixel manner. Furthermore, the missing pixel in the high-resolution image will be classified into three different types as shown in Figure 8.4,

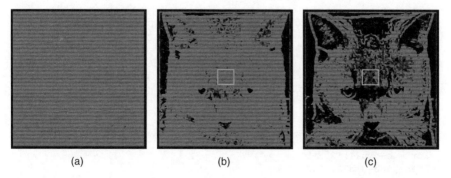

(a) (b) (c)

Figure 8.3 Distribution of pixels in up-sampled natural image *Cat* obtained by covariance based interpolation: (a) by considering full-ranked **C**, (b) by considering both full-ranked **C** and var(**w**) with $t = 8$ and (c) by considering both full-ranked **C** and var(**w**) with $t = 48$.

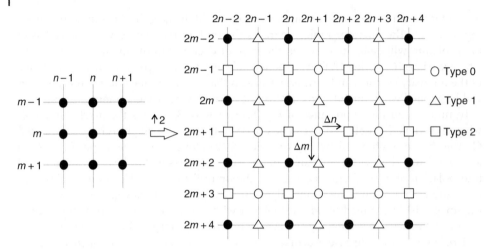

Figure 8.4 Three types of to-be-interpolated pixels in NEDI after resampling.

and each type is treated differently in order to provide the best construction of **C** for the pixel p_k under concern and hence the preservation of image structure between the low-resolution and high-resolution images. The MATLAB function nedi in Listing 8.3.2 shows the NEDI image interpolation framework.

MATLAB 8.3.2—NEDI image interpolation frame work.

```
function g = nedi(f,t,b)
  g = double(directus(f));
  [M,N]=size(g);
  for k = 0:3
    switch k
       case 0        % Estimation of Pixels at (2m+1,2n+1)
          pwin = ... % displacement coordinates in prediction window
          mwin = ... % displacement coordinates in mean covariance
                window
          dmn = [0,0];
       case 1        % Estimation of Pixels at (2m,2n+1)
          pwin = ... % displacement coordinates in prediction window
          mwin = ... % displacement coordinates in mean covariance
                window
          dmn = [1,0];
       case 2 % Estimation of Pixels at (2m+1,2n)
          pwin = ... % displacement coordinates in prediction window
          mwin = ... % displacement coordinates in mean covariance
                window
          dmn = [0,1];
    end;
    cwin = 2*pwin;
    for m=b-dmn(1):2:M-b
       for n=b-dmn(2):2:N-b
          g(m,n) = nedi_core(g,m,n,pwin,mwin,cwin,t);
  end; end; end; return;
```

The function begins with resampling the input low-resolution image f by direct inter-pixel zero padding with the function `directus()` to generate the high-resolution image lattice g. Within this general NEDI framework, the ordered vector dmn given by

$$\text{dmn} = \left[\begin{array}{c} \Delta m \\ \Delta n \end{array} \right] \tag{8.14}$$

will define a displacement vector from the interpolation pixel location (2m+1, 2n+1) as shown in Figure 8.4, which takes up values of $[0\ 0]^T$ for type 0 pixel estimation, $[1\ 0]^T$ for type 1 pixel estimation, and $[0\ 1]^T$ for type 2 pixel estimation. With this displacement vector, the nedi will be able to share the same interpolation `for` loop that invokes the nedi_core function to interpolate each missing pixel in the high-resolution image as shown in Listing 8.3.2.

MATLAB 8.3.3—The core function of the NEDI.

```
function [pixel] = nedi_core(g,m,n,pwin,mwin,cwin,t)
  [win xLR C] = nedi_window(g,m,n,pwin,mwin,cwin);
  [a] = nedi_weighting_factor(win,C,t);
  pixel = a'*xLR;
  pixel = nedi_correct(pixel,xLR);
return;
```

The MATLAB function nedi_core in Listing 8.3.3 forms the per-pixel NEDI. The covariance matrix $\mathbf{C}_\ell$ for each pixel p_ℓ within the mean covariance window mwin will be constructed and stored in the return vector C by the function call nedi_window. The function nedi_window will also generate the pixel intensity vectors win and xLR that contain the intensity of the pixels in the mean covariance window mwin and the prediction window pwin, respectively. The details of the two ordered matrices, mwin and pwin, and their generation methods will be discussed in Sections 8.3.1–8.3.3 in a sequel. Nevertheless, when the pixel intensity vectors and correlation matrix **C** are fed into the MATLAB function nedi_weighting_factor, it will generate the linear prediction weighting factor $\boldsymbol{\alpha}$ (in MATLAB a), such that the interpolating pixel intensity can be obtained by simple vector multiplication as in Eq. (8.11). It should be noted that a threshold t is supplied to the function to implement the checking depicted in Eqs. (8.12) and (8.13). The details can be found in Listing 8.3.1 to avoid annoying artifacts caused by applying covariance-based interpolation to smooth region. An iterative application of nedi_core with the appropriate window information for each high-resolution image missing pixel will complete the image interpolation process.

The readers might have one last observation that needs to be clarified before going to the details of the construction of windows for interpolation. There is a parameter b in the nedi function. This parameter specifies the boundary pixels to be ignored when processing the image. This is because the windows associated with the interpola-tion have finite size extended from the pixel under interpolation. As a result, there are chances that the pixels required by the windows are outside the image boundary and are thus undefined. The easiest way to handle this situation is not to process pixels close to the boundary that have the problem of undefined pixels within the window. This is the function of b. The desired value of b should be as small as possible but with all the pixels required by the window of the pixel under interpolation is still well defined.

8.3.1 Type 0 Estimation

Consider the estimation problem of the unknown pixel $g[2m + 1, 2n + 1]$ with $m, n \in \mathbb{Z}^+$ (the gray pixel within the prediction window drawn with solid line in Figure 8.5). The pixel displacement vector is set to

```
dmn = [0,0];
```

Without loss of generality, let us consider the interpolation being done with the pixel $[\hat{m}, \hat{n}]$. The ordered matrix `pwin` that stores the pixel displacement from $[\hat{m}, \hat{n}]$ to form the prediction window is given by

```
pwin = [-1 -1 1 1; -1 1 -1 1];
```

and the actual prediction window coordinates $[m, n]$ are given by

$$\begin{bmatrix} m \\ n \end{bmatrix} = \begin{bmatrix} \hat{m} \\ \hat{n} \end{bmatrix} + \begin{bmatrix} \texttt{pwin(1,:)} \\ \texttt{pwin(2,:)} \end{bmatrix}. \tag{8.15}$$

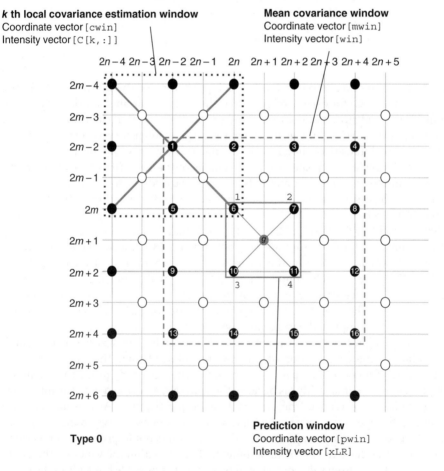

Figure 8.5 Illustration of pixels considered in MATLAB program of NEDI.

The prediction pixel intensity vector xLR can be extracted by direct matrix operation on g with $[m, n]$ (the pixel under interpolation), given by the following MATLAB code:

```
xLR = diag(g(m+pwin(1,:),n+pwin(2,:)));
```

Similarly, the coordinates of the pixels in the mean covariance window are given by

$$\begin{bmatrix} m \\ n \end{bmatrix} = \begin{bmatrix} \hat{m} \\ \hat{n} \end{bmatrix} + \begin{bmatrix} \texttt{mwin(1,:)} \\ \texttt{mwin(2,:)} \end{bmatrix}, \tag{8.16}$$

where the displacement matrix is given by

```
mwin = [-3 -3 -3 -3 -1 -1 -1 -1 1 1 1 1 3 3 3 3;
        -3 -1 1 3 -3 -1 1 3 -3 -1 1 3 -3 -1 1 3];
```

The mean covariance window pixel intensity vector **p** is implemented with the MATLAB variable win, which can be extracted by directly inputting the above coordinates into the high-resolution image *g* as

```
win = diag(g(m+mwin(1,:),n+mwin(2,:)));
```

Further displacing the mean covariance window pixels with cwin will obtain the coordinates of the pixels in the local covariance window, where cwin is given by

```
cwin=2*pwin;
```

such that it resembles the same geometric shape as that of the prediction window but doubled in size as shown in Figure 8.5. As a result, the pixel coordinates of the local covariance window associated with the *k*th pixel in the mean covariance window are given by

$$\begin{bmatrix} m \\ n \end{bmatrix} = \begin{bmatrix} \hat{m} \\ \hat{n} \end{bmatrix} + \begin{bmatrix} \texttt{win(1,k)} \\ \texttt{win(2,k)} \end{bmatrix} + \begin{bmatrix} \texttt{cwin(1,:)} \\ \texttt{cwin(2,:)} \end{bmatrix}. \tag{8.17}$$

The covariance vector associated with the *k*th pixel in the mean covariance window is therefore obtained from directly extracting *g* with the above coordinates, which can be implemented with the following MATLAB code:

```
C(:,k) = diag(g(m+wmn(1,k)+cwin(1,:),n+wmn(2,k)+cwin(2,:)));
```

such that all the *L* pixels in the mean covariance window will be stacked up to form a covariance estimation matrix C. The above discussed window formation methods are implemented in the nedi_window function, which will yield win,xLR,C for the computation of prediction coefficient **α** using the nedi_weighting_factor discussed in MATLAB Listing 8.3.1. The complete MATLAB implementation that generates the variety of windows is shown in Listing 8.3.4.

MATLAB 8.3.4—NEDI image interpolation windows.

```
function [win, xLR, C] = nedi_window(g,m,n,pwin,mwin,cwin)
xLR = diag(g(m+pwin(1,:),n+pwin(2,:)));
win = diag(g(m+mwin(1,:),n+mwin(2,:)));
for k=1:size(mwin,2)
    C(:,k) = diag(g(m+mwin(1,k)+cwin(1,:),n+mwin(2,k)+cwin(2,:)));
end; return;
```

While there is no special sequence that has to be followed by the pixels to construct the ordered matrices of the windows and the related intensity vector, the sequencing between ordered matrices and intensity vectors has to be consistent to avoid complicated program development. The pixels (both the coordinate-related ordered matrix and the intensity vector) of the developed MATLAB function `nedi_window` follow the numeric order listed in Figure 8.5.

8.3.2 Type 1 Estimation

Type 1 pixels are located at $g[2m, 2n + 1]$ with $m, n \in \mathbb{Z}^+$ (the gray pixel within the prediction window drawn in solid line in Figure 8.6). To share the same interpolation `for-loop` function as in MATLAB Listing 8.3.2, we shall construct a displacement vector

```
dmn = [1,0];
```

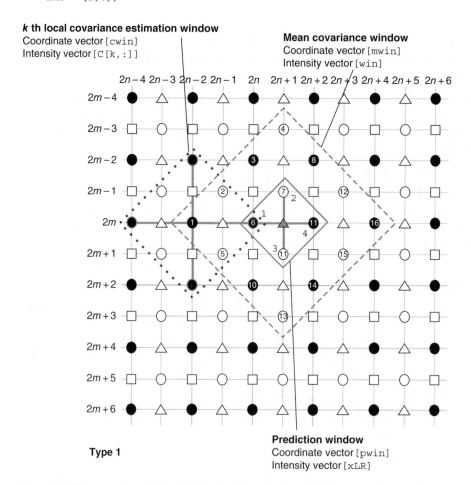

Figure 8.6 The rotated prediction windows for the estimation of unknown pixels at $[2m, 2n + 1]$ in NEDI.

such that

$$\begin{bmatrix} 2m+1 \\ 2n+1 \end{bmatrix} - \begin{bmatrix} 1 \\ 0 \end{bmatrix} = \begin{bmatrix} 2m \\ 2n+1 \end{bmatrix}. \tag{8.18}$$

It is easy to observe that the operation of displaced coordinate vector has the same form as that of type 0 pixels, where the same operation depicted in Eq. (8.15) can be applied.

It can be observed from Figure 8.5 that if the same prediction window as that in type 0 estimation is being applied to $g[2m, 2n+1]$, all the pixels covered by the prediction window are pixels with unknown intensity. As a result, a different prediction window has to be applied to interpolate pixels at locations $g[2m, 2n+1]$. Shown in Figure 8.6 is one of the many ways that can be applied to interpolate $g[2m, 2n+1]$ and is the way selected by Li and Orchard [40]. Compared with the prediction window for type 0 pixels in Figure 8.5, the prediction window in Figure 8.6 is rotated anticlockwise by 45°. As a result, the pixels covered by this prediction window are either low-resolution image pixels or type 0 pixels. In other words, if we perform type 0 pixel interpolation process first and then proceed to type 1 pixels, all the pixels within the prediction window in Figure 8.6 will be well defined. Such a prediction window is defined with the prediction window pixel displacement vector

```
pwin = [0 -1 1 0; -1 0 0 1];
```

The local covariance window cwin will be defined as cwin=2*pwin similar to that in type 0 pixels to resemble the same geometric shape as that of the prediction window but doubled in size as shown in Figure 8.6.

The mean covariance window pixel displacement matrix has to be altered in a similar way to make it consistent with that of the pwin. As shown in Figure 8.6, the mean covariance window pixel displacement matrix mwin should be defined as

```
mwin = [0 -1 -2 -3 1 0 -1 -2 2 1 0 -1 3 2 1 0;
        -3 -2 -1 0 -2 -1 0 1 -1 0 1 2 0 1 2 3];
```

where all the pixels covered by the mean covariance window are either low-resolution pixels or type 0 pixels and hence are well defined. The coordinates of all the pixels within the prediction window and the prediction pixel intensity vector xLR are generated using exactly the same method as that of type 0 pixels. Similarly, the mean covariance window pixel intensity vector **p** (and the associated MATLAB variable win) together with the covariance matrix **C** is also generated using the same method as that of type 0 pixels. As a result, a simple call to the MATLAB function nedi_window will be suffice to generate win, xLR, C, which are applied in the rest of the interpolation routines.

8.3.3 Type 2 Estimation

Type 2 pixels are those located at $g[2m+1, 2n]$ with $m, n \in \mathbb{Z}^+$ (the gray pixel within the prediction window drawn with solid line in Figure 8.7). Similar to the case of type 1 pixels, in order to make use of the same for-loop operation in the main interpolation framework in Listing 8.3.2, the coordinates of type 2 pixels will be constructed from displacing the coordinate of type 1 pixels with displacement vector set to

```
dmn = [0,1];
```

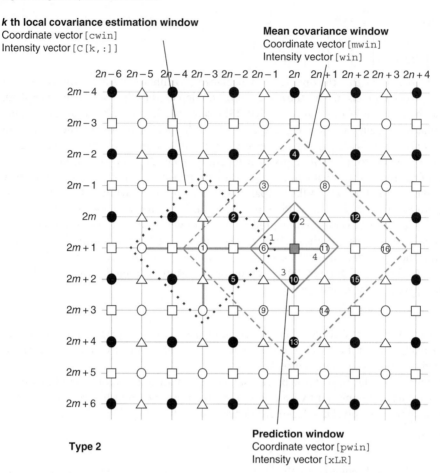

Type 2

Figure 8.7 The rotated prediction windows for the estimation of unknown pixels at $[2m + 1, 2n]$ in NEDI.

such that

$$\begin{bmatrix} 2m+1 \\ 2n+1 \end{bmatrix} - \begin{bmatrix} 0 \\ 1 \end{bmatrix} = \begin{bmatrix} 2m+1 \\ 2n \end{bmatrix}. \tag{8.19}$$

It is easy to observe that the displaced coordinate vector has the same form as that of type 2 pixels. Other requested information to complete the covariance-based interpolation will be the definition of the three types of windows. To avoid the windows being defined over unknown pixels, windows for type 2 pixels are defined in a similar fashion as that in type 1 pixels and are shown in Figure 8.7. In particular, the ordered displacement matrix of the prediction window is given by

```
pwin = [0 -1 1 0; -1 0 0 1];
```

with the local covariance window obtained as `cwin=2*pwin`. The mean covariance window is given by

```
mwin = [0 -1 -2 -3 1 0 -1 -2 2 1 0 -1 3 2 1 0;
       -3 -2 -1 0 -2 -1 0 1 -1 0 1 2 0 1 2 3];
```

With the above window definitions, a simple function call to `nedi_window` will generate `win,xLR,C` to be applied in the rest of the interpolation process.

8.3.4 Pixel Intensity Correction

Observed from the `nedi_core` in Listing 8.3.3, after `nedi_window`, the obtained `win,xLR,C` will be applied to generate the interpolation prediction coefficient α by the function call `nedi_weighting_factor` as discussed in Section 8.3. The interpolation is performed with the simple weighted sum operation `a'*xLR`. Normally, even if such multipoint linear prediction cannot capture the covariance structure of the image block, the interpolated pixel should be well within the dynamic range of the image in concern. In our example, all the interpolated pixels should be bounded in the range of [0,255]. However, similar to the DCT and wavelet-based image interpolation methods, there are cases where the interpolated pixels behave not as expected analytically. This might because of the numerical errors in the course of computation. When that happens, the interpolation methods discussed in previous chapters will apply `brightnorm` to normalize the brightness of the interpolated image, such that all the pixels are truncated to be larger or equal to 0, and the interpolated high-resolution image will be scaled, such that the normalized high-resolution image has the same dynamic range as that of the corresponding low-resolution image (note that the dynamic range of the low-resolution image might be smaller than [0, 255]).

The brightness normalization process for the covariance-based interpolated image to combat numerical computation error will not be as easy as that in `brightnorm`. This is because all the high-resolution pixels corresponding to pixels in the low-resolution image are preserved to be exactly the same. As a result, applying `brightnorm` to the covariance-based interpolated image will only produce an image with all the pixels with negative intensity being truncated to 0 and all the pixel with intensity higher than 255 being truncated to 255. This is not a desirable method to deal with the numerical error, because such method might induce salt and pepper noise, and long white and/or dark artificial lines to the processed image. Note that the dynamic range problem only happens in the interpolated pixels (as the other pixels are directly copied from the low-resolution image, which are assumed to be perfect). As a result, it is natural to consider modifying the interpolation method to alleviate this problem.

The MATLAB function `nedi_correct` in Listing 8.3.5 is designed to alleviate this dynamic range problem. With reference to `nedi_core` in Listing 8.3.3, after the pixel being interpolated by linear prediction with the prediction coefficients computed by covariance-based interpolation method using `nedi_weighting_factor`, the `nedi_correct` will be invoked with the interpolated pixel intensity together with the prediction window intensity vector as the input parameters. The interpolated pixel intensity will be checked if it is well within the allowable dynamic range (in our case [0, 255]). If it is, the correction process will end, and the covariance-based image interpolation will continue to process the next to be interpolated pixel. On the other hand, if the interpolated pixel intensity is outside the allowable dynamic range, the intensity of this pixel will be replaced with the average value of the prediction window intensity vector. As a result, the intensity of all the pixels passing out from `nedi_correct` will be well within the allowable dynamic range.

MATLAB 8.3.5—Correction of underestimation or overshoot pixel.

```
function new_val = nedi_correct(curr_val,xLR)
  num = size(xLR,1);
  if curr_val<0||curr_val>255
    a = ones(num,1)/num;
    new_val=a'*xLR;
  else new_val=curr_val;
end; return;
```

Note that this correction method is not the same as bilinear interpolation, but more closely related to mean value interpolation, because not all the prediction window pixels to the interpolated pixel distance are the same. Readers may argue that the nedi_correct might perform better if it is being implemented as an authentic bilinear interpolation instead of a simple mean value interpolation. The answer to this question has been left as an exercise for readers to find out.

8.3.5 MATLAB Implementation

Although the above discussions of the covariance-based image interpolation algorithm is originated from the NEDI image interpolation method, it is not exactly the same as the NEDI discussed in [40]. There are some minor differences, such as the way the windows are constructed and the number of pixels being applied to compute the mean covariance matrix **C**. However, we shall continue to call it NEDI for the credit of it being the basis of the discussed method. After putting all the discussed windows into the framework in Listing 8.3.2, the nedi is implemented with MATLAB Listing 8.3.6.

MATLAB 8.3.6—MATLAB implementation of NEDI.

```
function g = nedi(f,t,b)
  g = double(directus(f));
  [M,N]=size(g);
  for k = 0:3
    switch k
      case 0            % Estimation of Pixels at (2i,2j)
        pwin = [-1 -1 1 1; -1 1 -1 1]; % relative pixel coordinate in
                xLR
        mwin = [-3 -3 -3 -3 -1 -1 -1 -1 1 1 1 1 3 3 3 3;
                -3 -1 1 3 -3 -1 1 3 -3 -1 1 3 -3 -1 1 3];
        dmn = [0,0];
      case 1 % Estimation of Pixels at (2i-1,2j)
        pwin = [0 -1 1 0; -1 0 0 1]; % relative pixel coordinate in
                xLR
        mwin = [0 -1 -2 -3 1 0 -1 -2 2 1 0 -1 3 2 1 0;
                -3 -2 -1 0 -2 -1 0 1 -1 0 1 2 0 1 2 3];
        dmn = [1,0];
      case 2 % Estimation of Pixels at (2i,2j-1)
        pwin = [0 -1 1 0; -1 0 0 1]; % relative pixel coordinate in
                xLR
        mwin = [0 -1 -2 -3 1 0 -1 -2 2 1 0 -1 3 2 1 0;
                -3 -2 -1 0 -2 -1 0 1 -1 0 1 2 0 1 2 3];
```

```
        dmn = [0,1];
    end;
    cwin = 2*pwin;
    for m=b-dmn(1):2:M-b
        for n=b-dmn(2):2:N-b
            g(m,n) = nedi_core(g,m,n,pwin,mwin,cwin,t);
    end; end; end; return;
```

Figure 8.8 shows the NEDI interpolated synthetic image letter A from the size of 64×64 to 128×128 with threshold $t = 48$. It can be observed that the edge of the letter A is well preserved by NEDI. The comparison would be made more easy by studying the numerical results depicted in the intensity maps. When the NEDI is compared with the bilinear interpolation (MATLAB Listing 4.1.5 `biinterp(f,2)`) and the wavelet interpolation (MATLAB Listing 6.3.2 `wlrcs(f)` and MATLAB Listing 6.4.1 `brightnorm(f,g)`), the intensity maps of the selected region (enclosed by the white box) are taken from the original image (see Figure 8.8b), the NEDI interpolated image (see Figure 8.8c), the bilinear interpolated image (see Figure 8.8d,) and the wavelet interpolation image (see Figure 8.8e). It can be observed in Figure 8.8e that the wavelet interpolation preserves the sharpness across the edges, where the intensity in the dark region is "0" and the intensity in the gray region is "135," with only few pixels having the intensity values of "14." However, it can be observed that the detailed structure of the edge is distorted when compared with those in the other two methods. Both the interpolated images obtained by NEDI and the bilinear interpolation preserve more structure detail, while the NEDI interpolated image preserves the sharpness across the edge more effectively when compared with that obtained by the bilinear interpolation, or we can describe that the blurring artifact in the bilinear interpolated image is more significant. Nonetheless, we can observe from Figure 8.8c that the pixel values fluctuate

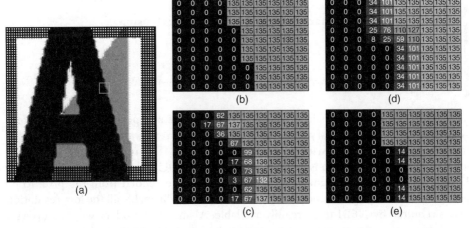

Figure 8.8 Interpolation of synthetic image letter A by different interpolation methods: (a) NEDI interpolated image without boundary extension, where the intensity map of the region enclosed by the box will be investigated; the intensity map of the selected region in (b) the original image; (c) the NEDI interpolated image; (d) the bilinear interpolated image; and (e) the zero-padded wavelet interpolated image.

more vigorously along the image edge, which is known to be the ringing artifact. Such artifact is due to the prediction error and the accumulation of error from the estimation of type 0 pixels to that of type 1 and 2 pixels.

It should be noted that the interpolation of the boundary pixels in Figure 8.8a is omitted, which generates the chessbox pattern enclosing the boundary. The dark pixels in the chessbox are the newly inserted zero pixels in the resampling process. The NEDI requires the formation of the prediction windows and mean covariance windows to perform linear prediction. Linear prediction error, as discussed, will occur when these windows extends over the boundary. Therefore, special treatment on the image boundary is required to avoid visual artifacts caused by linear prediction error along the boundary.

8.4 Boundary Extension

The NEDI image interpolation algorithm presented in Section 8.3 can achieve good image interpolation results because the weighting of the linear predictive interpolation assigned to neighboring pixels (within the prediction window pwin) is implicitly computed based on the image structure within a predefined local window (the covariance windows cwin) over the pixels on the mean covariance window (mwin). An obvious problem of the covariance-based image interpolation is the finite kernel size of the prediction window and also the local covariance window surrounding the prediction window. When the pixel to be interpolated is located on the image boundary, the pixels within the related windows will be located outside the image boundary and hence are undefined. To deal with undefined boundary pixel problem with operators of finite kernel size, Section 2.4.1 suggests us to perform boundary extension.

Let us consider a simple boundary extension scheme, the *periodic extension* as discussed in Section 2.4.1 with the following MATLAB source.

MATLAB 8.4.1—Boundary extension by periodic extension.

```
>> ext = 8;
>> temp = repmat(f,3,3);
>> [M N] = size(f);
>> fext = temp(M-ext+1:2*M+ext,N-ext+1:2*N+ext);
```

This MATLAB source takes in a low-resolution image f and performs periodic extension with extended boundary size ext=8 pixels. As a result, the boundary-extended image fext will have a size of $(M + 16) \times (N + 16)$. The reason why a boundary extension with 8 pixels is considered is because the NEDI implementation in MATLAB Listing 8.3.6 has a maximum window size of 11×11 extended from the pixel to be interpolated. Creating a boundary with size of 8 pixels will enable all the low-resolution pixels required by NEDI to be readily available. A smaller boundary will end up with NEDI processing nonexisting pixels outside the image boundary and hence cease to process. This boundary-extended image is a solution to create pixels outside the original image boundary, which will allow NEDI to interpolate pixels close to the original image boundary without ending up processing nonexisting pixels. The interpolated image is processed by the following MATLAB Listing 8.4.2 to extract an interpolated image with the size $[2M, 2N]$.

> **MATLAB 8.4.2—Invoke the NEDI with boundary-extended image and crop the interpolated image to size $2M \times 2N$.**
>
> ```
> >> g = nedi(fext,48,ext);
> >> g = g(2*ext+1:end-2*ext,2*ext+1:end-2*ext);
> ```

The last command in MATLAB Listing 8.4.2 will remove the pixels in the extended boundary and recover an image of size $2M \times 2N$. Shown in Figure 8.9a is the boundary-extended *Cat* low-resolution image (i.e. fext in MATLAB), where the original low-resolution image is being enclosed by the box. Those pixels out of the box are generated by periodic extension. The NEDI interpolates high-resolution image generated by the first line of the code shown in Listing 8.4.2 where the result is shown in Figure 8.9b with the boundary exhibits checkerboard noise because the image boundary is excluded in the interpolation due to insufficient pixels available to construct the required windows (same problem as that illustrated in Figure 8.8a). With proper treatment of the boundary pixels (i.e. the pixel cropping by the second line of Listing 8.4.2), the noisy boundary will be removed, and only pixels within the box in Figure 8.9b will remain to form the final interpolated image shown in Figure 8.9c. It is vivid that the boundary pixels are well interpolated in Figure 8.9c. Considering the comparison approach adopted in this book, the performance of an interpolation method is compared by first down-sampling the original image with a scaling factor of 2 and restoring it to the original size with the same scaling factor by the interpolation method under investigation. To compare the objective performance of the interpolation method, the final image would be required to acquire the same size as that of the original image. Hence, the cropping operation is essential to rectify the final image for objective performance (i.e. PSNR and SSIM) comparison.

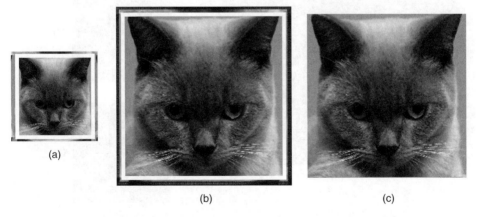

(a)

(b)

(c)

Figure 8.9 Boundary extension in NEDI: (a) original *Cat* image with extended boundary (i.e. in MATLAB fext), (b) the NEDI interpolated image showing the extended boundary, and (c) the NEDI interpolated image with the boundary pixels being removed.

The readers may argue that the NEDI might work better with other types of boundary extension, in particular the symmetric extension, because it does not introduce new pixel intensity discontinuities to the boundary-extended image when compared with that of periodic extended image. The answer to this question will be left as an exercise for the readers to find out.

Figure 8.10a shows the 2× interpolated result of the 256×256 *Cat* image to 512×512 by NEDI with the variance threshold of $t = 48$ and the boundary with $b = 8$ by the following function call:

```
>> g = nedi(f,48,8);
```

where the enlarged portions of the ear of the original high-resolution *Cat* image, the bilinear interpolated image using MATLAB Listing 4.1.5 with `biinterp(f,2)`, and the NEDI interpolated image are shown in sub-figures (b)–(d), respectively. It is vivid that the continuity of the hairs and the fur pattern is better preserved in the NEDI interpolated image when compared with that of the bilinear interpolated image. Although both NEDI and bilinear image interpolations are basically linear weighted interpolation methods, the weighting factor in the NEDI are adaptive per pixel and are tuned according to the orientation of the edges sustained by each pixel to preserve the continuity and sharpness of the edges. On the other hand, the bilinear interpolation has a nonadaptive weighting for all pixels, which flattened the high frequency components in the image.

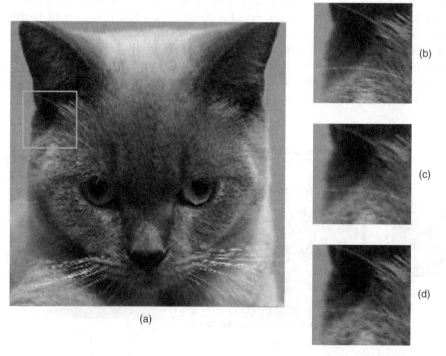

(b)

(c)

(d)

(a)

Figure 8.10 NEDI of natural image *Cat* by a factor of 2 and with threshold $t = 48$ (PSNR = 27.6027 dB, SSIM = 0.8248): (a) the full interpolated image, (b) zoom-in portion of the ear of the *Cat* image in original image, (c) zoom-in portion of the ear of the *Cat* image in the bilinear interpolated image, and (d) zoom-in portion of the ear of the *Cat* image in the NEDI interpolated image.

Furthermore, the readers should have noticed that the boundary pixels of the image with a width of 8 pixels have been excluded from the NEDI by setting b=8 when calling `nedi`, such that there will be sufficient boundary pixels for the proper construction of the local covariance window over the mean covariance window. In the case of MATLAB Listing 8.3.6, the maximum one-sided kernel size extended from the interpolation pixel is 6 pixels, and hence we reserved 8 pixels by setting b=8 to be sure that there will be sufficient boundary pixels. Ignoring the boundary pixels will result in checkerboard artifacts, around the boundary of the interpolated image. Since the interpolated image is corrupted with boundary pixels that cannot be interpolated, objective performance across the whole high-resolution image will not be fair nor meaningful. On the other hand, if we crop the image boundary pixels off from both the original image and the final image, the comparison will not be fair either. Therefore, special treatment on the image boundary will have to be applied such as to provide sufficient boundary pixels for window construction and at the same time to ensure the content integrity in the final cropped image.

Disregarding the superior edge preservation of NEDI, there are a few things that we want to investigate but cannot, which include the selection of threshold t and window size. The investigation on the optimal threshold value will be discussed in the coming section, where the use of image boundary extension to eliminate the non-interpolatable problem will allow us to compute the objective performance index for each interpolated image and use that as the index for comparison, thus sorting out the optimal value to be assigned to the threshold. Similarly, the current windows are constructed as 11×11 pixels surrounding the unknown pixels, and therefore the boundary has to be set to 8. Window of other sizes can also be applied to implement NEDI and will be discussed in later section after we developed a system to compute the objective performance index for NEDI and its derivatives.

8.5 Threshold Selection

Besides impulsive noise, sudden change in edge directions will also affect the efficiency of the covariance-based interpolation, as such changes are considered to be locally nonstationary. Applying covariance-based interpolation on noisy pixels or end of edges would result in unpleasant visual artifacts. NEDI avoids the use of covariance-based interpolation or noisy pixels or short segmented edges by examining the variance of the pixel intensity within the covariance estimation window as that in Eq. (8.13). However, this user-defined threshold is a global value applied to the entire image. A large threshold value shows better performance in bypassing the covariance-based interpolation on noisy pixels, but it will also remove some of the high frequency components because of the use of window averaging on the bypassed pixels. This can be illustrated by Figure 8.11, which shows the zoom-in portion of the forehead of the interpolated *Cat* image by NEDI using different t. The value of t governs how the unknown pixels are being interpolated. To compare the distribution of where the covariance-based interpolation is applied in the zoom-in portion, the corresponding distribution maps are shown in the same column with the white pixel in the distribution maps showing the pixel being interpolated by covariance-based interpolation. It can be observed that the image feature at the forehead of the *Cat* image is short edges in majority.

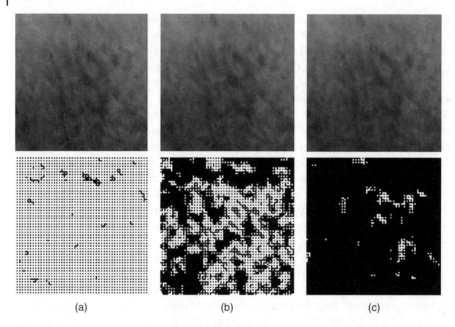

Figure 8.11 The zoom-in portion of the up-sampled *Cat* image taken from the forehead of the *Cat* image, in which the image is interpolated by NEDI using different thresholds t and boundary width of 8 pixels: (a) $t = 8$; (b) $t = 48$; and (c) $t = 128$. The corresponding distribution showing pixels interpolated by covariance-based interpolation is shown in the same column as that of the zoom-in image for comparison, where the white pixels in the distribution maps representing the pixels are interpolated by covariance-based interpolation.

The larger the t, the less pixels will be interpolated with covariance-based interpolation (the least white pixels in the distribution in Figure 8.11c) because more pixels are considered as pixels in smooth region. Hence, the interpolated image is observed to be more blurred. To overcome this disadvantage, Asuni and Giachetti [5] proposed to apply preconditional checks to the pixels in the covariance estimation window to determine if nonparametric interpolation or covariance-based interpolation should be applied to interpolate the unknown pixels. There are three preconditional checks that help to avoid the use of covariance-based interpolation on noisy nonuniform region or when there are discontinued edges in the covariance estimation window, including (i) selection of intensity levels, (ii) selection of connected pixels, and (iii) exclusion of uniform areas.

Table 8.1 summarizes the PSNR and SSIM of the interpolated *Cat* image by NEDI with respect to different thresholds. Since the natural *Cat* image has lots of texture, an increasing PSNR and SSIM are observed with increasing threshold. This implies that the PSNR and SSIM are improved with more and more pixels being interpolated with window averaging (i.e. non-covariance-based interpolation) with increasing threshold. However, this will result in more blurred and broken edges as that observed in Figure 8.11c. It should be noted that the trend on PSNR and SSIM versus threshold would vary upon different images.

Table 8.1 The PSNR and SSIM performance of a 2× *Cat* image interpolation to size 512 × 512 using the NEDI and periodic extension with various variance threshold values.

Variance threshold *t*	PSNR (dB)	SSIM
0	27.5644	0.8193
10	27.5685	0.8202
48	27.6027	0.8248
100	27.6516	0.8291
128	27.6780	0.8305
200	27.7328	0.8324
∞	28.1936	0.8358

8.6 Error Propagation Mitigation

Besides the boundary pixel estimation problem, the NEDI image interpolation also suffered from error propagation problem. The NEDI assumes local stationary of the covariance within these predefined covariance windows and the preservation of local regularity within the associated windows (covariance windows) in the low-resolution images and the interpolated high-resolution images. However, these assumptions and hence the interpolation method do suffer from a number of fallacies, which cause watercolor artifacts in fine texture regions and instability of the algorithm in smooth regions.

One of the fallacies of the NEDI implementation of the covariance-based image interpolation is the error propagation problem associated with the interpolation of type 1 and type 2 pixels. When interpolating type 1 and type 2 pixels, type 0 pixels are involved in the interpolation process. As a result, any interpolation error in type 0 pixels will cause similar prediction error in the estimation of type 1 and type 2 pixels. Although linear prediction error is inevitable, in the ideal case, the interpolation error of each pixel will be close to a white noise process. The HVS finds small power white noise corrupted image to be natural. However, the error propagation problem will cause a localized window of three pixels (types 0, 1, and 2) to have correlated errors, which when observed by HVS will be considered as unnatural watercolor-like artifacts. A simple approach can be applied to remedy this problem by modifying the prediction window for the interpolation of type 1 and type 2 pixels, such that the associated prediction window will only contain pixels from low-resolution image [20, 59]. Let us consider the case of type 2 pixels. Shown in Figure 8.12 are the modified window definitions for type 2 pixels, where only the low-resolution pixels (dark pixels) are utilized in the prediction window (solid line box). The mean covariance window (dashed line box) is modified accordingly to maintain the same geometric structure as that of the prediction window. The local covariance window (the dotted line box) is maintained to be `cwin=2*pwin` as that in NEDI implementation. With the above window definition, the fourth-order linear

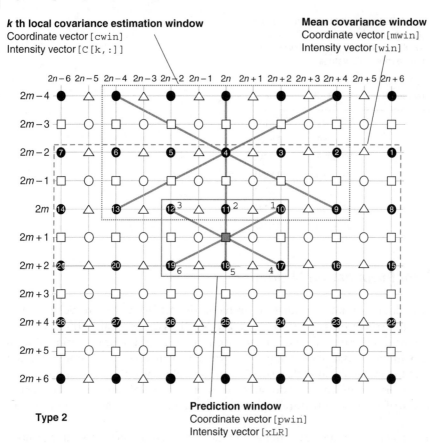

k th local covariance estimation window
Coordinate vector [cwin]
Intensity vector [C[k,:]]

Mean covariance window
Coordinate vector [mwin]
Intensity vector [win]

Type 2

Prediction window
Coordinate vector [pwin]
Intensity vector [xLR]

Figure 8.12 Illustration of the covariance window and local block of the second step of the MEDI method.

prediction problem is now changed to be a sixth-order linear prediction problem. The corresponding prediction window displacement matrix pwin as shown in Figure 8.12 is thus given by

```
pwin = [2 0 -2 2 0 -2; -1 -1 -1 1 1 1];
```

Similarly, the prediction window displacement matrix pwin for type 1 pixels is given by 90° rotation of that of type 2 pixels and can be obtained by swapping the two rows of the pwin for type 2 pixels, that is,

```
pwin = [-1 -1 -1 1 1 1; 2 0 -2 2 0 -2];
```

The mean covariance matrix for type 2 pixels has the same geometric shape as that of the prediction window as shown in Figure 8.12. The corresponding mean covariance displacement matrix is given by

```
mwin = [6   4   2   0  -2  -4  -6   6   4   2   0  -2  -4  -6   ...
        6   4   2   0  -2  -4  -6   6   4   2   0  -2  -4  -6;
       -3  -3  -3  -3  -3  -3  -3  -1  -1  -1  -1  -1  -1  -1   ...
        1   1   1   1   1   1   1   3   3   3   3   3   3   3];
```

In a similar manner, the mean covariance displacement matrix for type 1 pixels is obtained by swapping the two rows of mwin for type 2 pixels, which corresponds to the 90° rotation of that of type 2 pixels, that is,

```
mwin = [-3 -3 -3 -3 -3 -3 -3 -1 -1 -1 -1 -1 -1 -1 ...
         1  1  1  1  1  1  1  3  3  3  3  3  3  3;
         6  4  2  0 -2 -4 -6  6  4  2  0 -2 -4 -6 ...
         6  4  2  0 -2 -4 -6  6  4  2  0 -2 -4 -6];
```

The rest of the implementation is exactly the same as that of NEDI framework in MAT-LAB Listing 8.3.2. The final implementation is given by MATLAB Listing 8.6.1, which we shall call it as the *modified edge-directed interpolation* (MEDI) [59] for easy reference in this book.

MATLAB 8.6.1—MEDI, a modified NEDI image interpolation algorithm with windows defined on low-resolution pixels alone.

```
function g = medi(f,t,b)
  g = double(directus(f));
  [M,N]=size(g);
  for k = 0:3
    switch k
      case 0                  % Type 0 pixels
        pwin = [-1 -1 1 1; -1 1 -1 1];
        mwin = [-3 -3 -3 -3 -1 -1 -1 -1 1 1 1 1 3 3 3 3;
                -3 -1 1 3 -3 -1 1 3 -3 -1 1 3 -3 -1 1 3];
        dmn = [0,0];
      case 1                  % Type 1 pixels
        pwin = [-1 -1 -1 1 1 1; 2 0 -2 2 0 -2];
        mwin = [-3 -3 -3 -3 -3 -3 -3 -1 -1 -1 -1 -1 -1 -1 ...
                 1  1  1  1  1  1  1  3  3  3  3  3  3  3;
                 6  4  2  0 -2 -4 -6  6  4  2  0 -2 -4 -6 ...
                 6  4  2  0 -2 -4 -6  6  4  2  0 -2 -4 -6];
        dmn = [0,1];
      case 2                  % Type 2 pixels
        pwin = [2 0 -2 2 0 -2; -1 -1 -1 1 1 1];
        mwin = [6  4  2  0 -2 -4 -6  6  4  2  0 -2 -4 -6 ...
                6  4  2  0 -2 -4 -6  6  4  2  0 -2 -4 -6;
               -3 -3 -3 -3 -3 -3 -3 -1 -1 -1 -1 -1 -1 -1 ...
                1  1  1  1  1  1  1  3  3  3  3  3  3  3];
        dmn = [1,0];
    end;
    cwin = 2*pwin;
    for m=b-dmn(1):2:M-b
      for n=b-dmn(2):2:N-b
        g(m,n) = nedi_core(g,m,n,pwin,mwin,cwin,t);
end; end; end; return;
```

The MATLAB function medi can be simply invoked by g = medi(f,48,12) for the case of variance threshold set at $t = 48$ and with boundary width of 12 pixels. To remedy the boundary problem associated with the MEDI kernel, the boundary extension method as discussed in Section 8.4 can be applied. The MEDI interpolated *Cat* image with variance threshold set at $t = 48$ with periodic boundary extension to

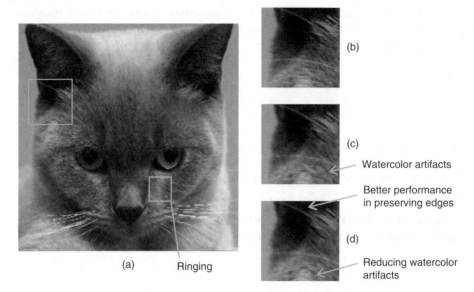

(a)   Ringing

(b)

(c)

Watercolor artifacts

Better performance
in preserving edges

(d)

Reducing watercolor
artifacts

Figure 8.13 A 512×512 2× MEDI interpolated *Cat* image with periodic boundary extension at $t = 48$ and $b = 12$ (PSNR = 27.8014 dB, SSIM = 0.8148). (a) The interpolated image, (b) zoom-in portion of the ear of the original high-resolution *Cat* image, (c) zoom-in portion of the ear of the NEDI interpolated *Cat* image, and (d) zoom-in portion of the ear of the MEDI interpolated *Cat* image.

handle boundary pixel problems is shown in Figure 8.13a, which is obtained with the following function call.

MATLAB 8.6.2—MEDI image interpolation with boundary extension.

```
>> ext = 12;
>> temp = repmat(f,3,3);
>> [M N] = size(f);
>> fext = temp(M-ext+1:2*M+ext,N-ext+1:2*N+ext);
>> g = medi(fext,48,ext);
>> g = g(2*ext+1:end-2*ext,2*ext+1:end-2*ext);
```

MEDI has improved the interpolation by modifying geometric structure prediction windows, mean covariance windows, and local covariance windows for type 1 and type 2 pixels, where only the low-resolution image pixels are considered in those windows, such that the prediction errors aroused in the course of the prediction of type 0 pixels will not propagate to the prediction of type 1 and type 2 pixels. The improvement can be more easily observed by studying the zoom-in portion of the ear of the *Cat* image shown in Figure 8.13d, where the same portion taken from the original image and the NEDI interpolated image are shown in Figures 8.13b,c, respectively. It can be observed in Figure 8.13d that the hairs at the upper part of the image are well preserved when compared with that of the NEDI, where more solid and sharp hairs are observed. The MEDI improves the prediction accuracy for type 1 and type 2 pixels, thus improving the interpolation performance along diagonal edges. It also can be observed that MEDI has successfully suppressed the watercolor artifacts when compared with the interpolated image obtained by NEDI as shown in Figure 8.13c, which is due to the copying of the image features in between neighboring pixels where the prediction of type 1 and type 2 pixels depends on the prediction results of type 0 pixels. With the modified windows in the MEDI, the prediction of each type of pixels acquires a specific set of low-resolution pixels, thus confining the image features to be interpolated within a predefined region. However, due to the larger size of the modified windows, any image features with size smaller than that of the windows would not be able to be well described by the covariance structure in the windows, thus resulting in local oscillation, which is also known as the ringing artifacts. It can be observed in Figure 8.13a that the face of the *Cat* image is degraded by ringing artifacts when compared with that obtained by NEDI (see Figure 8.10a).

Besides the subjective evaluation, let us also investigate the objective performance of the MEDI with respect to different values of t. A summary of the PSNR and SSIM performance of the MEDI interpolated *Cat* image with different t is shown in Table 8.2. It can be observed that the PSNR performance of the MEDI is generally improved when compared with that of the NEDI with $t < 200$, however the NEDI performs better in PSNR when t is further increased. It is because the prediction error propagation is suppressed with the use of modified windows, which reduces the errors across the entire image, especially in improving the prediction accuracy along edges, thus increasing the PSNR. When further increasing the t, more pixels would be interpolated by mean averaging in both the NEDI and the MEDI. However, it is more difficult to preserve the image structure with the large window size of the MEDI after the mean averaging operation (resulting blurred and broken edges). As a result, when the variance threshold is very large, the PSNR will decrease. Therefore, it is vivid that there is a trade-off between the suppression of prediction error in the covariance-based interpolation and the degradation of image structure in mean averaging of the larger window size in the MEDI. The SSIM is more effective in revealing the image structures embedded in the interpolated image. It is vivid to observe the variation in SSIM against increasing t. It can be observed that the SSIM in the MEDI interpolated *Cat* image turns out to be decreasing when t is greater than 48, while the PSNR is still increasing. In other words, the image structure degradation

Table 8.2 The PSNR and SSIM performance of a 2× *Cat* image interpolation to size 512 × 512 using the MEDI and periodic extension with various variance threshold values.

Variance threshold t	PSNR (dB)	SSIM
0	27.7930	0.8140
10	27.7942	0.8143
48	27.8014	0.8148
100	27.8082	0.8138
128	27.8125	0.8133
200	27.8204	0.8118
1000	27.8486	0.8034
5000	27.4806	0.7977
∞	27.3750	0.7983

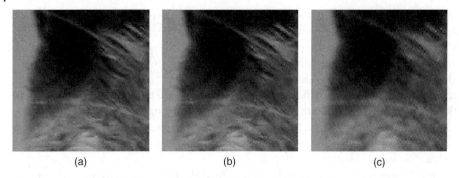

(a)	(b)	(c)

Figure 8.14 The zoom-in portion of the ear of the MEDI interpolated *Cat* image subject to different thresholds, namely, (a) $t = 48$, (b) $t = 200$, and (c) $t = 5000$, where the boundary extension in all images is $b = 12$.

brought by mean averaging begins to dominate the interpolation when t is large, which affects the objective performance of the MEDI. Figure 8.14 shows the zoom-in of the ears of the *Cat* image taken from the MEDI interpolated images with different thresholds t and with the same boundary extension of $b = 12$. It is vivid that the sharpness of the hairs (long edges) is best preserved in the case of $t = 48$. Subject to this t, the suppression of prediction errors by adopting enlarged windows is the most effective, and the image structure degradation in smooth region brought by mean averaging operation can be alleviated. However, with increasing t, more ringing artifacts are observed in the interpolated image due to the degraded image feature regulation under a large window size. In other words, the assumption of local stationary is less efficient with increased window size, though the interpolation is still a combination of the covariance-based interpolation and nonadaptive mean averaging interpolation. By further increasing $t = 5000$, the nonadaptive mean averaging interpolation takes over almost all the estimation of the unknown pixels; thus the image features are blurred especially with large window, which results in degradation in both subjective and objective (PSNR and SSIM) measures in the MEDI interpolated images when compared with that of the NEDI results.

8.7 Covariance Window Adaptation

Another situation where local image blocks do not follow local stationary can be demonstrated by the oversimplified image block example shown in Figure 8.15. Shown in Figure 8.15a is a local image block containing two edges ("Edge 1" and "Edge 2"). When the NEDI is applied to interpolate the gray pixel in the center of Figure 8.15a, the pixels within the box will form the prediction window, and the dashed box will form the mean covariance window. Figure 8.15b redraws the pixels within the prediction window, which clearly shows that it contains one edge (part of "Edge 1") only. Shown in Figure 8.15c are the pixels contained by the mean covariance window, which clearly shows that it contains "Edge 1" and part of "Edge 2." It is vivid that the covariance structure of the prediction window will not match with the covariance structure of the local image blocks within the mean covariance window. This *covariance mismatch* violates the geometric duality assumption between the high- and low-resolution images.

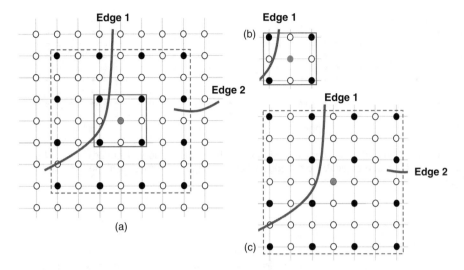

Figure 8.15 Illustration of covariance mismatch between prediction window and local covariance window corresponding to the gray pixel in (a); (b) prediction window contains Edge 1 only; (c) mean covariance window contains both Edge 1 and Edge 2.

As a result, the NEDI interpolated image block will have large interpolation error and undesirable interpolation artifacts. A careful investigation will find that there are two problems associated with the above *covariance mismatch* interpolation fallacies. The first problem is related to the structure of the windows, while the second one is about the spatial location of the windows relative to the pixel under interpolation.

8.7.1 Prediction Window Adaptation

One of the reasons leading to the *covariance mismatch* of the NEDI is the application of fixed window structure, both size and shape. As a result, one of the remedies is to modify the window to enclose the major feature only, such as to ensure that the low-resolution image and high-resolution image have similar covariance structures. Shown in Figure 8.16 are the modified prediction windows with the associated window shapes directed by the edge features within the local region [68]. There are four different sets of prediction windows adapting to edges with 0°, 90°, 45°, and 135° orientations as shown in the figure. The directionality of the prediction window is obtained by elongating the prediction window along the predefined edge direction and narrowing the prediction window in perpendicular to the predefined edge direction. Such window structures can partially alleviate the covariance mismatch problem and slightly improve the objective performance of the interpolated image. However, a lot of image features do not perfectly lie on 0°, 90°, 45°, and 135° (such as in the case of "Edge 1" in Figure 8.15). It can foresee that such image feature will not be completely enclosed by any one of the modified prediction windows in Figure 8.16, and hence the covariance mismatch problem remains. Directional windows that are spatially "wide" in shape are required to accommodate edge features that are not straightly straight line in shape. Another problem of the prediction window is the variation in size to accommodate edges in different sizes and orientations. As a window where the covariance estimation is biased, it will cause

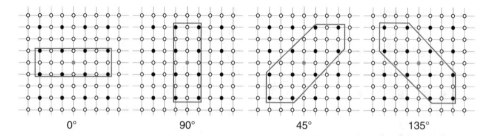

Figure 8.16 Directional adaptive prediction windows with elongation along the edge direction but reducing the width in perpendicular to the edge, where the edge are oriented in 0°, 90°, 45°, and 135° [68].

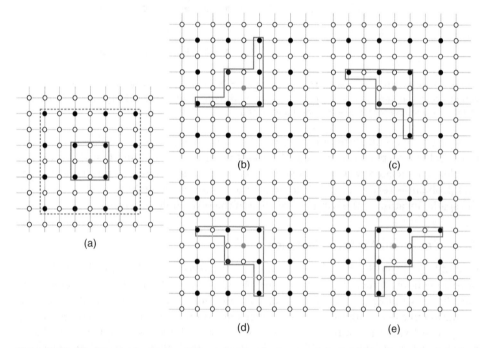

Figure 8.17 Directional adaptive prediction windows that are spatially "wide" in shape: (a) original prediction window and (b)–(e) the modified arrow-shaped prediction windows in different orientations but in the same size [68].

the covariance threshold to fail on detecting weak horizontal and vertical edges and falsely detect edge features as 45° and 135°. In other words, the consistency of prediction window shape is also important to the performance of the covariance-based image interpolation algorithm. Shown in Figure 8.17 is one of such prediction window structures.

Visually it is vivid that the arrow-shaped prediction windows in Figure 8.17 are consistent in shape and are directionally adaptive. Analytically the directional adaptation of the arrow-shaped prediction windows is obtained from the bias in covariance estimation provided by the spatial orientation of the windows. To determine which window should be applied, the intensity difference of each pair of pixels within each window is computed. The pixel pair with the largest intensity difference will decide the orientation of the edge, and the window that aligns with that pixel pair should be applied. In other words, the prediction window will only contain one pixel pair that are determined to be an edge and hence preserve the geometric regularity of the covariance estimation.

The prediction window adaptation does has its own drawback. Firstly, it is computationally expensive, as additional computations have to be performed to determine which prediction window should be applied. These additional computations are required to estimate the existence of an edge and the orientation of the edge should it exist. The determination of edge feature in these additional computations is a much worst problem than the edge detection problem discussed in Section 2.5 where the detector kernel size is small and hence the detection result is spatially accurate and is not susceptible to low noise level. On the other hand, the problem considered by the selection of prediction window has a much larger kernel size, and hence the result is highly susceptible to image noise. Secondly, the size adapted window does not resolve the problem of completely enclosing short featured image structure (short edge). In this case, the image structure within the covariance estimation window cannot be considered to be locally stationary.

8.7.2 Mean Covariance Window Adaptation

The prediction window adaptation will select a mean covariance window that covers only one image feature in the local image region. The adaptation of the prediction window ponders our question on adapting the mean covariance window to resolve the feature size problem, where the mean covariance window should cover one and only one image feature. As a result, using mean covariance window with size that is too large will capture features that should not coexist in the mean covariance window and the prediction window. However, if the mean covariance window size is too small, it will violate the assumption of local stationary within the mean covariance window. This has led to the development of adaptive window for covariance estimation [5]. The interpolation starts from an initial default window size, and the associated interpolation MSE is computed. The interpolation is then performed with a bigger mean covariance estimation window. If the interpolation MSE obtained from bigger mean covariance estimation window is smaller than that of smaller covariance estimation window, the one that achieves the smaller MSE will be adopted. The interpolation will keep performing with larger and larger mean covariance window size until a predefined maximum window size is achieved. The con of this method is the increase in computational complexity because of the iterative nature of the algorithm. The pro is that better interpolated image in both objective and subjective qualities is expected. The reality is that the quality of the image interpolated by this method varies. This is because the estimation of the MSE in the middle of each iteration will determine the performance of the final interpolated image, which is difficult to obtain accurately, if not impossible to obtain at all. Furthermore, increasing the size of the mean covariance window will seldom be locally stationary. The larger the mean covariance window, the more likely more than one image feature will be included within the window, hence implying nonstationary. As a result, the selection of mean covariance window size is an engineering trade-off between the preservation of covariance structure and the preservation of local stationary (which forms the basis of the geometric duality-based interpolation).

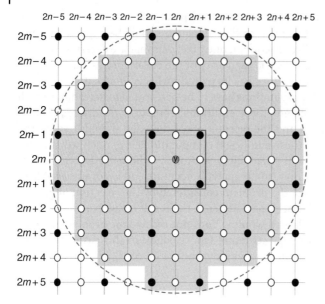

Figure 8.18 Windows of iNEDI [5], where the solid line windows are the low-resolution window and the dashed line windows is the mean covariance window.

Furthermore, the nonsymmetrical shape of the mean covariance window makes it directionally sensitive, just like the case of the prediction window. A simple solution to remedy the directional biasing problem of the mean covariance window is to use a circular window as that shown in Figure 8.18, which was proposed in [5]. Enhanced image interpolation results have been observed with this circular mean covariance window that is perfectly circular and has no directionality. The mirror has two faces; however, losing the directionality will require a large window to capture all the edge features inside the window to allow covariance-based image interpolation. As a result, the same old problem of nonstationary with large window size will pop out.

The perfect solution to the question requires a small mean covariance window that can enclose the local image feature (edge) and is unbiased directionally. At the same time, it should allow the covariance-based interpolation to exploit directional property of the image features enclosed within the mean covariance window for better image interpolation results. These requirements seem contradicting but somehow [59] proposed a mean covariance window generation and selection strategy that can almost perfectly achieve the above requirements.

8.7.3 Enhanced Modified Edge-Directed Interpolation (EMEDI)

To understand how to remedy the covariance mismatch problem, let us first review the problem using Figure 8.19. Figure 8.19a shows the prediction window and the mean covariance window adopted in the NEDI. If we allow the mean covariance window to vary its spatial location, we shall observe at least four different poses for the mean covariance windows with reference to the prediction window as shown in Figure 8.19b–e. These four mean covariance windows are displacement of the original

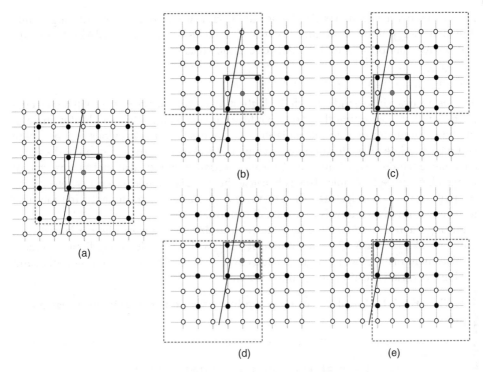

Figure 8.19 Illustration of different placements of covariance estimation window with respect to a fixed prediction window: (a) the placement adopted by the NEDI and (b)–(e) the other four placement variations.

covariance window where the center of the mean covariance window moves from $[m, n]$ (the interpolation pixel coordinate) to $[m + \texttt{cwin}(1,k), n + \texttt{cwin}(2,k)]$ for each pixel on the original mean covariance window indexed by the variable k. In all the cases, the mean covariance window does completely enclose the prediction window. These displaced mean covariance window placements have achieved different spatial biased, which provide estimation with directionality (similar to that in Figure 8.17). At the same time, they are unbiased covariance estimator when compared with each other, because they all have the same shape and are related to each other with a given rotation. Figure 8.20 illustrates the unbiased mean covariance window locations in our example. Among all the mean covariance estimation window, we should choose the one that can achieve the minimal covariance mismatch. Visually we can determine that the mean covariance window in Figure 8.19e will give the minimal covariance mismatch for the example in Figure 8.19. Analytically, the search for the best mean covariance window can be achieved by searching for the one that contains the strongest feature (edge). In other words, the search should be performed by computing the total energy of the covariance of each mean covariance window, which is given by

$$E_c = \sum (\text{cov}(\mathbf{c}))^2, \tag{8.20}$$

where $\texttt{cov}$ is the covariance operator for the 2D matrix and the $(\cdot)^2$ is a per-matrix element operation. MATLAB has a similar covariance computation function with the same name. The covariance matrix **C** is defined in the same way as that in the NEDI algorithm. The total energy of the covariance matrix can be computed by simple MATLAB manipulation. An example of the MATLAB code is shown as below:

```
>> covC = cov(C)
>> energyC = sum( covC(:).^2);
```

The mean covariance window with the highest mean covariance energy will be selected as the window containing the most significant image feature that would dominate in the linear prediction-based interpolation. As discussed in the previous section, there could be multiple image features coexisting in a local region. The selection of the mean covariance window with the largest mean covariance energy also makes this type of image block more favorable. This is because the covariance matrix energy reflects the strength of the image feature. The key to remedy the problem of capturing multiple features within the window is to use small window.

Putting them all together the best mean covariance window can be computed with the MATLAB Listing 8.7.1 for a given pixel $[m, n]$ with a predefined prediction window displacement matrix `pwin`, original mean covariance displacement window `mwin`, and the local covariance estimation window `cwin`.

> **MATLAB 8.7.1—Local covariance window selection to maximize covariance power.**
>
> ```
> function [winnum, maxE, bestwin, bestC] = emedi_select_win(g,m,n,pwin,
>     mwin,cwin)
>     [win xLR C] = nedi_window(g,m,n,pwin,mwin,cwin);
>     covC = cov(C);
>     maxE = sum(covC(:).^2);
>     bestwin = win; bestC = C; winnum = 0; % initialize the search
>         result
>     num=size(pwin,2);
>     for wins=1:num
>         [win xLR C] = nedi_window(g,m+cwin(1,wins),n+cwin(2,wins),pwin
>             ,mwin,cwin);
>         covC = cov(C);
>         energyC = sum(covC(:).^2);
>         if maxE < energyC
>             maxE = energyC; bestwin = win; bestC = C; winnum = wins;
>     end; end; return;
> ```

Within each iteration in the `for`-loop, the covariance matrix of a biased mean covariance window with center located in one of the original mean covariance window pixel will be constructed with the MATLAB function call to `nedi_window`, the same covariance matrix construction function used by the NEDI. The total covariance energy of the covariance matrix will be computed and compared with the largest total covariance energy `maxE` stored so far. If the computed total covariance energy is larger than `maxE`, it will replace `maxE`, and the current biased window will temporarily be the best mean covariance window. The mean covariance pixel intensity vector `bestwin` will be updated to be the pixel intensity of the current biased mean covariance window, such that `bestwin=win`. The best covariance estimation `bestC` will also be updated to be the current computed `C`. The above search will continue until each and every pixel in `[m+cwin(1,k),n+cwin(2,k)]` has been tested, where in MATLAB a counter parameter `wins` is defined to realize the parameter k to complete the window definition. This iterative search is initialized with the `maxE`, `bestC`, and `win` set to be equal to the total covariance energy, the estimated covariance, and mean covariance window pixel intensity vector of that of the original mean covariance window, respectively.

Figure 8.20 illustrates the spatial adaptation of the mean covariance windows for type 0 pixel, where 5 mean covariance windows are considered in this example. The window indexed by `winnum=0` is the original window. While there are four pairs of elements in `cwin`, there are the additional 4 displaced mean covariance windows (indexed by `winnum=1,2,3,and 4`) to be considered. This is a simple example showing the basic concept of alleviating the covariance mismatch problem by refining the mean covariance estimation window spatial location subject to the covariance structure carried by the mean covariance estimation window. By biasing the spatial location of the mean covariance estimation window, it effectively enlarges the coverage of the covariance structure estimation spatial area, without actually increasing the kernel size (window size) of the covariance estimation, hence maintaining the local stationary as that of the NEDI. Furthermore, there is no need to modify the shape of the prediction window nor the associated local covariance estimation window (in this example they are both squares in shape as that applied in the NEDI), while still be able to achieve all the benefits

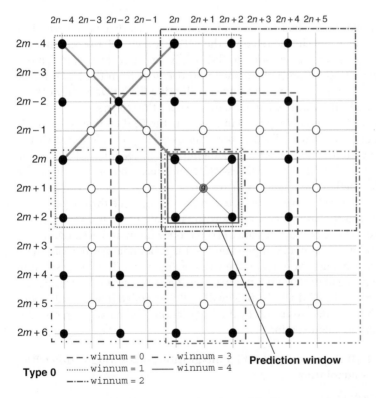

Figure 8.20 Illustration of the spatial adaptation of the five mean covariance windows adopted in the EMEDI for type 0 pixel. Noted the window `winnum=0` is same as that in the original NEDI. (*See insert for color representation of this figure.*)

of directionality, and space invariant mean covariance estimation window as that in Figures 8.16–8.18.

To implement a covariance-based image interpolation program that makes use of the best mean covariance window selection, we shall have to insert the function `emedi_select_win` after the window construction by `nedi_window` and before the construction of the linear prediction weighting factors by `nedi_weighting_factor`. The MATLAB function `emedi_core` listed in Listing 8.7.2 modifies the function `nedi_core` in Listing 8.3.3 implementing the core function for incorporating local covariance window with maximum covariance power in the interpolation.

> **MATLAB 8.7.2—EMEDI_CORE, a modified NEDI_CORE to incorporate local covariance window selection that maximizes covariance power.**
>
> ```
> function [pixel] = emedi_core(g,m,n,pwin,mwin,cwin,t)
>   [win xLR C] = nedi_window(g,m,n,pwin,mwin,cwin);
>   [winnum, maxE, bestwin, bestC] = emedi_select_win(g,m,n,pwin,mwin,
>       cwin);
>   [a] = nedi_weighting_factor(bestwin,bestC,t);
>   pixel = a'*xLR;
>   pixel = nedi_correct(pixel,xLR);
> return;
> ```

This core function can be applied to the same framework as that of the NEDI or the MEDI. In this example, we choose to adopt the MEDI framework to construct the *enhanced modified edge-directed interpolation* (EMEDI) image interpolation to demonstrate the progressive interpolation performance improvement from the NEDI to the MEDI and then to the EMEDI. The performance of adopting the NEDI framework for the construction of the EMEDI will be left as an exercise for the readers.

The MATLAB source listed in Listing 8.7.3 implements the EMEDI that is originally proposed by Tam et al. [59] and includes the above discussed improvement plus that of the MEDI. The MATLAB function `emedi` implements a 2× image interpolation using the EMEDI algorithm with user-defined threshold t and image border width b. The threshold will decide whether the weighting factors to be average filtered or to be computed by the covariance based approach depicted in Eq. (8.13), while the image border width will inform the interpolation algorithm how to take care of the image boundary. This is because the kernel size of the covariance estimation window and prediction window is not zero. Therefore, it cannot be applied on the image boundary; otherwise there will be undefined pixels being processed by the window functions. The low-resolution image is therefore required to perform boundary extension as discussed in Section 2.4.1 such that when operating the EMEDI, the pixel within the extended image border with the width of b will be excluded from the EMEDI operation. The detail of the border extension has been discussed in Section 8.4.

> **MATLAB 8.7.3—EMEDI, a modified MEDI image interpolation algorithm with covariance window adaptation.**
>
> ```
> function g = emedi(f,t,b)
>   g = double(directus(f));
> ```

```
[M,N]=size(g);
for k = 0:3
  switch k
    case 0                    % Type 0 pixels
      pwin = [-1 -1 1 1; -1 1 -1 1];
      mwin = [-3 -3 -3 -3 -1 -1 -1 -1 1 1 1 1 3 3 3 3;
              -3 -1 1 3 -3 -1 1 3 -3 -1 1 3 -3 -1 1 3];
      dmn = [0,0];
    case 1                    % Type 1 pixels
      pwin = [-1 -1 -1 1 1 1; 2 0 -2 2 0 -2];
      mwin = [-3 -3 -3 -3 -3 -3 -3 -1 -1 -1 -1 -1 -1 -1 ...
               1  1  1  1  1  1  1  3  3  3  3  3  3  3;
               6  4  2  0 -2 -4 -6  6  4  2  0 -2 -4 -6 ...
               6  4  2  0 -2 -4 -6  6  4  2  0 -2 -4 -6];
      dmn = [0,1];
    case 2                    % Type 2 pixels
      pwin = [2 0 -2 2 0 -2; -1 -1 -1 1 1 1];
      mwin = [6  4  2  0 -2 -4 -6  6  4  2  0 -2 -4 -6  ...
              6  4  2  0 -2 -4 -6  6  4  2  0 -2 -4 -6;
             -3 -3 -3 -3 -3 -3 -3 -1 -1 -1 -1 -1 -1 -1  ...
              1  1  1  1  1  1  1  3  3  3  3  3  3  3];
      dmn = [1,0];
  end;
  cwin = 2*pwin;
  for m=b-dmn(1):2:M-b
    for n=b-dmn(2):2:N-b
      g(m,n) = emedi_core(g,m,n,pwin,mwin,cwin,t);
end; end; end; return;
```

The MATLAB function `emedi` can be simply invoked by $g = \text{emedi}(f, 48, 20)$ for the case of threshold set at $t = 48$ and with boundary set at $b = 20$. To remedy the boundary problem associated with the EMEDI kernel, the boundary extension method as discussed in Section 8.4 can be applied. The EMEDI interpolated *Cat* image with $t = 48$ and $b = 20$ shown in Figure 8.21a, can be obtained with the following function call.

MATLAB 8.7.4—EMEDI image interpolation with boundary extension.

```
>> ext = 20;
>> temp = repmat(f,3,3);
>> [M N] = size(f);
>> fext = temp(M-ext+1:2*M+ext,N-ext+1:2*N+ext);
>> g = emedi(fext,48,ext);
>> g = g(2*ext+1:end-2*ext,2*ext+1:end-2*ext);
```

The EMEDI interpolated image is shown in Figure 8.21a. For comparison, the zoom-in portions of the ear of the *Cat* image extracted from the NEDI interpolated image, the MEDI interpolated image, and the EMEDI interpolated image are shown in Figure 8.21b–d, respectively. It can be observed from Figure 8.21d that the zoom-in image region of the ear of the *Cat* image has shown that the EMEDI image interpolation method can better preserve the image structure, when compared with that obtained by the MEDI as shown in Figure 8.21c. For comparison, the same image region of the NEDI

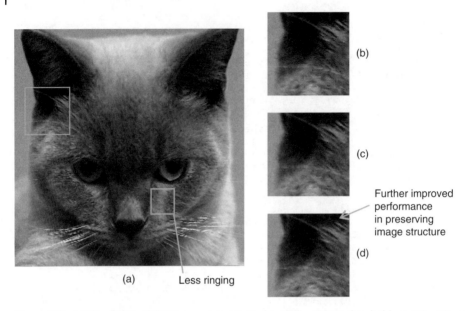

(b)

(c)

Further improved
performance
in preserving
image structure

(d)

(a)   Less ringing

Figure 8.21 A 512 × 512 2× EMEDI interpolated *Cat* image with variance threshold set at $t = 48$ and with the application of periodic boundary extension (PSNR = 27.8396 dB, SSIM = 0.8147). (a) The interpolated image, (b) zoom-in portion of the ear of the NEDI interpolated *Cat* image, (c) zoom-in portion of the ear of the MEDI interpolated *Cat* image, and (d) zoom-in portion of the ear of the EMEDI interpolated *Cat* image.

interpoated *Cat* image is shown in Figure 8.21b. The EMEDI interpolated image can preserve the image structure better because it adapts the covariance estimation window to the image feature. A larger window area is applied to search for the spatial location that has the highest regularity and hence can preserve the geometric duality better. This is being performed by searching the spatial location of the window with the highest covariance energy. To mitigate the covariance estimation error propagation problem, a bigger window is being adopted in the EMEDI. As a result, all the pixels being applied in the covariance estimation are directly obtained from the low-resolution image. The con of using a bigger window is the increased ringing artifacts in the interpolated image as observed in Figure 8.21a. This unwanted ringing artifacts can be suppressed by increasing the threshold t. The side effect of a bigger t is more likely that the image edge sharpness will get degraded. The selection of the best t is therefore a precise engineering trade-off problem between the edge sharpness and the ringing artifacts.

Having discussed the pros and cons about the EMEDI and the associated input parameters to the EMEDI, the objective quality of the 2× interpolated *Cat* image by the EMEDI has PNSR = 27.8396 dB, which is 0.24 dB better than that of the NEDI, in which the same $t = 48$ is applied. The improvement is attributed to the suppression of the covariance estimation error propagation in the NEDI. Furthermore, the SSIM of the interpolated image obtained by the EMEDI is 0.8147, which is also better than that of the NEDI. The improvement is attributed to the adaptivity of covariance

Table 8.3 The PSNR and SSIM performance of a 2× *Cat* image interpolation to size 512 × 512 using the EMEDI and periodic extension with various variance threshold values.

Variance threshold t	PSNR (dB)	SSIM
0	27.8350	0.8142
48	27.8396	0.8147
100	27.8414	0.8135
128	27.8428	0.8128
200	27.8465	0.8114
1000	27.8740	0.8027
5000	27.5751	0.7988
∞	27.3750	0.7977

estimation window, such that it can better preserve the covariance structure and hence the geometric duality between the low- and high-resolution image. Table 8.3 shows the summary of the PSNR and SSIM of the EMEDI interpolated images with the same boundary width but different threshold t. To further improve the SSIM, the covariance structure between the low- and high-resolution images should be better preserved, which in turn requires a low decision threshold t value, and hence new methods must be developed to suppress the increased ringing artifacts due to the use of small t. However, small t will make the EMEDI to consider weak edges or image noise as strong edges, and applies covariance-based interpolation on them, thus resulting in unpleasant subjective performance and degrading the PSNR result. In these circumstances, the greater the t, the better the PSNR. Therefore, the maxima of PSNR and SSIM as a function of threshold t are not collided, and they are image dependent, which should be carefully chosen. The next section will discuss how to improve the EMEDI through better preservation of covariance structure between the low- and high-resolution images by iterative error correction similar to those presented in Sections 5.6 and 6.4.

8.8 Iterative Covariance Correction

The covariance-based image interpolation, either the NEDI, the MEDI, or the EMEDI, is developed with the assumption of geometric duality between the low- and high-resolution images. It has been demonstrated in previous sections that even if the local image block within the covariance estimation window is locally stationary and regular, the local image block obtained from the NEDI, the MEDI, and the EMEDI interpolations will not have the same covariance structure as that of the low-resolution image block. There are a lot of reasons on the inefficiency of the interpolation algorithm such that the obtained local image block does not have the same covariance structure as that of the low-resolution image. One of the reasons will be that the interpolated pixel is obtained as the least squares solution of the estimated covariance structure, which is known to be sensitive to *outliers*, where we refer the outliers to noises in the image. A number of intermediate solutions have been presented in literature trying to remedy this poor estimation problem. The *robust NEDI* [42] incorporated a *nonlocal mean* method to optimize the linear prediction interpolation results, where the similarity of neighboring windows is compared with that of the current prediction window. When the covariance structure of the prediction window under concern is found to be similar to that of the neighboring windows, the prediction coefficients obtained from the original covariance estimation window and its neighboring windows with similar covariance structure will be mean filtered. The image obtained from these mean filtered prediction coefficients has found to be robust to image noises and be able to provide interpolated images with better objective and subjective qualities. However, similar to choosing a larger *t* to avoid noise being considered as image features, the mean filtered prediction will also cause degradation of structural details.

Before we can find a way to improve the local region of the high-resolution image to attain the same covariance structure as that of the corresponding low-resolution image region, we shall have to quantify the meaning of *covariance difference* analytically. The covariance structure difference between the covariance matrices of the corresponding low- and high-resolution image regions may not be compatible in dimension. As a result, we compare the total energy of the low- and high-resolution covariance matrices similar to that in Section 8.7.3. In particular, we shall compare the total energy of the low-resolution covariance matrix with the corresponding high-resolution covariance matrices under spatial displacements. The reason is the same as that discussed in Section 8.7.3, such that we shall allow the high-resolution covariance estimation to be spatially biased to capture the structure of the image feature for better preservation of the structural regularity. Given an interpolated pixel coordinate at [m,n], the spatial coordinates of the corresponding low-resolution image block are given by [m+lwin(1,:),n+lwin(2,:)] with the low-resolution pixel window spatial displacement vector lwin given by

```
hwin = [-1 -1 -1  0  0  0  1  1  1; -1  0  1 -1  0  1 -1  0  1];
lwin = [-3 -3 -3 -3 -1 -1 -1 -1  1  1  1  1  3  3  3  3;
        -3 -1  1  3 -3 -1  1  3 -3 -1  1  3 -3 -1  1  3];
```

for type 0 pixels. This particular choice of low-resolution window, which is the winnum=0 mean covariance window in Figure 8.20 surrounding the pixel to be interpolated, is shown in Figure 8.22. This specific window forms a fourth-order window with only the 4 × 4 low-resolution pixels (dark pixels) being considered. The second and third windows surrounding the interpolated pixel are not chosen because the second window containing only four low-resolution pixels is too small to capture image features, while the third window will include pixels from both high- and low-resolution images and hence does not fulfill our purpose. Similarly, the displacement vector hwin specifies the spatial coordinate displacement of the prediction window to extract the high-resolution pixel window, which forms a third-order system that covers 3 × 3 pixels surrounding the pixel to be interpolated, in which both low- and high-resolution pixels are considered. It is the difference in the order that makes direct comparison between the two covariance matrices impossible. We can either

Figure 8.22 Illustration of the examples of the biased covariance windows for high- and low-resolution image pixels.

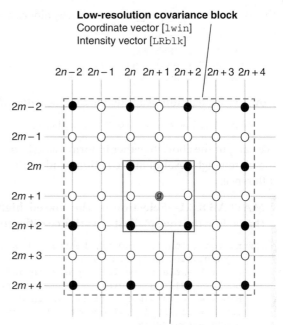

Low-resolution covariance block
Coordinate vector [lwin]
Intensity vector [LRblk]

2n−2 2n−1 2n 2n+1 2n+2 2n+3 2n+4

2m−2
2m−1
2m
2m+1
2m+2
2m+3
2m+4

Type 0 **High-resolution covariance block**
Coordinate vector [hwin]
Intensity vector [HRblk]

change the window size, or we can compare their total energy, and in this section we choose the latter one, which is also the easier one. The spatial coordinates for the high-resolution image block biased to the kth prediction pixels pwin(:,k) are given by [m+pwin(1,k)+hwin(1,:),n+pwin(2,k)+hwin(2,:)]. The corresponding lwin and hwin for type 1 pixels are given by

```
hwin = [-1 -1 -1  0  0  0  1  1  1  0  0  0  0  0  ...
         0  0 -1 -1 -1 -1 -1  0  0  0  0  0  1  1  1  1  1;
        -1  0  1 -1  0  1 -1  0  1  0  0  0  0  0  ...
         0  0 -2 -1  0  1  2 -2 -1  0  1  2 -2 -1  0  1  2];
lwin = [-3 -3 -3 -3 -3 -1 -1 -1 -1 -1  1  1  1  1  1  3  3  3  3  3;
        -4 -2  0  2  4 -4 -2  0  2  4 -4 -2  0  2  4 -4 -2  0  2  4];
```

and for type 2 pixels

```
hwin =[-2 -2 -2 -1 -1 -1  0  0  0  1  1  1  2  2  ...
        2  0 -1 -1 -1 -1 -1  0  0  0  0  0  1  1  1  1  1;
       -1  0  1 -1  0  1 -1  0  1 -1  0  1 -1  0  ...
        1  0 -2 -1  0  1  2 -2 -1  0  1  2 -2 -1  0  1  2];
lwin =[-4 -4 -4 -4 -2 -2 -2 -2  0  0  0  0  2  2  2  2  4  4  4  4;
       -3 -1  1  3 -3 -1  1  3 -3 -1  1  3 -3 -1  1  3 -3 -1  1  3];
```

Once the image block pixel coordinates are constructed, the low- and high-resolution image intensity vectors LRblk and HRblk, respectively, can be obtained by the following MATLAB code:

```
LRblk = [diag(g(m+lwin(1,:),n+lwin(2,:)))];
HRblk = [diag(g(m+pwin(1,k)+hwin(1,:),n+pwin(2,k)+hwin(2,:)))];
```

the total covariance energy of these image blocks are obtained with function call to cov

```
covLR = cov(LRblk);
covHR = cov(HRblk);
energyLR = sum( covLR(:).^2 );
energyHR = sum( covHR(:).^2 );
```

Now we can algorithmically define the *covariance difference* as

```
energyDiff = abs(energyHR-energyLR);
```

We can put the above together to form imedi_select_win in Listing 8.8.1 to select the biased high-resolution prediction window that can achieve the smallest covariance difference.

MATLAB 8.8.1—Selection of the biased high-resolution prediction window that achieving the smallest covariance difference in iMEDI.

```
function [winnum, minDiff, bestwin, bestC] = imedi_select_win(g,m,n,
     pwin,mwin,cwin,hwin,lwin)
          % extract the low-resolution and high-resolution image block
   LRblk = [diag(g(m+lwin(1,:),n+lwin(2,:)))];
   HRblk = [diag(g(m+hwin(1,:),n+hwin(2,:)))];
   covLR = cov(LRblk); % compute the covariance of the image blocks
   covHR = cov(HRblk);
          % compute the energies of the covariance matrices
   energyLR = sum(covLR(:).^2);
   energyHR = sum(covHR(:).^2);
   minDiff = abs(energyHR-energyLR);
          % init the best window number and order of the linear
               prediction
   winnum = 0;
   num=size(pwin,2);
   for wins=1:num
                  % extract the low-resolution and high-resolution image
                      block
     LRblk = [diag(g(m+lwin(1,:),n+lwin(2,:)))];
     HRblk = [diag(g(m+pwin(1,wins)+hwin(1,:),n+pwin(1,wins)+hwin(2,:))
              )];
                  % compute the covariance of the image blocks
     covLR = cov(LRblk);
     covHR = cov(HRblk);
                  % compute the energies of the covariance matrices
     energyLR = sum(covLR(:).^2);
     energyHR = sum(covHR(:).^2);
     energyDiff = abs(energyHR-energyLR);
     if energyDiff < minDiff
       minDiff = energyDiff;
       winnum = wins;
   end; end;
   if winnum == 0
     [bestwin bestxLR bestC] = nedi_window(g,m,n,pwin,mwin,cwin);
   else
     [bestwin bestxLR bestC] = nedi_window(g,m+cwin(1,winnum),n+cwin(2,
          winnum),pwin,mwin,cwin);
   end; return;
```

The function `imedi_select_win` is similar to `emedi_select_win` in Listing 8.7.1, where `emedi_select_win` adapts the mean covariance window, while `imedi_select_win` adapts the high-resolution prediction window. The biased high-resolution prediction window that can achieve the smallest covariance difference will be selected. If, for example, the smallest covariance difference is achieved by the *k*th biased high-resolution prediction window, prediction window should be displaced. However, for the purpose of implementation, it is easier to displace the interpolated pixel location from `[m,n]` to `[m+cwin(1,k),n+cwin(2,k)]` and hence the last `if-else` command in the MATLAB Listing 8.8.1. The `imedi_select_win` will return the pixel intensity vectors of the best selected mean covariance window `bestwin` and prediction window `bestxLR` and the associated covariance matrix `bestC`. These information will be fed into `nedi_weighting_factor` to generate the linear prediction coefficients, and so is the intensity of the pixel to be interpolated, in the same manner as that of the NEDI. The improved method is named *improved modified edge-directed interpolation* (iMEDI). All of these are implemented in the core function `imedi_core` in Listing 8.8.2, which will return the intensity of the interpolated pixel that achieves the minimal covariance difference.

MATLAB 8.8.2—iMEDI window generation.

```
function [pixel] = imedi_core(g,m,n,pwin,mwin,cwin,hwin,lwin,t)
  [win xLR C] = nedi_window(g,m,n,pwin,mwin,cwin);
  [winnum, minDiff, bestwin, bestC] = imedi_select_win(g,m,n,pwin,mwin
      ,cwin,hwin,lwin);
  [a] = nedi_weighting_factor(bestwin,bestC,t);
  pixel = a'*xLR;
  pixel = nedi_correct(pixel,xLR);
return;
```

A similar framework as that of `emedi` in Listing 8.7.3 is applied to implement the iMEDI interpolation in MATLAB source Listing 8.8.3.

MATLAB 8.8.3—2× image interpolation by iMEDI.

```
function g = imedi(g,t,b) % g is of high-resolution size
  [M,N]=size(g);
  for k = 0:3
    switch k
      case 0    % Type 0 pixels
        pwin = [-1 -1 1 1; -1 1 -1 1]; % same window as MEDI
        mwin = [-3 -3 -3 -3 -1 -1 -1 -1 1 1 1 1 3 3 3 3;
                -3 -1 1 3 -3 -1 1 3 -3 -1 1 3 -3 -1 1 3];
        hwin = [-1 -1 -1  0  0  0  1  1  1;
                -1  0  1 -1  0  1 -1  0  1];
        lwin = [-3 -3 -3 -3 -1 -1 -1 -1  1  1  1  1  3  3  3  3;
                -3 -1  1  3 -3 -1  1  3 -3 -1  1  3 -3 -1  1  3];
        dmn = [0,0];
      case 1    % Type 1 pixels
        pwin = [-1 -1 -1 1 1 1; 2 0 -2 2 0 -2];
        mwin = [-3 -3 -3 -3 -3 -3 -3 -1 -1 -1 -1 -1 -1 -1  ...
                 1  1  1  1  1  1  1  3  3  3  3  3  3  3;
```

```
                6   4   2   0 -2 -4 -6   6   4   2   0 -2 -4 -6  ...
                6   4   2   0 -2 -4 -6   6   4   2   0 -2 -4 -6];
     hwin = [-1 -1 -1   0   0   0   1   1   1   0   0   0   0   0  ...
             0   0 -1 -1 -1 -1 -1   0   0   0   0   0   1   1   1   1   1;
            -1   0   1 -1   0   1 -1   0   1   0   0   0   0   0  ...
             0   0 -2 -1   0   1   2 -2 -1   0   1   2 -2 -1   0   1   2];
     lwin = [-3 -3 -3 -3 -3 -1 -1 -1 -1 -1   1   1   1   1   1  ...
             1   3   3   3   3   3   3;
            -4 -2   0   2   4 -4 -2   0   2   4 -4 -2   0   2  ...
             4 -4 -2   0   2   4];
     dmn = [0,1];
  case 2     % Type 2 pixels
   pwin = [2   0 -2   2   0 -2; -1 -1 -1   1   1   1];
   mwin = [6   4   2   0 -2 -4 -6   6   4   2   0 -2 -4 -6  ...
           6   4   2   0 -2 -4 -6   6   4   2   0 -2 -4 -6;
          -3 -3 -3 -3 -3 -3 -3 -1 -1 -1 -1 -1 -1 -1  ...
           1   1   1   1   1   1   1   3   3   3   3   3   3   3];
   hwin =[-2 -2 -2 -1 -1 -1   0   0   0   1   1   1   2   2  ...
           2   0 -1 -1 -1 -1 -1   0   0   0   0   0   1   1   1   1   1;
          -1   0   1 -1   0   1 -1   0   1 -1   0   1 -1   0  ...
           1   0 -2 -1   0   1   2 -2 -1   0   1   2 -2 -1   0   1   2];
   lwin =[-4 -4 -4 -4 -2 -2 -2 -2   0   0   0   0   2   2  ...
           2   2   4   4   4   4;
          -3 -1   1   3 -3 -1   1   3 -3 -1   1   3 -3 -1  ...
           1   3 -3 -1   1   3];
     dmn = [1,0];
   end;
  cwin = 2*pwin;
  for m=b-dmn(1):2:M-b
    for n=b-dmn(2):2:N-b
      g(m,n) = imedi_core_new(g,m,n,pwin,mwin,cwin,hwin,lwin,t);
end; end; end; return;
```

Unlike `nedi`, `medi`, and `emedi`, the MATLAB function `imedi` does not interpolate image. Instead, the following function call

```
g1 = imedi(g,th,b);
```

takes in a high-resolution image g and generates another image g1 with the same resolution, where the pixels corresponding to the down-sampled version of g are preserved, while other pixels are interpolated to minimize the covariance difference between that of the down-sampled images. The rest of the parameters are defined to be the same as that in `nedi`. To smooth out the covariance difference problem, mean filtering should be applied to g1 and g, such as

```
>> g = (g+g1)./2;
```

which is known as dyadic averaging. If the mean filtered image is considered to be still suffering from covariance difference problem, the `imedi` can be invoked again, and another mean filtering can be performed. However, iterative application of dyadic averaging is biased to the last generated image and minimized the contribution from the first image. The equal weighting average should be applied in iterative covariance difference minimization that uses `imedi` to generate multiple high-resolution images in `for`-loop. As an example, at the $(k+1)$th loop that generates the $(k+1)$th high-resolution image g1 from the *k*th equal averaged image g, the equal weighting average image will be obtained as

```
>> g = (g.*k+g1);
>> g = g./(k+1);
```

Finally the iterative covariance difference minimization procedure is implemented with the MATLAB function imediloop in Listing 8.8.4 with details to be presented in the next section.

8.8.1 iMEDI Implementation

Putting them all together, the MATLAB function imediloop listed in Listing 8.8.4 implements a 2× image interpolation which iteratively minimizes the covariance difference of the interpolated high-resolution image obtained by medi with respect to the given low-resolution image.

MATLAB 8.8.4—Iterative application of iMEDI for 2× image interpolation.

```
function g=imediloop(f,th,b,i,tc)
   g = medi(f,th,b); % initial high-resolution image from MEDI
   mse = 0;
   for k=1:i
      g1 = imedi(g,th,b); % high-resolution image from IMEDI
      nmse = cmse(g,g1);
      if abs(nmse-mse)>tc % stop with small mse improvement
         g = (g.*k+g1);      % mean filtering over all additional images
         g = g./(k+1);
         mse = nmse;
      else break;
end; end; return;
```

The parameters in imediloop are defined to be the same as those in nedi. There are two newly added parameters, tc and i. The iterative covariance difference minimization will stop when the number of iteration equals i. The iteration will also come to a premature stop when the absolute difference of the mean squares difference between the mean filtered high-resolution images obtained at the *k*th iteration and that obtained at the $(k + 1)$th iteration is smaller than the predefined threshold tc. To compute the mean squares difference between two high-resolution images, the following MATLAB function cmse is created, which will take in the original high-resolution image oimg and the processed high-resolution image rimg and return the mean squares difference between these two images. In other words, the *k*th iteration image and the $(k + 1)$th image would be considered as oimg and rimg, respectively.

MATLAB 8.8.5—Mean squares difference of two images.

```
function returnVal = cmse(oimg, rimg)
   [orgM orgN] = size(oimg);
   [recM recN] = size(rimg);
   MSE = 0;
```

```
    if (orgM ~= recM) | (orgN ~= recM)
      returnVal = -1;
    end;
    for i = 1:recM
      for j = 1:recN
        MSE = ((round(double(oimg(i,j))) - round(double(rimg(i,j))))^2)
               /(recM*recN) + MSE;
    end; end;
    returnVal = MSE;
  return;
```

The 2× interpolated *Cat* image shown in Figure 8.23a is obtained with the following function call to `imediloop`:

```
>> g = imediloop(f,48,20,10,0.1);
```

The above parameters are for $t = 48$, image boundary width of 20, and a maximum of 10 iterations of covariance corrections with premature stop when the difference of the images in consecutive iteration measured by mean squares error is smaller than 0.1. For the *Cat* image with chosen $t = 48$, $b = 20$, and $tc = 0.1$, the iteration stops at the sixth iteration. It can be observed from the zoom-in image block of the ear of the *Cat* image shown in Figure 8.23d that taken from the iMEDI final image obtained at the sixth iteration, it can preserve the image structure better when compared with that obtained by the EMEDI as shown in Figure 8.23c. For comparison, the same image block

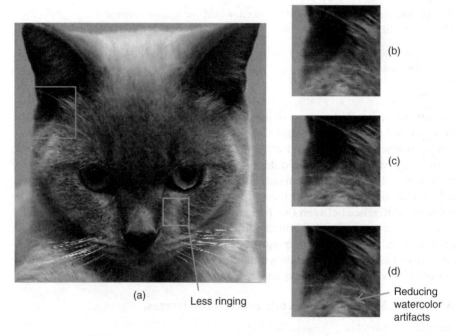

(b)

(c)

(d)

(a)

Less ringing

Reducing watercolor artifacts

Figure 8.23 iMEDI interpolation of the *Cat* image by a factor of 2 and with threshold $t = 48$ (PSNR = 27.9552 dB, SSIM = 0.8201) with five iterations: (a) the interpolated image, (b) zoom-in portion of the ear of the NEDI interpolated *Cat* image, (c) the EMEDI interpolated *Cat* image, and (d) the sixth iteration iMEDI interpolated *Cat* image.

Table 8.4 The PSNR and SSIM performance of a 2× *Cat* image interpolation to size 512 × 512 using the iMEDI and periodic extension with various variance threshold values

Variance threshold *t*	Total number of iMEDI iterations	PSNR (dB)	SSIM
0	6	27.9542	0.8203
48	6	27.9552	0.8201
100	6	27.9557	0.8184
1000	7	27.9010	0.8038
5000	4	27.4910	0.7984
∞	1	27.3750	0.7977

of the NEDI interpolated *Cat* image is shown in Figure 8.23b. The covariance correction in the iMEDI helps to preserve the image structure of the interpolated image to be almost the same as that of the low-resolution image. As a result, the edges are sharp, and the very few ringing nor checkerboard noises are observed in the interpolated image when compared with that obtained from the EMEDI and the NEDI. Both subjective and objective qualities of the sixth iteration iMEDI interpolated image are better than that of the EMEDI and the NEDI, where the PSNR equals 27.9552 dB, which is 0.1156 dB higher than that of the EMEDI, which achieves the best PSNR among all three methods. Moreover, the SSIM equals 0.8201, which is 0.0054 higher than that obtained by the EMEDI. This observation shows that the iterative error correction method can successfully improve the structure regularity of the covariance-based interpolation method.

Similar to all other covariance-based image interpolation algorithms, the performance of `imediloop` is *t* sensitive. Listed in Table 8.4 are the PSNR and SSIM of the 2× interpolated *Cat* image obtained with various threshold *t* values. It can be observed from the table that the PSNR and SSIM do not seem to agree with each other in this example. The PSNR of the `imediloop` interpolated *Cat* image achieves its highest value at $t = 48$, while the SSIM achieves its highest value at $t = 0$. This might be due to the fact that the Gaussian smoothing applied to compute SSIM (readers please refer to Section 3.3) has blurred the perfectly captured image features and hence compromised the SSIM value. Readers should also be able to observe from Table 8.4 and other tables in 8.1, 8.2, and 8.3 that the influence of *t* value on the final image quality is not as huge as that in the cases of the EMEDI, the MEDI, and the NEDI. This robustness is the result of the iterative covariance difference minimization. It can be observed that a satisfactory threshold immunity can be achieved when the number of iteration is more than 6 for the *Cat* image.

The first row in Figure 8.24 shows the normalized covariance energy difference maps for the iMEDI interpolated image taken from the third, the fifth, and the sixth iterations. The covariance energy difference maps are obtained by computing the difference in the total covariance energy in the `lwin` and the `hwin` windows. To show vivid variation in the energy difference maps, only the pixels on the difference maps where actual interpolated pixels exist will be considered, and those coupled to pixels inherited from original low-resolution image will be discarded. Moreover, the energy difference maps

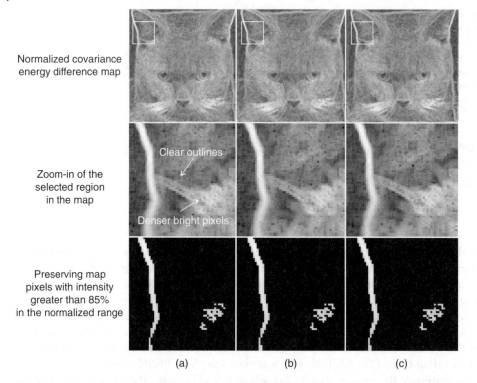

Figure 8.24 Covariance energy difference maps of the iMEDI interpolated *Cat* image at (a) the third iteration, (b) the fifth iteration, and (c) the sixth iteration.

taken from different iterations are converted into logarithmic scale and normalized by the built-in MATLAB function mat2gray into the range of [0, 1] all together, such that the intensity variation in the difference images reflects the variation in energy difference among all the three cases. It should be noted that the brighter the intensity of the pixels in Figure 8.24, the greater the energy difference and the lower the correlation between the two windows. It can be observed that the outlines of the *Cat* become more blurred as the iteration goes, which indicates that the covariance energy difference along image edges and features is reducing. This attributes to the prediction errors in the covariance-based interpolation along the image edges and features reducing along the iterations. This is also the objective of the iterative approach to minimize the mean squares error of the interpolated image, eventually improving the PSNR.

The second row in Figure 8.24 shows the zoom-in maps of the selected regions highlighted in the first row, where the region corresponding to the left ear of the *Cat* image is chosen. It should be noted that instead of directly enlarging the images presented in the first row, the selected regions from each of the difference maps are grouped together and undergone an independent normalization procedure for better comparison purpose. The white regions indicate the error concentrated regions. It can be observed that instead of clear outlines of the hairs as shown in the third iteration result, it becomes many patches stitched together as that shown in the sixth iteration result. Moreover, more dense bright regions are observed in the third iteration result. All these further show the improvement in the structural integrity brought by the iterative approach. To take a closer look of the dense region, the same set of zoom-in maps is further manipulated that only those pixels with intensity greater 0.85 are kept and presented in the third row in Figure 8.24. It can be observed that the covariance energy difference pixels are more closely packed with increasing iteration, while more unconnected pixels are observed in the third iteration result, which shows that the better image structure is preserved by increasing the iteration. By investigating the total energy difference in the manipulated maps, the total energy differences are 202.77, 202.79, and 201.93 for the third, fifth, and sixth iteration results, respectively, whereas the peak difference is 0.9996, 0.9999, and 1, respectively. This observation further shows that the iteration approach increases the interpolation errors in localized area but will generally lower the interpolation error in average when it converges.

The selection of the best t is important in all covariance-based edge-directed image interpolation methods. The subjective image quality between the interpolated images obtained by the iMEDI and the EMEDI is also similar, where the edges are sharp and there are very few artifacts in the interpolated image. Of course, there is minor difference between the texture-rich regions of the two interpolated images since the lower t value will invite more texture-rich region pixels to be interpolated by covariance-based interpolation, while they should be treated with nonparametric interpolation, such as the bilinear interpolation. Nevertheless, the iMEDI method with multiple iterations can achieve the best image quality. This improvement shows supreme performance in tackling the ringing artifacts in texture-rich regions, which is well presented in Figure 8.25. The ringing artifacts on the face of the *Cat* image in the iMEDI interpolated image are suppressed even when the same $t = 48$ is applied (Figure 8.25). Of course the con will be the high computation cost as the low-resolution image will have to go through multiple covariance-based image interpolations. However, as a household saying goes, "it is worthy to wait in line for good stuffs."

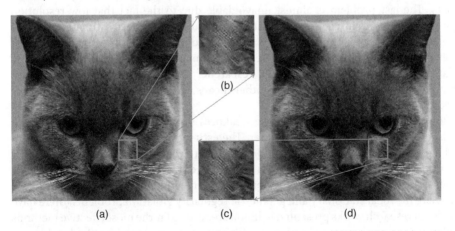

(a)   (c)   (d)

Figure 8.25 The iMEDI interpolation suppresses the ringing artifact when compared with that of EMEDI: (a) the EMEDI interpolated *Cat* image and (d) the iMEDI interpolated *Cat* image, where the same scaling factor of 2 and threshold $t = 48$ are applied. (b) and (c) are the corresponding zoom-in portion of the hairs of both interpolated images.

8.9 Summary

The idea of following edges during image interpolation has been considered in Chapter 7. This chapter discussed an alternative way to perform edge-directed image interpolation without generating an explicit edge map. The covariance-based image interpolation methods presented in this chapter are developed with two basic assumptions that a natural image is a second-order locally stationary Gaussian process and image edges acquire the geometric duality properties. The image features captured by local covariance of small image blocks (also known as the estimation window) are exploited to develop image interpolation algorithm. In particular, the geometric duality between the covariance of localized image block of low-resolution image and the corresponding high-resolution image is applied to allow the tuning of interpolation coefficients to match arbitrary oriented image features (edges) to perform a non-explicit edge-directed image interpolation. The statistical adaptive approach is able to accurately locate the image edges in all arbitrary orientation, thus preventing the edge mis-registration problem observed in those edge-directed interpolation methods using edge map. In particular we have used the NEDI and its variants as examples to present the development of covariance-based image interpolation methods.

The original NEDI works well and can produce high quality (both subjective and objective quality measures) image interpolation results until the assumptions break down. The assumptions will break down when the NEDI suffers from local stationary, covariance estimation error propagation, and inefficient estimation result that cannot preserve the geometric duality. The former one is caused by the covariance estimation windows being not able to co-align with the image features. It can also be caused by biased covariance estimation windows. The covariance estimation error propagation problem is caused by using part of the estimation results from pixels obtained in previous estimation for estimating unknown pixel values. As a result, the estimation error between these pixels will be correlated and results in clustered and easily detectable artifacts. The last problem is almost unavoidable due to the fact that low-resolution image does not contain all the information needed for a perfect estimation. This is also why image interpolation problem is an ill-posed problem. However, knowing that our objective is to interpolate a high-resolution image that preserves the geometric regularity of its low-resolution partner, researcher should come up with innovative solution, whether it is brute force or by other means, to enforce the interpolated image to strictly follow this property.

Various methods to remedy the above weakness of the NEDI algorithm have been discussed in literature and in this chapter. The estimation error propagation problem is tackled by using new estimation window structure that only makes use of the low-resolution image pixels [59], where we have presented the algorithm MEDI and showed that better interpolated images can be obtained when compared with that of the NEDI. To alleviate the local stationary and geometric regularity violation problems, there have been a lot of research works presented in literature, and so far the most effective methods will identify the appropriate covariance estimation window based on the local image covariance structure [59], nonlocal image covariance structure [19, 70], or resemblance of error minimization filter into the covariance matrix [30, 42]. All of these methods estimate the unknown pixel intensities in the same fashion as that of the NEDI, but the definition of the covariance estimation window adapts to the covariance structure of the image, such that it provides a better performance in preserving the local stationary and geometric regularity. In particular, the chapter chose the method presented in [59] to demonstrate the development and implementation of covariance-based image interpolation method with adaptive estimation window, such that the window is spatially adaptive to allow small-size estimation window that better preserves the local stationary of short edges, and small image features, while also having a large mean covariance estimation window size such as not to miss the existence of image features that constitute the covariance structure for interpolation that preserves the geometric regularity. The presented method is the EMEDI, which is built upon MEDI. Interpolated image with sharper and better edge continuity is observed, besides being able to achieve better objective performance.

The NEDI, MEDI, and EMEDI estimate the unknown pixels from neighboring pixels with optimal weighting factors obtained by linear prediction. The linear prediction is an analysis-by-synthesis process that produces the optimal weighting factors by minimizing the mean squares error obtained in prediction through Wiener filtering. Needless to say, prediction error is inevitable. As a result the geometric regularity is not preserved in strict sense. In this chapter we propose to resolve the problem by iterative covariance energy correction, such that the energy of the covariance matrices for all the interpolated pixels is compared with the corresponding energy of the covariance matrices of the low-resolution image. Should the difference between these two energies be larger than a given threshold, we shall interpolate that particular pixel again using the new covariance matrix obtained in the current high-resolution image. This will generate a new high-resolution image, which will be mean filtered with the high-resolution image in previous iteration to produce the final interpolated image. We demonstrated the implementation of such algorithm through the iMEDI, which is built upon the EMEDI. Better image interpolation results with high objective quality are obtained by the iMEDI interpolated images.

The possible improvement of covariance-based image interpolation method certainly will not stop here. One of the major improvements over the NEDI-based covariance-based image interpolation is the application of Markov random field to perform the interpolation [39]. We are glad to share some discussions with Dr. Min Li about developing a chapter in the initial version of this book for her image interpolation method. We feel very sorry that finally her work is not discussed in this book due to time and space restriction. Hopefully we can do that in the next edition of this book. More and more techniques will be developed in the future to produce better and better interpolated images. It is our purpose to show the theory, mathematics, algorithmic derivation, and MATLAB implementation to the readers such that they can make use of the presented information to develop their better and faster covariance-based image interpolation methods.

8.10 Exercises

8.1 The MATLAB function `nedi_correct` (Listing 8.3.5) adjusts the pixel intensity of an interpolated pixel to be bounded within the allowable dynamic range defined by the pixel intensity of the pixels in the prediction window via mean value interpolation. Create a function `nedi_correct_bilinear` to achieve the adjustment through bilinear interpolation and incorporate it into the `nedi`. Demonstrate and compare the performance of the new `nedi` algorithm by interpolating the *Cat* image.

8.2 Interpolate the image *Cat* by the NEDI using different boundary extension methods: (a) by constant extension, (b) by periodic extension, (c) by symmetric extension, and (d) by infinite extension. Compare their subjective and objective performance.

8.3 Compare the PSNR and SSIM of the interpolation of *Cat* image by the NEDI with different b: (a) $b = 8$, (b) $b = 12$, and (c) $b = 16$.

8.4 Compare the subjective and objective performance of the iMEDI with the use of different covariance-based interpolation methods to generate the initial high-resolution image by (a) the NEDI and (b) the EMEDI. Compare the number of iterations required for each of them to converge, the subjective performance, PSNR, SSIM, and CMSE of these two approaches using $b = 20$ and $t = 48$ against those of the original `imediloop`. (*Hint*: The `imediloop` function [in Listing 8.8.4] generates the initial high-resolution image g by `medi`.)

9

Partitioned Fractal Interpolation

The word *fractal* is chosen by Mandelbrot [46] to describe the field of study of *rough or fragmented geometric shapes that can be subdivided in parts, each of which is (at least approximately) a size reduced copy of the whole.* This might be because "fract," the Latin root of the word fractal, means broken. The main idea that stands behind fractal is the concept of *"self-similarity."* Fractal found applications in image processing with great success. This is attributed to the fact that objects in natural images are generally observed to be self-similar. There was great deal of hope and excitement over the application of fractal to compress natural images when it was first introduced in the 1980s. At that period of time, fractal has spurred considerable amount of research activities. Although fractal image coding is no longer considered to be a competitive method to compress images because the compression ratio is not good enough, it is worthy to study it as an alternate type of image interpolation scheme because of the natural-looking interpolation results. In this chapter, we shall study the application of fractal image coding to interpolate images. Fractal image coding considers images to be *"self-similar."* In other words, images are modeled as deterministic fractal objects, such that parts of an image are approximated by different parts of the same image, a direct result of the image being *self-similar.* As a consequence of the self-similarity, the fractal objects are scale independent. To understand the importance of scale independence, the readers should note that fractal objects are described with a simple recursion, such that images with different sizes can be generated from the associated fractal codes using the same recursion. This property makes changing image resolutions in fractal system very easy. The fractals have plenty other very interesting properties; however, it is not necessary for the readers to understand them all for the development of fractal-based image interpolation. Therefore, they will not be exploited here. Instead, we shall concentrate our discussions on *partitioned fractal image* (PFI) representation based on *iterated function system* (IFS). The word partition comes in from the fact that the image is partitioned into blocks and the search of self-similar fractal objects is performed over all the partitioned blocks that cover the whole image. The readers might have already noticed that the PFI is a block-based image processing algorithm. As a result, just like other block-based image interpolation algorithms discussed in Chapter 5, PFI-based image interpolation will suffer from blocking artifacts. A wonderful method that deals with blocking artifacts has been presented in Section 5.4, which is also applicable in PFI-based image interpolation. Despite the very complex theoretical background of the PFI-based image interpolation method, the objective performance of the interpolated

Digital Image Interpolation in MATLAB®, First Edition. Chi-Wah Kok and Wing-Shan Tam.
© 2019 John Wiley & Sons Singapore Pte. Ltd. Published 2019 by John Wiley & Sons Singapore Pte. Ltd.
Companion website: www.wiley.com/go/ditmatlab

images may not be as good as the methods presented in previous chapters. However, we would recommend the readers to enjoy the natural looking of the PFI-based image interpolation results. The PFI-based image interpolation usually achieves good subjective performance, which is one of the reasons why similar algorithms have been adopted into many commercial image enlargement softwares.

9.1 Iterated Function System

The fractal can be defined in a number of ways depending on the applications. When applied in image interpolation, we are interested in fractal defined by IFS. We shall not go through the complex mathematical derivation and shall take it for granted that the contractive affine transformation can generate fractal and hence forms an IFS. By repeating the contractive affine transformation an infinite number of times, any starting patterns will be transformed into the same structure at any level of details. In other words, the IFS allows us to zoom (interpolate) into the details of the structure. Having said that we shall skip the complex mathematics, we figure out that the readers will still need to be familiar with some basic mathematical tools and theorems before we can fearlessly apply the IFS to interpolate images.

9.1.1 Banach Fixed-Point Theorem

The convergence of the IFS defined by a contractive transformation is the result of the "fixed-point theorem." In here, we shall discuss the most basic fixed-point theorem in analysis, which is due to Banach and appeared in his PhD thesis (1920, published in 1922) [7].

Theorem 9.1   *Fixed-point theorem*: *Given a complete metric space (X, d) and a transformation $T : X \rightarrow X$ that satisfies*

$$d(T(x), T(y)) \leqslant c \cdot d(x, y), \tag{9.1}$$

for some $0 \leqslant c < 1$ and all $x, y \in X$. The transformation T has a unique fixed point x_f in X, where given any $x_0 \in X$, the sequence that iterates on $x_0, T(x_0), T(T(x_0)), \ldots$ converges to the fixed point x_f of T.

The fixed-point theorem is also known as the *Banach fixed-point theorem* and the *contraction transform theorem*. The transformation T that satisfies the fixed-point theorem is known as *contraction mapping*. A contraction shrinks distance by a uniform factor c less than 1 for all pairs of points. To get a grasp on the application of the fixed-point theorem, we shall review a high school problem of finding a high accuracy approximation to the irrational number $\sqrt{5}$ by Newton's method. Newton's method provides a scheme to construct the contraction transform where the associated fixed point is the solution of a system of equations.

Example 9.1   The solution of the equation $f(x) = 0$, with f being differentiable, can be approximated by Newton's method: find an approximate solution x_0, and then compute the following recursive sequence:

$$x_n = x_{n-1} - \frac{f(x_{n-1})}{f'(x_{n-1})}. \tag{9.2}$$

The contractive transform is given by

$$T(x) = x - \frac{f(x)}{f'(x)}. \tag{9.3}$$

Starting from some initial point x_0, the recursion will converge to $T(x_f) = x_f$, a fixed point of $T(x)$. When that happens, we shall have $T(x_f) = x_f = x_f - \frac{f(x_f)}{f'(x_f)}$, which implies $f(x_f) = 0$. In other words, the fixed point x_f is a solution of $f(x) = 0$.

To use Newton's method to estimate $\sqrt{5}$, we shall set $f(x) = x^2 - 5$ and seek a (positive) root of $f(x)$. The Newton recursion is thus given by

$$x_n = x_{n-1} - \frac{x_{n-1}^2 - 5}{2x_{n-1}} = \frac{1}{2}\left(x_{n-1} + \frac{5}{x_{n-1}}\right). \tag{9.4}$$

The contraction transform is given as $T(x) = \frac{1}{2}\left(x + \frac{5}{x}\right)$. The fixed point of T is $\sqrt{5}$. Starting with $x_0 = 1$, Table 9.1 listed x_n obtained in each iteration of Eq. (9.4), where it is vivid that the sequence converges to 2.236 068 in just five iterations. It can also be observed from the same table where three sequences are obtained from Eq. (9.4) with different x_0. All the sequences are observed to converge to 2.236 068 $\approx \sqrt{5}$. On the other hand, the number of iterations required for each sequence to converge is observed to be different. In fact the number of iterations required for the sequence to convergence depends on the distance between x_0 and $\sqrt{5}$.

Example 9.1 not only forms an IFS that converges to $\sqrt{5}$. A closer examination will reveal the fact that the number $\sqrt{5}$ is now represented by the contraction transform in Eq. (9.4). In fact any number $\sqrt{a}$ can be approximated with an IFS defined by Eq. (9.4) with a simple change of variable. If we use a polynomial representation system to describe the corresponding IFS, Eq. (9.4) can be rewritten as $(0.5, (-1, a), (1, 1))$,

Table 9.1 Approximation of $\sqrt{5}$ by Newton's method.

n	x_n	x_n	x_n
0	1	2	5
1	3.000 000	2.250 000	2.625 000
2	2.333 333	2.236 111	2.264 881
3	2.238 095	2.236 068	2.236 251
4	2.236 069	2.236 068	2.236 068
5	2.236 068	2.236 068	2.236 068
6	2.236 068	2.236 068	2.236 068

where the first coefficient 0.5 is the scaling or magnitude transformation. The following 2-tuple list the order of x and the corresponding coefficients. As an example, the tuple $(-1, a)$ represent the term $\frac{a}{x}$. This polynomial representation provided us an alternative representation of the number $\sqrt{a}$ and is a more efficient (compact) way to store the number $\sqrt{a}$, which by definition would require an infinite space to store all the decimal places. Such representation also provides us a way to zoom into $\sqrt{a}$. The accuracy of approximation to $\sqrt{a}$ depends on the number of iterations applied to compute Eq. (9.4). More details of $\sqrt{a}$ can be revealed if we allow Eq. (9.4) to iterate a few more times. This detail *"zoom-in"* property is what makes IFS an interesting image interpolation method. The image interpolation problem can be casted as the problem of finding the contraction transform that forms an IFS with the associated fixed point approximates the given image. After that, we can use the contraction transform and the associated IFS to zoom into the details of the fixed point (the given image), which will provide us the interpolated image.

9.2 Partitioned Iterative Function System

The direct application of the IFS would suggest the representation of any given image as contractive transformation of itself. Among various methods to construct the contraction transform, we are in particular interested in the *affine transform*.

Theorem 9.2 *Affine map*: The affine transform in $\mathbb{R}^N \to \mathbb{R}^N$ defined as $T(x) = Ax + b$ with $x, b \in \mathbb{R}^N$ and $A \in \mathbb{R}^{N \times N}$ is a contractive transform, with respect to the norm $\mathbb{R}^N$ that induces the matrix norm when

$$|T| < 1, \tag{9.5}$$

with the given matrix norm.

Theorem 9.2 can be easily proved by considering $x, y \in \mathbb{R}^N$ and then $|T(x) - T(y)| = |A(x - y)| \leqslant |A| \cdot |x - y| = |A| \cdot d(x, y)$, which implies T is contractive by Theorem 9.1. According to Hutchinson [31], given a collection Ω of affine and contractive transforms T_i, with $i = 1, 2, \ldots, \ell$ in a complete metric space $(\mathbb{R}^N, d)$, the following union of contractive transforms

$$\Omega = \{\mathbb{R}^N, T_i : \quad i = 1, 2, \ldots, \ell\}, \tag{9.6}$$

is also a contractive transform. The IFS fractal image representation makes use of the superposition of all small fixed point of each contractive transform T_i to approximate a given image. Such system represented by Ω is known as a *partitioned iterated function system* (PIFS), because the image is being partitioned into blocks and each partitioned block is being represented by a contractive transform T_i. Such an image representation is shown to be efficient. This is because natural images do not satisfy self-similarity in strict sense and many images (particularly photographs), such as the *Cat* image, do have areas that are almost self-similar. The similarity of parts of an image provides the inspiration for the concept of a PIFS, which is a block-based fractal image representation scheme that exploits local self-similarities within the image [32]. The PIFS is similar to an IFS, except that the contractive transforms have restricted domains that exploit the inherent local self-similarities of the image. The flexibility of PIFS permits the construction of more general measures that do not have to be strictly self-similar in a global sense [8]. In practice, this means that an image f can be represented by PIFS with N_r partitioned small regions, or also known as *range blocks*, r_i, that spans over f:

$$f = \bigcup_{i=1}^{N_r} r_i. \tag{9.7}$$

Each of the r_i is matched as closely as possible to the affine transform of one of several larger regions, known as *domain blocks*, $d_j : j = 1, \ldots, N_d$ of the image. It should be noted that each range block can be considered as a sub-image, in which the indices i and j refer to the order of the range blocks and domain blocks in their corresponding collections. It is assumed that the blocks are ordered according to their appearance in the original image following by row and then column. Each range block will be matched against all the domain blocks in the original image. The best match result yields the contractive transformation, T_i, which maps part of the original image onto that range block r_i. A PIFS encodes N_r sub-images r_i, where the fixed-point associated contractive transform T_i for each r_i will then be superimposed to produce a single image. As a result, the union of the contractive transforms is sufficed to represent the fixed-point image, which in turn is an approximation of the original image:

$$f \approx f_f = \bigcup_{i=1}^{N_r} T_i(d_{\alpha(i)}), \tag{9.8}$$

where $\alpha(i)$ is the mapping that gives the best domain block index for the ith range block. With reference to the contractive mapping fixed-point theorem, the union of contractive mappings in Eq. (9.8) has a unique fixed point f_f, called the attractor of the PIFS. Therefore, if we can find a PIFS such that its attractor is as close to the image f as possible, we can obtain a good approximation of the image f and represent it with a union of affine transforms. Furthermore, Banach's fixed-point theorem 9.1 told us that the series of iterates $f_{k+1} = \bigcup_{i=1}^{N_r} T_i(d_{k,\alpha(i)})$ is a convergent series, where $d_{k,j}$ is the jth domain block extracted from the image f_k obtained at the kth iteration. Starting with any arbitrary initial f_0, these series will converge to the unique fixed point f_f. A natural solution to find T_i and $\alpha(i)$ for the PIFS representation of f with the contractive transform constrained to be affine transform defined in Theorem 9.2 can be obtained by rewriting Eq. (9.8) as

$$f_f = \bigcup_{i=1}^{N_r} (A_i d_{\alpha(i)} + b_i)$$

$$= \sum_{i=1}^{N_r} P_i (A_i d_{\alpha(i)} + b_i)$$

$$= \sum_{i=1}^{N_r} \sum_{j=1}^{N_d} P_i (A_i S_{i,j} f_f + b_i)$$

$$= \mathbf{A} f_f + \mathbf{b}$$

$$(\mathbf{A} - \mathbf{I}) f_f = \mathbf{b}$$

$$f_f = (\mathbf{A} - \mathbf{I})^{-1} \mathbf{b}, \tag{9.9}$$

where P_i is the translation operator putting the affine transformed domain block to the ith range block position and $S_{i,j}$ is the domain block extraction operator that extracts the $\alpha(i)$th domain block with $S_{i,j} = 1$ when $j = \alpha(i)$; otherwise, $S_{i,j} = 0$ when $j \neq \alpha(i)$. The matrix $\mathbf{A}$ summed all the matrix products of $P_iA_iS_{i,j}$ together, and $\mathbf{b}$ is a matrix that lumped all the translated scalar P_ib_i together to form a matrix. If the fixed point f_f converges to the original image f exactly, Eq. (9.9) can be rewritten as $f = (\mathbf{A} - \mathbf{I})^{-1}\mathbf{b}$. In other words, the PIFS is now posed as an inverse problem for finding $\mathbf{A}$ and $\mathbf{b}$ as shown in Eq. 9.9, where $(\mathbf{A}, \mathbf{b})$ serves as the fractal representation for f. However, solving this inverse problem is difficult. In particular, most real-world objects are rarely entirely self-similar. As a result, $f_f \neq f$, and hence the inverse problem in Eq. (9.9) is ill-posed. Fortunately, Barnslay shows that we do not have to solve the inverse problem. A good PIFS representation with f_f that approximates f can be found by the application of collage theorem [8].

Theorem 9.3 **Collage theorem**: Given an IFS with contractive transform T, contraction factor $c \in (0, 1)$, and fixed point x_f, let x and $\epsilon > 0$ be chosen such that

$$d(x, T(x)) \leqslant \epsilon, \tag{9.10}$$

then

$$d(x, x_f) \leqslant \frac{\epsilon}{1 - c}. \tag{9.11}$$

According to Theorem 9.3, the closer is the collage $T(f)$ (first-order approximation of the fixed point) to the original image f, the better is the constructed PIFS, and hence the attractor f_f is closer to the original image f. In other words, when constructing the PIFS (the fractal encoding process), one can focus on minimizing the distance $d(T(f), f)$, and this will result in minimizing the distortion $d(f, f_f)$, which is the goal of fractal representation of the original image f. The quantitative distance measure $d(T(f), f)$ is called the *collage error*. The computational complexity of fractal representation is significantly reduced by the minimization of the collage error instead of the distance between the original image and the attractor (the fixed point f_f). With respect to each range block $r_i \in f$, the PIFS is constructed by finding the domain block d_j and the corresponding affine transform matrix A_i and b_i that satisfies

$$d(r_i, T(d_j)) = \min_{j, A_i, b_i} d(r_i, A_i d_j + b_i I). \tag{9.12}$$

The above is a direct application of the *collage theorem*, a simple consequence of the Banach fixed-point theorem, which ensures the fixed point f_f is close to f if also the distortion $\bigcup_{i=1}^{N_r} d(r_i, T(d_j))$ between the original image and its collage $T(d_j)$ is small. A union of these contractive transforms for all the partitioned blocks will form the PIFS. In other words, the PIFS is formed by the set of surjective functions that maps the jth domain block to the ith range block. The procedure that achieves the "best" match is known as the *fractal encoding*.

The mapping between i and j, the affine transform A_i, and the shift b_i are sufficient to define the IFS. However, this solution does not give the optimal results. It is vivid that the larger the range block block size of r_i, the fewer the bits are required to store the fractal code and hence provide higher coding gain. On the other hand, the larger the block size, the poorer the fractal approximation (the fixed point) of the original image, and hence, the lower the quality of the fractal encoded image. Considering the purpose of this book, the fractal code is used to zoom into the image, thus providing us an interpolated image. Therefore, small block size is desired. However, the structural property advantages of fractal image representation can only be observed with large block size. This creates a design dilemma in choosing the right block size for better original image resemblance or better structural quality of the interpolated image. Subsequent section will show you that a block size of 4×4 and 8×8 will be sufficient for the job depending on the interpolation ratio r. Various other methods to improve the IFS performance will be discussed in later sections.

The fractal image encoding method in Eq. (9.12) is a simplified implementation of the first fully automatic method for fractal encoding presented by Jacquin [32], which forms the basis for many fractal encoding methods. All other methods can be treated as improvements to the Jacquin method. This chapter will present the fractal IFS representation of natural image by the Jacquin method. However, there are still a few practical issues left unaddressed before we can successfully implement Jacquin fractal encoding method, and that will be addressed in subsequent sections. The problems to be addressed include what kind of partitioning for the image should be used, how does one find the best match block pairs from the partitioned blocks, and the associated grayscale transform that will "*optimally*" transform this "*best match*" block for each range block.

9.3 Encoding

In the ideal case, the partition of the encoding image into parts should be performed to optimize the matching of one part with another. However, such an intelligent approach would need a human to drive it. A fully automatic approach is only possible if a fixed partition of the image is applied. In a simple PIFS image encoder, the image is partitioned in two ways to generate the *range blocks* r_i, often with uniform size and non-overlapping, and the *domain blocks* d_i, with larger size than that of the range blocks and usually overlapping.

9.3.1 Range Block Partition

The image can be partitioned by different ways to obtain the range blocks, and they can be summarized into three major streams with the partitions shown in Figure 9.1 for the *Cat* image:

Uniform partition: As shown in Figure 9.1a, this is a simple partition method as all the blocks have the same size but are inefficient in terms of coding performance. A MATLAB example of the uniform partition is shown in Listing 9.3.1, where the range block RBlk is obtained from the image array f as

```
RBlk = im2col(f,[blocksize blocksize],'distinct');
```

with im2col rearranges each distinct blocksize × blocksize block partitioned from the image array f to form one column in RBlk. As a result, the number of

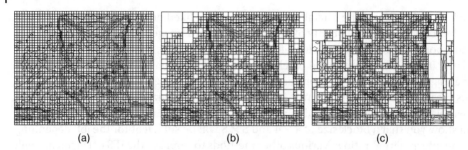

(a)   (b)   (c)

Figure 9.1 Three different range block partition methods for the *Cat* image with the edges of the *Cat* overlay the partitions - (a) uniform, (b) quadtree, and (c) HV partition – to show their relationships.

columns in `RBlk` is M/blocksize · N/blocksize, and hence the total size of `RBlk` is

$$(\texttt{blocksize}\cdot\texttt{blocksize})\quad\times\quad(\text{M/blocksize}\cdot\text{N/blocksize}).$$

Quadtree partition: As shown in Figure 9.1b, this is a relative simple and efficient partition method, where the partitioned blocks are squares with adaptive sizes based on the information content of the localized image region.

HV partition: As shown in Figure 9.1c, this is an advanced and efficient partition method that partitions the image into quadrangle blocks with adaptive sizes based on the information content of the localized image region.

The following discussion will concentrate on uniform partition, while the quadtree partition will be left to be explored by the readers after the readers finished reading this book. The HV partition should be the most efficient way to generate the range blocks. However, the HV partition has the deficiency of the possibility of leave out regions, such that highly sophisticated algorithm is required to ensure the non-overlap partitioned blocks will fully cover the input image. Therefore, HV partition is seldom used in practice.

9.3.2 Domain Block Partition

When the range block is obtained by uniform partition, the most frequently used domain block partition strategy is uniform partition with overlap, which provides optimal partition result, but is extremely computational expensive. The domain blocks are usually assumed to be twice the length and width (hence four time the area) of the range blocks. An example of generating the domain blocks `DBlk` by this strategy is shown in the following MATLAB code.

```
DBlk = im2col(f, [blocksize*2 blocksize*2],'sliding');
```

with the size of each domain block being $(2\cdot\texttt{blocksize})\times(2\cdot\texttt{blocksize})$, which is twice (containing four times more pixels) of that of the range block. This code makes use of the `sliding` command, where each sliding will extract a $(2\cdot\texttt{blocksize})\times(2\cdot\texttt{blocksize})$ block from the image array f. As a result, the total number of domain blocks is given by `sizeDBlk` $= (\text{M}-2\cdot\texttt{blocksize}+1)\times(\text{N}-2\cdot\texttt{blocksize}+1))$, and they are all stored column by column within the matrix `DBlk`. In other words, the number of columns in `DBlk` is

$(M - 2 \cdot \texttt{blocksize} + 1) \cdot (N - 2 \cdot \texttt{blocksize} + 1)$. Therefore, the total size of $\texttt{DBlk}$ is given by

$$(2 \cdot \texttt{blocksize} \cdot 2 \cdot \texttt{blocksize}) \quad \times \quad ((M - 2 \cdot \texttt{blocksize} + 1)$$
$$\cdot (N - 2 \cdot \texttt{blocksize} + 1)).$$

This domain block partition method is being applied in the fractal image encoder listed in the MATLAB code Listing 9.3.1.

To simplify the encoding process, the affine transform will be performed on all the domain blocks, and the transformed blocks will be stored in $\texttt{codebook}$. In this case, the PIFS image encoding process will become the process of finding a surjective function $c_i \rightarrow r_i$ from a particular block c_i in the $\texttt{codebook}$ to the range blocks r_i. This surjective function will find the best matching codebook block for each range block with respect to a given matching criteria. Various matching criteria can be applied, which essentially affects the complexity and the quality of the fractal image representation. In the rest of the chapter, the matching criterion applied to illustrate the theory and implementation of PIFS encoding is the $\mathcal{L}^2$ distance between c_i and r_i. The mapping that provides the least squares distance will be the best matching pair. Naturally, the larger the codebook, the better the matching between the codebook blocks, and the range blocks can be obtained. However, a large codebook will require more memory to store the indices that specify the locations of the best match codebook blocks. From a computation efficiency viewpoint, compromises between the domain pool size (the codebook size) and the fidelity must be established. The following section will discuss codebook generated with various isometric affine transforms, but the implementation example will only concentrate on codebook generated with domain blocks directly extracted from the given image without performing any isometric affine transformation.

9.3.3 Codebook Generation

A codebook (also known as domain block pool) is a collection of the domain blocks $\texttt{DBlk}$. Since all the blocks within the codebook will be compared with the range blocks, therefore, they should be size compatible. In other words, we have to either interpolate the range block to make it as big as that of the domain blocks or down-sample the domain blocks to make it as small as the range blocks. It will be difficult if not impossible to prove either method to be the theoretical optimal method. As a result, the one that has the lower computational complexity will usually be adopted. Note that the smaller the block size, the lower the computational complexity. Therefore, we shall adopt the approach of down-sampling the domain blocks to generate the codebook. With reference to Section 2.7.3, there exist a large number of image block down-sampling algorithms. To ease our discussions, we shall adopt the bilinear down-sampling method, which can be easily achieved by the MATLAB built-in function $\texttt{imresize}$. As a result, the codebook, $\texttt{codebook}$, obtained from the down-sampled domain blocks, is obtained as

```
codebook= zeros(dimRBlk, sizeDBlk);
for i = 1: sizeDBlk
   blk = reshape(DBlk(:,i), [blocksize*2 blocksize*2]);
   codebook(:,i) = double(imresize(blk,0.5,'bilinear'));
end
```

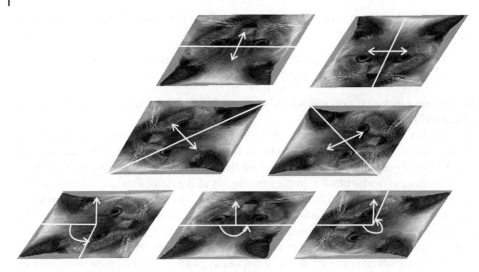

Figure 9.2 The seven different isometries – affine transformations.

where the variable `dimRBlk=blocksize*blocksize` is the dimension of the range block and `sizeDBlk` is the total number of domain blocks extracted from the image.

Besides the down-sampled domain blocks, the codebook can be enriched by incorporating various affine transformed down-sampled domain blocks as the codebook vectors. While there are infinitely many different types of affine transformations that can be applied to enrich the content of the codebook, the most frequently applied affine transformations for codebook generation are the isometric affine transformations as shown in Figure 9.2 that include four rotations, a horizontal flipping, a vertical flipping, and two diagonal flippings. All these transformations are isometries of the original decimated domain blocks. Should any subset of these isometries be considered to form a codebook, the codeword can be indexed with an additional parameter ℓ with $0 \leqslant \ell \leqslant 7$, where $\ell = 0$ is the original domain block, such that the surjective mapping that describes the PIFS becomes $i \to (j, \ell)$ between the ith range block and the jth domain block with ℓth affine transformation.

The overall idea would be more clearly presented by considering Figure 9.3. Figure 9.3 illustrates the generation of the `codebook`. The generation process begins with the partition of the original image into domain blocks. All the domain blocks in the image have the same block size. The domain blocks are taken sequentially from the top left corner (the [1,1] coordinates in MATLAB format) and slide through the image in a row-then-by-column manner, until the last domain block with the top left corner pixel located at $[(M - 2 * \text{blocksize} + 1), (N - 2 * \text{blocksize} + 1)]$, such that all the pixels in the original image are covered. The top left corner coordinate of the block extracted from the original image that forms the domain block, together with the affine transformed contents (in our case, the down-sampled domain blocks), will be stored in each column vector of the `codebook`. As a result, a simple `codebook` with domain pool that does not contain any isometric affine transform blocks will have $(M - 2 * \text{blocksize} + 1) \times (N - 2 * \text{blocksize} + 1)$ than many columns, where the total codebook size is given by `blocksize` $\times$ `blocksize` $\times (M - 2 * \text{blocksize} +1) \times (N - 2 * \text{blocksize} +1)$. It should be noted that when other isometric affine transformed blocks are also included

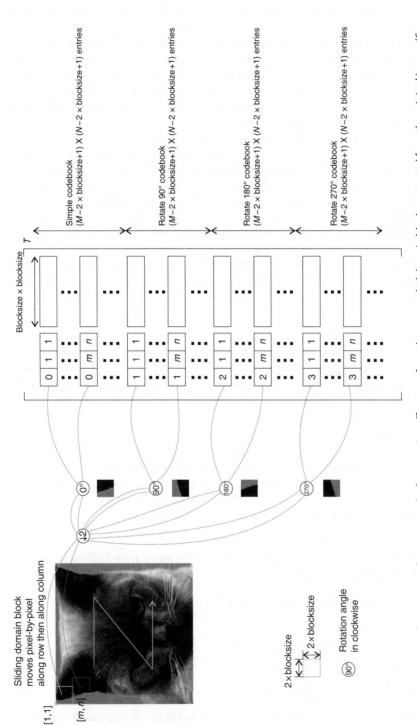

Figure 9.3 Generation of codebook that contains the four rotation affine transform down-sampled domain blocks extracted from the original image. (*See insert for color representation of this figure.*)

in the domain pool, the columns of the simple codebook will be concatenated with the affined transformed vectors. An example of the formation of codebook that contains four rotations of the down-sampled domain blocks is shown in Figure 9.3. To allow an efficient presentation of the figure, the domain pool stored in the codebook is shown in a row-by-row form with the overall codebook being transposed with the transpose operator T shown at the top right corner of the codebook such that it reflects the actual implementation of the codebook in MATLAB presented in this chapter, which is in the form of column-by-column storage.

It is believed that a large codebook will result in very good PIFS image representation quality. However, a large codebook will cost high computational complexity to find the best match block within the codebook for a given range block. In most applications, including those to be presented in this chapter, compromise between the size of the codebook and the PIFS representation image quality has been made. It will be shown in the example presented in this chapter that even with simple codebook (such that the codebook does not contain any affine transformed codeword of the down-sampled domain blocks), good image interpolation results can be obtained. It has been shown in [41] that allowing more rotations and shrinking factors or more domain blocks will not improve the performance of the fractal image representation significantly. As a result, we shall concentrate the following discussions with this simple codebook.

9.3.4 Grayscale Scaling

To complete the affine transform on the codeword in the codebook for finding the best match codeword for a given image block, we have to scale and offset the codewords, where the optimal scaling and gray-level offset can be obtained with direct application of the collage theorem in Eq. (9.10). The collage error $e_{i,j}$ of the codeword c_j in the codebook for the range block r_i is given by

$$e_{i,j}^2 = \min_{a_{i,j}, b_{i,j}} r_i - (a_{i,j} \cdot c_j + b_{i,j})^2. \tag{9.13}$$

The parameter pair $(a_{i,j}, b_{i,j})$ performs gray-level scaling and offset on the codeword c_j to minimize the squares distance with the given range block r_i. To implement Eq. (9.13) with the ith range block iRBLK, and the jth codeword in codebook(:,j) in MAT-LAB, the grayscale transformed block tBLK can be obtained as

$$\text{tBLK} = a * \text{codebook}(:,j) + b, \quad \text{with } |a| \leqslant 1. \tag{9.14}$$

The optimal grayscale transform pair is given by the solution of the linear equations (assuming a unique solution exist)

$$a_{i,j} = \frac{\text{dimRBlk} \sum_{m,n} (r_i[m,n]c_j[m,n]) - \left(\sum_{m,n} r_i[m,n]\right)\left(\sum_{m,n} c_j[m,n]\right)}{\text{dimRBlk} \sum_{m,n} c_j^2[m,n] - \left(\sum_{m,n} c_j[m,n]\right)^2}, \tag{9.15}$$

$$b_{i,j} = \frac{\sum_{m,n} r_i[m,n] - a_{i,j} \sum_{m,n} c_j[m,n]}{\text{dimRBlk}}, \tag{9.16}$$

where the summation is performed over each scalar entry in the codeword. There is one complication, however, about the contractivity of the fractal transform operator T dependent upon the scaling coefficient a. There is no simple relationship between the $\mathcal{L}^2$ contractivity factor, a, and b because of the local nature of the surjective mapping.

However, in the $\mathcal{L}^\infty$ norm, contractivity is guaranteed if all the grayscale scaling factors a associated with all range blocks satisfy the condition $|a| < 1$. For this reason, most fractal coding algorithms "clamp" the coefficients a to be $a = \text{sign}(a) \cdot \min(|a|, 1)$. As a result, the associated fractal transform is contractive in $\mathcal{L}^\infty$, hence almost always contractive in $\mathcal{L}^2$, due to the equivalence of the norms in finite pixel space.

The optimal grayscale transform of each range block is computed for each codeword inside the codebook in order to find the closest codeword to each range block. This optimality search is performed by storing all collage errors $e_{i,j}$ for all c_j in the codebook with a given range block r_i. These stored collage errors will be compared, and the minimum is chosen where the associated surjective mapping $i \mapsto j$ forms the contractive transform. This surjective mapping pair (i, j) for all i that covering the image, together with the grayscale scaling parameter pair $(a_{i,j}, b_{i,j})$, will form the complete PIFS to describe the input image. The 4-tuple $(i, j, a_{i,j}, b_{i,j})$ will be the PIFS encoding result and is also known as the *fractal codebook*. With the 4-tuple stored in predetermined orders associated with i, it is possible to simplify the 4-tuple to 3-tuple (j, a, b). In particular, the 3-tuple is what we needed to construct the PIFS representation for the given image. Readers should distinguish the difference between the codebook in Section 9.3.3, which is the *domain pool*, and the *fractal codebook* of the 3-tuple (j, a, b), which is the PIFS representation parameter set.

Instead of solving Eqs. (9.15) and (9.16), the squares distance between the ith range block iRBLK, and the jth codeword in the codebook, and the associated parameter pairs $(a(i), b(i))$ can be easily obtained by the pseudo inverse function in MATLAB. The implementation of the formation of $a(i)$ and $b(i)$ from downDBLK is shown below:

```
jDBlk = [codebook(:,j),ones(dimRBlk,1)];
lse = jDBlk\iRBlk;
estRBlk = jDBlk * lse;
err = estRBlk - iRBlk;
mse = sum(err.^2);
a(i) = lse(1);
b(i) = lse(2);
```

The best match domain block for the ith range block iRBlk can be obtained by exhaustive search among all the down-sampled domain blocks within the codebook to find the jth block codebook(:,j) that achieves the smallest mse.

As a summary, the encoding process is illustrated in Figure 9.4. The original image is partitioned into a serial of range blocks. For simplicity, the ordering of the range blocks is made exactly the same to that of the domain blocks, but the block size of the range block is smaller than that of the domain blocks. All entries in the codebook will be considered in the encoding for each of the range block r_i. However, in our example, the sizes of the row and column dimensions of the domain block are both twice of those of the range block; the block content of the domain block is down-sampled to form c_j, which has the same block size as that of the range block r_i. Both r_i and c_j are applied in the generation of the gray-level scaling $a_{i,j}$ and offset $b_{i,j}$ parameters. The adjusted c_j will be compared with r_j for the collage error $e_{i,j}^2$. The encoding of that particular r_i will be accomplished when the minimum $e_{i,j}^2$ is achieved. The row coordinate and column coordinate of c_j gives minimum $e_{i,j}^2$ for r_i will be stored in the ith element in the column vectors i and j, respectively. The corresponding $a_{i,j}$ and $b_{i,j}$ will be stored in the ith element in the column vectors a and b, respectively. The four-column vector that contains i, j, a, and b is the fractal codebook. It should be noted that the ith elements in the fractal codebook

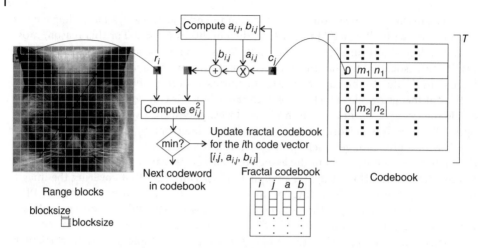

Figure 9.4 Fractal encoding by matching range blocks with grayscale transformed domain blocks from the codebook.

will be updated when a smaller $e_{i,j}^2$ comes in. The encoding process will be done when all entries in the codebook are considered, and the encoding will proceed to the next range block.

9.3.5 Fractal Encoding Implementation

This section will put together all the MATLAB source from Sections 9.3.1 to 9.3.3 to form the fractal encoding MATLAB program, encodeFractal. For demonstration purposes, the codebook constructed from the down-sampled domain block presented in the MATLAB function encodeFractal will not consider any isometry transformations. The codebook will be simply constructed from the down-sampled domain blocks alone. This will limit the codebook size and hence the quality of the PIFS image representation. The construction of PIFS using codebook formed with all the seven isometries of the down-sampled domain blocks will leave for the readers to explore for themselves. The output of the encodeFractal function will include the best match domain block indexed by the vector [col, row] of the original image, which is also the top left-hand pixel coordinate of the block in the image to the extracted domain block. Together with the grayscale scaling and offset given by a and b, these four parameters (row, col, a, b) are all we need to describe the original image f in the PIFS.

> **MATLAB 9.3.1—Fractal image encoding with scaling only.**
>
> ```
> function [row, col, a, b] = encodeFractal(f, blocksize)
>    [M N] = size(f);
>    dimRBlk = blocksize*blocksize;
>    blocksize2 = blocksize*2;
>
>    RBlk = im2col(f,[blocksize blocksize],'distinct');  % range blocks
>    sizeRBlk = size(RBlk, 2);
> ```

```
    DBlk = im2col(f,[blocksize2 blocksize2],'sliding'); % domain blocks
    sizeDBlk = size(DBlk, 2);

    codebook = zeros(dimRBlk, sizeDBlk);    % codebook generation
    for i = 1: sizeDBlk
        blk = reshape(DBlk(:,i), [blocksize2 blocksize2]);
        downblk = double(imresize(blk,0.5,'bilinear'));
        codebook(:,i) = downblk(:);
    end;

    besti = zeros(1, sizeRBlk);      % grayscale scaling
    a = zeros(1, sizeRBlk);
    b = zeros(1, sizeRBlk);
    lse = zeros(2, sizeDBlk);
    estRBlk = zeros(dimRBlk, sizeDBlk);

    for i = 1: sizeRBlk           % encode each range block
        iRBlk = double(RBlk(:,i));
        for j = 1:sizeDBlk           % exhaustive search each domain block
            jDBlk = [codebook(:,j), ones(dimRBlk,1)];
            lse(:,j) = jDBlk\iRBlk;
            estRBlk(:,j) = jDBlk*lse(:,j);
        end
        err = estRBlk - repmat(iRBlk, 1, sizeDBlk);
        mse = sum(err.^2,1);
        [minMSE, besti(i)] = min(mse); % best domain block search
        a(i) = lse(1,besti(i));
        b(i) = lse(2,besti(i));
    end
    [col, row] = ind2sub([M-blocksize2+1, N-blocksize2+1], besti);
end
```

The proper calling of the function `encodeFractal` with range block block size 8 is

```
>> f = imread('cat256.png');
>> blocksize = 8;
>> [row,col,a,b] = encodeFractal(f,blocksize);
```

where the code vectors [`row`, `col`, `a`, `b`] are the fractal code that completely defines the PIFS to represent the image f. There are a lot of things that can be done with this fractal code. In the following sections, we shall first discuss how to reconstruct an approximated image f from the fixed point described by the fractal code [`row`, `col`, `a`, `b`]. We shall then extend the reconstruction result to create an interpolated image g with interpolation ratio of 2.

9.4   Decoding

The fractal code generated by the PIFS encoding process described the relations between different parts of the image, which is independent of the size and resolution of the image. With a given fractal code that defines the collection of contractive transforms $\bigcup T$ (the affine transform described by the domain block location [`col`, `row`] and the associated grayscale scaling and offset by (`a`, `b`)), the fixed point f_f can be obtained by simple iteration of the union of the contractive transforms. Starting with an arbitrary image f_0, one forms the iteration sequence $f_{k+1} = \bigcup T(f_k)$. With the contractive transform constrained to be simple affine transform as considered in previous section, the decoding procedure can be constructed by recovering the range blocks of the $(k + 1)$th decoded image f_{k+1} from the codebook of the decoded image f_k. A decoding loop of the above procedure will be performed until specified quality parameter is fulfilled and is detailed in the following steps:

1. Construct the codebook using the down-sampled domain blocks from the previously decoded image. The codebook generation routine should be the same as that used in the PIFS encoder. Furthermore, if there is no previously decoded image, the "previously decoded image" can be initialed by any image, including the dark (zero matrix) image

   ```
   finit=zeros(M,N);
   ```

   where $M \times N$ is the size of the decoded image. For our purpose of image interpolation, the initial image can be the original image f, such as to reduce the decoding time (readers can refer to Example 9.1 for the number of iterations for the PIFS decoding to convert related to the distance between the initial image and the fixed-point image).

2. Form the ith range block from the code vector indexed by besti

   ```
   besti = sub2ind([M-blocksize2+1, N-blocksize2+1], col, row);
   ```

   extracted from the codebook with gray-level scaling by a and addition of brightness shift b on each pixel of the code vector of the recovered range block as the following MATLAB code:

   ```
   RBlk = repmat(a,dimRBlk,1).*codebook(:,besti)+repmat(b,dimRBlk,1);
   ```

3. Glue all the range blocks together to form the fractal decoded image at the kth iteration:

   ```
   g = col2im(RBlk,[blocksize blocksize],[M N],'distinct');
   ```

4. If the number of iteration is smaller than a predefined number, and if the differences between the images in consecutive loops is larger than a specified tolerance, then go back to step 1 for the $(k + 2)$th fractal decoding iteration using the kth fractal decoded image g as the start image.

This iterative decoding procedure does not require exhaustive search, nor matrix inverse computation; therefore, it is vivid that the decoding procedure requires a fraction of the computational complexity when compared with the fractal encoding procedure. Most of the computation time will be used to construct the codebook from the decoded image g in each loop. A MATLAB implementation of the fractal image decoding procedure that uses codebook without isometric transforms that matches with that applied in the PIFS code generated from MATLAB Listing 9.3.1 is shown in Listing 9.4.1.

> **MATLAB 9.4.1—Fractal image decoding with scaling only.**
>
> ```
> function [g codebook]=decodeFractal(row, col, a, b, blocksize, finit, q)
>     [M N] = size(finit);
> ```

```
g = finit;                       % initial image
dimRBlk = blocksize*blocksize;
blocksize2=blocksize*2;

besti = sub2ind([M-blocksize2+1, N-blocksize2+1], col, row);
for l = 1:q
  DBlk = im2col(g,[blocksize2 blocksize2],'sliding');
  sizeDBlk = size(DBlk,2);
  codebook = zeros(dimRBlk, sizeDBlk);
for i = 1: sizeDBlk      % codebook generation
  blk = reshape(DBlk(:,i), [blocksize2 blocksize2]);
  downblk = double(imresize(blk,0.5,'bilinear'));
  codebook(:,i) = downblk(:);
end
  % range blocks generation through affine transform
RBlk = repmat(a, dimRBlk,1).*codebook(:,besti) + repmat(b, dimRBlk
     ,1);
  g = col2im(RBlk,[blocksize blocksize],[M N],'distinct');
  imgName = ['output-',num2str(blocksize),'-', num2str(l),'.png'];
  imwrite(uint8(g), imgName);
end; end
```

The proper calling of the function `decodeFractal` to regenerate the 256×256 PIFS decoded *Cat* image with `blocksize=8` from a given PIFS encoding data of `[row,col,a,b]` with a dark initial image is

```
>> finit=zeros(256,256);
>> blocksize = 8;
>> n = 20;
>> img = decodeFractal(row,col,a,b,blocksize,finit,n);
```

where the decoder will stop after `n=20` decoding iterations. Shown in Figure 9.5 is the decoded image. The *fractal* nature of the decoded image is vivid from Figure 9.5a, which is the decoded image obtained from the third iteration. Blocks with similar features as that of the original image are being put together, and it is possible to identify the *Cat* image from Figure 9.5a. The image in Figure 9.5b is obtained with two more iterations. The *Cat* image is almost completely reconstructed from the PIFS decoding iterations. The decoded image obtained from the seventh iteration as shown in Figure 9.5c has already faithfully reconstructed the *Cat* image, and only minimal difference can be

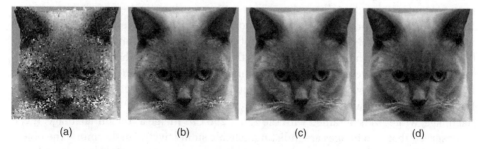

(a)   (b)   (c)   (d)

Figure 9.5 *Cat* image of size 256 × 256 encoded with 8 × 8 range block fractal and decoded under different iterations with constant initial image being a 0 matrix: (a) the third iteration, (b) the fifth iteration, (c) the seventh iteration, and (d) the twentieth iteration.

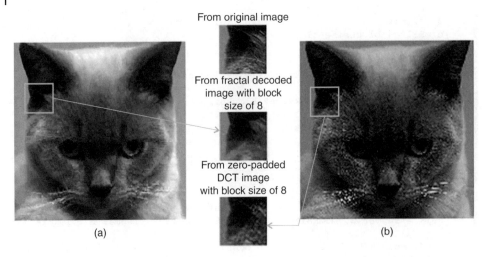

Figure 9.6 Comparison of *Cat* image of size 256 × 256 generated by (a) fractal decoding with 20 iterations and `blocksize=8`; (b) 8 × 8 DCT that retain the low frequency 4 × 4 DCT coefficients and zero padded all other high frequency coefficients.

found between these seventh iteration PIFS decoded image and that obtained from the twentieth iteration PIFS decoded image as shown in Figure 9.5d.

Compared with the classical DCT-based coder (Chapter 5) as shown in Figure 9.6b, the image in Figure 9.6a obtained from fractal decoding with the *Cat* image encoded with `blocksize=8` at the twentieth iteration which has compression ratio compatible to that of the DCT image coding with 8 × 8 DCT block size and retaining only the 4 × 4 low frequency coefficients block. Observed from Figure 9.6a, the fractal PIFS is superior in encoding edges as well as low frequency image content but lack of perceivable texture. Due to the exploitation of scaling invariance (the domain blocks are scaled down by a factor of 2), the modeling of image areas with high frequency details is inferior when compared with that obtained from the DCT-based coder. However, such details are irregular in nature; as a result, such kind of impairments is visually concealed, given that there is no well-known, recognizable geometrical pattern within the photo, such as text characters or geometrical figures. As a result, the HVS will perceive the decoded image from fractal coder to has no or minor artifacts as long as the decoded image content is *similar* to the original. This makes fractal image coding more attractive for natural image coding. The PSNR and SSIM values of the fractal decoded image are 26.54 dB and 0.726, respectively, which is not as good as that obtained from other image encoders.

Finally, we shall investigate the effect of initial image to the fixed-point image. Shown in Figure 9.7 are the twentieth iteration fractal decoded images obtained from the same fractal codebook but with different initial images. Figure 9.7a is obtained with a dark initial image, while (b) is obtained with the 256 × 256 *Cat* image as the initial image. It can be observed that two images are indistinguishable subjectively. Furthermore, the objective performance of both decoded images is the same, with the PSNR equals 26.54 dB and SSIM equals 0.726. The only difference is the number of iterations required to obtain the fixed-point image as shown in Figure 9.7a,b, where fifteen iterations are required

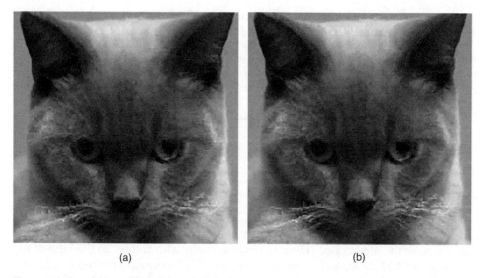

(a) (b)

Figure 9.7 Comparison of fractal decoded *Cat* image of size 256 × 256 obtained from the same fractal codebook but with different initial images at the twentieth iteration, where the same block size of 8 × 8 is applied in the decoding: (a) initial image with all pixel intensity at 0 and (b) the original *Cat* image as initial image, where both the decoded images have the same PSNR and SSIM at 26.54 dB and 0.726, respectively.

for the dark initial image to converge to the fixed-point *Cat* image, while it takes nine iterations for the *Cat* image to converge to the fixed-point *Cat* image. These observation can be conjectured from the discussions presented in Example 9.1.

9.4.1 Does Size Matter

As discussed in Section 9.3, both the PIFS representation quality and the computational complexity of the PIFS encoding process depend on the range block block size. We encoded and decoded the *Cat* image using MATLAB functions Listings 9.3.1 and 9.4.1 and a dark (zero matrix) initial image but with two different range block block sizes, 4 × 4 and 8 × 8. The encoding and decoding particulars are listed in Tables 9.2

Table 9.2 Fractal image representation of the 256 × 256 *Cat* image with range block block sizes of 4 × 4 and 8 × 8, respectively, running `encodeFractal` with MATLAB R2016b on MS Windows 7 PC with Quad Core Xeon E5520 at 2.27 GHz and 8 GB RAM.

Block size	4 × 4	8 × 8
Time to encode	15 min	3 min
Size of codebook	16 × 62,001 double	64 × 58,081 double
Fractal code size	0.375 byte/pixel	0.07 byte/pixel

The fractal codebook is computed with each component in the `row, col` vectors to be 8-bit data and each component in the `a, b` vectors to be both quantized to 16-bit data.

Table 9.3 256 × 256 *Cat* image reconstructed from fractal image representation using range block block sizes of 4 × 4 and 8 × 8, respectively, with blank initial reference image running `decodeFractal` with MATLAB R2016b on MS Windows 7 PC with Quad Core Xeon E5520 at 2.27 GHz and 8 GB RAM.

Block size	4 × 4 double	8 × 8 double
Size of `codebook`	16 × 62,001 double	64 × 58,081 double
Number of iterations	30	20
Time to decode	50 min	5 min
PSNR	31.00 dB	25.54 dB

and 9.3, respectively. It can be observed that the increase in the range block block size does increase the memory consumption exponentially with respect to the ratio of the two range block block sizes. However, the number of code vectors in the codebook is still comparable (which is basically comparable with the total number of pixels in the image). As a result, as long as the computational devices (the computer than runs the MATLAB) have enough memory, it is expected that the encoding time should be comparable with respect to the codebook size. On the other hand, the larger the range block block size, the smaller the number of range blocks required to be encoded, and the reduction should be comparable to the ratio of the two range block block sizes. As a result, an overall reduction in the encoding time of the fractal encoding process with range block block size 8 × 8 by a factor of almost 5 is observed when compared to that with range block block size 4 × 4. When we examine the computational performance gain of fractal encoding with range block block size equals 8 × 8, it can be observed from Listing 9.3.1 that the larger the range block block size, the smaller the encoded fractal codes, and the reduction follows directly from the range block block size ratio.

If we further investigate the fractal decoding process, we shall find that the codebook size required in the fractal decoder should be of the same size as that in the fractal encoder. As a result, the decoding complexity will depend on the number of range blocks, which partially explained the long decoding time of the PIFS decoding with range block block size 4 × 4 when compared to that with 8 × 8. Another reason on the long PIFS decoding time for the case with range block block size 4 × 4 is caused by the slow convergence, where almost doubled the number of iterations are required before the decoding algorithm converges. The fast convergence of the PIFS decoding with range block block size 8 × 8 is because of the fact that some of the range blocks with details are not fractal. When they are considered as fractal objects, the image details within these blocks will be washed out. As a result, the PIFS decoding converges fast with large range block block size. On the other hand, most of the small range block (4 × 4) are fractal blocks and will require long convergence time. The pros of small range block are the preservation of image details as observed in Figure 9.8, which is also reflected in the PSNR of the decoded images as listed in Table 9.3. It will be difficult to find a balance between the range block block size and the other performance parameters. In the rest of this chapter, we shall keep using range block block size 8 × 8 (`blocksize=8`), because

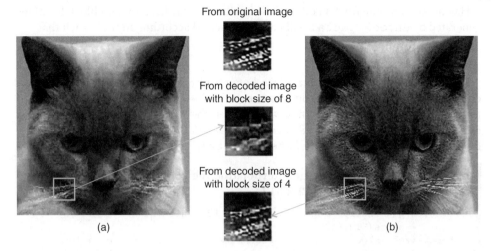

Figure 9.8 *Cat* image of size 256 × 256 with (a) 8 × 8 range block fractal encoding and decoded with 30 iterations and a 0 matrix initial image, and the associated zoom-in image block of the whiskers of the *Cat*, and (b) the same block from 20 iterations fractal decoded image with 4 × 4 range block.

of the computational complexity advantages, which does not affect us to present the theories and concepts that we desired.

9.5   Decoding with Interpolation

The main idea of the fractal image interpolation is rather simple. It is based on the assumption that the fractal coding is really a fractal process and the fractal code's attractor is a fractal object. Such that by iterating a deterministic transformation on some initial image, a deterministic fractal image will be obtained. The transforms that build the fractal code describe relations between different parts of the image, which is independent of the size and resolution of the image being processed. This means that the image can be decoded to any resolution, higher or lower than that of the original image.

The ability of using fractal code to interpolate image has been developed in [27, 28, 53] and is known as *"fractal zoom."* It is known as "zoom" because the fractal decoded and enlarged image does not necessary preserve the pixel intensity corresponding to the low-resolution image. As a result, according to Section 1.4, the "zoom" algorithm is not an interpolation algorithm, but a fitting algorithm. More about the fractal zoom will be discussed in subsequent section. In the meantime, let us concentrate on fractal zoom, which decodes the PIFS codes to arbitrary resolutions. For magnification, the range block blocksize has to be increased, while for image shrinkage the range block blocksize has to decrease. In particular, in our discussions within Section 9.3, the interpolation ratio is fixed to be 2 ($r = 2$). As a result, the blocksize in decode-Fractal should be doubled:

```
>> blocksize = blocksize * 2;
```

Having said that the fractal code will be unchanged, the best domain block locations generated by `encodeFractal` will have to be scaled according to the *r*, such that

```
>> col = (col-1)*2 +1;
>> row = (row-1)*2 +1;
```

Finally, although the initial image can be an arbitrary image (in the following, we choose the zero matrix), it has to be the same size as the interpolated image when applied to the PIFS transform. Putting these all together, the MATLAB source to generate a 512×512 *Cat* image from a PIFS encoded 256×256 *Cat* image with encoding range block `blocksize=8` is given by `interpFractal`.

> **MATLAB 9.5.1—Fractal image interpolating the 256×256 PIFS encoded *Cat* image with scaling only to 512×512.**
>
> ```
> function g = interpFractal(row,col,a,b,blocksize,n)
>   finit = zeros(512,512);
>   blocksize = blocksize*2;    % blocksize  x2 for 2x interpolation
>   col = (col-1)*2 +1;         % scale the best domain block locations
>   row = (row-1)*2 +1;
>   g = decodeFractal(row,col,a,b,blocksize,finit,n);
> end
> ```

The fractal zoom-in *Cat* image shown in Figure 9.9 is the result of applying the fractal codeword `[row,col,a,b]` obtained from `encodeFractal(f,8)` with the MATLAB function call

```
g = interpFractal(row,col,a,b,8,20);
```

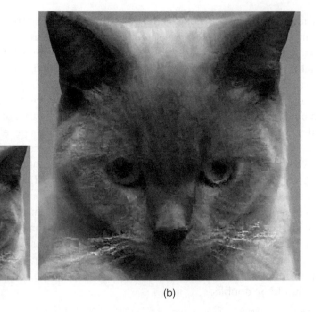

(a)   (b)

Figure 9.9 Fractal zoom-in *Cat* image in (a) same size as that of original image (i.e. 256×256) and (b) an enlargement to the size of 512×512, with both images decoded with identical range block block size of 8×8, dark image as initial image, and the number of iteration is 20 (PSNR = 25.2715 dB, SSIM = 0.6290).

It should be noted that the fractal zooming does not preserve the pixel values and hence performs very bad in traditional objective measures, where PSNR and SSIM are 25.2715 dB and 0.6290, respectively. On the other hand, the fractal zoom-in image performs very good with subjective assessments. Visually, it is vivid that the fractal zoom-in image can provide acute preservation of edges without serration effects and increased brilliance when compared with other methods in previous chapters. In summary, the fractal zoom-in image is observed to process the following properties:

1. When edges are well approximated at the original resolution, they are sharp and fairly well preserved in the interpolated image.
2. Edges do not always match well at block boundaries.
3. The non-fractal blocks are less visually satisfactory, where "notches" are created by non-fractal blocks, which are propagated by iterations onto neighboring blocks.

The loss in details of the non-fractal blocks is mostly caused by the fact that the fractal coding is a lossy process and the coding error is magnified in the decoding stage during zooming. As a result, a special treatment of this error would be necessary to enable the fractal image interpolation to compete with the classical interpolation methods with respect to objective performance assessments. Back propagation and overlapping range blocks can all be used to suppress the blocking artifacts, which appear in the zoom-in image as grid overlay.

9.5.1 From Fitting to Interpolation

Although the PIFS image representation is based on the assumption that the image can be treated as a fractal object, almost all real-world images do not satisfy the self-similarity property. The consequence is that the PIFS decoded image will be lossy and the interpolated image obtained from the application of PIFS cannot guarantee the preservation of the original pixel values. As a result, the traditional fractal zooming can only be considered as fitting (as discussed in Section 1.4) instead of interpolation. When that happens, Section 5.6 suggests a back propagation algorithm to recover the original pixel values in the interpolated image. Similar algorithm can be applied in PIFS image interpolation problem. However, we understand that the fractal decoding depends on the invariant of the affine transformation performed by the fractal encoding process, instead of the underlying image. We have demonstrated this property by initializing the PIFS decoding process with zero matrix, and bilinear interpolated original images, where the fractal decoding algorithm converges to images that are almost exactly the same. As a result, instead of considering the adjustment of the fractal decoded image by iterative fractal interpolation of difference images as in Section 5.6, we can modify the fractal decoded image in each iteration with

```
>> g(1:2:M,1:2:N)=f;
```

such that all pixels corresponding to the original image are replaced by that of the original image in the intermediate decoded interpolated image in each iteration as shown in the following MATLAB function `exactinterpFractal`.

MATLAB 9.5.2—Fractal interpolation with low-resolution image interleave layer.

```
function [g] = exactinterpFractal(row, col, a, b, blocksize, f, q)
   [M,N] = size(f);            % double the size of the image
   M = 2*M; N = 2*N;
   g = zeros(M,N);             % initial image
   g(1:2:M,1:2:N)=f;
   blocksize = blocksize*2;    % double the blocksize
   blocksize2 = blocksize*2;
   dimRBlk = blocksize*blocksize;
      col = (col-1)*2 +1;         % scale the best domain block locations
      row = (row-1)*2 +1;
      besti = sub2ind([M-blocksize2+1, N-blocksize2+1], col, row);
      for l = 1:q
      DBlk = im2col(g,[blocksize2 blocksize2],'sliding');
      sizeDBlk = size(DBlk,2);
      codebook = zeros(dimRBlk, sizeDBlk);
      for i = 1: sizeDBlk       % codebook construction
        blk = reshape(DBlk(:,i), [blocksize2 blocksize2]);
        downblk = double(imresize(blk,0.5,'bilinear'));
        codebook(:,i) = downblk(:);
      end
      clear DBLK; clear blk; clear downblk;       % Free up memory
      % range blocks generation through affine transform
      RBlk = repmat(a, dimRBlk,1).*codebook(:,besti)+repmat(b,dimRBlk,1)
         ;
      g = col2im(RBlk,[blocksize blocksize],[M N],'distinct');
      g(1:2:M,1:2:N)=f;
         imgName = ['output-',num2str(blocksize),'-',num2str(l),'.png
            '];
         imwrite(uint8(g), imgName);
   end end
```

Similar algorithm has been considered in [21] where the *enhancement layer* is introduced in the fractal decoding process, which is essentially the same as the interleave layer in the MATLAB function `exactinterpFractal`. The interpolated *Cat* image is shown in Figure 9.10, where it is vivid that the interpolated image has more details and less artifacts than that obtained by `interpFractal` shown in Figure 9.9. It is interesting to notice the subjective quality of the interpolated image with PSNR = 26.41 dB and SSIM = 0.7231, which are both not as good as that obtained from the simple fractal zooming method with the zoom-in image presented in Figure 9.9. This is because the pixel replacement scheme does not follow the self-similar property of fractal image representation, which may end up with distinct pixel values (also known as shot noise) to be observed in the interpolated image. Such artifacts will affect the performance of the constructed domain pool for the next iteration and hence the final image object quality. Furthermore, this pixel replacement procedure in the decoding process does not alter the block processing nature of the PIFS image representation, and hence the interpolated image is still observed to be blocky.

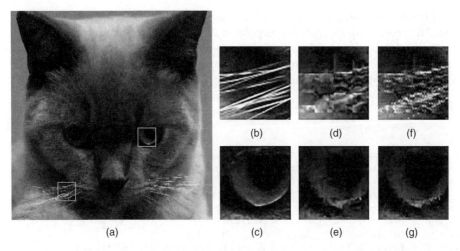

Figure 9.10 Fractal interpolated *Cat* image by a factor of 2 to 512 × 512 at the fifteenth iteration with range block block size of 8 × 8 interleaved with low-resolution *Cat* image pixel layer (PSNR = 26.41 dB, SSIM = 0.7231): (a) the full interpolated image; zoom-in portion of the whiskers of (b) the original *Cat* image, (d) the interpolated image by `interpFractal`, and (f) the interpolated image by `exactinterpFractal`; zoom-in portion of the eye of (c) the original *Cat* image, (e) the interpolated image by `interpFractal`, and (g) the interpolated image by `exactinterpFractal`.

9.6 Overlapping

Fractal image representation technique is a block-based technique, and hence blocking fractal artifact is observed to be heavy and considered to be the most important visual artifact in the decoded image. When this technique is applied to interpolate an image, the blocking artifact is emphasized and is usually highly visible. To alleviate the blocking artifact, the *overlapping* technique considered in Section 5.4 by classical DCT-based image interpolation can be applied to fractal image interpolation, such that the fractal image interpolation results obtained from images that are shifts of one another such that they have different range block boundaries are averaged to alleviate the discontinuities around the range block boundaries. A set of images that are shifts of the original image can be obtained easily by the MATLAB functions `npart`, `mpart`, and `dpart` discussed in Section 5.4. Similar to that of the DCT image interpolation considered in Section 5.4, the shift should be equal to half of the range block block size. A set of PIFS image coding results from the original and shifted images can be obtained from

```
>> f = double(imread('cat256.png'));
>> blocksize = 8;
>> [row,col,a,b] = encodeFractal(f,blocksize);
>> fn = npart(f,blocksize);
>> [rown,coln,an,bn] = encodeFractal(fn,blocksize);
>> fm = mpart(f,blocksize);
>> [rowm,colm,am,bm] = encodeFractal(fm,blocksize);
>> fd = dpart(f,blocksize);
>> [rowd,cold,ad,bd] = encodeFractal(fd,blocksize);
```

The PIFS image coding results of each shifted image will generate one interpolated image. After rectifying the fractal interpolated shifted images (by padding the boundary with the fractal decoded image of the non-shifted image) to be the same as that obtained from the non-shifted image, all the images will be averaged to produce the final overlapped interpolated image as shown by the following MATLAB script:

```
>> f = double(imread('cat256.png'));
>> blocksize = 8;
>> L = blocksize/2;
>> i = 15;
>> g = exactinterpFractal(row,col,a,b,blocksize,f,i);
>> gn = exactinterpFractal(rown,coln,an,bn,blocksize,fn,i);
>> gm = exactinterpFractal(rowm,colm,am,bm,blocksize,fm,i);
>> gd = exactinterpFractal(rowd,cold,ad,bd,blocksize,fd,i);
>> [M N] = size(g);
>> pgn = [g(1:M,1:2*L) gn g(1:M,N-2*L+1:N)];
>> pgm = [g(1:2*L,1:N); gm; g(M-2*L+1:M,1:N)];
>> pgd = [g(1:2*L,1:N); g(2*L+1:M-2*L,1:2*L) gd g(2*L:M-2*L-1,N-2*L+1:N);
         g(M-2*L+1:N,1:N)];
>> aveg = (g+pgn+pgm+pgd)/4;
```

As discussed in Section 5.4, such operation is equivalent to the application of mean filtering to the overlapped images of the "non-shifted" and "shifted" images. We shall expect the blocking artifact be alleviated and the image quality be further improved. The interpolated image of the above MATLAB script is shown in Figure 9.11, with the

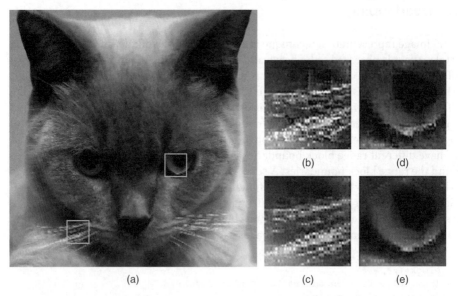

(a)   (b)   (d)   (c)   (e)

Figure 9.11 2× interpolated *Cat* image by mean filtering a set of four cyclic spin fractal decoding images (original plus three other shifted images) with doubled range block block size (i.e. 16 × 16) and interleaved low-resolution image pixels using exactinterpFractal function (PSNR = 27.39 dB, SSIM = 0.7662): (a) the full interpolated image; zoom-in portion of the whiskers of the *Cat* image obtained from (b) exactinterpFractal without mean filtering (same as Figure 9.10c) and (c) mean filtering shifted fractal decoded images; zoom-in portion of the eye of the *Cat* image obtained from (d) exactinterpFractal without mean filtering (same as Figure 9.10g) and (e) mean filtering shifted fractal decoded images.

zoom-in image in Figure 9.11c and Figure 9.11d. Note that the PIFS decoding is being implemented with `exactinterpFractal`, and thus the obtained images are all interpolated images and hence the average image in Figure 9.11a. It can be observed that the blockiness of the interpolated image has largely suppressed, and the details of the texture rich regions of the *Cat* images can be preserved. Besides the blocking artifacts, the shot noise problem due to the interleave layer in `exactinterpFractal` has also been suppressed. This is because the location of the shot noise pixels is different in fractal decoded images with different shifts. As a result, the averaging action among fractal decoded images with different shot noise pixel locations helps to reduce the shot noise intensity to an HVS non-observable level. The good performance of this image interpolation scheme is also observed in the objective performance measures, where both the PSNR (27.39 dB) and SSIM (0.7662) are better than other fractal zooming/interpolation methods presented in this chapter. This almost perfect fractal image interpolation scheme does come with the very high price of exceptionally high computational complexity and possible high memory requirement. Readers who try to execute the MATLAB script to generate the fractal decoded shifted images may need to clear the memory of the MATLAB space by saving the required code vector into file, such as to free up enough memory for the next fractal decoding to execute.

9.7 Summary

This chapter has shown that fractal image interpolation has the potential to generate high quality interpolated images. One of the major weaknesses of the fractal image interpolation is the use of fixed size range and domain image blocks. There are regions in images that are more difficult to cope with (such as the eye region of the *Cat* image), which will require a mechanism to adapt the block size. One of such methods is to use quadtree decomposition as discussed in Section 9.3.1. Unfortunately variable block size fractal image interpolation suffers from huge encoding complexity. Actually even for range block with uniform size, the search space to be investigated is spanned by the amount of domain block locations, which equals to the number of pixels in the image, and the variations of all affine transform applied to the domain pool for codebook generation. Therefore, the key to make fractal image interpolation to work is to find methods to reduce the search effort to an acceptable level for real-world implementation in everyday home computer. This involves intelligent search methods to be investigated by the readers. In summary, the fractal image interpolation can produce excellent interpolation results for natural image, where very sharp edges can be obtained with almost nil ringing artifacts. The cons are the very high computational complexity and processing memory requirement, whether it is being applied alone or mixed with various artifacts reduction techniques.

As the last chapter of the book, readers should have noticed two facts about image interpolation. First, image interpolation is an ill-posed problem with infinitely many solutions due to the lack of information presented in the low-resolution image. Second, various interpolation techniques and artifact reduction methods can be mixed to achieve better interpolation results. However, mixing different interpolation methods and artifact reduction methods together does not always work. But when it works, the result will usually be very pleasing. The major fallacies of such mix and match methods will be the increase in computational complexity. Because such scheme is usually iterative, the very high computational complexity interpolation algorithm will have to be performed for many more times before a *perfect interpolated image* can be obtained. Therefore, the design of an image interpolation algorithm is to find the best trade-off between the appearance of artifacts (the unfortunate results of a series of wrong assumptions) and the computational complexity.

9.8 Exercises

9.1 Show that if a contraction function f in Eq. (9.1) has a fixed point, then it must be unique.

9.2 Replace the `imresize` function in Listings 9.3.1, 9.4.1, and 9.5.2 with a new function `bilinearinterp`, where the function call `g=bilinearinterp(f, [m n])` will interpolate or down-sample the image block `f` of arbitrary size to `g` with size `[m n]`. Compare the subjective and objective fractal reconstructed image and fractal zoom-in image generated with these new functions with that obtained by the original functions.

9.3 Change the MATLAB code Listing 9.3.1 to allow domain block flip horizontally and vertically as the allowable affine transform.

9.4 Revise the MATLAB code Listing 9.5.1 to allow arbitrary zoom ratio using any method that can you think of.

Appendix

MATLAB Functions List

The following is a list of all the MATLAB sources that are applied to generate the figures presenting the simulation results in this book. All MATLAB sources have been tested with MATLAB 2016B. If you are using MATLAB in other versions, beware that you may need to modify the sources, as MATLAB do update the language from time to time.

Figure	Listing	Filename	Function
2.7	2.3.3	freqshiftplot	2D spatial frequency plot with shift
2.14	2.5.1	sobel	Sobel edge image extraction
	2.7.1	directds	Down-sampler with down-sampling ratio $1/r$
	2.7.2	sincds	Sinc filter down-sampler with down-sampling ratio $1/2$
	2.7.3	aveds	Averaging filter down-sampler with down-sampling ratio $1/2$
	3.2.1	imageerr	Error image generation
	3.2.2	mae	Mean absolute error
	3.2.3	mse	Mean squares error
	3.2.4	rmse	Root mean squares error
	3.2.5	psnr	Peak signal-to-noise ratio
	3.2.6	epsnr	Edge peak signal-to-noise ratio
	3.3.1	mssim	Mean structural similarity
	4.1.1	directus	Low-resolution to high-resolution image 2× resampling by zero padding
	4.1.2	nnfilter	Nearest neighbor interpolation by 2D convolution
4.4 4.5a	4.1.3	nn	Nearest neighbor interpolation with ratio 2
	4.1.4	bi2x2	Pixelwise bilinear interpolation

(Continued)

Digital Image Interpolation in MATLAB®, First Edition. Chi-Wah Kok and Wing-Shan Tam.
© 2019 John Wiley & Sons Singapore Pte. Ltd. Published 2019 by John Wiley & Sons Singapore Pte. Ltd.
Companion website: www.wiley.com/go/ditmatlab

Figure	Listing	Filename	Function
4.8 4.9a	4.1.5	`biinterp`	Bilinear image interpolation with ratio r
4.14 4.15a	4.1.6	`bicubic`	Bicubic image interpolation with ratio 2
	4.1.7	`bicubic4x4`	Pixelwise bicubic interpolation
	4.4.1	`rotatenn`	Image rotation by nearest neighbor interpolation
4.21a		`rotatenn40`	40° *Cat* image rotation by nearest neighbor interpolation
	4.4.2	`rotatebi`	Image rotation by bilinear interpolation
4.21b		`rotatebi40`	40° *Cat* image rotation by bilinear interpolation
4.22		`rotate9`	Structure integrity test by 9 rotations of the Cat image with $2\pi/9$
	5.1.1	`dftinterp`	Fourier interpolation of 1D signal sequence to length K
5.4a	5.1.2	`zpfft`	2× image interpolation by DFT zero padding
5.5	5.1.3	`dftramp8`	8× interpolation of a discrete ramp by DFT zero padding
	5.2.1	`dctkernel`	Length N DCT kernel
5.6	5.2.2	`dctramp8`	8× interpolation of a discrete ramp by DCT zero padding
	5.3.1	`zeropad2`	Zero padding a $[M, N]$ block to $[2M, 2N]$
5.7a	5.3.2	`blockdct`	Forward 8×8 DCT block processing
	5.3.3	`blockidct`	8×8 inverse DCT block processing
5.8 5.9	5.3.4	`dctx2`	2× image interpolation with $L \times L$ block DCT zero padded to $2L \times 2L$
	5.3.5	`brightnorm`	Image dynamic range normalization with respect to a given reference image
5.10b	5.4.1	`npart`	Return an image with the first $L/2$ and the last $L/2$ columns discarded
5.10c	5.4.2	`mpart`	Return an image with the first $L/2$ and the last $L/2$ rows discarded
5.10d	5.4.3	`dpart`	Return an image with the first $L/2$ and the last $L/2$ columns and the first $L/2$ and last $L/2$ rows discarded
5.11	5.4.5	`dctcs`	2×image interpolation with 8×8 DCT block zero padding and half block size cyclic spin
5.12a		`vzdctx2`	2× image interpolation with mean filtering 8×8 block DCT zero padding and half block vertical 8×8 block DCT zero padding
5.13 5.14a		`mzdctx2`	2× image interpolation with mean filtering 8×8 block DCT zero padding and 3 half block cyclic spin block DCT zero padding

Figure	Listing	Filename	Function
	5.5.1	eidctkernel	$K \times N$ EIDCT kernel matrix
	5.5.2	eidct	$r\times$ interpolated image by DFT zero padding through DCT transformed coefficients using EIDCT
5.15a	5.5.3	mzdcteidct	2× image interpolation with mean filtering 8×8 block DCT zero padding and DFT zero padding through EIDCT
5.18	5.6.1	dctx2bp	2× image interpolation by 8×8 block DCT zero padding with direct down-sampling iterative error compensation
6.4a	6.1.1	twoddwtex	2D DWT dyadic decomposition image
6.6a	6.2.1	wzp	2× image interpolation by wavelet zero padding
6.7a	6.2.2	wbp	2× image interpolation by wavelet bilinear interpolation
6.9a	6.2.3	wazp	2× image interpolation by wavelet alternate zero
6.10a	6.2.4	wazp15	2× image interpolation by wavelet alternate zero with LL band divided by 1.5
6.11a	6.2.5	wrazp	2× image interpolation by wavelet alternate zero with regularity preserving subband scaling
6.13a	6.3.1	wzpcs	2× image interpolation by mean filtering wavelet alternate zero with regularity preserving and wavelet zero padding cyclic spinning
6.15a	6.3.2	wlrcs	2× image interpolation by mean filtering wavelet alternate zero and cyclic spinning wavelet zero padding with LL bands replaced low-resolution image cyclic spinning
6.16a		wzplrcs	2× image interpolation by mean filtering wzpcs and wlrcs
6.18a	6.4.1	wecor	2× image interpolation by wavelet zero padding iterative error correction
	7.2.1	ease1d	1D EASE interpolation
	7.2.2	directus1d	1D direct up-sample by zero padding
	7.2.3	ease2d	Pointwise 2D EASE interpolation
7.10 7.11a	7.2.4	ease	2× image interpolation by EASE
	8.3.1	nedi_weighting_factor	Weighted average interpolation weighting factors
	8.3.3	nedi_core	The core function of the NEDI
	8.3.4	nedi_window	NEDI image interpolation windows
	8.3.5	nedi_correct	Correction of underestimation or overshoot pixel

(Continued)

Figure	Listing	Filename	Function
8.8 8.10	8.3.6	`nedi`	NEDI 2× image interpolation
8.9a	8.4.1	`nedi_pe`	Image boundary extension by periodic extension
8.9b 8.9c	8.4.2	`nedi_pe_crop`	NEDI 2× image interpolation with periodic boundary extension and crop the interpolated image to size $2M \times 2N$
	8.6.1	`medi`	MEDI, a modified NEDI with windows defined on low-resolution pixels alone
8.13a	8.6.2	`medi_call`	MEDI image interpolation with boundary extension
	8.7.1	`emedi_select_win`	Local covariance window selection to maximize covariance power
	8.7.2	`emedi_core`	EMEDI core, a modified NEDI core to incorporate local covariance window selection that maximizes covariance power
	8.7.3	`emedi`	EMEDI, a modified MEDI with covariance window adaptation
8.21a	8.7.4	`emedi_call`	EMEDI image interpolation with periodic boundary extension
	8.8.1	`imedi_select_win`	Selection of biased high-resolution prediction window that achieves the smallest covariance difference in iMEDI
	8.8.2	`imedi_core`	iMEDI window generation
	8.8.3	`imedi`	iMEDI 2× image interpolation
8.23a	8.8.4	`imediloop`	
	8.8.5	`cmse`	Mean squared difference of two images
	9.3.1	`encodeFractal`	Fractal image encoding with scaling only
	9.4.1	`decodeFractal`	Fractal image decoding with scaling only
9.5 9.8		`decodeFractal_call`	Fractal image decoding function call
9.9a	9.5.1	`interpFractal`	2× zoom-in image using fractal with doubled range block size using scaling only
9.10a	9.5.2	`exactinterpFractal`	2× interpolated image using fractal with doubled range block size using scaling only and interleave with low-resolution image pixel replacement layer
9.11a		`encodeFractalcs`	Fractal image encoding with scaling only for a set of cyclic spin images
9.11a		`decodeFractalcs`	2× image interpolation by mean filtering a set of four cyclic spin fractal decoding images with doubled range block size and interleaved low-resolution image pixels

Bibliography

1 Recommendation J.144 (03/04) (2001). Objective perceptual video quality measurement techniques for digital cable television in the presence of a full reference. *International Telecommunication Union, Telecommunication standardization sector*.

2 Ahmed, N., Natarajan, T., and Rao, K.R. (1974). On image processing and a discrete cosine transform. *IEEE Transactions on Computers* 90–93.

3 Allebach, J. and Wong, P.W. (1996). Edge-directed interpolation. In: *Proceeding of the 3rd IEEE International Conference on Image Processing*, vol. 2, 707–710.

4 Antonini, M., Barlaud, M., Mathieu, P., and Daubechies, I. (1992). Image coding using wavelet transform. *IEEE Transactions on Image Processing* 1 (2): 205–220.

5 Asuni, N. and Giachetti, A. (2008). Accuracy improvements and artifacts removal in edge based image interpolation. *Proceedings of the 3rd International Conference of Computer Vision Theory and Applications*.

6 Ayazifar, B. and Lim, J.S. (1992). PEL-adaptive model-based interpolation of spatially sub-sampled images. In: *Proceeding of the IEEE International Conference on Acoustic, Speech and Signal Processing*, vol. 3, 181–184.

7 Banach, S. (1922). Sur les operations dans les ensembles abstraits et leur application aux equations integrales. *Fundamenta Mathematicae* 3: 133–181.

8 Barnsley, M.F., Elton, J.H., and Hardin, D.P. (1989). Recurrent iterated function systems. *Constructive Approximation* 5: 3–31.

9 Bayer, B.E. (1976). Color imaging array. US Patent 3,971,065.

10 Recommendation ITU-R BT.601-5 (1995). Studio encoding parameters of digital television for standard 4:3 and wide-screen 16:9 aspect ratios. *ITU-T*.

11 Carey, W.K., Chuang, D.B., and Hemami, S.S. (1999). Regularity-preserving image interpolation. *IEEE Transactions on Image Processing* 8 (9): 1293–1297.

12 Carrato, S., Ramponi, G., and Marsi, S. (1996). A simple edge-sensitive image interpolation filter. In: *Proceeding of the IEEE International Conference on Image Processing*, vol. 3, 711–714.

13 Carrato, S. and Tenze, L. (2000). A high quality 2x image interpolator. *IEEE Signal Processing Letters* 7 (6): 132–134.

14 Celik, T. and Kusetogullari, H. (2009). Self-sampled image resolution enhancement using dual-tree complex wavelet transform. *Proceedings of the European Signal Processing Conference*.

15 Celik, T. and Tjahjadi, T. (2010). Image resolution enhancement using dual-tree complex wavelet transform. *IEEE Transactions on Geoscience and Remote Sensing* 7 (3): 554–557.

Digital Image Interpolation in MATLAB®, First Edition. Chi-Wah Kok and Wing-Shan Tam.
© 2019 John Wiley & Sons Singapore Pte. Ltd. Published 2019 by John Wiley & Sons Singapore Pte. Ltd.
Companion website: www.wiley.com/go/ditmatlab

16 Cha, Y. and Kim, S. (2006). The error-amended sharp edge (EASE) scheme for image zooming. *IEEE Transactions on Image Processing* 16 (6): 1496–1505.

17 Chan, R.H., Chan, T.F., Shen, L., and Shen, Z. (2003). Wavelet algorithm for high-resolution image reconstruction. *SIAM Journal on Scientific Computing* 24 (4): 1408–1432.

18 Chang, S.G., Cvetkovic, Z., and Vetterli, M. (1995). Resolution enhancement of images using wavelet transform extrema interpolation. In: *Proceedings of the IEEE International Conference on Acoustic, Speech, and Signal Processing*, 2379–2382.

19 Chen, W., Tian, Q., Liu, J., and Wang, Q. (2014). Nonlocal low-rank matrix completion for image interpolation using edge detection and neural network. *Signal, Image and Video Processing* 8 (4): 657–663.

20 Chen, X.Q., Zhang, J., and Wu, L.N. (2003). Improvement of a nonlinear image interpolation method based on heat diffusion equation. In: *Proceedings of the International Conference on Machine Learning and Cybernetics*, vol. 5, 2911–2914.

21 Chung, K.-H., Fung, Y.-H., and Chan, Y.-H. (2003). Image enlargement using fractal. In: *Proceedings of the International Conference on Acoustic, Speech, and Signal Processing*, vol. 6, 273–276.

22 Daubechies, I. (1992). *Ten Lectures on Wavelets*. SIAM Press.

23 Doyle, T. and Looymans, M. (1990). Progressive scan conversion using edge information. In: *Signal Processing of HDTV II* (ed. L. Chairiglione), 711–721. The Netherlands: Elsevier.

24 Dube, S. and Hong, L. (2000). An adaptive algorithm for image resolution enhancement. In: *Proceedings of the IEEE 34th Asilomar Conference on Signals, Systems and Computers*, vol. 2, 1731–1734.

25 Dugad, R. and Ahuja, N. (2001). A fast scheme for image size change in the compressed domain. *IEEE Transactions on Circuits Systems for Video Technology* 11 (4): 461–474.

26 Eckert, M.P. and Bradley, A.P. (1998). Perceptual quality metrics applied to still image compression. *Signal Processing* 70 (11): 177–200.

27 Fisher, Y. (1995). *Fractal Image Compression – Theory and Applications*. Springer-Verlag.

28 Gharavi-Alkhansari, M., DeNardo, R., Tenda, Y., and Huang, T.S. (1997). Resolution enhancement of images using fractal coding. In: *Proceedings of SPICE Visual Communications and Image Processing*, vol. 3024, 1089–1100.

29 Hse, Y.-F. and Chen, Y.-C. (1997). Rational interpolation by extendible inverse discrete cosine transform. *IET Electronics Letters* 33 (21): 1774–1775.

30 Hung, K.W. and Siu, W.C. (2012). Robust soft-decision interpolation using weighted least squares. *IEEE Transactions on Image Processing* 21 (3): 1061–1069.

31 Hutchinson, J. (1981). Fractals and self-similarity. *Indiana University Journal of Mathematics* 30, 713–747.

32 Jacquin, A.E. (1992). Image coding based on a fractal theory of iterated contractive image transformations. *IEEE Transactions on Image Processing* 1 (1): 18–30.

33 Jawerth, B. and Sweldens, W. (1995). Biorthogonal smooth local trigonometric bases. *Journal of Fourier Analysis and Applications* 2 (2): 109–133.

34 Jensen, K. and Anastassiou, D. (1995). Subpixel edge localization and the interpolation of still images. *IEEE Transactions on Image Processing* 4: 285–295.

35 Kay, S.M. (1998). *Fundamentals of Statistical Signal Processing: Detection Theory*, vol. II. Prentice Hall.

36 Keys, R. (1981). Cubic convolution interpolation for digital image processing. *IEEE Transactions on Acoustics Speech and Signal Processing* 29 (6): 1153–1160.

37 Kok, C.-W. (1997). Fast algorithm for computing discrete cosine transform. *IEEE Transactions on Signal Processing* 45 (3): 757–760.

38 Lee, S.W. and Paik, J.K. (1993). Image interpolation using adaptive fast B-spline filtering. In: *Proceeding of the IEEE International Conference on Acoustic, Speech, and Signal Processing*, vol. 5, 177–180.

39 Li, M. and Nguyen, T.Q. (2008). Markov random field model-based edge-directed image interpolation. *IEEE Transactions on Image Processing* 17 (7): 1121–1128.

40 Li, X. and Orchard, M.T. (2001). New edge-directed interpolation. *IEEE Transactions on Image Processing* 10 (10): 1521–1527.

41 Lu, N. (1997). *Fractal Imaging*. Academic Press.

42 Mai, Z., Rajan, J., Verhoye, M., and Sijbers, J. (2011). Robust edge-directed interpolation of magnetic resonance images. In: *Proceedings of the 4th International Conference on Biomedical Engineering and Informatics (BMEI) 2011*, vol. 1, 472–476.

43 Mallat, S.G. (1998). *A Wavelet Tour of Signal Processing*. Academic Press.

44 Mallat, S. and Zhong, S. (1992). Characterization of signals from multiscale edges. *IEEE Transactions on Pattern Analysis and Machine Intelligence* 14 (7): 710–732.

45 Malvar, H.S. (1990). Lapped transforms for efficient transform/subband coding. *IEEE Transactions on Acoustics Speech and Signal Processing* 38 (6): 969–978.

46 Mandelbrot, B.B. (1982). *The Fractal Geometry of Nature*. W.H. Freeman and Company.

47 Morse, B.S. and Schwartzwald, D. (1998). Isophote-based interpolation. In: *Proceeding of the IEEE International Conference on Image Processing*, vol. 3, 227–231.

48 Mukherjee, J. and Mitra, S.K. (2005). Arbitrary resizing of images in the DCT space. *IEE Proceedings on Visual, Image, and Signal Processing* 152 (2): 155–164.

49 Nguyen, N. and Milanfar, P. (2000). An efficient wavelet based algorithm for image superresolution. In: *Proceedings of the International Conference on Image Processing*, 351–354.

50 Nicolier, F. and Truchetet, F. (2000). Image magnification using decimated orthogonal wavelet transform. In: *Proceedings of the International Conference on Image Processing*, 355–358.

51 Ohm, J. (ed.) (2015). *Multimedia Signal Coding and Transmission*. Springer-Verlag.

52 Pennebaker, W.B. and Mitchell, J.L. (1993). *JPEG - Still Image Data Compression Standard*, 3e. Springer.

53 Polidori, E. and Dugelay, J.L. (1997). Zooming using iterated function. *Fractals* 5 (Supplementary Issue): 111–123.

54 Ratakonda, K. and Ahuja, N. (1998). POCS based adaptive image magnification. In: *Proceeding of the IEEE International Conference on Image Processing*, vol. 3, 203–207.

55 Reichenbach, S.E. and Geng, F. (2003). Two-dimensional cubic convolution. *IEEE Transactions on Image Processing* 12 (8): 857–865.

56 Shannon, C.E. (1948). A mathematical theory of communication. *The Bell System Technical Journal* 27: 379–423.

57 Shi, H. and Ward, R. (2002). Canny edge based image expansion. In: *Proceedings of the IEEE International Symposium on Circuits and Systems*, vol. 1, 785–788.

58 Strang, G. and Nguyen, T.Q. (1998). *Wavelets and Filter Banks*. Wellesley-Cambridge Press.

59 Tam, W.-S., Kok, C.-W., and Siu, W.-C. (2010). Modified edge-directed interpolation for images. *Journal of Electronic Imaging* 19 (1): 013011.

60 Temizel, A. and Vlachos, T. (2005). Wavelet domain image resolution enhancement using cycle-spinning. *Electronics Letters* 41 (3): 119–121.

61 Thevenaz, P., Blu, T., and Unser, M. (2000). Interpolation revisited (medical images application). *IEEE Transactions on Medical Imaging* 19 (7): 739–758.

62 Tsai, P.-S. and Acharya, T. (2006). Image up-sampling using discrete wavelet transform. *Proceeding of the 2006 Joint Conference on Information Sciences*.

63 Wang, Z., Bovik, A.C., Sheikh, H.R., and Simonelli, E.P. (2004). Image quality assessment: from error visibility to structural similarity. *IEEE Transactions on Image Processing* 13 (4): 600–612.

64 Winkler, S. (1999). Issues in vision modeling for perceptual video quality assessment. *Signal Processing* 78: 231–252.

65 Wu, X. and Zhang, X. (2005). Image interpolation using texture orientation map and kernel Fisher discriminant. In: *Proceedings of the International Conference on Image Processing*, 49–52.

66 Wyszecki, G. and Stiles, W.S. (1982). *Color Science*. Wiley.

67 Xi, J. and Chicharo, J.F. (2000). Computing running DCTs and DSTs based on their second-order shift properties. *IEEE Transactions on Circuits and Systems I: Fundamental Theory and Applications* 47 (5): 779–783.

68 Yamaguchi, R., Murakami, H., Wada, N., and Koike, A. (2013). Improvement of pixel interpolation accuracy based on edge direction for high resolution imaging. *Journal of the Faculty of Science and Technology, Seikei University* 50 (1): 45–50.

69 Yoo, H. and Jeong, J. (2002). Direction-oriented interpolation and its application to de-interlacing. *IEEE Transactions on Consumer Electronics* 48 (4): 954–962.

70 Zhang, X., Ma, S., Gao, W. et al. (2009). Nonlocal edge-directed interpolation. In: *Advances in Multimedia Information Processing - PCM 2009, Lecture Notes in Computer Science*, vol. 5879 (ed. P. Muneesawang, F. Wu, I. Kumazawa et al.), 1197–1207. Berlin, Heidelberg: Springer-Verlag.

Index

Digital Image Interpolation in MATLAB®, First Edition. Chi-Wah Kok and Wing-Shan Tam.
© 2019 John Wiley & Sons Singapore Pte. Ltd. Published 2019 by John Wiley & Sons Singapore Pte. Ltd.
Companion website: www.wiley.com/go/ditmatlab